Immigrant Women
in the United States

**Recent Titles in
Bibliographies and Indexes in Women's Studies**

Women in China: A Selected and Annotated Bibliography
Karen T. Wei

Women Writers of Spain: An Annotated Bio-Bibliographical Guide
Carolyn L. Galerstein and Kathleen McNerney, editors

The Equal Rights Amendment: An Annotated Bibliography of the Issues, 1976-1985
Renee Feinberg, compiler

Childbearing Among Hispanics in the United States: An Annotated Bibliography
Katherine F. Darabi, compiler

Women Writers of Spanish America: An Annotated Bio-Bibliographical Guide
Diane E. Marting, editor

Women in Ireland: An Annotated Bibliography
Anna Brady, compiler

Psychological and Medical Aspects of Induced Abortion: A Selective, Annotated Bibliography, 1970-1986
Eugenia B. Winter, compiler

Women Writers of Germany, Austria, and Switzerland: An Annotated Bio-Bibliographical Guide
Elke Frederiksen, editor

IMMIGRANT WOMEN IN THE UNITED STATES

A Selectively Annotated Multidisciplinary Bibliography

Compiled by
Donna Gabaccia

Bibliographies and Indexes in Women's Studies, Number 9

Greenwood Press
New York • Westport, Connecticut • London

Library of Congress Cataloging-in-Publication Data

Gabaccia, Donna R.
  Immigrant women in the United States : a selectively annotated multidisciplinary bibliography / compiled by Donna Gabaccia.
    p.   cm. — (Bibliographies and indexes in women's studies, ISSN 0742-6941 ; no. 9)
  ISBN 0-313-26452-X (lib. bdg. : alk. paper)
  1. Women immigrants—United States—Bibliography. I. Title.
II. Series.
Z7164.I3G33   1989
[JV6346.W7]
016.32573′082—dc20   89-17191

British Library Cataloguing in Publication Data is available.

Copyright © 1989 by Donna Gabaccia

All rights reserved. No portion of this book may be reproduced, by any process or technique, without the express written consent of the publisher.

Library of Congress Catalog Card Number: 89-17191
ISBN: 0-313-26452-X
ISSN: 0742-6941

First published in 1989

Greenwood Press, Inc.
88 Post Road West, Westport, Connecticut 06881

Printed in the United States of America

The paper used in this book complies with the Permanent Paper Standard issued by the National Information Standards Organization (Z39.48-1984).

10 9 8 7 6 5 4 3 2 1

For My Great-Grandmother, Margherita DeDerizzi Moersch
and
For My Grandmother Maria Strata Gabaccia

Contents

Introduction and Acknowledgments	ix
CHAPTER 1 Bibliography	1
CHAPTER 2 General Works	9
CHAPTER 3 Migration	23
CHAPTER 4 Family	35
CHAPTER 5 Work	67
CHAPTER 6 Working Together	99
CHAPTER 7 Body	119
CHAPTER 8 Mind	139
CHAPTER 9 Cultural Change	157
CHAPTER 10 Biography	169
CHAPTER 11 Autobiography	215
CHAPTER 12 Fiction	259
Indices	283
Author Index	283

Index of Persons	299
Group Index	305
Subject Index	313

Introduction and Acknowledgments

Awareness of cultural diversity, the growth of women's studies, and the arrival of this nation's third wave of immigrants in the 1970s and 1980s have all contributed to strong recent interest in female immigrants in this country. Immigrant Women in the United States is the second bibliography on this topic to appear in five years. It differs from an earlier work by Francesco Cordasco, The Immigrant Woman in North America (Metuchen, N.J.: The Scarecrow Press, 1985), in a number of ways. Its coverage is wider, including recent published work and dissertations appearing before 1989, and from a broader range of disciplines. It is narrower only in its exclusive focus on the United States. Unlike Cordasco's bibliography, Immigrant Women in the United States also includes research reports on Mexican immigrant women; it nearly doubles Cordasco's listings of biography and autobiography; and it includes a selection of fictional works that tell the stories of immigrant women in the United States.

Ninety years ago, studies of immigrant women were undertaken almost exclusively by social welfare workers or sociologists of the Chicago school. Today, by contrast, study of immigrant women is underway in almost all disciplines in the humanities and the social sciences, and in policy- and service-oriented fields. Historians and biographers have written the most, often focusing on the lives of notable women or on the large population of southern and eastern Europeans who came to the United States at the turn of the century. Studies from literary, epidemiological, psychological, or demographic perspectives are increasing in numbers, while sociologists remain concerned with female immigration, in particular the most recently arrived immigrants from Asia, Central and South America, and the Caribbean.

Only rarely are researchers aware of the full range of work already completed on immigrant women. Fragmentation is typical of immigration studies generally, as scholars usually focus on only one group, following either their ethnic loyalties or their language skills. Disciplinary divisions are common: scholars do not always read or react to research published outside their own field, whatever it is. The result is that students of immigrant women have as yet produced few comparative works, and even fewer works of synthesis. Historians have been concerned with the transplantation of families and the formation of ethnic communities, while sociologists moved from an earlier concern with assimilation to studies of sex and ethnicity in segmented job markets; somewhat independently, scholars in women's studies have outlined distinctive female experiences or sought authentic women's voices. Diverging research agendas and paradigms and specialized vocabularies deeply divide historians, sociologists, and students of literature who nevertheless share a common topic.

Immigrant Women in the United States is a multidisciplinary bibliography. My hope is that a bibliography that provides access to the broad range of work in this field will facilitate communication across disciplinary boundaries, encourage comparison and synthesis.

Because this bibliography is multidisciplinary, it does not claim to include every significant publication on immigrant women in the United States. The bibliography covers scholarly secondary materials in English--books, articles, and dissertations--but omits popular publications, unpublished works, working papers, and most primary sources. Bibliographies, autobiographies, and fiction are handled in separate chapters. Worth noting, but not falling within the scope of this bibliography, are small but growing scholarly literatures on immigrant women in languages other than English. These are usually written and published in the many homelands from which women came.

Rather than grouping citations by nationality group, discipline, or time period, Immigrant Women in the United States tries to encourage interdisciplinary research by organizing scholarly publications by topic. A wide range of themes are considered, with separate chapters on general works, migration, family life, work, collective action of various types, women's bodies and minds, cultural and generational change, and biography. Although a large literature covers female lives in the many nations from which women emigrated, I have included citations to this literature only in cases where migration to the United States is explicitly treated. My inclusion of a work under one topic or another may sometimes strike a reader as arbitrary. For reasons of convenience, I have grouped important published collections of oral history with traditional biographies and autobiographies.

In addition to topical chapters that cover the scholarly literatures, Immigrant Women in the United States includes chapters on published autobiographies and substantial fictional works that present portraits of individual women immigrants. Along with biographies, these are necessary sources for scholars interested in female subjectivity, experience, and voice. I have not catalogued the many scholarly or literary works written by immigrant women unless they address the topic of immigrant women directly. Similarly, I have not attempted to cover systematically all scholarly analysis of the thought and writings of immigrant women authors, although this might be a worthwhile undertaking. I have, however, included in the fiction, autobiography, and biography chapters some literary studies that analyze selected writings of immigrant women; included here are studies in which either the books analyzed or the analysis of the writer's life sheds some light on being foreign and female in the United States.

Unfortunately, students of immigrant women do not currently have, and this bibliography cannot provide, a comprehensive introduction to the wide array of primary sources of interest to them. These are numerous and varied enough to deserve a bibliography of their own. Chapter 1, on bibliography, provides some introduction to this topic. In addition, this introduction can point researchers in a number of useful directions.

Manuscript and archive collections on immigrant women easily number in the hundreds. Obvious starting places are the specialized collections of the Immigration History Research Center at the University of Minnesota, the Balch Institute in Philadelphia, the Center for Migration Studies on Staten Island, and the Schlesinger Library at Radcliffe College. (A helpful introduction, The Immigration History Research Center: A Guide to Collections by Joel Wurl, is being published by Greenwood Press.) Beyond these collections--which specialize in materials on either women or immigrants--nearly every major repository in the country contains at least some holdings on immigrant women. Especially large collections are available at the New York Public Library, the American Jewish Archives, Mugar Library at Boston University, the Harvard University Theater Collection, the Library of Congress, the Minnesota Historical Society, the National Archives, and the Wisconsin State Historical Society. Dozens of smaller libraries and historical societies maintain rich holdings on some time periods or on particular groups well represented in their area. The sisterhoods of the Catholic church, many of which were either founded or brought to the United States by foreign-born women, maintain sizable, if sometimes out-of-the-way archives.

Published or microfilmed primary sources are probably equally numerous. Countless national, state, and local government publications include statistical data or anecdotal materials on immigrant women, as do the reports of even more numerous private religious, ethnic, and charitable societies. In addition, the careful scholar ought not to ignore English and foreign-language publications specifically addressed to female readers. My informal count suggests that well over fifty newspapers and periodicals were published in the United States for immigrant women; most were written in their native tongues.

INTRODUCTION

Any work that focuses on immigrants faces some complex issues of definition, and this bibliography was no exception: which women would be included and which excluded? The term immigrant itself is used in several ways, and it is more widely used in some fields (like history) than in others. In sociology and women's studies, by contrast, racial or ethnic minority and class are sometimes preferred to nationality, religion, or cultural ethnic group as analytical categories.

For the purposes of this bibliography, I have considered as immigrants those who voluntarily cross a national boundary to live or work temporarily or permanently in the United States, as well as the daughters of such immigrants. Thereby excluded are women who came to British North America prior to the Revolution, and African women who were brought against their will. This definition reflects my own belief that the experiences of colonizers, on the one hand, and slaves, on the other, did differ in significant ways from those of voluntary immigrants arriving after the formative years and independence of the United States.

Also excluded from consideration by this definition are present-day Puerto Rican women. While Puerto Ricans share with most immigrants the experience of being culturally distinctive, their U.S. citizenship also makes their migration patterns and political adjustment in the United States somewhat different from immigrants in general.

Finally, I decided to include studies of U.S.-born daughters of foreign-born parents in this bibliography. On the one hand, the native-born (second-generation) daughter is sometimes indistinguishable in attitudes and behavior from the foreign-born (first-generation) female who comes to the United States at an early age. On the other hand, inclusion of the second generation in any study of immigration opens up unique possibilities for considering culture change, integration, assimilation, and acculturation--all topics that have been subjects of considerable research and controversy in sociology and history.

Defining categories complicated some other decisions about which materials to include in this bibliography. In many fields, immigrant women are studied indirectly either as members of this nation's racial, religious, and ethnic minority groups or as members of the working class. Studies of Jewish Americans and Asian Americans usually single out the foreign-born or second- generation groups within the general population for special consideration, probably because these groups are viewed as of recent and foreign origin. But this is not the case in studies of other minorities or of the working class of the United States.

Studies of Afro-Americans, for example, rarely identify or analyze a foreign-born component of the minority group, and until very recently immigrants were, in fact, only a tiny minority within this minority. The arrival of Haitians, Jamaicans, and other Central and South Americans of African descent is, however, changing the composition of the Afro-American minority population considerably in American cities today.

Immigrants have long made up a sizable percentage of Hispanics in the United States, and an even larger percentage of the overlapping group called Latinos, but separate consideration of the foreign-born in studies of these ethnic groups varies immensely. This is especially true of research on Mexican-Americans and Chicanas in the United States. Some deny that birth place distinguishes foreign- from native-born Chicanas in the U.S. Southwest, which was once part of Mexico. Others see Chicanas, regardless of birthplace, as a native-born minority much like the Native Americans from whom many are descended. As a result, it is sometimes difficult to identify immigrants (as defined above) in studies of these groups.

Finally, the foreign-born were usually a significant portion of the working class of the United States in the years before World War I. Studies of working-class women, then, often are studies of immigrant women. Again, however, the women are not easily identifiable as immigrants, since studies of the working class do not always distinguish among culturally distinctive nationality groups, or among the several generations that made up this population.

Immigrant Women in the United States covers the large social scientific literature on minority women and the growing historical one on working-class women, but it covers them selectively. It cites mainly those studies of minority and working-class women which allow at least some identification of the foreign-born or second-generation women within the larger group. Some studies of minority women do clearly identify the women studied as immigrants. Others, particularly in Chicano studies, provide information about residence, education, and language use which indirectly identify the foreign born. In the many questionable cases, I have tried to err on the side of inclusiveness. Still, by excluding many studies of working-class and minority women, I have undoubtedly excluded some works that might be helpful to scholars interested in immigrant women, and readers should be aware of this as they use the bibliography.

My own hope is that students of minority and working-class women will increasingly consider also the relevance of nativity, nationality, culture, religion, and generation for the groups they study. It is quite likely that this will happen in studies of Afro-American women in the years ahead. As the number of nonwhite immigrants has grown in recent years, the internal dynamics of minority communities has begun to reflect their presence, and scholarship should eventually reflect this transformation as well. Female majorities among recent immigrants and the growth of migration from the Third World mean that we should see many exciting studies of the interaction of gender, race, ethnicity, and nativity in the years ahead. I hope that those studying this latest wave of immigration into the

United States will draw upon the considerable historical literature on immigrant women that is also compiled in the chapters that follow.

Even though I have worked in immigration history since the mid-1970s, I found the completion of a bibliography of this type a daunting task. Fortunately, I enjoyed the help of countless librarians (particularly at Mercy College, the Immigration History Research Center, and the New York Public Library) and the support of a computer-literate husband. The enthusiastic responses of many professional colleagues helped me keep with the task during the more painstaking moments. Mercy College provided some financial support for the project with a Faculty Development Grant in 1988.

Still, my biggest debt in this project is to my German and American students. Confronting women's history and immigration history, often for the first time, they helped me recognize just how useful a bibliography on this topic could be. Their need first motivated me to start a project I might otherwise not have considered. I hope they will use and benefit from the finished work.

Immigrant Women
in the United States

1

Bibliography

INTRODUCTION

Almost every bibliography on immigrant groups contains at least some listings on women; similarly, many general bibliographies on women in the United States refer to important works on immigrant women. Rather than try to draw together the entire bibliographic literature on these two large topics, this chapter lists bibliographies with substantial materials on immigrant women in the fields of literature, women's studies, ethnic studies, history, and a number of the social sciences.

Works cited in other chapters sometimes also contain good bibliographies or bibliographic essays. I have tried to indicate this in annotations.

Good finding guides to sources for the study of immigrants are still rare, and this is especially true when the topic is narrowed to sources for the study of immigrant women. Particularly desirable would be a bibliography that covers archive and manuscript collections on individual immigrant women and the organizations of foreign-born females. A guide to oral-history collections which include transcripts and tapes from interviews with immigrant women would be useful, as would a list of the periodical press aimed at women with native tongues other than English. A bibliography of studies of immigrant women in languages other than English would also probably reveal several dozen works of this type.

CITATIONS

1. Addis, Patricia. <u>Through a Woman's I: An Annotated Bibliography of American Women's Autobiographical Writings, 1946-1976</u>. Metuchen, N.J.: Scarecrow Press, 1983.

2   IMMIGRANT WOMEN IN THE U.S.

2. Arthur and Elizabeth Schlesinger Library on the History of Women in America. <u>The Manuscript Inventories and the Catalogs of Manuscripts, Books and Pictures</u>. Boston: G.K. Hall, 1973.

A helpful guide to an archive with a broad collection of materials on immigrant women.

3. Brana-Shute, Rosemary and Rosemarijn Hoefte. <u>A Bibliography of Caribbean Migration and Caribbean Immigrant Communities</u>. Gainesville: University of Florida Libraries in cooperation with the Center for Latin American Studies, 1983.

4. Buhle, Mari Jo. <u>Women and the American Left: A Guide to Sources</u>. Boston, Mass.: G.K. Hall, 1983.

Especially good on immigrant labor activists.

5. Cabello-Argandona, Roberto et al., eds. <u>The Chicana: The Comprehensive Bibliographic Study</u>. Los Angeles; Chicano Studies Center, University of California, 1976.

6. Candelaria, Cordelia. "Six Reference Works on Mexican-American Women: A Review Essay." <u>Frontiers: A Journal of Women Studies</u> 5 (Summer 1980): 75-80.

7. Candelaria, Cordelia. <u>Chicano Poetry: A Critical Introduction</u>. Westport, Conn.: Greenwood Press, 1986.

Includes good listings of poets, both native- and foreign-born.

8. Cantor, Aviva. <u>The Jewish Woman, 1900-1980: A Bibliography</u>. Fresh Meadows, N.Y.: Biblio Press, 1981.

Many entries included on the immigrant generation.

9. Caroli, Betty B. "Italian Women in America: Sources for Study." <u>Italian Americana</u> 2 (1976): 242-254.

10. Casal, Lourdes and Andres R. Hernandez. "Cubans in the U.S.: A Survey of the Literature." <u>Cuban Studies/Estudios Cubanos</u> 5 (1975): 25-51.

Includes some materials on family role changes and women's employment.

11. Center for Afroamerican and African Studies, University of Michigan. <u>Black Immigration and Ethnicity in the United States, An Annotated Bibliography</u>. Westport, Connecticut: Greenwood Press, 1985.

12. Center for Research on Women. <u>Selected Bibliography of Social Science Readings on Women of Color</u>. Memphis: Memphis State University, 1984.

13. Chai, Alice Y. "Toward a Holistic Paradigm for Asian-American Women's Studies: A Synthesis of Feminist Scholarship and Women of Color's Feminist Politics." (Special Issue: Rethinking Sisterhood: Unity in Diversity) Women's Studies International Forum 8, 1 (1985): 59-66.

Outlines a course and suggests methods of studying linkages of sexism, racism, classism, and homophobia.

14. Cohen Stuart, Bertie A. Women in the Caribbean: A Bibliography. The Hague: Department of Caribbean Studies, Royal Institute of Linguistics and Anthropology, 1979.

Although the focus is the homelands, one section addresses migration issues.

15. Cook, Patsy A., ed. Directory of Oral History Programs in the United States. Sanford, N.D.: Microfilming Corp. of America, 1982.

Identifies collections of materials on immigrants and women.

16. Cordasco, Francesco. The Immigrant Woman in North America; An Annotated Bibliography of Selected References. Metuchen, N.J.: Scarecrow Press, 1985.

Bibliography and General References; Autobiographies, Biographies and Reminiscences; The Workplace and Political Encounters; Immigrant Women and Progressive Reformers; The Family, Immigrant Child and Educational Influences; Miscellanea. A heavily annotated, but somewhat idiosyncratic collection; not all works contain significant information on immigrants.

17. Cotera, Martha P. Latina Sourcebook: Bibliography of Mexican American, Cuban, Puerto Rican and other Hispanic Women Materials in the U.S. Austin, Tx: Information Systems Development, 1982.

A good introduction to unpublished and pamphlet materials.

18. D'Andrea, Vaneeta-Marie. "Ethnic Women: A Critique of the Literature, 1971-1981." Ethnic and Racial Studies 9 (April 1986): 235-246.

Reviews citations on Asian-American, European-American, Native American, and Spanish-American women in Women's Studies Abstracts.

19. Darabi, Katherine F., comp. Childbearing among Hispanics in the United States, An Annotated Bibliography. New York: Greenwood Press, 1987.

The bibliography does not distinguish between native and foreign-born Chicanas, but both annotations and index single out Colombians, Central and South Americans, Cubans, and Dominicans. Annotations sometimes identify Mexican-born and second-generation.

4   IMMIGRANT WOMEN IN THE U.S.

20. de Caro, Francis A. *Women and Folklore, a Bibliographic Survey*. Westport, Conn.: Greenwood Press, 1983.

Although little known to scholars in other disciplines, folklorists have done considerable work on both women and immigrant groups.

21. Doi, Mary L. et al. *Pacific/Asian American Research: An Annotated Bibliography*. Bibliographical Series, No. 1. Chicago: Pacific/Asian American Mental Health Research Center, 1981.

A comprehensive bibliography with citations on sex roles, marriage roles, wife abuse, war brides, professional women, and prostitution.

22. Duffy, Susan. *Shirley Chisholm: A Bibliography of Writings by and About Her*. Metuchen, NJ: The Scarecrow Press, 1988.

Chisholm is the second-generation child of Barbadian and Guyanan immigrants.

23. Elwell, Ellen S. and Edward R. Levenson, ed. *The Jewish Women's Studies Guide*. Fresh Meadows, N.Y.: Biblio Press, 1982.

Good attention to the immigrant generation.

24. Fairbanks, Carol and Sara B. Sundberg. *Farm Women on the Prairie Frontier: A Sourcebook for Canada and the United States*. Metuchen, N.J. and London: The Scarecrow Press, 1983.

Discussion of women immigrants in both countries as well as a helpful bibliography on the individuals and groups who settled in rural areas.

25. Gilbert, V.F. and D.S. Tatla. *Women's Studies, A Bibliography of Dissertations, 1870-1982*. Oxford and New York: Basil Blackwell, 1985.

26. Greenberg, Blu. "Recent Literature on Jewish Women." *Jewish Book Annual* 35 (1977-78): 97-107.

A review essay.

27. Hinding, Andrea, ed. *Women's History Sources, A Guide to Archives and Manuscript Collections in the United States*. New York and London: R.R. Bowker Co., 1979.

Although not every important collection on immigrant women can be found here, this is the best starting place for those interested in archive materials and manuscript collections.

BIBLIOGRAPHY   5

28. Hoerder, Dirk and Christiane Harzig. *The Immigrant Labor Press in North America, 1840s-1970s: An Annotated Bibliography*. New York: Greenwood Press, 1987.

A good starting place for those interested in periodicals aimed at immigrant women readers.

29. Hoglund, A. William. *Immigrants and their Children in the United States, a Bibliography of Doctoral Dissertations, 1885-1982*. New York and London: Garland Publishing Co., 1986.

A good starting place, this bibliography is nevertheless difficult to use: the index lists only ethnic and nationality groups; there is no index entry on women or other topics.

30. Holte, James C. *The Ethnic I: A Sourcebook for Ethnic-American Autobiography*. New York: Greenwood Press, 1988.

31. Houston, Helen R. *The Afro-American Novel, 1965-1975: A Descriptive Bibliography of Primary and Secondary Material*. Troy, N.Y.: Whitston Publishing Co., 1973.

Contains a bibliography of Paule Marshall's writings, and critical literature about them.

32. Immigration History Research Center, University of Minnesota. "Recapturing History: Immigrant Women and Their Daughters." *Spectrum* 3, (July 1980): 1-11.

Surveys the holdings of this important archive and library collection.

33. Inglehart, Babette and Anthony R. Mangione. *The Image of Pluralism in American Literature: The American Experience of European Ethnic Groups*. New York: American Jewish Committee Institute on Pluralism and Group Identity, 1974.

Good introduction to fiction by and about immigrants, including immigrant women.

34. James, Edward T., ed. *Papers of the Women's Trade Union League and its Principal Leaders: Guide to the Microfilm Edition*. Woodbridge, Conn.: Published for the Schlesinger Library, Radcliffe College by Research Publications, 1981.

Describes important paper collections, including those of foreign-born and second-generation women like Margaret Dreier Robins, Leonora O'Reilly, Rose Schneidermann, and Mary Anderson in the Schlesinger Library; also summarizes holdings of the Women's Trade Union League, which undertook organizing efforts among immigrant women workers.

6   IMMIGRANT WOMEN IN THE U.S.

35. Kaplan, Louis. *A Bibliography of American Autobiographies*. Madison: The University of Wisconsin Press, 1961.

Although the index groups entries for particular immigrant groups, not all the autobiographies by immigrant women cited are properly indexed.

36. Kennedy, Susan E. *America's White Working-Class Women; A Historical Bibliography*. New York and London: Garland Publishing, 1981.

Includes a separate section on immigrants.

37. Kerst, Catherine H. *Ethnic Folklife Dissertations from the United States and Canada, 1960-1980, A Selected, Annotated Bibliography*. Washington: American Folklife Center, Library of Congress, 1986.

38. Koske, Mary, comp. and Suzanna Moody, ed. *Guide to the Minnesota Finnish American Family History Collection* Minneapolis: University of Minnesota, Immigration History Research Center, 1985.

Describes a sizeable collection with much material on Finnish women.

39. Leuchter, Sara, with the assistance of Jean L. Lettofsky. *Guide to Wisconsin Survivors of the Holocaust: A Documentation Project of the Wisconsin Jewish Archives*. Madison: State Historical Society of Wisconsin, 1983.

Mainly Eastern European Jews.

40. Loeb, Catherine. "La Chicana: A Bibliographic Survey." *Frontiers* 5 (Summer 1980): 59-74.

41. Meier, Matt S., comp. *Bibliography of Mexican American History*. Westport, Conn.: Greenwood Press, 1984.

Contains an index entry on Chicanas.

42. Momeni, Jamshid A. *Demography of Racial and Ethnic Minorities in the United States, An Annotated Bibliography with a Review Essay*. Westport, Connecticut: Greenwood Press, 1984.

Sufficiently annotated so that studies of the foreign-born can be identified.

43. Mortimer, Delores M. "Women and Migration: A Bibliography." Pp. 364-482 *Female Immigrants to the United States: Caribbean, Latin American and African Experiences*. Ed. Delores Mortimer and Roy Bryce-Laporte. Washington, D.C.: Research Institute on Immigration and Ethnic Studies, Smithsonian Institute, 1981.

Includes both case studies and theoretical works.

44. Oshana, Maryann. *Women of Color: Filmography of Minority and Third World Women.* New York: Garland, 1985.

A list of films which included portrayals of women of many backgrounds: Mexican, Latin American, West Indian, Jamaican, Asian, Japanese, Filipino, Eurasian, Middle Eastern, Turkish, Persian, Afghan. Although not all these women were immigrants, the work nevertheless provides an interesting and important way of studying stereotypes in this very popular fictional medium.

45. Portillo, Cristina et al. *Bibliography of Writings on La Mujer.* Berkeley: University of California at Berkeley, Chicano Studies Library, December 1976.

46. Roucek, Joseph S. *The Immigrant in Fiction and Biography.* New York: Bureau for Intercultural Education, 1945.

Short annotations identify those works with a focus on women and/or family life.

47. Skardal, Dorothy. "The Scandinavian Immigrant Writer in America." *Norwegian-American Studies* 21 (1962): 14-63.

Covers English and foreign-language publications, press and fiction, with good attention to women.

48. Soltow, Martha J. et al. *Women in American Labor History, 1825-1935: An Annotated Bibliography.* Lansing, Mich.: Michigan State University, School of Labor and Industrial Relations, 1972.

49. Stoner, K. Lynn. *Latinas of the Americas, A Source Book.* New York: Garland Publishing, 1988.

50. Talbot, Jane M. and Gilbert R. Cruz. *A Comprehensive Chicano Bibliography, 1960-1970.* Austin, Tex.: Jenkins Publishing, 1973.

Separate sections on machismo, women, marriage, and the family.

51. Thomas, Evangeline, CSJ. *Women Religious History Sources, A Guide to Repositories in the United States.* New York and London: R.R. Bowker Co., 1983.

A guide to published works and archive collections which have been little used even by Catholic historians.

52. Truillo, Roberto G. and Andres Rodriguez. *Literatura Chicana: Creative and Critical Writings through 1984.* Oakland, Calif.: Floricanto Press, 1985.

Includes a useful listing of writings by women.

53. United Nations High Commissioner for Refugees and the Refugee Policy Group for the United Nations Decade for Women. <u>A Selected and Annotated Bibliography on Refugee Women</u>. Geneva: Refugee Policy Group, 1985.

Contains many references to unpublished materials on a wide range of refugee groups.

54. William E. Wiener Oral History Library. <u>Catalogue of Memoirs of the William E. Wiener Oral History Library</u>. New York: American Jewish Committee, 1978.

Describes the considerable holdings in this repository; including a group of interviews with Holocaust survivors and their second-generation children and a group that concentrates on women's experiences in the Eastern European homelands.

55. Woo, Merle and Nellie Wong. "Bibliography of Asian American Women Writers." <u>Three Asian American Writers Speak Out on Feminism</u>. San Francisco: Karen Brodine, 1980.

2

General Works

INTRODUCTION

Included in this chapter are three types of works. Some general studies of immigrants or of American women contain enough information on immigrant women to merit mention. The former typically include information on the work patterns of the foreign-born woman; women's role in building the immigrant or ethnic community is also sometimes covered. Historical studies of American women normally include information about immigrants from southern and eastern Europe for the years between 1880 and 1920; these were the peak years of immigration into the United States, but they were also the years when middle-class female reformers worked most closely in settlement houses and in the labor movement with the foreign-born. By contrast, studies of contemporary American women sometimes include information on immigrants in sections on racial and ethnic minorities in the United States today.

In addition, there are increasing numbers of studies of immigrant women of particular groups; these often range broadly over many topics, offering preliminary surveys. Only a few, like Hasia Diner's Erin's Daughters, may be regarded as definitive. Many of these studies are by historians, and they focus on immigrant women in the nineteenth and early twentieth centuries. We currently have more monographic studies of eastern European Jewish women than of other groups. A number of anthologies that focus on one group are also included in this chapter.

Finally, a small number of monographs offer comparison and synthesis by covering many aspects of the lives of women of many immigrant groups. With a few exceptions, these are preliminary efforts, focusing almost exclusively on the immigrants of the past. In this chapter, I cite only those few works that were completed by a single author or several authors working together. I have not included anthologies of articles on many groups, but have instead cited individual articles separately by topic.

10   IMMIGRANT WOMEN IN THE U.S.

CITATIONS

56. Abbott, Grace. "A Study of Greeks in Chicago". American Journal of Sociology 15 (November 1909): 349-393.

Good attention to women throughout; notes low proportion of women in this group.

57. Abbott, Grace. The Immigrant and the Community. New York: The Century Co., 1917.

Good attention to women in many areas. See "The Special Problems of the Immigrant Girl" plus case materials scattered through most other chapters; information on midwives also included.

58. Addams, Jane. Democracy and Social Ethics. New York: The MacMillan Co., 1902.

Includes information on immigrant women as charity-givers, wage workers, and the second-generation daughters' strained relationships to parents.

59. Addams, Jane. Twenty Years at Hull House. New York: MacMillan, 1910.

Contains a small amount of anecdotal material on several subjects, including culture change in the first and second generations, the lives of second-generation girls, and the handicrafts of immigrant women.

60. Almquist, Elizabeth M. "Race and Ethnicity in the Lives of Minority Women." Pp. 423-453 Women: A Feminist Perspective. Ed. Jo Freeman. 3rd Ed. Palo Alto, Cal.: Mayfield Publishing, 1984.

General account with information on Mexican, Filipino, Cuban, Japanese, and Chinese women. Notes difficulty of distinguishing native- from foreign-born Mexicans. A section on Asian-American women discusses their relations to native-born women.

61. Aquino, Belinda. "The History of Filipino Women in Hawaii." Bridge 7 (Spring 1979): 17-21.

62. Armitage, Susan and Elizabeth Jameson. The Woman's West. Norman: University of Oklahoma Press, 1987.

Miscellaneous information; see pictures of Jules and Mary Sandoz, Lebanese Wedding Couple, 1907, and poster recruiting British women as migrants to Canada.

63. Arrinaga, Esther K. "Contributions of Korean Immigrant Women." Montage. Ed. Nancy F. Young and Judy R. Parrish. Honolulu: University of Hawaii Press, 1977.

64. Balch, Emily. Our Slavic Fellow Citizens. Philadelphia: William F. Fell, 1910.

Good attention to women throughout.

65. Baum, Charlotte, Paula Hyman, and Sonya Michel. The Jewish Woman in America. New York: New American Library, 1975.

Good attention to a wide range of topics in the lives of the immigrant and second generation.

66. Blea, Irene I. Toward a Chicano Social Science. Westport, Ct.: Greenwood Press, 1988.

Includes a general chapter on Mexican-American female experience.

67. Blegen, Theodore. "Immigrant Women and The American Frontier." Norwegian-American Historical Association Studies and Records 5 (1930): 26-29.

Focus is on Scandinavian women in the upper Midwest.

68. Bodnar, John. The Transplanted: A History of Immigrants in Urban America. Bloomington: Indiana University Press, 1985.

Focuses on those aspects of women's lives that most resemble men's--as workers and labor, community, or church activists. Little on reproduction, family dynamics, or domesticity.

69. Bogen, Elizabeth. Immigration in New York. New York: Praeger, 1987.

Contains information on women's educational levels, work, and sex ratios among recent immigrant groups.

70. Breckinridge, Sophonisba P. New Homes for Old. New York: Harper Brothers, 1921.

A rich source on immigrant women from many groups, but especially Eastern Europeans. Includes sections on family life, care of the home, consumer patterns, and childrearing, and a good list of women's ethnic organizations.

71. Buchanan, Susan H. "Haitian Women in New York City." Migration Today 7 (September 1979): 19-25, 39.

Notes mixed results for women in the new world: life becomes harder in some ways. Some attention to the migration process; why women predominate (at least among legal immigrants); domestic work; double burden of family work; marriage; single motherhood.

12   IMMIGRANT WOMEN IN THE U.S.

72. Bukowczyk, John J. *And My Children Did Not Know Me; A History of the Polish-Americans*. Bloomington: Indiana University Press, 1987.

Some information on women in workplace, family, and community.

73. Caroli, Betty B. et al. *The Italian Immigrant Woman in North America*. Toronto: The Multicultural History Society of Ontario, 1978.

This anthology covers a wide range of topics, from family and work experiences to immigrant women's interaction with the native-born and activism in community groups.

74. Castro, Mary G. "Colombian Voices in the Big Apple." *Migration Today* 10 (1982): 22-32.

75. Catholic Institute for International Relations. *The Labour Trade: Filipino Migrant Workers Around the World*. London: Russell Press, 1987.

A chapter on U.S. contains good information on women; excellent pictorial material on a variety of topics.

76. Chih, Ginger. *The History of Chinese Immigrant Women, 1850-1940*. North Bergen, NJ: by the author, 1977.

77. Chinese Historical Society. *The Life, Influence, and Role of the Chinese in the U.S., 1776-1960*. San Francisco: Chinese Historical Society, 1975.

See especially the biography of Dr. Hu King, and "The Life, Influences, and Role of the Chinese Women in the United States."

78. Clinton, Catherine. *The Other Civil War, American Women in the Nineteenth Century*. New York: Hill and Wang, 1984.

One chapter is entitled "Natives and Immigrants." Book also includes information on Frances Wright, Elizabeth Blackwell, Maria Zakrzewska, Emma Goldman, and Rose Pastor Stokes."

79. Cohen, Lucy. "Latinas Lead the Way." Pp. 179-202 *Female Immigrants to the United States: Caribbean, Latin American and African Experiences*. Ed. Delores Mortimer and Roy Bryce-Laporte. Washington, D.C.: Research Institute on Immigration and Ethnic Studies, Smithsonian Institute, 1981.

A general article with information on migration, work, family, stress, and health.

80. Cole, Johnnetta B. "Commonalities and Differences." Pp. 1-30 *All American Women; Lines that Divide, Ties that Bind*. Ed. Johnnetta B. Cole. New York and London: The Free Press and Collier Macmillan Publishers, 1986.

GENERAL WORKS   13

81. Cole, Marie C. *The Girl of Foreign Background*. The Woman's Press, 1934.

A study completed by the YWCA.

82. Cotera, Marta. *Profile of the Mexican American Women*. Austin: National Educational Laboratory, 1976.

A preliminary survey.

83. Cotera, Martha P. *Diosa y Hembra, The History and Heritage of Chicanas in the United States*. Austin, Texas: Information Systems Development, 1976.

Wide-ranging but preliminary survey.

84. Daniel, Robert L. *American Women in the 20th Century, The Festival of Life*. San Diego and New York: Harcourt Brace Jovanovich, 1987.

Considerable but scattered information on immigrant women, past and present, of many backgrounds.

85. Diner, Hasia R. *Erin's Daughters in America; Irish Immigrant Women in the Nineteenth Century*. Baltimore and London: The Johns Hopkins University Press, 1983.

The Irish were the only nineteenth-century immigrant group in which women outnumbered men. Covers a wide range of topics, including homeland, migration, family, work, social problems, women's communities and community activism, male/female relations, and Irish perspectives on the woman question.

86. Ding, Barbara. "Researching Chinese American Women: Difficult But Needed." *East/West* November 18, 1981: 4-5.

87. Doran, Terry et al. *A Road Well Traveled: Three Generations of Cuban American Women*. Newton, MA: Education Development Center, Women's Educational Equity Act Publishing Center, 1988.

88. Erickson, Charlotte. "English Women Immigrants in America in the Nineteenth Century: Expectations and Reality". Fawcett Library Papers 7. London: LLRS Publications 1983.

Although quite general, also contains a number of case histories.

89. Ewen, Elizabeth. *Immigrant Women in the Land of Dollars; Life and Culture on the Lower East Side, 1890-1925*. New York: Monthly Review Press, 1985.

Attention to a wide variety of topics relating to lives of Italian and Eastern European Jewish women; best chapters are on popular culture and the meaning of Americanization and American myths for immigrant women.

14   IMMIGRANT WOMEN IN THE U.S.

90. Foner, Nancy. "Sex Roles and Sensibilities: Jamaican Women in New York and London." Pp. 133-151 International Migration, The Female Experience. Ed. Rita J. Simon and Caroline B. Brettell. Totowa, N.J.: Rowman & Allanheld, 1985.

General account finds some differences from men; while women feel victimized by men, they also accept inequalities that seem oppressive to outsiders.

91. Fujitomi, Irene and Diane Wong. "The New Asian American Woman." Pp. 236-248 Female Psychology: The Emerging Self. Ed. Sue Cox. Chicago: Science Research Associates, 1976.

Sections on Chinese and Japanese immigrants, contrasts these to newer and more modern women of later generations.

92. Gee, Emma. "Issei: The First Women." Civil Rights Digest 6 (Spring 1974): 48-53.

93. Glanz, Rudolf. The Jewish Woman in America: Two Female Immigrant Generations, 1820-1929. 2 Vol. New York: KTAV Publishing House and National Council of Jewish Women, 1976.

Attention to both German Jewish and Eastern European Jewish immigrants and second generation.

94. Glueck, Sheldon and Eleanor T. Five Hundred Delinquent Women. New York: Alfred A. Knopf, 1934.

Sixty percent of those studied were foreign-born or women of the second generation. Case studies of Portuguese, Irish, and French-Canadian women are included.

95. Gonzalez, Rosalinda M. "Distinctions in Western Women's Experiences: Ethnicity, Class, and Social Change." Pp. 237-252 The Woman's West. Ed. Susan Armitage and Elizabeth Jameson. Norman: University of Oklahoma Press, 1987.

Discusses Mexican immigrants and Chicanas, arguing for the importance of a class perspective on their lives.

96. Gurak, Douglas T. and Mary M. Kritz. "Dominican and Colombian Women in New York City." Migration Today 10, 3/4(1982): 14-21.

A study of two of the fastest-growing groups in New York; women are a majority in both--57 percent of Dominicans and 66 percent of Colombians. Surveys demographic characteristics; notes that nuclear family is more typical of Colombians.

97. Herzfeld, Elsa G. *Family Monographs: The History of Twenty-Four Families Living in the Middle-West Side of New York City*. New York: James Kempster Printing, 1905.

Case histories of Irish, German, British, and one Russian Jewish family; includes much information on women, work, health, death, and housekeeping.

98. Horowitz, Ruth. *Honor and the American Dream: Culture and Identity in a Chicano Community*. New Brunswick, N.J.: Rutgers University Press, 1983.

Focus is on growing up in Chicago, immigrant and second generation, with good attention to women and sexuality.

99. Hyman, Paula. "Culture and Gender: Women in the Immigrant Jewish Community." Pp. 157-78 *The Legacy of Jewish Immigration: 1881 and Its Impact*. Ed. David Berger. New York: Brooklyn College Press, 1983.

Very general account.

100. Ichioka, Yuji. "Amerika Nadeshiko: Japanese Immigrant Women in the United States, 1900-1924." *Pacific Historical Review* 49 (1980): 339-357.

101. Ichioka, Yuji. *The Issei, The World of the First Generation Japanese Immigrants, 1885-1924*. New York and London: The Free Press, 1988.

Contains some general information on women, especially the early prostitutes.

102. Jameson, Elizabeth. "Toward a Multicultural History of Women in the Western United States." *SIGNS: Journal of Women in Culture and Society* 13 (Summer 1988): 761-791.

Reviews the literature on Mexican-American, Chinese-American, and Japanese-American women in the West; notes that foreign-born were one-quarter to one-third of western population before 1900; distinguishes foreign-born from Euro-American women of second generation.

103. Kataoka, Susan M. "Issei Women: A Study in Subordinate Status." Unpublished Ph.D. Dissertation, University of California, Los Angeles, 1977. Order Number 77 30928.

Notes women's active participation in migration. Wage-earning did not change family balance of power. Japanese women did encounter institutionalized discrimination.

104. Kennedy, Susan E. *If All We Did was to Weep at Home: A History of White Working-Class Women in America*. Bloomington: Indiana University Press, 1979.

See especially the chapter on immigrant women from several cultures.

16 IMMIGRANT WOMEN IN THE U.S.

105. Kerber, Linda K. and Jane DeHart-Mathews. *Women's America, Refocusing the Past.* 2nd. Ed. New York and Oxford: Oxford University Press, 1987.

Contains considerable information about female immigrants of many backgrounds, especially for the years 1880-1920.

106. Kumagai, Gloria L. "The Asian Woman in America." *Explorations in Ethnic Studies* 1 (July 1978): 27-39.

Information about picture brides, work patterns, and other topics.

107. Kumagai, Gloria. "The Asian Woman in America." *Bridge* 6 (Winter 1978): 16-20.

Argues that traditional values of submission led to exploitation and weakened capacity for resistance.

108. LaGuerre, Michael S. *American Odyssey: Haitians in New York City.* Ithaca, N.Y.: Cornell University Press, 1984.

Attention to women in all facets of life.

109. Lasker, Bruno. *Filipino Immigration to Continental United States and Hawaii.* Chicago: University of Chicago Press, 1931.

Contains a small amount of information on women, sex and age composition of migrants, sexual relations, and intermarriage.

110. Liu, William T. *Transition to Nowhere, Vietnamese Refugees in America.* Nashville: Charter House Publishers, 1979.

Includes some information on women's representation, family groups, female headed households (20 percent), and women's mental health.

111. Loomis, A. W. "Chinese Women in California." *Overland Monthly* 10 (April 1969): 343-351.

112. MacLean, Annie M. "Life in the Pennsylvania Coal Fields with Particular Reference to Women." *American Journal of Sociology* 14 (Nov. 1908): 329-351.

Sixty percent of those studied were Slavs; includes some information on women's clubs and church clubs; and on women's work in house and mill.

113. Marcus, Jacob R. *The American Jewish Woman, 1654-1980.* New York and Cincinnati: KTAV Publishing House and American Jewish Archives, 1981.

Besides treating a wide range of subjects, an introduction to the lives of lesser-known immigrant and second-generation women; includes a helpful bibliography.

GENERAL WORKS   17

114. Matsumoto, Valerie. "Japanese American Women during World War II." Frontiers 8 (1984): 6-14.

Focus is on internment.

115. Mirandé, Alfredo and Evangelina Enriquez. La Chicana, The Mexican-American Woman. Chicago and London: The University of Chicago Press, 1979.

Includes chapters on the Mexican cultural heritage; family, work and education; images in literature; and feminism. The authors discuss terminology in studies of these women, but do not themselves distinguish foreign- from native-born Chicanas.

116. Mirandé, Alfredo. The Chicano Experience, An Alternative Perspective. Notre Dame, Ind.: University of Notre Dame Press, 1985.

Includes information on women in chapters on family and on machismo. Some attention to women immigrants, although the work does not generally distinguish foreign- from native-born, because of indigenous Native American roots of both.

117. Mitchell, Florence S. "From Refugee to Rebuilder: Cambodian Women in America." Unpublished Ph.D. Dissertation, Syracuse University, 1987. Order Number DA 8806696.

Based on interviews with seven women.

118. Miyasaki, Gai. Montage: An Ethnic History of Women in Hawaii. Honolulu: University of Hawaii Press, 1977.

119. Mora, Magdalena et al., eds. The Mexican Woman. Los Angeles: Aztlán Publications, Chicano Studies Center, University of California, 1977.

120. Morawska, Eva. For Bread with Butter, The Life-World of East Central Europeans in Johnstown, Pennsylvania, 1890-1940. Cambridge: Cambridge University Press, 1985.

Some scattered attention to women.

121. Mortimer, Delores M. "Race, Ethnicity, and Sex in the Recent Immigration." Pp. xi-lxvii Female Immigrants to the United States: Caribbean, Latin American and African Experiences. Ed. Delores Mortimer and Roy Bryce-Laporte. Washington, D.C.: Research Institute on Immigration and Ethnic Studies, Smithsonian Institute, 1981.

Believes that immigrant women will influence development of ethnicity in these groups, and will contribute to struggle toward sexual equality.

18   IMMIGRANT WOMEN IN THE U.S.

122. Neidle, Cecyle. *America's Immigrant Women: Their Contribution to the Development of a Nation from 1609 to the Present*. New York: Hippocrene Books, 1975.

The emphasis is on the lives of notable immigrant women.

123. Pehotsky, Bessie. *The Slavic Immigrant Woman*. Cincinnati: Powell & White, 1925.

Includes chapters on homelands, peasant women, migration, community work among Russian women, the home departments of the churches, girlhood, work and home conditions in the U.S., the boarder problem, and childbirth and the midwife. Makes suggestions as to how American social agencies might better serve the immigrant woman and on how missions might reach her.

124. Pickle, Linda S. "Stereotypes and Reality: Nineteenth-Century German Women in Missouri." *Missouri Historical Review* 79 (April 1985): 291-312.

Focus is on rural life. The stereotype is of good, laborious, and submissive housewives; the evidence presented is far more complex.

125. Pido, Antonio J.A. *The Philippinos in America: Macro/Micro Dimensions of Immigration and Integration*. New York: Center for Migration Studies, 1986.

Includes sections on the status of women in the homeland, familial and social relations in the U.S., and immigration of women (they outnumber men).

126. Ragsdale, Crystal S. "The German Woman in Frontier Texas." Pp. 144-156 *German Culture in Texas: A Free Earth; Essays from the 1978 Southwest Symposium*. Ed. Glen E. Lich and Dona B. Reeves. Boston: Twayne Publishers, 1980.

A very general account.

127. Reid, Ira D. *The Negro Immigrant: His Background, Characteristics and Social Adjustment, 1899-1937*. New York: Columbia University Press, 1939.

Includes some comments on sex composition of immigrants from the Caribbean, on women's naturalization and imprisonment, and on fertility and intermarriage.

128. Ryan, Mary P. *Womanhood in America, From Colonial Times to the Present*. Third Edition. New York: Franklin Watts, 1983.

Includes scattered references to immigrant women.

129. Rynearson, Ann M. and Pamela A. DeVoe. "Refugee Women in a Vertical Village: Lowland Laotians in St. Louis." *Social Thought* 10,3 (1984): 33-48.

GENERAL WORKS   19

130. Saiki, Patsy S.   Japanese Women in Hawaii, the First 100 Years. Honolulu: Kisaku, 1985.

Although not a sophisticated account, still gives a sense of the issues and chronology.

131. Scarpaci, Jean V.   "La Contadina: The Plaything of the Middle Class Woman Historian." Journal of Ethnic Studies 9 (Summer 1981): 21-38.

Critical of what she calls women historians' "history by empathy."

132. Seller, Maxine, ed. Immigrant Women. Philadelphia: Temple University Press, 1981.

Primarily a collection of documents, but with commentary that is worth reading since it represents a first effort at revision of long-standing stereotypes.

133. Seller, Maxine. "Putting Women into American Jewish History." Frontiers 5 (Spring 1980): 59-62.

How to integrate materials on women into Jewish studies courses.

134. Simkhovitch, Mary K.   The City Worker's World in America. New York: The MacMillan Co., 1917.

The focus is on immigrant families, with attention to family, education, work, leisure, health, politics, and religion. Women are considered throughout.

135. Stansell, Christine. "Women, Children, and the Uses of the Streets: Class and Gender Conflicts in New York City, 1850-1860." Feminist Studies 8 (1982): 309-336.

Little attention to nationality, but most of the women and children studied were probably immigrant and second-generation Irish and Germans.

136. Stansell, Christine. City of Women; Sex and Class in New York, 1789-1860. New York: Alfred A. Knopf, 1986.

Most of the women studied are immigrant and second-generation Irish and Germans, but author is not particularly interested in nationality or ethnicity; good description of middle-class efforts to domesticate working-class women to their own patterns of appropriate motherly behavior.

137. Sunoo, Harold Hakwon and Sonia Shin Sunoo. "The Heritage of the First Korean Women Immigrants in the United States: 1903-1924." Korean Christian Scholars Journal 2 (1977): 158-163.

20   IMMIGRANT WOMEN IN THE U.S.

138. Sunoo, Sonia Shin. "Korean Women Pioneers of the Pacific Northwest." Oregon Historical Quarterly 79 (Spring 1978): 51-63.

A general account of early settlers.

139. Teodor, Luis V., Jr. Out of this Struggle: The Filipinos in Hawaii. Honolulu: University Press of Hawaii, 1983.

Includes a general chapter on women in homeland and in Hawaii.

140. Tobenkin, Elias. "The Immigrant Girl in Chicago." Survey 23 (1909): 189-204.

141. True, Reiko Homma. "The Profile of Asian American Women." Pp. 124-135 Female Psychology, the Emerging Self. Ed. Sue Cox. New York: St. Martin's Press, 1981.

Includes notes on immigrant and subsequent generations; emphasizes stereotypes: "sexy"; "modest"; "dragon lady."

142. Tsai, Shih-shan Henry. The Chinese Experience in America. Bloomington: Indiana University Press, 1987.

Includes a small amount of information on immigrant women in contemporary American society.

143. U.S. Commission on Civil Rights, ed. Civil Rights Issues of Asian and Pacific Americans: Myths and Realities. Washington, D.C.: Government Printing Office, 1980.

See section "Women's Issues" which contains scattered information on foreign-born women, military wives, and other topics.

144. Wargelin Brown, K. Marianne. "The Legacy of Mummu's Granddaughters, Finnish American Women's History." Pp. 14-40 Women Who Dared: The History of Finnish American Women. Ed. Carl Ross and K. Marianne Wargelin Brown. St. Paul, Minnesota: Immigration History Research Center, 1986.

145. Weatherford, Doris. Foreign and Female: Immigrant Women in America, 1840-1938. New York: Schocken Books, 1986.

An unsuccessful effort at synthesis, with chapters on body and soul, morality, domesticity, work, cultural conflicts, and family. Does not cover the experience of Asian immigrants.

146. Weinberg, Sydney S. *The World of Our Mothers, Lives of Jewish Immigrant Women.* Chapel Hill: North Carolina University Press, 1988.

Based on oral histories, the book covers shtetl life, emigration, Americanization, family relations, education work, marriage, and social mobility; the focus is on Eastern European Jews.

147. Wing Siu Luk, Judith. "What was Her Life Like?" *Bu Gao Ban* Winter/Spring, 1985.

General account on Chinese immigrant women.

148. Winsey, Valentine Rossilli. "The Italian Immigrant Woman Who Arrived in the United States Before World War I." Pp. 199-210 *Studies in Italian American Social History; Essays in Honor of Leonard Covello.* Ed. Francesco Cordasco. Totowa, N.J.: Rowman and Littlefield, 1975.

A very general and anecdotal account.

149. Woloch, Nancy. *Women and the American Experience.* New York: Alfred A. Knopf, 1984.

Includes good information on immigrant women 1880-1920, but almost nothing on contemporary arrivals; some attention as well to notable immigrant women Emma Goldman and Frances Wright and second-generation woman Margaret Sanger.

150. Woods, Robert A. and Albert E. Kennedy. *Young Working Girls: A Summary of Evidence From Two Thousand Social Workers.* Boston: Houghton Mifflin, 1913.

Some attention to Irish, Italian, and Syrian girls, especially in the treatment of home life, sexuality, and recreation.

151. Yang, Eun Sik. "Korean Women in America: 1903-1930." Pp. 167-182 *Korean Women in Transition: At Home and Abroad.* Ed. Eui-Young Yu and Earl H. Phillips. Los Angeles: Center for Korean-American and Korean Studies, California State University, 1987.

152. Yang, Eun Sik. "Korean Women of America: From Subordination to Partnership, 1903-1930." *Amerasia* 11 (1984): 1-28.

About one-third of early arrivals were women, mainly wives settling in Hawaii. Includes information on picture brides and women's organizations. Argues that arrival of women was "pivotal in transforming Korean immigrants from temporary to permanent settlers."

153. Yoshika, Robert B. "Stereotyping Asian American Women." *Civil Rights Digest* 6 (Spring 1974): 45.

Recounts how stereotypes emerged during the early migration years.

22   IMMIGRANT WOMEN IN THE U.S.

154. Yung, Judy. "Chinese Women of America: 1834-1982." <u>Bu Gao Ban</u> (Winter/Spring, 1985).

155. Yung, Judy. <u>Chinese Women of America: A Pictorial History</u>. Seattle: University of Washington Press, 1986.

Narrative covers a broad range of topics.

3

Migration

INTRODUCTION

The study of women's migration to the United States remains a much neglected topic. In this area, social scientists who study contemporary women immigrants lead the way, perhaps because women currently are the majority of all immigrants entering the United States. Studies of the migration of the female minority in the past are less numerous. Theoretical work on women and migration worldwide has made great strides in the past fifteen years, but only a few sociologists who study women immigrants in the United States have made much use of it.

Studies of the homelands from which women depart sometimes include information about their emigration, or the impact of male migration upon their lives. A few works of this type are included in this chapter.

Readers interested in women's migration should also refer to index entries for undocumented immigrants and refugees. Studies which treat the lives of undocumented and refugee women in the United States occasionally also shed some indirect light on the migration process itself.

A number of studies of female migration emphasize the importance of changing U.S. immigration law in encouraging or discouraging the migration of women as family members and spouses. This is a topic that needs further exploration, especially for the years before 1965. A number of important changes in law in the late nineteenth and the first half of the twentieth century had differential impact on male and female immigrants. In addition, the manner in which the United States handled the citizenship of married women immigrants changed during this time. All of these changes deserve further attention.

CITATIONS

156. Ahern, Susan et al. "Migration and La Mujer Fuerte." _Migration Today_ 13, 1 (1985): 14-20.

Traces the impact of male Mexican migration on the women left behind. Although the husband arranged for others to help a wife before he departed, she gradually took over more responsibilities and became a "strong woman." Conflicts with her son resulted. The strong woman reverted to traditional behavior when the husband returned.

157. Alcantara, Ruben R. _Sakada: Filipino Adaptation in Hawaii_. Washington, D.C.: University Press of America, 1981.

Offers some analysis of the scarcity of women among immigrants before 1946, and the arrival of wives thereafter.

158. Archdeacon, Thomas J. _Becoming American, An Ethnic History_. New York: The Free Press, 1983.

Gives some attention to the changing sex ratio among immigrants arriving in the U.S. over the centuries.

159. Baca, Reynaldo and Dexter Bryan. "Mexican Undocumented Women Workers in Los Angeles: A Research Note." Pp. 297-313 _Female Immigrants to the United States: Caribbean, Latin American and African Experiences_. Ed. Delores Mortimer and Roy Bryce-Laporte. Washington, D.C.: Research Institute on Immigration and Ethnic Studies, Smithsonian Institute, 1981.

More illegal women than usual were found in this study. They resembled men in their occupational backgrounds, but were more dependent on friends and family for making living arrangement.

160. Baines, Dudley. _Migration in a Mature Economy: Emigration and Internal Migration in England and Wales, 1861-1900_. New York: Cambridge University Press, 1985.

Summarizes sex ratio among immigrants leaving for the U.S.

161. Barkan, Elliott R. "Whom Shall We Integrate?: A Comparative Analysis of the Immigration and Naturalization Trends of Asians Before and After the 1965 Immigration Act (1951-1978)." _Journal of American Ethnic History_ 3 (Fall 1983): 29-57.

One section shows the impact of the 1965 immigration law on immigrant gender ratios; women immigrants naturalized at a later average age than men.

162. Beale, Jenny. **Women in Ireland: Voices of Change**. Bloomington: Indiana University Press, 1987.

See especially the chapter "Maidens and Myths: Women in Rural Life" which includes some information on women's emigration.

163. Bean, Frank, et al. "The Number of Illegal Migrants of Mexican Origin in the United States: Sex Ratio-Based Estimates for 1980." **Demography** 20 (February 1980): 99-109.

164. Blake, Judith. **Family Structure in Jamaica: The Social Context of Reproduction**. New York: The Free Press of Glencoe, 1961.

The focus is changing family patterns (with good attention to women) during the period when male migration predominated.

165. Bolles, Lynn A. "'Goin' Abroad': Working Class Jamaican Women and Migration." Pp. 56-85 **Female Immigrants to the United States: Caribbean, Latin American and African Experiences**. Ed. Delores M. Mortimer and Roy S. Bryce-Laporte. Washington, D.C.: Smithsonian Institution, Research Institute on Immigration and Ethnic Studies, 1981.

Notes emigration to several destinations, including the U.S. The focus is on the factors that cause migration, especially women's unemployment.

166. Breckinridge, Sophonisba P. **The Family and the State**. Chicago: University of Chicago Press, 1934.

Mainly a collection of family-law documents, but see section "The Citizenship of Married Women" which discusses the Cable Act and its impact.

167. Brody, Eugene B. **Sex, Contraception and Motherhood in Jamaica**. Cambridge and London: Harvard University Press, 1981.

Good information on women and family in the homeland; notes also the increasing importance of migration to the U.S.

168. Browning, Harley L. and Nestor Rodriguez. "The Migration of Mexican Indocumentados as a Settlement Process: Implications for Work." Pp. 277-297 **Hispanics in the U.S. Economy**. Ed. Georges Borjas and Marta Tienda. Orlando and New York: Academic Press, 1985.

Includes breakdowns by type of migration, age and sex. Seems to regard the arrival of women as indicator of permanent settlement; relatively few women were discovered among undocumented migrants.

169. Bryce-Laporte, Roy S. "Introduction: The New Immigration: The Female Majority." Pp. vii-xxxix *Female Immigrants to the United States*. Ed. Delores M. Mortimer and Roy S. Bryce-Laporte. Washington, DC: Smithsonian Institution, Research Institute on Immigration and Ethnic Studies, 1981.

The majority of immigrants since 1965 have been women.

170. Burgess, Judith and Meryl James-Gray. "Migration and Sex Roles: A Comparison of Black and Indian Trinidadians in New York City." Pp. 86-112 *Female Immigrants to the United States: Caribbean, Latin American and African Experiences*. Ed. Delores M. Mortimer and Roy S. Bryce-Laporte. Washington, D.C.: Smithsonian Institution, Research Institute on Immigration and Ethnic Studies, 1981.

Blacks were concerned with obtaining white collar and professional jobs, while Indians wanted jobs with immediate monetary returns.

171. Chaney, Elsa M. "Women Who Go and the Women Who Stay Behind." *Migration Today* 10 (1982): 6-14.

Although this essay does not focus on the U.S., it provides good background for understanding women's gradual but recent switch from temporary to long-term migration in the world as a whole.

172. Cohen, Lucy M. "The Female Factor in Resettlement." *Society* 14 (Sept./Oct. 1977): 27-30.

Focus is on migration from the Caribbean and Central and South America; in these groups women were often pioneer migrants in their families. Most were upwardly mobile, of working-class backgrounds with high commitment to work; many were married women leaving children behind.

173. Cortes, Carlos, ed. *The Latin American Brain Drain to the United States*. New York: Arno Press, 1980.

Includes some information on migration of nurses, but provides no systematic breakdowns by sex in general treatment of brain-drain migrants.

174. Cuddy, Dennis L., ed. *Contemporary American Immigration, Interpretive Essays (Non-Europeans)*. Boston: Twayne, 1982.

Includes chapters on each group; those on Chinese and Japanese include some information on sex ratios among migrants and on war brides.

175. De Jong, Gordon F. et al. "Family Reunification and Philippine Migration to the United States: The Immigrants' Perspective." International Migration Review 20 (Fall 1986): 598-611.

Studies impact of U.S. immigration law on make-up of migrant population. Those migrating under family reunification provisions were older, less well educated and more heavily female.

176. Dominguez, Virginia R. From Neighbor to Stranger: The Dilemma of Caribbean Peoples in the United States. New Haven: Antilles Research Program, 1975.

Contains some information on the sex ratio and age distribution of female immigrants from Barbados, Jamaica, Trinidad and Tobago, and other West Indian countries in the 1960s and 1970s.

177. Donato, Katharine and Andrea Tyree. "Family Reunification, Health Professionals, and the Sex Composition of Immigrants to the United States." Sociology and Social Research 70, 3 (April 1986): 226-230.

Significant migrations of nurses and female health-care workers did not explain predominance of women among recent immigrants; family reunification provisions of U.S. immigration law had a bigger impact.

178. Fjellman, Stephen M. and Hugh Gladwin. "Haitian Family Patterns of Migration to South Florida." Human Organization 44 (Winter 1985): 301-12.

Analyzes seven family histories to show how extended kinship linked individuals scattered over many countries; women were frequently the pioneer migrants to a particular destination.

179. Gabaccia, Donna R. "Kinship, Culture and Migration: A Sicilian Example." Journal of American Ethnic History 3 (1984): 39-53.

Contrasts differing kin networks of male and female migrants.

180. Garrison, Vivian and Carol I. Weiss. "Dominican Family Networks and United States Immigration Policy: A Case Study." International Migration Review 13 (Summer 1979): 264-83.

Case study of one family; good attention to women. Dominicans defined families more broadly than did U.S. immigration law.

181. Gill, Margaret. Women, Work and Development. Cave Hill, Barbados: Institute of Social and Economic Research (Eastern Caribbean), University of West Indies, 1984.

Contains a short section on women and migration.

28   IMMIGRANT WOMEN IN THE U.S.

182. González, Nancie L. "Garifuna Settlement in New York: A New Frontier." International Migration Review 13 (Summer 1979): 255-263.

Good attention to women; migration to New York was simply a continuation of older migratory patterns.

183. González, Nancie L. "Multiple Migratory Experiences of Dominican Women." Anthropological Quarterly 49 (January 1976): 36-44.

Prostitution, domestic service, and garment work (in the U.S.) were the only jobs open to women. Residence in U.S. opened new opportunities.

184. González, Nancie L. Black Carib Household Structure, A Study of Migration and Modernization. Seattle and London: University of Washington Press, 1969.

Good attention to women, family roles, work, and the organization of migration.

185. Gordon, Monica H. "Caribbean Migration: A Perspective on Women." Pp. 14-55 Female Immigrants to the United States. Ed. Delores M. Mortimer and Roy S. Bryce-Laporte. Washington, D.C.: Smithsonian Institution, Research Institute for Ethnic Studies, 1981.

Stresses importance of economic motives for migration; English-speaking Caribbean women met family obligations (including non-legal ones) and tried to improve themselves by moving.

186. Grey, Donna. "Caribbean Women and the Brain Drain." P. 171 Female Immigrants to the United States: Caribbean, Latin American and African Experiences. Ed. Delores M. Mortimer and Roy S. Bryce-Laporte. Washington, D.C.: Smithsonian Institution, Research Institute on Immigration and Ethnic Studies, 1981.

A brief note on an important, but little-studied, topic.

187. Houstoun, Marion et al. "Female Predominance of Immigration to the United States since 1930: A First Look." International Migration Review 18 (Winter 1984): 908-965.

Predominance of women was a result of legal preferences for wives, and later, other family members under U.S. immigration law.

188. Hvidt, Kristian. Flight to America: The Social Background of 300,000 Danish Emigrants. New York: Academic Press, 1975.

Focus is on characteristics of migrants in nineteenth century; see chapter on gender.

189. Jackson, Pauline. "Women in 19th Century Irish Emigration." International Migration Review 18 (Winter 1984): 1004-1020.

This was the only nineteenth-century migration in which women outnumbered men.

190. Jung, B. "Chinese Immigrant Women." Civil Rights Digest 6 (Spring 1974): 46-47.

The Chinese Exclusion Act of 1882 produced seriously unbalanced sex ratios in Chinese communities by making it almost impossible for women to enter the U.S. legally.

191. Kaups, Matti. "The Finns in the Copper and Iron Ore Mines of the Western Great Lakes Region, 1864-1905: Some Preliminary Observations." Pp. 55-88 The Finnish Experience in the Western Great Lakes Region: New Perspectives. Ed. Michael Karni. Vammala: Institute for Migration of Turku Finland, 1975.

Contrasts differing male and female migration patterns, and resulting wide variations in sex ratios among migrants to particular destinations. Women were most likely to settle in farming communities.

192. Kellor, Francis A. "The Protection of Immigrant Women." Atlantic 101 (Feb. 1908): 246-255.

Emphasizes the special problems faced by women during migration.

193. Kennedy, Robert E. The Irish: Emigration, Marriage and Fertility. Berkeley: University of California Press, 1973.

Some attention to women, and to linkage between marriage customs and female migration.

194. LaGuerre, Michael S. "The Impact of Migration on the Haitian Family and Household Organization." Pp. 446-481 Family and Kinship in Middle America and the Caribbean. Ed. Arnaud F. Marks and Rene A. Romer. Willemstad: Institute of Higher Studies in Curacao, 1978.

Eight case studies of how families and households left behind managed when men migrated; good attention to women.

195. Larson, Eric M. "International Migration and the Labor Force: A Study of Members of Migrant Households Versus Members of Domestic Households in the Dominican Republic." Unpublished Ph.D. Dissertation, The University of Texas at Austin, 1987. Order Number DA 8717463.

Some attention to women in both types of families.

196. Massey, Douglas S. and Katherine M. Schnabel. "Background Characteristics of Undocumented Hispanic Migrants to the United States: A Review of Recent Research." *Migration Today* 11 (1983): 9-13.

Most undocumented migrants studied were Mexicans; only 10 percent of those apprehended by U.S. Immigration and Naturalization Service were women.

197. Massey, Douglas S. and Katherine M. Schnabel. "Recent Trends in Hispanic Immigration to the United States." *International Migration Review* 17 (1983): 212-244.

Analyzes age and sex of Mexican, Cuban, and South American immigrants; females outnumbered males in all groups--but only slightly among Mexicans.

198. Massiah, Joycelin. *Employed Women in Barbados: A Demographic Profile, 1946-1970.* Cave Hill, Barbados: Institute of Social and Economic Research (Eastern Caribbean), University of the West Indies, 1984.

Includes a section on migration. Migrating men were apt to be gone for long periods 1891-1921 and 1946-60. This led to increased economic independence of women; after 1960, women migrants outnumbered men.

199. Mendez, Paz P. et al. *The Filipino Family in Transition: A Study in Culture and Education.* Mendiola, Manila: Centro Escolar University Research and Development Center, 1984.

Focus is on homeland; some analysis of impact of migration on family ties and patterns; good attention to women throughout.

200. Meyerowitz, Joanne. "Women and Migration: Autonomous Female Migrants to Chicago, 1880-1930," *Journal of Urban History* 13 (February 1987): 197-206.

Only a small proportion of those studied were Scandinavian, Polish, Canadian, and Irish women; autonomous migration was more characteristic of native- than of foreign-born.

201. Morokvasic, Mirjana. "Birds of Passage are also Women..." *International Migration Review* 18 (Winter 1984): 886-907.

Although not limited to analysis of migration to the U.S., this article offers important background for understanding general world-wide patterns in female migration.

202. Nolan, Janet A. "Ourselves Alone: Female Emigration from Ireland, 1885-1920." Unpublished Ph.D. Dissertation, The University of Connecticut, 1986. Order Number DA 8710271.

Focuses on the large number of unmarried Irish women traveling alone to the U.S.

203. Oh, Tai K. The Asian Brain Drain: A Factual and Causal Analysis. San Francisco: R & E Research Associates, 1977.

Analyzes foreign students; only 20 percent were women.

204. Otterbein, Keith F. "Caribbean Family Organization: A Comparative Analysis." American Anthropologist 67 (February 1965): 66-79.

Offers an explanation for the important economic role of women in Caribbean; traces patterns to male absenteeism, sometimes related to male labor migration.

205. Pang, Henry. "The Sex Composition of the Japanese American Population." Journal of Sex Research 4 (November 1968): 313-315.

Once male-dominated, the sex ratio of this group dropped 1950-1960 because of the migration of military brides.

206. Papademetriou, Demetrios G. and Nicholas Di Marzio. "Profile of Unapprehended Undocumented Aliens in Northern New Jersey: A Research Note." International Migration Review 19 (Winter 1985): 746-759.

Relatively few women were found in this population.

207. Peffer, George A. "Forbidden Families: Emigration Experiences of Chinese Women Under the Page Law, 1875-1882." Journal of American Ethnic History 6 Fall (1986): 28-46.

Author argues that this law, widely assumed to be ineffective, nevertheless diminished the number of women migrants traveling to U.S. to join husbands after its passage.

208. Pollock, Nancy J. "Women and Division of Labor: A Jamaican Example." American Anthropologist 74 (June 1972): 689-692.

Male migration encouraged women to depend upon each other for support during one phase of life cycle.

209. Rasmussen, Janet E. "Sisters Across the Sea: Early Norwegian Feminists and Their American Connections." Women's Studies International 5, no. 6 (1982): 647-654.

Information about the feminist movement in the U.S. encouraged some Norwegian women to emigrate.

210. Reichert, Josh and Douglas S. Massey. "Patterns of U.S. Migration from a Mexican Sending Community: A Comparison of Legal and Illegal Migrants." International Migration Review 13 (Winter 1979): 599-623.

Men seriously outnumbered women among illegal immigrants but only slightly among legal; legal migrants were much more likely to bring wives, children, and other dependents.

32   IMMIGRANT WOMEN IN THE U.S.

211. Sassen-Koob, Saskia. "Notes on the Incorporation of Third World Women into Wage-Labor Through Immigration and Off-Shore Production." *International Migration Review* 18 (Winter 1984): 1144-1167.

Notes women's growing importance in migration streams worldwide; these developed with women's growing involvement in production throughout the world.

212. Scheper-Hughes, Nancy. "Inheritance of the Meek: Land, Labor and Love in Western Ireland." *Marxist Perspectives* 5 (1979): 46-77.

A good source for understanding the consequences of migration for family and marriage patterns among those who remained behind.

213. Scheper-Hughes, Nancy. *Saints, Scholars, and Schizophrenics: Mental Illness in Rural Ireland*. Berkeley: University of California Press, 1979.

Focus is on contemporary Ireland, but traces the impact of past migrations on sex roles and male/female relations, celibacy, birth order, and inheritance; see especially the chapter "The People Left Behind."

214. Seivwright, Mary. "Project Report on Factors Affecting Mass Migration of Jamaican Nurses to the United States." *The Jamaican Nurse* 5 (August and December 1965): 8-13.

215. Shukert, Elfrieda B. and Barbara S. Scibetta. *War Brides of World War II*. Novato, Cal.: Presidio Press, 1988.

Groups considered include English, Australian, French, Italian, German, Chinese, and Japanese. The focus is on the homeland, courtship, and migration experience, not life in the U.S.

216. Simon, Rita J. and Caroline B. Brettell, eds. *International Migration, the Female Experience*. Totowa, N.J.: Rowman and Allanheld, 1985.

Although only a few articles focus on the U.S., the introduction provides a good introduction to themes of theoretical interest to all students of women and migration.

217. Smith, M. Estellie. "Networks and Migration Resettlement: Cherchez la Femme." *Anthropological Quarterly* 49 (January 1976): 20-27.

Portuguese women often built the social networks that facilitated migration to New England.

218. Smith, M. Estellie. "The Portuguese Female Immigrant: The 'Marginal Man'." International Migration Review 14 (Spring 1980): 77-92.

Focus is Azoreans who migrated to New England; women were mediators and "nags," who instigated migration even if they themselves did not migrate.

219. Sung, Betty L. "Changing Chinese." Society 14 (September/October 1977): 44-49.

The number of women immigrants now exceeds that of men, a significant change in this nationality group.

220. Tyree, Andrea and Katharine M. Donato. "A Demographic Overview of the International Migration of Women." Pp. 21-44 International Migration, The Female Experience. Ed. Rita J. Simon and Caroline B. Brettell. Totowa, N.J.: Rowman & Allanheld, 1985.

Focus is on contemporary migration, comparing U.S. to some other receiving countries.

221. Tyree, Andrea and Katherine M. Donato. "The Sex Composition of Legal Immigrants to the United States." Sociology and Social Research 69 (July 1985): 577-84.

Provides breakdown by nationality groups for 1979. Family reunification encouraged female migration, but Mexican women in U.S. also "imported" bridegrooms from their homeland.

222. Waltz, Waldo E. The Nationality of Married Women: A Study of Domestic Policies and International Legislation. University of Illinois Studies in the Social Sciences 22, 1 (1937).

Includes some information on the Cable Act, which required immigrant women to obtain citizenship independent of their husbands.

223. Wiest, Raymond E. "Wage Migration and the Household in a Mexican Town." Journal of Anthropological Research 29 (Autumn 1973): 180-209.

A study of migration as a family strategy. Women's migration rates were low. Compares the women left behind by male migration to the better-studied Caribbean case.

224. Yung, Judy. "'A Bowlful of Tears': Chinese Women Immigrants on Angel Island." Frontiers 2 (Summer 1977): 52-55.

Study of women who arrived after 1882, and of their sometimes-lengthy detainment as a result of the Chinese Exclusion Act.

4

Family

INTRODUCTION

In both the social sciences and in history, the centrality of family in the lives of immigrant women has been an important theme, regardless of the kinds of sources used. Scholars in many disciplines use the model of the family economy, and focus on the changing balance of work and family in women's lives. For this reason, the reader interested in women as family members is advised to consult Chapter 5 on work, where research on housework (which might be considered a dimension of family life) is also cited. The reader should also refer to index entries on particular aspects of family life, since information on family can often be found in works cited elsewhere in this bibliography.

Some dimensions of women's family experiences have been treated in far greater depth than others. For example, we know far more about intermarriage than we do about childrearing or courtship.

Generally, scholarly studies have portrayed families as important and supportive resources for immigrant women, and they have emphasized family and kinship as arenas where wives and mothers enjoyed influence and authority. A smaller but growing body of literature drawing on feminist theory focuses instead on the family as a place of conflict and potential or actual exploitation. The female-headed household is a topic of some interest in both cases, especially to those scholars who study contemporary migrations.

Among historians, the study of the family as a flexible but enduring institution was an important element in rewriting the history of ethnic communities in the United States, and in explaining their persistence. This approach, however, has not always brought the immigrant woman into particularly sharp focus. In the social sciences, by contrast, there has been a switch from studies of family breakdown and pathology among immigrants to a focus on roles within the family as determined by gender, age, and generation. Family roles, like intermarriage rates, are sometimes studied in order to gauge cultural change and the degree of integration or adaptation to life in the United States.

A highly specialized literature on fertility is not cited in this chapter but in Chapter 7 on "The Body." Although one would not want to exclude the topic from a bibliography on immigrant women, quantitative studies of fertility rarely reveal much about women's subjective experiences as wives, mothers, or daughters.

CITATIONS

225. Adams, Paul L. and Jeffrey H. Horovitz. "Coping Patterns of Mothers of Poor Boys." Child Psychiatry & Human Development 10 (Spring 1980):

The mothers of Cuban boys are compared to Afro-American mothers.

226. Adler, Peter et al. "Familiar Correlates of Gang Membership: An Exploratory Study of Mexican-American Youth." Hispanic Journal of Behavioral Sciences 6 (March 1984): 65-76.

Among other family characteristics, mothers of gang members were more dissatisfied and fatalistic than control groups.

227. Afoa, Ioane A. "Divorce Counseling with Samoan Couples." Unpublished Ph.D. Dissertation, School of Theology at Claremont, Sociology, 1980. Order Number 8018693.

The focus is on pastoral counseling of both sexes.

228. Aguirre, Benigno E. "The Marital Stability of Cubans in the United States." Ethnicity 8 (Dec 1981): 387-405.

Females married after arrival in the U.S. have stable marriages. Notes modernity of marriages.

229. Aguirre-Lopez, Benigno E. "The Marital Stability of Cuban Immigrants: 1970." Unpublished Ph.D. Dissertation, Ohio State University, 1977. Order Number 7731811.

Found that women's marital stability decreased with increasing instrumental ability.

230. Alba, Richard D. "Assimilation among American Catholics." Unpublished Ph. D. Dissertation, Columbia University, 1974. Order Number 75-16,095.

Focus is on increasing intermarriage by generation among Irish and Italians; notes corresponding weakening of ethnic identity.

231. Albornoz, Jaime I. "A Comparative Survey of Self-Concept, Marital Adjustment, and Reactions toward Infidelity in Intracultural and Intercultural Marriages." Unpublished Ph.D. Dissertation, United States International University, 1979. Order Number 7924555.

Considers intermarriage between Latin Americans and Caucasians, differentiating men and women. Women ranked lower than men in self-concept, marital adjustment, and infidelity.

232. Alcalay, Rina. "Hispanic Women in the United States: Family and Work Relations." *Migration Today* 12, 3 (1984): 13-20.

No attention to generation, but does contrast Mexican-American, Puerto Rican, and Cuban-American patterns. A common theme for Hispanics is woman's authority and importance within extended family.

233. Alvarez, Robert R., Jr. *Familia, Migration and Adaptation in Baja and Alta California, 1880-1975.* Berkeley: University of California Press, 1987.

Mexican migrants to California; women appear mainly as parts of family networks.

234. Armstrong, M. Jocelyn. "Ethnicity and Sex Role Socialization: A Comparative Example Using Life History Data from Hawaii." *Sex Roles: A Journal of Research* 10 (February 1984): 157-181.

Compares two second-generation women, one Portuguese and one Chinese, including good information on childrearing (both women were raised by their grandmothers).

235. Bakke, E. Wight. *Citizens Without Work: A Study of the Effects of Unemployment upon the Workers' Social Relations and Practices.* New Haven: Yale University Press, 1940.

Although little systematic attention is given to national origin, this study of New Haven includes interesting material on foreign-born and second generation women. See section II for case material on a patriarchal Italian family and "A Polish Mother Becomes Head of a Family."

236. Barron, Milton L. *People Who Intermarry: Intermarriage in a New England Industrial Community.* Syracuse, N.Y.: Syracuse University Press, 1946.

A study of Derby, Conn., which includes breakdowns by sex for Italian, Irish, Polish, British, Russian, and many smaller groups.

237. Benoit, Virgil. "A French-Canadian Community in the Minnesota Red River Valley." Minnesota History 44 (Winter 1975): 279-289.

Some attention to women in family and spiritual life of community.

238. Benson, Paulette and Joanne Altschuler. The Jewish Family: Past, Present and Future. Denver: Alternatives in Religious Education, 1979.

Some attention to immigrant Eastern European Jews and women in family roles.

239. Berman, Louis. Sex Role Patterns in the Jewish Family. New York: Thomas Yoseloff, 1968.

See chapter on sex-role patterning. Some attention to homeland, immigrant generation, and matricentricity. See also chapter on sexuality.

240. Bernard, Richard N. The Melting Pot and the Altar. Minneapolis: University of Minnesota Press, 1980.

Tabular data broken down by sex. Notes considerable endogamy into second generation, especially among Eastern Europeans. (Groups studied include German, Norwegian, Canadian, and Irish.)

241. Bienstock, Beverly G. "The Changing Image of the American Jewish Mother." Pp. 173-91 Changing Images of the Family. Ed. Virginia Tufte and Barbara Myerhoff. New Haven and London: Yale University Press, 1979.

One section concerns immigrants; focus is the Jewish mother in literature, emphasizing women's expanded economic and familial responsibilities.

242. Blau, Zena S. "In Defense of the Jewish Mother." Midstream 18 (February 1967): 42-49.

Focus is "die Yiddishe Mameh." Notes that delayed emotional independence from mother may encourage educational achievement.

243. Bloch, Harriet. "Changing Domestic Roles Among Polish Immigrant Women." Anthropological Quarterly 49 (January 1976): 3-10.

Case study of Poles in the homeland and in New Jersey; shows how increasing importance of wage-earning leads to dissatisfactions with family life; women's commitment to improving family economic status worked against female solidarity.

244. Bodnar, John. Workers' World; Kinship, Community, and Protest in an Industrial Society, 1900-1940. Baltimore and London: The Johns Hopkins University Press, 1982.

Based on oral histories with Italians, Poles, Croatians, Slovenians, and Lithuanians. One third of interviews with women; women's memories included in part I, which focuses on family and kinship ties.

245. Borah, Woodrow and Sherburne F. Cook. "Marriage and Legitimacy in Mexican Culture: Mexico and California." California Law Review 54 (May 1966): 946-1006.

Traces Spanish and Mexican customs from colonial period to the present, focusing on the frequency of irregular and informal unions which result in high illegitimacy rates under U.S. law; found common-law marriage relatively common among Mexicans in California.

246. Boyd, Carol J. "Relationships among the Correlates within the Construct of Mother-Daughter Identification: Mutual Identification, Attachment, Conflict and Identity in Adult Polish-American Women." Unpublished Ph.D. Dissertation, Wayne State University, 1987. Order Number DA 8714530.

247. Brandt, Lillian. Five Hundred and Seventy-four Deserters and Their Families. New York: The Charity Organization Society, 1905.

The largest groups of families affected by desertion were native-born, followed by Irish and English Canadians. Other groups were poorly represented.

248. Bressler, Marvin. "Selected Family Patterns in W.I. Thomas' Unfinished Study of the Bintl Brief." American Sociological Review 17 (October 1952): 563-71.

Some attention to marriage and childbearing among Eastern European Jewish women.

249. Bryan, Dorothy P. "Nigerian Women and Child-Rearing Practices in Washington, D.C.: A Summary of Research Findings and Implications." Pp. 157-170 Female Immigrants to the United States. Ed. Delores M. Mortimer and Roy S. Bryce-Laporte. Washington, D.C.: Smithsonian Institution, Research Institute for Ethnic Studies, 1981.

Topics covered include pregnancy, feeding, toilet training and discipline.

250. Bryant, Carol A. "The Impact of Kin, Friend and Neighbor Networks on Infant Feeding Practices: Cuban, Puerto Rican and Anglo Families in Florida." Social Science and Medicine 16, 20 (1982): 1757-1765.

Others seriously influenced mothers' decisions about child's feeding.

40   IMMIGRANT WOMEN IN THE U.S.

251. Burki, Elizabeth A. "Cambodian and Laotian Mothers and Daughters in Chicago: Surviving Crises and Renegotiating Identities." Unpublished Ph.D. Dissertation, Northwestern University, 1988. Order Number DA 8423625.

252. Burma, John H. "Interethnic Marriage in Los Angeles, 1948-1959." Social Forces 42 (December 1963): 156-165.

Discusses Japanese and Chinese immigrants. Finds that unbalanced sex ratios led to greater endogamy among women; notes also the impact of large numbers of Japanese war brides.

253. Burma, John H. et al. "A Comparison of the Occupational Status of Intramarrying and Intermarrying Couples: A Research Note." Sociology and Social Research 54 (1970): 508-519.

Compares Japanese- and Chinese-Americans by sex and generation.

254. Byington, Margaret F. Homestead: The Households of a Mill Town. Vol. 4 The Pittsburgh Survey. New York: Russell Sage Foundation, Charities Publication Committee, 1910.

Main group studied is Slavs. See especially chapters "Of Human Relationships," "Table and Dinner Pail," "Family Life of the Slavs."

255. Cappozzoli, Mary J. "Three Generations of Italian American Women in Nassau County, New York, 1925-1981." Unpublished Ph.D. Dissertation, Lehigh University, 1985. Order Number DA 8505012.

Based on oral histories. Compares Italian to other women in county, and finds evidence of familism and a tradition of male superiority. For the third generation, the meaning of ethnicity diminished to names and food recipes.

256. Casas, J. Manuel and Silvia Ortiz. "Exploring the Applicability of the Dyadic Adjustment Scale for Assessing Level of Marital Adjustment with Mexican Americans." Journal of Marriage and the Family 47 (November 1985): 1023-27.

Compares men and women and native- and foreign-born, noting significant differences in both.

257. Casgupta, Shamita D. "Marching to a Different Drummer? Sex Roles of Asian Indian Women in the United States." Women and Therapy 5 (Summer 1986): 297-322.

Homemakers seemed to abide by traditional roles, even though they were aware of their inequities. Found differences in sex roles for women employed in male-dominated and female-dominated occupations.

258. Castellano, Vianne and Myron H. Dembo. "The Relationship of Father Absence and Antisocial Behavior to Social Egocentrism in Adolescent Mexican American Females." Journal of Youth and Adolescence 10 (February 1981): 77-84.

Most of the girls studied were second-generation.

259. Catapusan, Benicio T. "Filipino Intermarriage Problems in the United States." Sociology and Social Research 22 (January-February 1938): 265-272.

Men were more likely than women to marry out in Los Angeles, often with Mexican immigrant women.

260. Cavan, Ruth S. and Katherine H. Ranck. The Family and the Depression: A Study of One Hundred Chicago Families. Chicago: University of Chicago Press, 1938.

Russian- and Polish-born families were the largest immigrant groups studied in this Chicago work; good attention to women and their family roles, but little systematic attention to nationality group or generation.

261. Chai, Alice Y. "Sexual Division of Labor in the Contexts of Nuclear Family and Cultural Ideology among Korean Student Couples in Hawaii." Humboldt Journal of Social Relations 10 (Spring/Summer 1983): 153-74.

Women found the burden of childrearing particularly heavy because they had few female relatives to help them; well-educated wives willingly took menial jobs to support husbands, and when they did so husbands did more domestic work in response. Women wanted more help than they actually got.

262. Char, Walter F. and John F. McDermott. "Family Relationships: Different Attitudes of Adolescent Boys and Girls." Medical Aspects of Human Sexuality 21 (August 1987): 36-42.

Examines generational differences and sexual and familial attitudes of Japanese-Americans in Hawaii.

263. Chavez, John and Raymond Buriel. "Reinforcing Children's Effort: A Comparison of Immigrant, Native-Born Mexican-American and Euro-American Mothers." Hispanic Journal of Behavioral Sciences 8 (June 1986): 127-142.

Contrasts differing methods used by immigrant and second-generation Mexican mothers.

264. Choi, Elizabeth S. C. "Mother-Infant Interaction Among Korean and American Mothers." Unpublished Ph.D. Dissertation, University of Texas at Austin, 1981. Order Number 81 19274.

Found rapid change toward bottle-feeding among immigrant mothers.

42   IMMIGRANT WOMEN IN THE U.S.

265. Claghorn, Kate H. *The Immigrant's Day in Court*. New York: Harper and Brothers, 1923.

See sections on family troubles (includes information on women's work for boarders); violence resulting from family trouble and from "irregular" sexual relations. Also includes a section on important immigrant strikes, including those of women workers.

266. Cohen, Jessica L. "A Comparison of Norms and Behaviors of Childrearing in Jewish and Italian Mothers." Unpublished Ph.D. Dissertation, Syracuse University, 1977. Order Number 7811640.

No attention to generation, but the dates when women married suggest that most were second-generation. Found that close friendship was limited to members of own ethnic group.

267. Cohen, Lizabeth A. "Embellishing a Life of Labor: An Interpretation of the Material Culture of American Working-Class Homes, 1885-1915." *Journal of American Culture* 3 (Winter 1980): 752-775.

Much evidence comes from Italian, Russian Jewish, and Slavic homes. Good attention to Americanization efforts aimed at home life of immigrant women by social settlement workers.

268. Colcord, Joanna C. *Broken Homes: A Study of Family Desertion*. New York: Russell Sage Foundation, 1919.

Includes a chart that gives nationality backgrounds of 480 deserting men and their families in New York; contrasts to all social work cases of same period. The largest group of deserted families were Italians.

269. Connor, John W. "Family Bonds, Maternal Closeness and the Suppression of Sexuality in Three Generations of Japanese Americans." *Ethos* 4 (Summer 1976): 189-221.

Sacramento Japanese had higher attachment to their mothers than Caucasians.

270. Connor, John W. *A Study of the Marital Stability of Japanese War Brides*. San Francisco: R & E Research Associates, 1976.

271. Cook, Sherburne F. "Type of Marriage Ceremony as a Carryover in Acculturation of Mexicans in the United States." *Ethnohistory* 23 (Winter 1976): 45-63.

No special attention to women, although obviously they were involved: notes preference for civil marriage ceremonies.

272. Cromwell, Vicky L. and Ronald E. Cromwell. "Perceived Dominance in Decision-Making and Conflict Resolution among Anglo, Black and Chicano Couples." Journal of Marriage and the Family 40 (November 1978): 749-59.

Kansas City Mexicans, many of whom are probably immigrant and second-generation. Found conflict between men and women over childrearing decisions, but deny that men made most decisions for family.

273. D'Andrea, Vaneeta-Marie. "The Social Role Identity of Italian-American Women: An Analysis and Comparison of Familial and Religious Expectations". Pp. 61-68 The Family and Community Life of Italian Americans. Ed. Richard N. Juliani. Staten Island: The Italian American Historical Association, 1983.

Some attention to immigrant generation. Power that mothers enjoyed in families explains why so few felt need to free themselves from family bonds.

274. de Cubas, Mercedes M. and Tiffany Field. "Teaching Interactions of Black and Cuban Teenage Mothers and their Infants." Early Childhood Development and Care 16 (July 1984): 41-56.

Cuban mothers talked more to their children as they demonstrated a task.

275. del Castillo, R. Griswold. "La Familia Chicano: Social Changes in the Chicano Family of Los Angeles, 1850-1880." Journal of Ethnic Studies 3 (Spring 1975): 41-58.

Some attention to women, especially as heads of households.

276. Dubnoff, Steven J. "The Family and Absence from Work: Irish Workers in a Lowell, Massachusetts Cotton Mill, 1860." Unpublished Ph.D. Dissertation, Brandeis University, 1976. Order Number 76-25,299.

Considerable attention to Irish female-headed households.

277. Eisenbruch, Maurice. "Cross-Cultural Aspects of Bereavement: II. Ethnic and Cultural Variations in the Development of Bereavement Practices." Culture, Medicine and Psychiatry 8 (December 1984): 315-347.

Widowhood among Chinese, Southeast Asian refugees, Haitian, Italian, Greek, and Spanish-speaking groups.

278. Endo, Russell and Dale Hirokawa. "Japanese American Intermarriage." Free Inquiry in Creative Sociology 11 (November 1983): 159-166.

Rates increased with each generation, but women married out more frequently than men in all.

279. Escovar, Luis and Peggy. "Retrospective Perception of Parental Child-Rearing Practices in Three Culturally Different College Groups." <u>International Journal of Intercultural Relations</u> 9, 1 (1985): 31-49.

Cuban-Americans are compared to other Hispanics and non-Hispanics. Cuban mothers more resembled non-Hispanic Americans than they did mothers in Latin American countries.

280. Esparza, Ricardo. "The Value of Children among Lower Class Mexican, Mexican American and Anglo Couples." Unpublished Ph.D. Dissertation, University of Michigan, 1977. Order Number 77-17,991.

Found variation across ethnic and religious lines, regarding not only the value of children, but also the preference for boys over girls and the intended family size.

281. Fitzgerald, Daniel F. "International Marriage: A Focus on Japanese-American Marriage and Families." Unpublished Ph.D. Dissertation, University of Northern Colorado, 1986. Order Number DA 8629374.

Study was undertaken to assist American Defense Department workers who were considering marrying a Japanese or other foreign citizen. The assumption of the study is that the military person is a male soldier.

282. Fridkis, Ari L. "Desertion in the American Jewish Immigrant Family: The Work of the National Desertion Bureau in Cooperation with the Industrial Removal Office." <u>American Jewish History</u> 71 (December 1981): 285-299.

Notes conflicts of religious and secular divorce practices, which resulted in high rates of desertion among Eastern European Jews.

283. Friedman, Reena S. "'Send Me My Husband Who Is In New York City': Husband Desertion in the American Jewish Immigrant Community, 1900-1926." <u>Jewish Social Studies</u> 44 (Winter 1982): 1-18.

Desertion was common among Eastern European Jews; 15 percent of United Hebrew Charities relief funds went to deserted wives.

284. Frisbie, W. Parker et al. "Nativity and Household-Family Structure Among the Mexican-Origin Population of the United States." Pp. 74-99 <u>Mexican Immigrants and the Mexican American Community: An Evolving Relationship</u>. Ed. R. de la Garza and H. Browning. Austin: The University of Texas Press, 1985.

Emphasizes the differences between immigrant households and those of general Mexican-American population. Includes information on female-headed households and fertility.

FAMILY   45

285. Frisbie, W. Parker. "Variations in Patterns of Marital Instability among Hispanics." <u>Journal of Marriage and the Family</u> 48 (February 1986): 99-106.

Based on study of ever-married women in 1980 census. Contrasts low rates of divorce among Mexican-Americans and Cubans to higher rates among Puerto Ricans and Afro-Americans.

286. Gabaccia, Donna R. <u>From Sicily to Elizabeth Street: Housing and Social Change among Italian Immigrants.</u> Albany: State University of New York Press, 1984.

Studies changes in family life that accompanied move from Italy's large urban villages to a tenement neighborhood in New York; good attention to women and their work.

287. Gambino, Richard. <u>Blood of my Blood, The Dilemma of the Italian-American.</u> New York: Doubleday, 1974.

Some attention to immigrant generation; see especially "La Serietà--The Ideal of Womanliness" and "Sex."

288. Glasco, Laurence A. "The Life Cycles and Household Structure of American Ethnic Groups: Irish, German and Native-Born Whites in Buffalo, New York, 1855." <u>Journal of Urban History</u> 1 (May 1975): 339-364.

Separate sections on native-born, Irish, and German women, with attention to fertility and household composition, age at leaving home.

289. Glenn, Evelyn N. "Split Household, Small Producer and Dual Wage Earner: An Analysis of Chinese-American Family Strategies," <u>Journal of Marriage and the Family</u> 45 (February 1983): 35-46.

Three family patterns emerged over time, with differing roles for wives--wage-earning work outside the family, participation in family business, housework only.

290. Glick, C. "Interracial Marriage and Ad-mixture in Hawaii." <u>Social Biology</u> 17 (1970): 278-91.

Rates of intermarriage among Japanese and Chinese increased with each generation.

291. Goldschieder, Frances K. "Family Patterns Among the U.S. Yiddish-Mother-Tongue Subpopulation: 1970." Pp. 172-183 <u>The Jewish Family: Myths and Reality</u>. Ed. Steven Cohen and Paula F. Hyman. New York and London: Holmes & Meier, 1986.

Found extent and duration of marriage higher than U.S. average but fertility lower than average.

292. Gonzalez, Rosalinda M. "Chicanas and Mexican Immigrant Families, 1920-1940: Women's Subordination and Family Exploitation." Pp. 59-84 Decades of Discontent: the Women's Movement, 1920-1940. Ed. Lois Scharf and Joan M. Jensen. Westport, Conn.: Greenwood Press, 1983.

Women workers were often recruited as part of family groups, allowing maintenance of traditional forms of subordination.

293. Gordon, Linda. Heroines of their Own Lives, The Politics and History of Family Violence. New York: Viking Press, 1988.

Many of the cases studied were of foreign-born families and women. An appendix provides some statistical breakdowns on violence by national origin, but text pays little attention to ethnicity, except to note that female drunkenness was common only among Irish and that the most extreme examples of patriarchal control over wives and daughters came from Italians families.

294. Grant, Geraldine. "Immigrant Family Stability: Some Preliminary Thoughts." Journal of Children in Contemporary Society 15 (Spring 1983): 27-37.

Notes increased importance of nuclear family, and rapid change in husband/wife relations.

295. Gray, Ellen and John Cosgrove. "Ethnocentric Perception of Childrearing Practices in Protective Services." Child Abuse and Neglect 9, 3 (1985): 389-396.

Interviews with Mexican, Filipino, Japanese, Samoan, and Vietnamese-Americans show delegation of responsibility to child and dominance/submission in parent/child relations are areas of potential misunderstanding.

296. Griswold del Castillo, Richard. La Familia, Chicano Families in the Urban Southwest, 1848 to the Present. Notre Dame: Notre Dame University Press, 1985.

Good attention to women in Tucson, Los Angeles, San Antonio, and Santa Fe--roughly one-third of whom were foreign-born. Includes comparisons to other immigrant groups. Female-headed households were common even though female employment was low. See especially chapter 5 on immigration and intermarriage and chapter 6 on childrearing, discipline, and sex.

297. Guinnane, Timothy W. "Migration, Marriage, and Household Formation: The Irish at the Turn of the Century." Unpublished Ph.D. Dissertation, Stanford University 1987. Order Number DA 8800945.

Compares Irish and Irish immigrants in the U.S. The author doubts that a distinctive Irish culture influenced marriage patterns in the U.S.

298. Gupta, Omprakash K. and Savitri. "A Study of the Influence of American Culture on the Child-Rearing Attitudes of Indian Mothers." <u>Indian Journal of Social Work</u> 46 (April 1985): 95-104.

Found no significant differences in Indian immigrant mothers and native-born American women.

299. Gurak, Douglas. "Family Formation and Marital Selectivity Among Colombian and Dominican Immigrants in New York City." <u>International Migration Review</u> 21 (Summer 1987): 274-298.

300. Haddad, Safia F. "The Women's Role in the Socialization of Syrian-Americans in Chicago". Pp. 84-101 <u>The Arab Americans: Studies in Assimilation</u>. Ed. Elaine C. Habopian and Add Paden. AAUG Monograph Series no. 1. Wilmette, Ill.: Medina University Press, 1969.

Emphasizes wife as money-maker and consumer, and documents increasing companionship between husbands and wives.

301. Hall, Elizabeth L. <u>Mothers' Assistance in Philadelphia: Actual and Potential Costs: A Study of 1010 Families</u>. Hanover, N.H.: The Sociological Press, 1933.

About one-third of the mothers were foreign-born, mainly Italian, Irish, Russian, and Polish; focus is on mother as caretaker and wage-earner.

302. Hampsten, Elizabeth. "A German-Russian Family in North Dakota." <u>Heritage of the Great Plains</u> 20 (Winter 1987): 1-8.

303. Hareven, Tamara. "Family and Work Patterns of Immigrant Laborers in a Planned Industrial Community." Pp. 47-65 <u>Immigrants in Industrial America, 1850-1920</u>. Ed. Richard L Ehrlich. Charlottesville: University Press of Virginia for the Eleutherian Mills-Hagley Foundation and Balch Institute, 1977.

Some attention to foreign-born women.

304. Hareven, Tamara. <u>Family Time and Industrial TIme: The Relationship between the Family and Work in a New England Industrial Community</u>. Cambridge and New York: Cambridge University Press, 1982.

Much on the work and family lives of French-Canadian, Greek, Polish, and British women immigrants.

305. Harzler, Kaye and Juan N. Franco. "Ethnicity, Division of Household Tasks and Equity in Marital Roles: A Comparison of Anglo- and Mexican-American Couples." *Hispanic Journal of Behavioral Sciences* 7 (December 1985): 333-344.

Contrasts more and less acculturated college student couples; found that Mexican-American women wanted husbands to do more housework.

306. Hawkes, Glenn R. and Minna Taylor. "Power Structure in Mexican and Mexican-American Farm Laborer Families." *Journal of Marriage and the Family* 37 (1975): 807-811.

The most common form of decisionmaking was egalitarian, not patriarchal; the only decision made mainly by the man was where the family lived.

307. Hayner, Norman S. and Charles N. Reynolds. "Chinese Family Life in America." *American Sociological Review* 2 (October 1937): 630-637.

Emphasizes the unbalanced sex ratio, the separation of women and men during migration, and the impact of patriarchal mores on women remaining in China.

308. Heer, David. "The Marital Status of Second-Generation Americans." *American Sociological Review* 26, 2 (1961): 233-241.

Data presented by age and sex for twenty-three countries of parental origin; latest marriage was among Irish, earliest among Mexican.

309. Helmbold, Lois R. "Beyond the Family Economy: The Impact of the Great Depression on Black and White Working Class Women." *Feminist Studies* 13 (Fall 1987): 629-656.

Some examples given are from immigrant and second-generation women; the article is primarily a critique of the family economy, showing instead how women sought independence from familial constraints.

310. Hendricks, Glenn. *The Dominican Diaspora*. New York: Columbia University Press, 1972.

See the chapter "Adaptation of Social Structures: Household, Marriage, Role," which includes some information on women. Notes the special importance of virginity for young women.

311. Herzfeld, Elsa. "The Tenement House Family." *The Independent* 59 (Dec. 1905): 1520-23.

Notes national differences in house decor among Germans and Irish in New York; attention is given to women as workers and as mothers.

FAMILY   49

312. Higa, Masanori. "A Comparative Study of Three Groups of 'Japanese' Mothers: Attitudes toward Child Rearing." Pp. 16-25 Youth, Socialization and Mental Health.   Vol. III Mental Health Research in Asia and the Pacific. Ed. William P. Lebra. Honolulu: University of Hawaii Press, 1974.

Compares U.S. and Hawaii immigrants to Japanese nationals. Immigrant mothers considered their children Americans, while Hawaiian Japanese mothers encouraged children to excel to avoid disgracing their race.

313. Humphrey, Norman.   "The Changing Structure of the Detroit Mexican Family: An Index of Acculturation." American Sociological Review 9 (December 1944): 622-626.

Emphasizes conflict between husbands and wives, and between husband and children over degree of patriarchal authority and control.

314. Ikels, Charlotte. "Parental Perspectives on the Significance of Marriage."   Journal of Marriage and the Family 47 (May 1985): 253-264.

Compares Chinese and Irish; most immigrant mothers and fathers expected children to support them in old age, but few tried to control children's marriages or careers.

315. Johnson, Colleen L. "Interdependence, Reciprocity, and Indebtedness: An Analysis of Japanese American Kinship Relations." Journal of Marriage and the Family 39 (May 1977): 351-364.

Based on interviews with Japanese wives in Honolulu; contrasts exchanges in immigrant and second generations. Although little attention paid to gender, women seemed to assume responsibility for organizing reciprocity.

316. Johnson, Colleen L. "The Japanese-American Family and Community in Honolulu: Generational Continuities in Ethnic Affiliation."   Unpublished Ph.D. Dissertation, Syracuse University, 1972. Order Number DA 73-9537.

Interviews about family and kinship relations with mothers of three generations.

317. Johnson, Colleen L.   Growing Up and Growing Old in Italian-American Families. New Brunswick, N.J.:   Rutgers University Press, 1985.

Based on interviews with wives, mainly second-generation and middle-class; attention to both childrearing and aging.

318. Johnson, Elizabeth S. "Role Expectations and Role Realities of Older Italian Mothers and Their Daughters." International Journal of Aging and Human Development 14 (1981-82): 271-276.

High degree of consensus about appropriate roles for daughters in second generation.

50   IMMIGRANT WOMEN IN THE U.S.

319. Jones, Robert C. "Ethnic Family Patterns: The Mexican Family in the United States." American Journal of Sociology 53 (May 1948): 450-452.

Emphasizes the sharp division of labor by sex within the family.

320. Karsh, Audrey R. "Mothers and Daughters of Old San Diego." Western States Jewish History 19 (April 1987): 264-270.

General information on family relations among immigrants and second-generation Jews.

321. Keefe, Susan E., et al. "The Mexican-American Extended Family as an Emotional Support System." Human Organization 38 (Summer 1979): 144-152.

This California study finds Anglos as likely as Mexicans to see family as a source of support, but notes that Mexicans had more relatives available to support them. Mexican women of three generations depended primarily on other female family members, but there was significant variation by generation. Some women preferred friends for support.

322. Kennedy, J. C. Wages and Family Budgets in the Chicago Stockyards District, With Wage Statistics from Other Industries Employing Unskilled Labor. Vol. 3 A Study of Chicago's Stockyards Community. Chicago: University of Chicago Press, 1914.

Mainly a study of Polish, Lithuanian, and Slovak families, with attention to women's wage-earning and family responsibilities. Budgets include information on women's clothing and brides' costs for weddings.

323. Kikumura, Akemi and Harry H. Kitano. "Interracial Marriage: A Picture of the Japanese Americans." Journal of Social Issues 29, 2 (1973): 67-81.

Data presented by sex and generation; notes increasing rates of intermarriage for men and women, and tendency to marry other Asian groups.

324. Kim, Bok-Lim C. "Asian Wives of U.S. Servicemen: Women in Shadows." Amerasia Journal 4, no. 1 (1977): 91-116.

Study of Japanese, Korean, and Vietnamese wives suggests more difficulties than found in some previous studies; makes policy suggestions.

325. Kim, Bok-Lim C. "Casework with Japanese and Korean Wives of Americans." Social Casework 53 (May 1972): 273-279.

Emphasizes women's strengths; argues that case workers should not interpret submission as dependency. Found that most women overcame initial difficulties.

326. Kim, Bok-Lim C. "Korean Americans: An Emerging Immigrant Community." Civil Rights Digest 9 (Fall 1976): 39-41.

Includes information on military and war brides.

327. Kim, Bok-Lim C. "Pioneers in Intermarriage: Korean Women in the United States." Pp. 59-95 Korean Women in a Struggle for Humanization. Ed. Harold Hakwon Sunoo and Dong Soo Kim. Memphis, Tenn.: Association of Korean Christian Scholars in North America, 1978.

328. Kim, Bok-Lim. Plight of Asian Wives of Americans. Urbana: University of Illinois, 1975.

329. Kitano, Harry H. "Differential Child-Rearing Attitudes Between First and Second Generation Japanese in the United States." Journal of Social Psychology 53 (1961): 13-19.

Significant differences found, but explained mainly by higher levels of education of the second generation.

330. Kitano, Harry H. "Inter- and Intragenerational Differences in Maternal Attitudes Toward Child Rearing." Journal of Social Psychology 63 (August 1964): 215-110.

Compares Japanese women in U.S. and Japan. Generation and age were more important than homeland in shaping women's attitudes.

331. Kitano, Harry H. and Lynn H. Chai. "Korean Interracial Marriage." Marriage and Family Review 5 (Spring 1982): 75-89.

Females married out at a higher rate that men.

332. Kitano, Harry H. and Wai-Tsang Yeung. "Chinese Interracial Marriage." Marriage and Family Review 5 (Spring 1982): 35-48.

Rapid rise in out-marriage for both sexes.

333. Kitano, Harry H. et al. "Asian-American Interracial Marriage." Journal of Marriage and the Family 46 (February 1984): 179-90.

Rates of intermarriage given for Chinese (41 percent), Japanese (60 percent), and Koreans (28 percent). Women in all groups were more likely than men to marry out. Intermarriage increased with generation, and this explained differences between groups since Japanese were mainly third-generation.

52   IMMIGRANT WOMEN IN THE U.S.

334. Kuchner, Joan R.F.   "Chinese-American and European-American: A Cross-Cultural Study of Infant and Mother." Unpublished Ph.D. Dissertation, University of Chicago, 1981. <u>Dissertation Abstracts</u>   44: 1151B. No Order Number given.

Both groups were middle-class; the study identifies differing maternal and child behaviors in two groups.

335. Lamphere, Louise et al. "Kin Networks and Strategies of Working-Class Portuguese Families in a New England Town." Pp. 219-149 <u>The Versatility of Kinship</u>. Ed. Linda Cordell and Stephen Beckerman. New York: Academic Press, 1980.

Shows the role of women in maintaining extended family networks.

336. Landes, Ruth and Mark Zborowski.   "Hypotheses Concerning the Eastern European Family." <u>Psychiatry</u> 13 (1950): 447-464.

Although focus is on Jewish family in homeland shtetl), study is still of interest since it is based on an early effort at oral history (128 interviews, of which 74 were women) with first- and second-generation Eastern European Jews.

337. Laosa, Luis M.   "Maternal Teaching Strategies in Chicano Families of Varied Educational and Socioeconomic Levels." <u>Child Development</u> 49 (December 1978): 1129-35.

Los Angeles study of 43 mothers with overall low level of education. Found that better educated mothers praised, while less well educated mothers taught by offering themselves as examples.

338. Law, Timothy.   "Differential Childrearing Attitudes and Practices of Chinese-American Mothers." Unpublished Ph.D. Dissertation, Claremont Graduate School, 1973.   Order Number 74-967.

Compares foreign- and native-born, finding that native-born were "more democratic and permissive," while less accepting of maternal role.

339. Lee, Sung-Ja C.   "Housing Adjustment of Korean Families in American Society."   Unpublished Ph.D. Dissertation, The Florida State University, 1982. Order Number DA 9225205.

Found that elderly and working women wanted an "on-dol" (a room with floor heating); kitchen structure should also be redesigned to accommodate differing needs of Korean women.

340. Leon, J.L.   "Sex-Ethnic Marriage in Hawaii: A Nonmetric Multidimensional Analysis." <u>Journal of Marriage and the Family</u> 37 (1975): 775-781.

While intermarriage increased for both sexes, marriages tended to cluster among Asians of several backgrounds.

341. Leonard, Karen and Bruce LaBrack. "Conflict and Compatibility in Punjabi-Mexican Immigrant Families in Rural California, 1915-1965." Journal of Marriage and the Family 46 (1984): 527-537.

Immigrant male Punjabs (Hindi) married immigrant or second-generation Mexican women. Often they married sisters or sets of related women (mothers/daughters). Spanish or English, never Punjabi, was language at home.

342. Leonard, Karen. "Marriage and Family Life Among Early Asian Indian Immigrants." Population Review 25 (1982): 67-75.

343. Lewin, Ellen. Mothers and Children: Latin American Immigrants in San Francisco. New York: Arno Press, 1980.

Mexicans and Central Americans used a form of "marian altruism" to create bonds with children which they regarded as more reliable than those with their husbands.

344. Li, Peter S. "Fictive Kinship, Conjugal Tie and Kinship Chain among Chinese Immigrants in the United States." Journal of Comparative Family Studies 8 (Spring 1977): 47-64.

Paper sons and hasty marriages were common responses to changing immigration law. Includes information on sex ratio among immigrants yearly in nineteenth century.

345. Li-Repac, Diana C. "The Impact of Acculturation on the Child-Rearing Attitudes and Practices of Chinese-American Families: Consequences for the Attachment Process." Unpublished Ph.D. Dissertation, University of California, Berkeley, 1982. Order Number DA 8300573.

The parents of infants twelve to eighteen months old were studied. Childrearing was more restrictive and controlling than typical of American families.

346. Lobodzinska, Barbara. "A Cross-Cultural Study of Mixed Marriage in Poland and the United States." International Journal of Sociology of the Family 15 (Spring-Autumn, 1985): 94-117.

Notes the importance of marriage as a way of acquiring permanent residence in the U.S. A U.S. husband and a Polish wife more often succeeded because of complementary beliefs about men's marital privileges.

347. Lopata, Helen Z. "Widowhood in Polonia." Polish American Studies 34 (Autumn 1977): 7-25.

348. Lopata, Helen Z. Occupation Housewife. New York: Oxford University Press, 1971.

A suburban Chicago study in which about one-quarter of the women studied were second-generation women (31 percent Catholic; 16 percent Jewish); some attention is given to the impact of immigrant backgrounds on these women.

349. Lyman, Stanford M. "Marriage and the Family Among Chinese Immigrants to America, 1850-1960." Phylon 29, 4 (1968): 321-330.

The consequences of the unbalanced sex ratio are emphasized.

350. Markides, Kyriakos S. and S.K. Hoppe. "Marital Satisfaction in Three Generations of Mexican Americans." Social Science Quarterly 66 (March 1985): 147-54.

Found decreasing marital satisfaction among women from younger to older generations.

351. Mars, Amy I. "AMAE: Indulgence and Nurturance in Japanese American Families." Unpublished Ph.D. Dissertation, University of California, Los Angeles, 1986. Order Number DA 8621114.

352. Martinez, Marco A. "Conversation Asymmetry between Mexican Mothers and their Children." Hispanic Journal of Behavioral Sciences 3 (December 1981): 329-346.

No generation given, but all were Spanish speakers. Mothers took leadership in maintaining conversation.

353. Martinez, Marco A. "Dialogues Among Children and Between Children and their Mothers." Child Development 58 (August 1987): 1035-43.

Immigrant Mexican mothers regulated conversation with their children to extend the length of interaction; children used same technique, symmetrically, with each other.

354. Masuoka, Jitsuichi. "The Life Cycle of an Immigrant Institution in Hawaii: The Family." Social Forces 23 (October, 1944): 60-64.

Includes some interviews with Japanese women; emphasizes generational conflicts.

355. Matsumoto, Valerie J. "The Cortez Colony: Family, Farm and Community among Japanese Americans, 1919-1982." Unpublished Ph.D. Dissertation, Stanford University, 1986. Order Number DA 8608184.

Examines gender roles within families.

FAMILY   55

356. McGoldrick, Monica et al. <u>Ethnicity and Family Therapy</u>. New York: The Guilford Press, 1982.

Some information on women's family roles among West Indians, Mexicans, Cubans, Asians, French Canadians, Germans, Greeks, Iranians, Irish, Italians, Polish, Portuguese, British, Vietnamese, and Chinese.

357. Melody, Sister Laura. "Mexican American Mothers' Teaching Style and their Children's Need for Structure." Unpublished Ph.D. Dissertation, University of Illinois, Urbana, 1975. Order Number 76-6872.

Women used a wide variety of teaching styles, some of which produced children with low need for classroom structure.

358. Miller, Michael V. "Variations in Mexican American Family Life: A Review Synthesis of Empirical Research." <u>Aztlán</u> 9 (1978): 209-231.

Refers to both immigrant and second generation, considering machismo, women's roles, and intermarriage.

359. Mindel, Charles H. et al. <u>Ethnic Families in America, Patterns and Variations</u>. 3rd ed. New York: Elsevier, 1988.

Some attention to immigrant and second generation in separate essays on Polish, Irish, Italian, Mexican, Cuban, Korean, Chinese, Japanese, Vietnamese, Jewish, and Arab families.

360. Mirandé, Alfredo. "The Chicano Family: A Reanalysis of Conflicting Views." <u>Journal of Marriage and the Family</u> 39 (November 1977): 747-756.

Contrasts traditional negative view of male-dominated family with more positive stereotype of nurturing secure families; notes that violence against women was often posited in traditional view; summarizes mother-son and mother-daughter relations; notes that important of girl gangs in second generation.

361. Mitchell, Albert G. "Irish Family Patterns in Nineteenth-Century Ireland and Lowell, Massachusetts." Unpublished Ph. D. Dissertation, Boston University, 1976. Order Number 76-21,294.

Some attention to Irish women as wives and mothers, few of whom worked. Generation changes noted in intermarriage and the keeping of boarders.

362. Mittelbach, Frank G. and Joan W. Moore. "Ethnic Endogamy--the Case of Mexican Americans." American Journal of Sociology 74 (July 1968): 50-62.

Three generations are considered; older men preferred Mexican brides, but the same was not true of older women; endogamous marriages were usually between those of similar generation. Exogamy was higher among women, especially after the first generation.

363. Monroe, Day. Chicago Families: A Study of Unpublished Census Data. Chicago: University of Chicago Press, 1932.

About half of the homemakers studied were foreign-born; includes information on child-rearing, second-generation girls, and the employment of working wives.

364. More, Louise B. Wage Earners' Budgets: A Study of Standards and Cost of Living in New York City. New York: H. Holt and Co., 1907.

Data collected from 35 Irish, 15 English, 17 German, 15 Italian, 4 French, 4 Scandinavian, 2 Swiss, one Cuban, one Austrian, and one Scottish wives.

365. Morgan, Myfanwy and Hilda H. Golden. "Immigrant Families in an Industrial City: A Study of Households in Holyoke, 1880." Journal of Family History 4 (Spring 1979): 59-67.

Some attention to women's fertility and to women-headed households in Irish and French-Canadian families in Holyoke, Mass.

366. Murguia, Edward and W. Parker Frisbie. "Trends in Mexican American Intermarriage: Recent Findings in Perspective." Social Science Quarterly 58 (December 1977): 374-389.

No attention to generation, but contrasts men and women's patterns; finds increasing exogamy for both over time.

367. Murillo, Nathan. "The Mexican American Family." Pp. 97-108. Chicanos: Social and Psychological Perspectives. Ed. Nathaniel N. Wagner and Marsha J. Haug. Saint Louis: Mosby, 1971.

Some attention to women's family roles.

368. Newlin-Haus, Esther M. "A Comparison of Proxemic and Selected Communication Behavior of Anglo-American and Hmong Refugee Mother-Infant Pairs." Unpublished Ph.D. Dissertation, Indiana University, 1982. Order Number DA 8300862.

Hmong mothers touched their babies more, but no differences in infant vocalization resulted.

FAMILY 57

369. Oh, Heisik. "Marriage Enrichment in the Korean Immigrant Church." Unpublished Ph.D. Dissertation, School of Theology at Claremont, 1987. Order Number DA 8723909.

Notes conflict over Confucian family values, arranged marriages, and women's new aspirations.

370. Panunzio, Constantine. "Intermarriage in Los Angeles, 1924-33." American Journal of Sociology 47 (March 1942): 690-701.

Summarizes rates for Mexican, Japanese, Chinese, and Filipino immigrants. Found higher rates of intermarriage than elsewhere. Notes impact of sex ratio on intermarriage--where men outnumbered women, they were more likely to marry into other groups.

371. Parkman, M. A. and J. Sawyer. "Dimensions of Ethnic Intermarriage in Hawaii." American Sociological Review 32 (1967): 593-607.

Korean intermarriages increased over time, presumably along with generational changes.

372. Parot, Joseph J. "The 'Serdeczna Matko' of the Sweatshops: Marital and Family Crises of Immigrant Working-Class Women in Late Nineteenth Century Chicago." Pp. 155-184 The Polish Presence in Canada and America. Ed. Frank Renkiewicz. Toronto: The Multicultural Society of Ontario, 1982.

Also contains notes on women's wage-earning.

373. Peñalosa, Fernando. "Mexican Family Roles." Journal of Marriage and the Family 30 (November 1968): 680-689.

Although focus is family in Mexico, article was written to provide background necessary for understanding Mexicans in the U.S. Emphasizes female submission to male, mother's preparation of son for domination and independence, and closeness of mother/daughter tie.

374. Pessar, Patricia. "Social Relations within the Family in the Dominican Republic and United States: Continuity and Change." Hispanics in New York: Religious, Cultural and Social Experiences. Ed. Office of Pastoral Research. New York: Archdiocese of New York, 1982.

375. Pleck, Elizabeth H. "Challenges to Traditional Authority in Immigrant Families." Pp. 504-517 The American Family in Social-Historical Perspective. Ed. Michael Gordon. 3rd Ed. New York: St. Martin's Press, 1983.

Neighbors, wives, and children sought U.S. agencies' aid in intervening with abusive fathers, who resented American laws prohibiting wife or child abuse; notes that second generation clearly rejected father's right to use violence against family members.

376. Pleck, Elizabeth H. "The Old World, New Rights, and the Limited Rebellion: Challenges to Traditional Authority in Immigrant Families." Research in the Interweave of Social Roles 3 (1983): 91-112.

Finds that changing consciousness about women and children led immigrants to turn to outside agencies for assistance in combatting family violence.

377. Pleck, Elizabeth H. Domestic Tyranny; The Making of American Social Policy against Family Violence from Colonial Times to the Present. New York and Oxford: Oxford University Press, 1987.

Scattered references to violence in Irish, German, Russian, and Polish immigrant families,

378. Proudian, Armine. "Perceived Parental Power and Parental Identification among Armenian-American Adolescents." Psychological Reports 53 (December 1983): 1101-1102.

Second-generation girls perceived mothers as having more power than did boys.

379. Ramos, Reyes. "A Case in Point: An Ethno-methodological Study of a Poor Mexican Family." Social Science Quarterly 53 (March 1973): 905-919.

A study of a female-headed family on welfare.

380. Ratliff, Bascom W. et al. "Intercultural Marriage: The Korean American Experience." Social Casework 59 (April 1978): 221-226.

A report by military social workers.

381. Reed, Ruth. The Illegitimate Family in New York City: Its Treatment by Social and Health Agencies. New York: Columbia University Press, 1934.

Includes information about Irish (30 percent of the cases), British West Indians (10.5 percent) and Germans (13 percent), as well as some on Russians and Poles.

382. Richardson, Frank D. "Ministries to Asian Wives of Servicemen: A 1975 Inquiry." Military Chaplain's Review Winter 1976: 1-14.

Tacoma, Washington study contrasts Asians' and chaplains' differing viewpoints on family relations.

383. Richmond, Marie L. "Beyond Resource Theory: Another Look at Factors Enabling Women to Affect Family Interaction." *Journal of Marriage and the Family* 38 (May 1976): 257-265.

Study of Cubans showing that acculturation (including acceptance of egalitarian ethos) has greater effect on women's increased participation in decision-making than do the wages they contribute to the family.

384. Richmond, Marie L. *Immigrant Adaptation and Family Structure Among Cubans in Miami, Florida*. New York: Arno Press, 1980.

Based on interviews with 120 wives; wives' wages led to more egalitarian marriages and decision-making.

385. Risdon, Randall. "A Study of Interracial Marriages Based on Data for Los Angeles County." *Sociology and Social Research* 39 (November 1954): 92-95.

Filipino and Chinese men were more likely to intermarry than women, while Japanese women more likely to intermarry than men.

386. Rooney, Elizabeth. "Polish-Americans and Family Disorganization." *American Catholic Sociological Review* 18 (March 1957): 47-63.

Disputes Znaniecki and Thomas's contention that marital discord and broken marriages were common among Poles.

387. Rothbell, Gladys. "The Jewish Mother: Social Construction of a Popular Image." Pp. 118-128 *The Jewish Family: Myths and Reality*. Ed. Steven Cohen and Paula F. Hyman. New York and London: Holmes & Meier, 1986.

Analyzes American jokes about mothers, concluding that they were invented and first spread by Jewish men.

388. Ryan, Lawrence. "Some Czech-American Forms of Divination and Supplication." *Journal of American Folklore* 69 (July-August 1956): 281-285.

Includes customs of girls wanting to predict who their future husbands will be.

389. Schnepp, Gerald J. and Agnes M. Yui. "Cultural and Marital Adjustment of Japanese War Brides." *American Journal of Sociology* 61 (July 1955): 48-50.

Finds that marriages were not hasty, and that little cultural conflict resulted.

60   IMMIGRANT WOMEN IN THE U.S.

390. Schultz, Sandra L. "Intermarriage in a Greek-American Community: An Analysis of Ethnic Boundaries." Unpublished Ph.D. Dissertation, University of Arizona, 1977. Order Number 7805675.

Based on extensive interviews with first- and second-generation men and women. Intermarriage was very common and unproblematic.

391. Schwartz, Laura A. "Immigrant Voices from Home, Work and Community: Women and Family in the Migration Process, 1890-1938." Unpublished Ph.D. Dissertation, State University of New York, Stony Brook, 1984. Order Number DA 8420706.

Study based on 200 life histories done by the W.P.A. in Connecticut in the 1930s with Hungarians, Slovaks, Poles, Italians, and Jews. Emphasizes that family became an active coping mechanism for women.

392. Schwarz, Geraldine. "Family Cohesion in a Norwegian-American Settlement." Pp. 1-6 Conversations with the Recent Past: Northeast Iowa Oral History Project. Ed. Luis Torres. Decorah, Iowa: Luther College Press, 1975.

Based on interviews with second-generation women.

393. Schwieder, Dorothy. Black Diamonds: Life and Work in Iowa's Coal Mining Communities, 1895-1925. Ames: Iowa State University Press, 1983.

Chapters on family and on women include considerable information on the lives of the many Italians in these communities.

394. Seder, Doris L. "The Influence of Cultural Identification on Family Behavior." Unpublished Ph.D. Dissertation, Brandeis University, 1966. Order Number 66-9451.

Focus is the marital interaction of Greek couples with strong ties to their homeland culture.

395. Shin, Eui-Hang. "Interracially Married Korean Women in the United States: An Analysis Based on Hypergamy-Exchange Theory." Pp. 249-274 Korean Women in Transition: At Home and Abroad. Ed. Eui-Young Yu and Earl H. Phillips. Los Angeles: Center for Korean-American and Korean Studies, California State University, 1987.

396. Siddiqui, Musab U. and Earl Y. Reeves. "A Comparative Study of Mate Selection Criteria among Indians in India and the United States." International Journal of Comparative Sociology 27 (September-December 1986): 226-233.

Caste, income and religion mattered more than occupation in both places; gender differences persisted with migration to the U.S.

FAMILY   61

397. Slayton, Robert A. Back of the Yards, The Making of a Local Democracy. Chicago and London: The University of Chicago Press, 1986.

Scattered references to immigrant Polish and Mexican women in Chicago; see especially chapter 3, "Arenas of Life: Women and the Household."

398. Smith, Jacquelen M. "Planning for Homeless Children: A Study of Chinese Girls Adopted into American Families." Unpublished Ph.D. Dissertation, Harvard University, 1970.

399. Smith, Judith E. "Our Own Kind: Family and Community Networks in Providence." Radical History Review 17 (Spring 1978): 99-120.

Examines cooperation and conflict, and women's work, within Jewish and Italian families.

400. Smith, Judith E. Family Connections; A History of Italian and Jewish Immigrant Lives in Providence, Rhode Island 1900-1940. Albany: State University of New York Press, 1985.

Good attention to male/female differences, cooperation and conflict, and second generation in Jewish and Italian families.

401. Spargo, John. The Bitter Cry of the Children. New York and London: The Macmillan Company, 1906.

Studies the effect of poverty on childhood, including scattered references to foreign-born women, whom the author regards as generally unsatisfactory mothers. Includes good pictures of girl "little mothers".

402. Staples, Robert. "The Mexican American Family: Its Modification Over Time and Space." Phylon 32 (Summer 1971): 179-192.

Although study pays good attention to gender and courtship, it does not specify which generation is being studied.

403. Stein, Howard F. "An Ethno-Historic Study of Slovak-American Identity." Unpublished Ph.D. Dissertation, University of Pittsburgh, 1972. Order Number DA 731663.

Examines first to fourth generations, including direct observation of childrearing and interviews with mothers.

404. Stein, Howard. "The Slovak-American 'Swaddling Ethos': Homeostat for Family Dynamics and Cultural Continuity." Family Process 17 (March 1978): 31-45.

Childrearing in this group encourages dependency on extended family and results in perpetuation of the ethnic tradition. Based on study of a multigeneration Slovak family.

62   IMMIGRANT WOMEN IN THE U.S.

405. Strauss, Anselm L. "Strain and Harmony in American-Japanese War Bride Marriages." Pp. 268-281 The Blending American: Patterns of Intermarriage. Ed. Milton L. Barron. Chicago: Quadrangle Books, 1972.

Found intermarried war-bride couples no more strained than others, and sources of strains similar to other marriages. Notes that Japanese brides had few occupational expectations, but expected steadiness of their husbands.

406. Strom, Robert et al. "The Adjustment of Korean Immigrant Families." Educational and Psychological Research 6 (Summer 1986): 213-227.

Assesses the child-rearing expectations of mothers and fathers of preschool children. Gender differences were found; the influence of length of time in the country is also noted.

407. Szapocznik, Jose. "Role Conflict Resolution in Cuban Mothers." Unpublished Ph.D. Dissertation, University of Miami, 1977. Order Number 77-21,898.

Cuban mothers resolved conflicts in ways theory has not considered.

408. Tienda, Marta and R. Angel. "Headship and Household Composition among Blacks, Hispanics, and Other Whites." Social Forces 6 (December 1982): 508-31.

Found higher rates of female-headed households among Mexicans, Central and South American Hispanics, and native-born Afro-Americans; in all cases associated with economic hardship.

409. Tinker, John N. "Intermarriage and Ethnic Boundaries: The Japanese American Case." Journal of Social Issues 29,2 (1973): 49-66.

Found decreasing intermarriage by females over time.

410. Toll, William. "The Female Life Cycle and the Measure of Social Change: Portland, Oregon, 1880-1930." American Jewish History 72, 3 (March 1983): 309-332.

Study of German Jews and second generation; focus is on women's lives and the demographic transformation of the community.

411. Torgoff, Stella de Rosa. "Immigrant Women, The Family, and Work, 1850-1950." Trends in History 2 (1982): 31-47.

412. Tsutakawa, Mayumi. "A Chest of Kimonos--A Female Family History." Pp. 156-165 Gathering Ground: New Writing and Art by Northwest Women of Color. Ed. Jo Cochran et al. Seattle: Seal Press, 1984.

The focus is on the women in a Japanese family. Much of the rest of the book is fiction and poetry.

413. Van Deusen, John et al. "Southeast Asian Social and Cultural Customs: Similarities and Differences, Parts I and II." Journal of Refugee Resettlement 1 (1981): 20-39.

Focus is the marriage customs of Vietnamese, Cambodian, Hmong, and Laotian refugees.

414. Walkowitz, Daniel. "Working-Class Women in the Gilded Age: Factory, Community and Family Life Among Cohoes, NY Cotton Workers." Journal of Social History 5 (1972): 464-490.

Main groups studied were British, Irish, and French-Canadians.

415. Weinberg, Sydney S. "Jewish Mothers and Immigrant Daughters: Positive and Negative Role Models." Journal of American Ethnic History 6 (Spring 1987): 39-55.

Based on oral histories; all women emphasized the importance of their mothers as role models even if negative ones; emphasizes importance of birth order in determining a daughter's family responsibilities.

416. Williams, Brett. "Why Migrant Women Feed Their Husbands Tamales: Foodways as a Basis for a Revisionist View of Tejano Family Life." Pp. 113-126 Ethnic and Regional Foodways in the United States, The Performance of Group Identity. Ed. Linda Keller Brown and Kay Mussell. Knoxville: The University of Tennessee Press, 1984.

Focus is on Mexican women as food preparers.

417. Williams, Phyllis. South Italian Folkways in Europe and America. New York: Russell and Russell, 1938.

Includes information on women throughout, but see especially chapter on Marriage and the Family.

418. Wold, Clynonia N. et al. "Marital Therapy with a Vietnamese Couple: A Cross-cultural Melange." Family Therapy 4 (1977): 337-346.

Language and divergent ways of thinking were only two difficulties in counseling this man and wife.

419. Wolfenstein, Martha. "Two Types of Jewish Mothers." Pp. 424-440 Childhood in Contemporary Cultures. Ed. Margaret Mead and M. Wolfenstein. Chicago: University of Chicago Press, 1955.

Includes case studies of a Russian-Jewish mother and a second-generation woman of Eastern European Jewish parents. The second-generation woman encouraged independence in her children much earlier.

420. Wong, Bernard. "Family, Kinship and Ethnic Identity of the Chinese in N.Y. City, with Comparative Remarks on the Chinese in Lima, Peru and Manila, Philippines." Journal of Comparative Family Studies 16 (Summer 1985): 231-254.

Notes the growing importance of the husband-wife bond for all migrated Chinese.

421. Wong, Sandra M.J. "For the Sake of Kinship: The Overseas Family." Unpublished Ph.D. Dissertation, Stanford University, 1987. Order Number DA 8723121.

Based on interviews with twenty men and women from Canton living in San Francisco. Argues that the female-managed household provides new power and influence for women in families.

422. Yanigisako, Sylvia J. "Women-Centered Kin Networks in Urban Bilateral Kinship." American Ethnologist 4 (1977): 207-226.

Focus is on how Japanese women bound extended family groups together.

423. Yans-McLaughlin, Virginia. Family and Community: Italian Immigrants in Buffalo, 880-1930. Ithaca: Cornell University Press, 1977.

Good attention to women, especially in their family roles.

424. Yeung, Wai-Tsang. "Chinese Outmarriage in Los Angeles County." Unpublished D.S.W. Dissertation, University of California, Los Angeles, 1982. Order Number DA 8219784.

Found increasing rates of outmarriage for women in second and third generations.

425. Yim, Sun B. "Korean Battered Wives: A Sociological and Psychological Analysis of Conjugal Violence in Korean Immigrant Families." Pp. 171-199 Korean Women in a Struggle for Humanization. Ed. Harold Hakwon Sunoo and Dong Soo Kim. Memphis, Tenn.: Association of Korean Christian Scholars in North America, 1978.

426. Yu, Eui-Young. "Korean-American Women: Demographic Profile and Family Roles." Pp. 183-198 Korean Women in Transition: At Home and Abroad. Ed. Eui-Young Yu and Earl H. Phillips. Los Angeles: Center for Korean-American and Korean Studies, California State University, 1987.

FAMILY 65

427. Zeskind, Philip S. "Cross-Cultural Differences in Maternal Perceptions of Cries of Low- and High-Risk Infants." Child Development 54 (October 1983): 1119-1128.

Cuban women resembled native-born whites on some ratings, and native-born Afro-Americans on others.

428. Zinn, Maxine B. "Chicano Family Research: Conceptual Distortions and Alternative Directions." Journal of Ethnic Studies 7 (Fall 1979): 59-71.

Latest studies show men are not so "macho" or women so submissive as earlier believed; some attention to second generation.

5

Work

INTRODUCTION

The work that immigrant women do for wages has always been a central topic in the study of immigration, while unwaged work performed within the family or household has received less attention. Included in this chapter are studies of waged and unwaged work, as well as studies that focus on immigrant women as participants or organizers of family businesses. Studies of labor activism, however, are cited in Chapter 6, "Working Together."

In the past, immigrant women and their daughters formed a sizeable proportion of the female work force in the United States, and both their rates of labor force participation and their patterns of working across the life cycle differed from native-born American women's. With time, differences between foreign-born and native-born women's work have diminished, largely because of changes in the lives of native-born women. On the other hand, foreign-born women in the United States today still can be found disproportionately in certain types of jobs.

A number of important themes seem to be shared across the disciplines in studies of immigrant women as wage workers. One of these involves the segmentation of the labor market and the clustering of immigrant women in particular kinds of employment, both in the past and in the present. Both the garment industry and domestic service have been studied as important employers of foreign-born women. The employment patterns of the female second generation are less well understood, however, and this stands in clear contrast to a very significant historical literature on occupational mobility among second-generation men.

A second theme which has intrigued both historians and social scientists is the impact of waged work on immigrant women's family position and "emancipation." Many scholars have argued that women wage-earners are more likely to participate in family decision-making, but this seems to apply only to working wives, not working daughters. The impact of a wife's wage-earning on household responsibilities is even less clear. And many studies find no evidence that women's working for wages alone changes group ideology about "women's place."

Because work and family are so frequently studied in relation to each other, the reader is advised to consult Chapter 4, "The Family," and to check index entries on particular types of work.

CITATIONS

429. Abbott, Edith and Sophonisba P. Breckinridge. "Women in Industry: The Chicago Stockyards." Journal of Political Economy 19 (October 1911): 632-654.

Irish women working in food processing were disturbed when Slavic women took jobs requiring them to work with knives, since these jobs had previously been men's and such work was seen as "degrading" to women.

430. Abbott, Edith. Women in Industry, A Study in American Economic History. New York and London: D. Appleton and Co, 1910.

Identifies clusters of women of particular backgrounds in a variety of industries and jobs.

431. Abeles, Schwartz, Hackel and Silverblatt, Inc. The Chinatown Garment Study. New York: ILGWU, 1983.

432. Ablon, Joan. "Samoans in Stateside Nursing." Nursing Outlook 18 (December 1970): 33-34.

Found a concentration of immigrant nurses in geriatric care.

433. Abyaneh, Parvin. "Post-Migration Economic Role of Females and Patriarchy in Immigrant Iranian Families." Unpublished Ph.D. Dissertation, University of California, Riverside, 1986. Order Number DA8706975.

Found differing modes of adaptation in families where women were full-time housewives, where women worked in family-run businesses, and where women worked outside the home or in nonfamily enterprises; those employed in family businesses experienced patriarchy to the greatest degree.

434. Addams, Jane. A New Conscience and an Ancient Evil. New York: MacMillan, 1913.

Includes some case studies of foreign-born girls and commentary on the particular vulnerability of immigrant women during travel. Points to domestic service as the most frequent prior occupation of prostitutes.

435. Aldrich, Mark and Randy Albelda. "Determinants of Working Women's Wages During the Progressive Era." Explorations in Economic History 27 (October 1980): 323-341.

Contrasts the earnings of old immigrants and new, and describes limitation of new immigrant women to a narrow range of jobs.

436. Anh, Nguyen Thi. "Occupational Adjustment of Vietnamese Refugees in Los Angeles and Orange Counties: Education and Jobs." Unpublished Ed.D. Dissertation, University Of California, Los Angeles, 1982. Order Number DA 8219630.

Notes variation by sex. Women's ability to understand the language, more than men's, has influence on type of job taken.

437. Anthony, Katharine. Mothers Who Must Earn. New York: Russell Sage Foundation, Survey Associates, 1914.

Good attention also to family life of the immigrant and second-generation Irish and German, Italian, and English immigrant women studied.

438. Ashbury, Herbert. The Barbary Coast. New York: Capricorn, 1968.

See "The Slaves of Chinatown," which focuses on early prostitutes.

439. Auten, Nellie M. "Some Phases of the Sweating System in the Garment Trades of Chicago." American Journal of Sociology 6 (March 1901): 604-645.

Includes some attention to the many groups, including women, involved in this type of work: Swedes, Bohemians, Italians, Austrian and Russian Jews, Germans, and Poles.

440. Bach, Robert L. and Rita Carroll-Seguin. "Labor Force Participation, Household Composition and Sponsorship among Southeast Asian Refugees." International Migration Review 20 (Summer 1986): 381-404.

Found women's work rates were about fifty percentage points lower than men.

441. Badillo-Veiga, Amerigo et al. "Undocumented Immigrant Workers in New York City." NACLA Report of the Americas 13 (November-December 1979): 2-46.

Based on fifty interviews, this article includes good coverage of women, especially at work.

442. Baum, Charlotte. "What Made Yetta Work? The Economic Role of Eastern European Jewish Women in the Family." Response 18 (1973): 32-38.

443. Beyers, Marjorie. "Exploration of Factors Affecting the Achievement of Licensure for Foreign-Educated Nurses." Unpublished Ph.D. Dissertation, Northwestern University, 1979. Order Number 7927194.

Explores the training and the testing of Filipino nurses.

444. Blackwelder, Julia K. "Women in the Work Force: Atlanta, New Orleans, and San Antonio, 1930 to 1940." Journal of Urban History 4 (1978): 331-358.

Compares foreign-born white women to Afro-American, native-born whites, and other races. Finds evidence of female-headed households among San Antonio's Chicana workers.

445. Blackwelder, Julia K. Women of the Depression, Caste and Culture in San Antonio, 1929-1939. College Station, Tex: Texas A & M Press, 1984.

Good attention to work and family experiences of Mexican women. Proportion of foreign-born among Mexican is not clear. Compares experiences of Afro-American, Mexican-American, and Anglo. In addition, statistical material in appendices distinguishes foreign-born from other Anglos.

446. Blewett, Mary H. Men, Women and Work: Class, Gender, and Protest in the New England Shoe Industry, 1780-1910. Urbana, Il: University of Illinois Press, 1988.

Immigrant women, especially Irish and French Canadian, a significant component of the work force studied. Some information on relationship between foreign-born and native-born in labor protest.

447. Bloom, Florence T. "Struggling and Surviving--the Life Style of European Immigrant Breadwinning Mothers in American Industrial cities, 1900-1930." Women's Studies International Forum 8, 6 (1985): 609-620.

Emphasizes how patriarchy prevented women from seeking change in traditional families.

448. Bodnar, John, et al. Lives of Their Own: Blacks, Italians and Poles in Pittsburgh, 1900-1960. Urbana: University of Illinois Press, 1981.

Includes information on Polish and Italian work and family patterns.

449. Bodnar, John. "Socialization and Adaptation: Immigrant Families in Scranton, 1880-1890". Pennsylvania History 43 (April 1976): 147-162.

Some attention to the work of second-generation daughters of Irish and Welsh immigrants.

450. Bonacich, Edna M. and Jae-Hong Park. "Korean Immigrant Working Women in the Early 1980s." Pp. 219-248 Korean Women in Transition: At Home and Abroad. Ed. Eui-Young Yu and Earl H. Phillips. Los Angeles: Center for Korean-American and Korean Studies, California State University, 1987.

451. Boris, Eileen. "Regulating Industrial Homework: The Triumph of 'Sacred Motherhood.'" Journal of American History 71 (1985): 745-763.

Notes that many homeworkers--often foreign-born or second-generation women--wished to continue work at home. Traces the reform movement to eliminate work from home.

452. Bose, Christine E. "Household Resources and U.S. Women's Work: Factors Affecting Gainful Employment at the Turn of the Century." American Sociological Review 49 (1984): 474-490.

Found that ethnicity made little difference in the paid employment of wives; all families depended heavily on daughters' wages. Southern and Eastern European wives were more likely to keep boarders than native-born or northern or western Europeans. Considers immigrants of a wide range of backgrounds.

453. Boyd, Monica. "Occupations of Female Immigrants and North-American Immigration Statistics." International Migration Review 10 (Spring 1976): 73-80.

Compares employment among recent women immigrants in U.S. and Canada.

454. Briody, Elizabeth K. "Patterns of Household Immigration into South Texas." International Migration Review 21 (Spring 1987): 27-47.

Found changing attitudes toward Mexican women and children when they became wage-earners to offset general downward mobility.

455. Buck, Rinker. "The New Sweatshops: A Penny For Your Collar." Pp. 34-37 Selected Readings on U.S. Immigration Policy and Law: A Compendium. Ed. Congressional Research Service. Washington: U.S. Government Printing Office, 1980.

456. Butler, Elizabeth B. Women and the Trades: Pittsburgh, 1907-1908. Vol. 1. The Pittsburgh Survey. Ed. Paul Underwood. New York: Russell Sage Foundation, Charities Publication Committee, 1909.

Good information on Irish, Poles, Italians, Slavs, and Eastern European Jews working in food processing, cleaning, needle trades, and commerce.

457. Campbell, Helen S. **Prisoners of Poverty: Women Wage Earners, Their Trades and Their Lives.** Boston: Roberts Brothers, 1890.

Some information on Irish workers, see especially "The Case of Rose Haggerty" (a second-generation woman), "Domestic Service and its Problems," and "The Widow Maloney's Boarders."

458. Cardenas, Gilbert et al. "Undocumented Immigrant Women in the Houston Labor Force." **California Sociologist** 5 (Summer 1982): 98-118.

Mexican women without proper residence documentation concentrated in the "other" economy, over half in domestic service.

459. Carliner, Geoffrey. "Female Labor Force Participation Rates for Nine Ethnic Groups." **Journal of Human Resources** 16 (Spring 1981): 286-193.

Compares Mexican, Cuban, Japanese, Chinese, and Filipina wives. Filipina wives had the highest rates of labor-force participation (50 percent), while only about a third of Chicana wives worked for wages. Notes relationship between high fertility rates and low rates of labor-force participation.

460. Carpenter, Margaret. "Addressing the Needs of Women Refugees." **World Refugeé Survey** 1981: 42-44.

Includes a section on U.S. programs to aid women refugees; notes that women were to receive job training, too.

461. Cartwright, O.G. **The Middle West Side: Mothers Who Must Earn.** New York: Russell Sage Foundation, 1914.

Many of the women studied are immigrant and second-generation Irish and German.

462. Casal, Lourdes (with Yolanda Prieto). "Black Cubans in the United States: Basic Demographic Information." Pp. 314-348 **Female Immigrants to the United States: Caribbean, Latin American and African Experiences.** Ed. Delores Mortimer and Roy Bryce-Laporte. Washington, D.C.: Research Institute on Immigration and Ethnic Studies, Smithsonian Institute, 1981.

Poorer in Cuba, black Cuban women were underrepresented in the early migration. A Miami sample showed Black Cuban women overrepresented in service and industrial work, but they were also more likely to be working as professionals than Cuban immigrant women generally.

463. Castro, Felipe G. et al. "Long-Term Stress Among Latino Women after a Plant Closure." Sociology and Social Research 71 (January 1987): 85-88.

Study of Mexican women workers in a tuna processing plant. Found considerable stress that did not dwindle quickly.

464. Castro, Mary G. "Work Versus Life: Colombian Women in New York." Pp. 231-259 Women and Change in Latin America. Ed. June Nash and Helen Safa. South Hadley, Mass.: Bergin and Garvey Publishers, 1986.

Based on survey data of 98 women and some in-depth interviews with eight, the study found that most women assessed the impact of migration positively.

465. Chai, Alice Y. "Freed from the Elders but Locked into Labor: Korean Immigrant Women in Hawaii." Women's Studies 13, 3 (1987): 223-34.

466. Chavez, Leo. "Households, Migration and Labor Market Participation: The Adaptation of Mexicans to Life in the United States." Urban Anthropology 14 (Winter 1985): 301-46.

Provides breakdowns of employment by sex and legal status; notes extremely flexible household structures of those studied.

467. Cheng, Lucie. "Free, Indentured, Enslaved: Chinese Prostitutes in Nineteenth-Century America." Pp. 402-434 Labor Immigration Under Capitalism; Asian Workers in the United States Before World War II. Ed. Lucie Cheng and Edna Bonacich. Berkeley, Los Angeles and London: University of California Press, 1984.

Emphasizes the frequent survival of semifeudal structures among nonwhites and immigrants well into the 20th century. Prostitution helped maintain labor force of single young men and provided arena for immense entrepreneurial profits.

468. Chiswick, Barry R. "Immigrant Earnings Patterns by Sex, Race and Ethnic Groups." Monthly Labor Review 103 (October 1980): 22-25.

Found that immigrant women achieved wage parity with native-born women more quickly than did men, but also notes the great earning disadvantage of Asian women married to U.S. servicemen.

469. Chung, Hyo Jin. " A Study of Korean Nurse Immigrants' Adaptation Experience to the Nursing Profession in the Los Angeles Area." Unpublished Ph.D. Dissertation, University of California, Los Angeles, 1986. Order Number DA 8621264.

470. Clark, Sue A. and Edith Wyatt. <u>Making Both Ends Meet: The Income and Outlay of New York Working Girls</u>. New York: MacMillan, 1911.

Provides good information on the nationality of employees; includes chapters on shopgirls (some of whom were immigrants), on the shirtwaist and cloak makers' strikes, and on laundry workers.

471. Cohen, Lucy M. and Mary A. Grossnickle, eds. <u>Immigrants and Refugees in a Changing Nation: Research and Training, Proceedings of a Conference held at the Catholic University of America (Washington, DC, May 13-14, 1982)</u>. Washington D.C.: Catholic University of America Press, 1983.

Includes material on refugee women's work and immigrant women artists.

472. Cohen, Miriam J. "From Workshop to Office: Italian Women and Family Strategies in New York City, 1901-1950." Unpublished Ph. D. Dissertation, University of Michigan, 1978. Order Number 790748.

Focus is work and education in immigrant and second generations.

473. Colen, Shellee. "'With Respect and Feelings,' Voices of West Indian Child Care and Domestic Workers in New York City." Pp. 46-70 <u>All American Women; Lines that Divide, Ties that Bind</u>. Ed. Johnnetta B. Cole. New York and London: The Free Press and Collier Macmillan Publishers, 1986.

A look at the subjective feelings involved in domestic service.

474. Consumers' League of New York. <u>Behind the Scenes in a Hotel</u>. New York: Consumers' League, 1922.

Two-thirds of the women studied were foreign-born, mainly Austro-Hungarians. The focus of the study is their working conditions.

475. Cooney, Rosemary S. "Changing Labor Force Participation of Mexican-American Wives: A Comparison with Anglos and Blacks." <u>Social Science Quarterly</u> 56 (Summer 1975): 252-261.

Finds that rates were increasing; the best-educated women and mothers of pre-schoolers worked at rates higher than Anglo women.

476. Cooney, Rosemary S. and Vilma Ortiz. "Nativity, National Origin and Hispanic Female Labor Force Participation." <u>Social Science Quarterly</u> 64 (1978): 510-523.

Notes considerable variation within group.

477. Cross, Gary and Peter R. Shergold. "The Family Economy and the Market: Wages and Residence of Pennsylvania Women in the 1890s. Journal of Family History 11, 3 (1986): 245-265.

Found that immigrant daughters were more likely than native-born to live with parents, even if they earned wages that might have purchased autonomy.

478. Culp, Alice B. A Case Study of the Living Conditions of Thirty-five Mexican Families in Los Angeles with Special Reference to Mexican Children. San Francisco: R & E Research Associates, 1971; orig. publ. 1921.

A biased study which nevertheless presents some data on working Mexican mothers (about one-quarter of all).

479. Davis, Susan G. "Women's Roles in a Company Town: New York Mills, 1900-1951." New York Folklore 4 (Summer/Winter1978): 35-47.

The focus is Poles; oral histories revealed that wage work was common even after marriage. Women also kept boarders and grew much of family food.

480. Dickinson, Joan Y. The Role of the Immigrant Women in the U.S. Labor Force, 1890-1910. New York: Arno Press, 1980.

Attention to a wide range of immigrant groups, including Germans, French-Canadians, Hungarians, English, Bohemians, Irish, Italians, Lithuanians, Polish, Scandinavian, Russians, and Russian Jews.

481. Dillon, Richard. The Hatchet Men, 1881-1906. New York: Ballantine Books, 1972.

See section on slave girls, which describes Chinese prostitution.

482. Dixon, Marlene et al. "Theoretical Perspectives on Chicanas, Mexicanas, and the Transnational Working Class." Contemporary Marxism 11 (Fall 1985): 46-76.

Notes the super-exploitation of household labor and wage-labor within a transnational labor reserve.

483. Dublin, Louis I. "Infant Mortality in Fall River, Massachusetts." American Statistical Association Journal 14 (June 1915): 505-517.

Found higher mortality among children of Portuguese mothers, presumably because they worked in mills during pregnancy.

484. Dudden, Faye E. *Serving Women; Household Service in Nineteenth-Century America.* Middletown, Conn.: Wesleyan University Press, 1983.

Information on Irish, German, Chinese, and Scandinavian women as domestic servants.

485. Early, Frances H. "The French-Canadian Family Economy and Standard-of-Living in Lowell, Massachusetts, 1870." *Journal of Family History* 7 (Summer 1982): 190-99.

Emphasizes continuity with Canadian farm patterns, especially dependence on child labor; some attention to women and girls as wage-earners.

486. Edelheit, Martha. "Conversations and Reminiscences." *Heresies* 4 (Winter 1978): 72-87.

Based on interviews with immigrant women about their handiwork and role as food preparers.

487. Fernández-Kelly, M. Patricia and Anna M. Garcia. "The Making of an Underground Economy: Hispanic Women, Home Work, and the Advanced Capitalist State." *Urban Anthropology* 14 (Spring-Fall 1985): 59-90.

Compares Mexican women in Los Angeles and Cuban women in Miami. Found that factory work became more important as employer of Hispanic women, which was the opposite of trend in general population.

488. Ferree, Myra M. "Employment without Liberation: Cuban Women in the United States." *Social Science Quarterly* 60 (1978): 35-50.

Found that work did not significantly change ideology about women or division of labor within family.

489. Fuentes, Annette and Barbara Ehrenreich. *Women in the Global Factory.* Boston: South End Press, 1985.

See chapter on "Made in the U.S.," which focuses on Caribbean, Asian, and Central American women working in garments and in electronics plants in Silicon Valley.

490. Furio, Colomba M. "Immigrant Women in Industry: A Case Study, The Italian Immigrant Women and the Garment Industry, 1880-1950." Unpublished Ph. D. Dissertation, New York University, 1979. Order Number 8010282.

Focuses on the emotional tug of war between family and class identities among workers and labor activists.

491. García, Mario T. "The Chicana in American History: The Mexican Women of El Paso, 1880-1920--A Case Study." Pacific Historical Review 49 (May 1980): 315-337.

Wives earned wages only when it could be combined with traditional domestic responsibilities; notes the importance of laundering and domestic work and recounts events of a laundry strike.

492. Gentry, Curt. Madams of San Francisco. Garden City: Doubleday, 1964.

Includes information on Ah Toy, a Chinese woman who operated a successful brothel, and the life of the French madam, Eleanore Dumont.

493. Ginger, Ray. "Labor in a Massachusetts Cotton Mill, 1853-1860". Business History Review 28,1 (1954): 67-91.

Focus is Scottish women weavers: notes contradictory evidence on living standards; real incomes in Holyoke were high by Scottish standards, but turnover was also very rapid.

494. Glenn, Evelyn N. "Occupational Ghettoization: Japanese American Women and Domestic Service, 1905-1970." Ethnicity 8 (1981): 351-386.

The focus is on segmentation of labor market, and immigrant women's limitation to housework.

495. Glenn, Evelyn N. "The Dialectics of Wage Work: Japanese American Women and Domestic Service, 1905-1940." Pp. 470-514 Labor Immigration Under Capitalism; Asian Workers in the United States Before World War II. Ed. Lucie Cheng and Edna Bonacich. Berkeley, Los Angeles and London: University of California Press, 1984.

496. Glenn, Evelyn N. "Women, Labor Migration and Household Work: Japanese American Women in the Pre-War Period. Pp. 93-114 Ingredients for Women's Employment Policy. Ed. Christine Bose and Glenna Spitze. Albany: State University of New York Press, 1987.

Found that immigrants reproduced household-based economies in farms and small businesses. Emphasizes differences from European migrants. Domestic workers and their families experienced more change as consequence of wage-earning.

497. Glenn, Evelyn N. Issei, Nisei, Warbride; Three Generations of Japanese American Women in Domestic Service. Philadelphia: Temple University Press, 1986.

Includes chapters on migration, settlement, labor market, domestic work, coping, family life, and gender in generational groups.

78   IMMIGRANT WOMEN IN THE U.S.

498. Glenn, Susan A. "The Working Life of Immigrants: Women in the American Garment Industry, 1880-1920." Unpublished Ph.D. Dissertation, University of California, Berkeley, 1983. Order Number DA 8413400.

The focus is on Jewish women workers; notes shift from mother to daughter as supporter of family.

499. Griffen, Clyde and Sally Griffen. Natives and Newcomers: The Ordering of Opportunity in Mid-Nineteenth Century Poughkeepsie. Cambridge: Harvard University Press, 1978.

Some information on German, British and Irish women as wage-earners.

500. Groneman, Carol. "Working-Class Immigrant Women in Mid-Nineteenth-Century New York: The Irish Woman's Experience." Journal of Urban History 4 (1978):255-174.

Main focus is work and family experiences.

501. Groneman, Carole. "She Earns as a Child--She Pays as Man: Women Workers in a Mid-Nineteenth Century New York Community." Pp. 33-46 Immigrants in Industrial America, 1850-1920. Ed. Richard L. Ehrlich. Charlottesville, N.C.: University Press of Virginia for the Eleutherian Mills-Hagley Foundation and Balch Institute, 1977.

Main focus is Irish women.

502. Grubb, Farley. "Immigrant Servant Labor: Their Occupational and Geographic Distribution in the Late Eighteenth-Century Mid-Atlantic Economy." Social Science History 9 (Summer 1985): 249-276.

Most were Irish and German women, going to Philadelphia and other cities.

503. Hancock, Paula. "The Effect of Welfare Eligibility on the Labor Force Participation of Women of Mexican Origin in California." Population Research and Policy Review 5, 2 (1986): 163-185.

Examines the relation of labor-force participation and various welfare programs in several groups of women, including those without legal residence.

504. Hareven, Tamara K. "Family Time and Industrial Time: Family and Work in a Planned Corporation Town, 1900-1924." Journal of Urban History 1 (May 1975): 365-389.

Some attention to marriage and work for immigrant women; argues that women's work "articulated to the family cycle."

505. Hareven, Tamara K. "The Laborers of Manchester, New Hampshire, 1912-1922: The Role of Family and Ethnicity in Adjustment to Industrial Life." Labor History 16 (Spring 1975): 249-265.

A small amount of information on the particular work patterns of women.

506. Hareven, Tamara K. and Randolph Langenbach. Amoskeag: Life and Work in an American Factory City. New York: Pantheon Books, 1978.

Based on oral histories, with considerable interpretation of work experiences. Most informants were French Canadian immigrants and second-generation, about half female.

507. Hartman, Harriet and Moshe. "The Effect of Immigration on Women's Roles in Various Countries." The International Journal of Sociology and Social Policy 3,3 (1983): 86-103.

Compares Canada, Israel, and the U.S. Finds that employed immigrant women held distinctive and lower occupations in all three countries, even after many years of residence.

508. Haug, Madeleine J. "Miami's Garment Industry and Its Workers." Pp. 173-190 Research in the Sociology of Work, A Research Annual. Ed. Ida H. Simpson and Richard L. Simpson. Greenwich, Conn.: JAI Press, 1983.

Found that employers preferred immigrant females to native-born Afro-Americans as employees. Argues that garment manufacturing has located in Miami because of Cuban female work force. Found both sweatshops and homework.

509. Havira, Barbara S. "Factories and Workers in Three Michigan Towns: 1880-1920." Unpublished Ph.D. Dissertation, Michigan State University, 1986. Order Number DA8700477.

Many of the workers studied were immigrant women; their work was for family needs, not mobility.

510. Hines, David. "Vietnamese Refugee Women in the U.S. Labor Force: Continuity or Change?" Pp. 62-75 International Migration, The Female Experience. Ed. Rita J. Simon and Caroline B. Bretell. Totowa, N.J.: Rowman & Allanheld, 1985.

Found that women's labor force participation had been increasing in Vietnam and continued to increase in U.S. Differentiates among Chinese, Laotian, Hmong, Khmer, and Vietnamese women.

80   IMMIGRANT WOMEN IN THE U.S.

511. Hirata, Lucy C. "Chinese Immigrant Women in Nineteenth Century California." Pp. 224-44 <u>Women of America, A History</u>. Ed. Carol R. Berkin and Mary Beth Norton. Boston: Houghton Mifflin, 1979.

Much information on prostitution.

512. Hirayama, Kasumi K. "Effects of the Employment of Vietnamese Refugee Wives on their Family Roles and Mental Health." Unpublished D.S.W. Dissertation, University of Pennsylvania, 1980. Order Number 8023466.

Found alarming numbers of women under stress; employment of wife led to new division of labor for housework tasks only; employment and mental health were positively related.

513. Hirayama, Kasumi K. "Evaluating Effects of the Employment of Vietnamese Refugee Wives on Their Family Roles and Mental Health." <u>California Sociologist</u> 5,1 (Winter 1982): 96-110.

Found that husbands of working wives did more housework and child care. Working or not, women reported loneliness and a sense of loss and isolation. Stress resulted when the husband's income is low; it was not a function of the wife's employment.

514. Hobson, Barbara M. <u>Uneasy Virtue, the Politics of Prostitution and the American Reform Tradition</u>. New York: Basic Books, 1987.

See especially pp. 88-94 on immigrant prostitutes in Boston, New York, and Philadelphia. Irish, British, and Canadian women were overrepresented as prostitutes.

515. Hoffman, Klaus. "Sewing is for Women, Horses are for Men: The Role of German Russian Women." Pp. 131-144 <u>Germans from Russia in Colorado</u>. Ed. Sidney Heitman. Ann Arbor: Western Social Science Association, 1978.

Explores the division of labor within the family. Emphasizes the limited realm of women outside the home.

516. Houghteling, Leila. <u>The Income and Standard of Living of Unskilled Laborers in Chicago</u>. Chicago: University of Chicago Press, 1927.

Mainly a budget and food study; gives some information about boarding and working mothers, especially among Poles.

517. Hughes, Gwendolyn S. <u>Mothers in Industry: Wage-Earning by Mothers in Philadelphia</u>. New York: New Republic, 1925.

About two-thirds of the women studied were foreign-born and second-generation, mainly Irish and Polish; explores impact of mothers' work on family life.

518. Humphrey, Norman D. "The Housing and Household Practices of Detroit Mexicans." Social Forces 24 (May 1946): 433-437.

Notes that poor housing was sometimes blamed on women's lack of housekeeping standards; emphasizes that overcrowding was the result of poverty; as soon as the economic situation of a family improved, they attained American standards in their homes.

519. Ichioka, Yuji. "Ameyuki-San: Japanese Prostitutes in Nineteenth-Century America." Amerasia Journal 4, 1 (1977): 1-21.

The first significant group of Japanese women coming to the U.S. were brought to work as prostitutes.

520. Irwin, Elizabeth A. "The Story of a Transplanted Industry: Lace Workers of the Italian Quarter of New York." Craftsman 12 (1907): 404-409.

521. Jensen, Joan M. Loosening the Bonds, Mid-Atlantic Farm Women, 1750-1850. New Haven: Yale University Press, 1986.

Some attention to Irish women as rural farm laborers.

522. Johnson, Audrey. "Ethnic, Racial Attitudes Among Professional and Managerial Black Women: Research Note." Pp. 143-156 Female Immigrants to the United States. Eds. Delores M. Mortimer and Roy S. Bryce-Laporte. Washington, D.C.: Smithsonian Institution, Research Institute for Ethnic Studies, 1981.

Professional women were well represented among women from the Caribbean. They were much more aware of class differences than native-born Afro-Americans.

523. Johnson, Carmen A. "Mexican American Women in the Labor Force and Lowered Fertility." American Journal of Public Health 66, 12 (1976): 1186-8.

Emphasizes influence of education, age, and mother tongue on employment and childbearing.

524. Joseph, Judith L. V. "The Nafkeh and the Lady: Jews, Prostitutes and Progressives in New York City, 1900-1930." Unpublished Ph.D. Dissertation, State University of New York, Stony Brook, 1986. Order Number DA 8614616.

Focus is on Jewish prostitutes and the efforts of Jewish women's organizations to combat Jewish prostitution.

525. Joyce, Richard E. and Chester L. Hunt. "Philippine Nurses and the Brain Drain." Social Science and Medicine 16 (1982): 1223-1233.

Compares recent to earlier arrivals for socioeconomic backgrounds and plans to return.

82   IMMIGRANT WOMEN IN THE U.S.

526. Katz, Naomi and David S. Kemnitzer. "Fast Forward: The Internationalization of Silicon Valley." Pp. 332-345 <u>Women, Men and the International Division of Labor</u>. Ed. June Nash and Maria P. Fernández-Kelly. Albany, NY: State University of New York Press, 1983.

Most of work force was female, and about half of the women were from the Third World, mainly recently arrived Asians.

527. Katzman, David. <u>Seven Days a Week: Women and Domestic Service in Industrializing America</u>. New York: Oxford University Press, 1978.

Good attention to immigrants, especially Irish, contrasts their work experiences to native Afro-Americans; includes a bibliographical note on immigrant women as domestics.

528. Kay, Chung Y. "At the Palace: Work, Ethnicity and Gender in a Chinese Restaurant." <u>Studies in Sexual Politics</u> 3 (1985): 1-83.

A study of ethnicity and gender in work culture. Notes the importance of language for both creating and overcoming problems of ethnicity.

529. Kellor, Frances A. "The Immigrant Woman". <u>Atlantic</u> 100 (Sept. 1907): 401-407.

Emphasizes that they came to the U.S. to work, but preferred industry to domestic service.

530. Kennedy, Susan E. "Poverty, Respectability, and Ability to Work." <u>International Journal of Women's Studies</u> 2 (September/October 1979): 401-414.

Focus is on native-born women reformers and their attention to the particular problems of immigrant women.

531. Kessler-Harris, Alice. <u>Out to Work, A History of Wage-Earning Women in the United States</u>. New York: Oxford University Press, 1982.

Although the focus is working-class women, they are distinguished by ethnic and national background, providing one of the more differentiated views of women's wage-earning work currently available.

532. Kessner, Thomas and Betty B. Caroli. "New Immigrant Women at Work: Italians and Jews in New York City." <u>Journal of Ethnic Studies</u> 5 (Winter 1978): 19-32.

Wives of both groups preferred domesticity, but Italian wives worked more frequently than Eastern European Jews. Among daughters and second-generation, however, Jewish girls more likely to work than Italians and to take jobs similar to those of their brothers.

533. Kim, Elaine H. "With Silk Wings, Asian American Women at Work." Pp. 95-100 All American Women; Lines that Divide, Ties that Bind. Ed. Johnnetta B. Cole. New York and London: The Free Press and Collier Macmillan Publishers, 1986.

Includes some information about the particular patterns of the immigrant generation.

534. Kim, Illsoo. New Urban Immigrants: The Korean Community in New York City. Princeton, N.J.: Princeton University Press, 1981.

Contains miscellaneous information about women as workers; some attention to the work contracts of health care workers.

535. Kim, Kwang Chung and Won Moo Hurh. "Employment of Korean Immigrant Wives and the Division of Household Tasks." Pp. 199-218 Korean Women in Transition: At Home and Abroad. Ed. Eui-Young Yu and Earl H. Phillips. Los Angeles: Center for Korean-American and Korean Studies, California State University, 1987.

536. Klaczynska, Barbara M. "Working Women in Philadelphia, 1900-1930." Unpublished Ph.D. Dissertation, Temple University, 1975. Order Number 75-28,230.

Polish, Jewish, Irish, and native-born women. Notes switch from home-based to factory work for immigrant women.

537. Klaczynska, Barbara. "Why Women Work: A Comparison of Various Groups in Philadelphia: 1910-1930." Labor History 17 (Winter 1976): 73-87.

Compares Irish, Afro-American, native-born, Polish, Jewish, and Italian women, emphasizing the different choices they made about jobs.

538. Klausner, Patricia R. "The Politics of Massage Parlor Prostitution: The International Traffic in Women for Prostitution into New York City, 1970-present." Unpublished Ph.D. Dissertation, University of Delaware, 1987. Order Number DA 8719536.

Notes recruitment of Latin American and Korean women workers.

539. Kleinberg, Susan J. "Technology and Women's Work: The Lives of Working Class Women in Pittsburgh, 1870-1900." Labor History 17 (Winter 1976): 58-72.

Most of the working-class women studied were immigrants, but this is not given any attention. The meaning and practice of domesticity and housework in a town dominated by men's industry is the focus.

84   IMMIGRANT WOMEN IN THE U.S.

540. Kleinberg, Susan J. "Technology's Stepdaughters, the Impact of Industrialization upon Working Class Women, Pittsburgh, 1865-1890." Unpublished Ph.D. Dissertation, University of Pittsburgh, 1973. Order Number 74-18,447.

No attention to nationality, but most were foreign-born and second-generation women. Pittsburgh's economy prevented women's move from domesticity into wage-earning.

541. Kneeland, George J. Commercialized Prostitution in New York City. New York: The Century Co., 1913.

Contains some analysis of the nativity and ethnic backgrounds of prostitutes. Eastern European Jews and Irish women were the largest foreign-born groups.

542. Kossoudji, Sherrie A. and Susan I. Ranney. "The Labor Market Experience of Female Migrants: The Case of Temporary Mexican Migration to the U.S." International Migration Review 18 (Winter 1984) : 1120-1143.

Found that many undocumented women were single or divorced, and most worked as domestics.

543. Krause, Corinne A. "Italian, Jewish and Slavic Grandmothers in Pittsburgh: Their Economic Roles." Frontiers 2 (Summer 1977): 18-28.

Found Slavic women most and Italian women least likely to work outside home.

544. Lamphere, Louise et al. "The Economic Struggle of Female Factory Workers: A Comparison of French, Polish, and Portuguese Immigrants." Pp. 12-152 National Institution of Education Conference on the Educational and Occupational Needs of White Ethnic Women. Washington, D.C.: U.S. Government Printing Office, 1980.

545. Lamphere, Louise. "Bringing the Family to Work: Women's Culture on the Shop Floor." Feminist Studies 11 (Fall 1985): 519-540.

Compares women in a Southwest factory to Portuguese in New England. Argues that resistance culture drew on outside roles, including friendship and family relations. The work context determined whether the family was "brought to work." Employers could also coopt family-style relations in workplace.

546. Lamphere, Louise. "Fighting the Piece-Rate System: New Dimensions of an Old Struggle in the Apparel Industry." Pp. 257-276 Case Studies in the Labor Process. Ed. Andrew Zimbalist. New York: Monthly Review, 1979.

Study of Portuguese sewers. New technology had little impact upon the basic conflict over piecework rate and productivity.

547. Lamphere, Louise. "From Working Daughters to Working Mothers: Production and Reproduction in an Industrial Community." American Ethnologist 13 (1986): 118-130.

Focus on several immigrant generations in one mill town.

548. Lamphere, Louise. "Working Mothers and Family Strategies: Portuguese and Colombian Immigrant Women in a New England Community." Pp. 266-283 International Migration, The Female Experience. Ed. Rita J. Simon and Caroline B. Bretell. Totowa, N.J.: Rowman & Allanheld, 1985.

Emphasizes the importance of the economy in shaping women's decisions about work and family; notes switch from wage-earning daughters to wage-earning mothers.

549. Lamphere, Louise. From Working Daughters to Working Mothers; Immigrant Women in a New England Industrial Community. Ithaca and London: Cornell University Press, 1987.

Compares Polish, French-Canadian, Portuguese, Colombian, English, and Italian women's wage-earning patterns. Found that the work done by women was "a product of a group's location in a particular niche within the local economy rather than a reflection of different values."

550. Lan, Dean. "Chinatown Sweatshops". Pp. 347-358 Counterpoint: Perspectives on Asian America. Ed. Emma Gee. Los Angeles: University of California, 1976.

Focus is San Francisco's garment industry. Includes data on employment by sex and some information about women's participation in union.

551. Lasser, Carol S. "Mistress, Maid and Market: The Transformation of Domestic Service in New England, 1790-1870." Unpublished Ph.D. Dissertation, Harvard University, 1982. Order Number DA8216219.

One chapter focuses on Irish women.

552. Lasser, Carol. "The Domestic Balance of Power: Relations Between Mistress and Maid in Nineteenth-Century New England." Labor History 28 (Winter 1987): 5-22.

Found that native-born women were reluctant to take Irish domestics and believed that immigrant women became less compliant when exposed to American democratic ideals. Notes growing distance between employer and maid after 1830.

553. Laughlin, Clara E. The Work-a-Day Girl: A Study of Some Present-Day Conditions. New York: Fleming H. Revell, 1913.

Theme is that low wages led women to immorality. Many of the case studies seem to be Irish and Eastern European Jewish women. Good pictures.

554. Leiserson, William M. *Adjusting Immigrant and Industry*. New York: Harper and Brothers, 1924.

See the chapter "Special Problems of the Immigrant Women" which includes information on work, family roles, and home life.

555. Levorson, Barbara. "Our Bread and Meat." *Norwegian American Studies* 22 (1965): 178-197.

Includes good information on women as farm workers, food growers, and food preparers.

556. MacLean, Annie M. *Women Workers and Society*. Chicago: A.C. McClurg, 1916.

Some attention to nationality of women workers.

557. Mancuso, Arlene. "Women of Old Town." Unpublished Ed.D Dissertation, Columbia University, 1977. Order Number 77-14,741.

Second-generation Italian wives and mothers drew on extensive kin and friendship networks for information and power; the women made key decisions for the family group.

558. Manning, Caroline. *The Immigrant Woman and Her Job*. U.S. Department of Labor Women's Bureau Bulletin No. 74. Reprinted New York: Arno Press, 1970.

Focus is on Southern and Eastern Europeans--their work, family life, and education. Includes some interview materials.

559. Maram, Sheldon L. *Hispanic Workers in the Garment and Restaurant Industries in Los Angeles County: A Social and Economic Profile*. La Jolla, Cal.: Program in U.S.-Mexican Studies, University of California at San Diego, 1980.

The majority in both industries were undocumented immigrants. Most expected to stay in U.S., were young, unmarried, and with little education. In garments, most were women; in restaurants, most were men.

560. McInnis, Kathleen M. "Income Packaging Strategies among Native and Foreign Born Female Heads of Household." Unpublished Ph.D. Dissertation, The University of Wisconsin, Madison, 1987. Order Number DA 8712428.

Immigrant women who headed households were more likely to be employed and less likely to receive welfare than native-born women.

561. Medina, Celia and Maria R. Reyes. "Dilemmas of Chicana Counselors." *Social work* 21 (November 1976): 515-517.

A study of Spanish-speaking counselors, finds they often suffered from "the over-compassion trap."

562. Melloh, Ardith K. "Life in Early New Sweden, Iowa". *The Swedish Pioneer Historical Quarterly* 32 (April 1981): 124-146.

Notes changes in Swedish women's farm work as men assumed care and milking of dairy animals.

563. Mensch, Jean U. "Social Pathology in Urban America: Desertion, Prostitution, Gambling, Drugs and Crime among East European Jews in New York City between 1881 and World War I." Unpublished Ph.D. Dissertation, Columbia University, 1983.

564. Miraflor, Clarita G. "The Philippine Nurse: Implications for Orientation and in-Service Education for Foreign Nurses in the United States." Unpublished Ph.D. Dissertation, Loyola University of Chicago, 1976. Order Number 76-11,719.

Motives for migration included furthering education, improving technical skills, and financial improvement. Adjustment problems included difficulties communicating and learning hospital procedures.

565. Modell, John and Tamara K. Hareven. "Urbanization and the Malleable Household: An Examination of Boarding and Lodging in American Families." *Journal of Marriage and the Family* 35 (August 1973): 467-479.

Contrasts native-born and foreign-born women and men. Boarding was not a sign of family breakdown, but a way of maintaining family relations and economies, as children entered and left the home.

566. Montero, Darrel. "The Vietnamese Refugees in America: Toward a Theory of Spontaneous International Migration." *International Migration Review* 13 (Winter 1979): 624-648.

Includes data on labor force participation by women.

567. Mormino, Gary R. and George E. Pozzetta. "Immigrant Women in Tampa: The Italian Experience, 1890-1930. *Florida Historical Quarterly* 61 (July 1982): 296-312.

Women cigar workers.

568. Mormino, Gary R. and George E. Pozzetta. *The Immigrant World of Ybor City; Italians and Their Latin Neighbors in Tampa, 1885-1985.* Urbana and Chicago: University of Illinois Press, 1987.

Based in part on oral histories, but few were with women. Some information about women cigar workers.

569. Naff, Alixa. *Becoming American: The Early Arab Immigrant Experience.* Carbondale: Southern Illinois University Press, 1985.

Good coverage of Arab women in work and family roles.

88   IMMIGRANT WOMEN IN THE U.S.

570. Nasaw, David. *Children of the City: At Work and At Play*. Garden City, N.Y.: Doubleday, 1985.

One chapter focuses on girls, mainly of second generation. Information about leisure as well as wage-earning.

571. Neu, Irene D. "The Jewish Businesswoman in America." *American Jewish Historical Quarterly* 66 (September 1976): 137-154.

Tells of German Jewish peddlers, and Russian Jewish women who as breadwinners became involved in business.

572. Nguyen, Thuy T. et al. "Food Habits and Preference of Vietnamese Children." *Journal of School Health* 53 (February 1983): 144-47.

Notes that Vietnamese mothers needed nutritional education.

573. Odencrantz, Louise. *Italian Women in Industry: A Study of Conditions in New York City*. New York: Russell Sage Foundation, 1919.

574. Ogden, Annegret. *The Great American Housewife; From Helpmate to Wage Earner, 1776-1986*. Westport, Conn. and London: Greenwood Press, 1986.

A chapter on pioneers covers both rural women and immigrants in cities.

575. Ong, Paul M. "Immigrant Wives' Labor Force Participation." *Industrial Relations* 26 (Fall 1987): 296-303.

Study of Chinese in California; assimilation effected labor-force participation rates only when women live outside of a Chinese ethnic economy.

576. Ortiz, Vilma and Rosemary S. Cooney. "Sex-Role Attitudes and Labor Force Participation among Young Hispanic Females and Non-Hispanic White Females." *Social Science Quarterly* 65 (June 1984): 392-400.

Traditional attitudes towards sex roles (i.e., domesticity of wives) were strongly held only in the first generation. Educational achievement, not attitudes, explained the lower labor-force participation rates of second- and third-generation Hispanic women when compared to white non-Hispanics.

577. Paradise, Viola. "The Jewish Immigrant Girl in Chicago." *Survey* 30 (1913): 703.

Large numbers worked in the garment industry.

578. Parker, Cornelia S. *Working with the Working Woman*. New York: Harper and Brothers, 1922.

The author took various jobs in order to report on working conditions and coworkers, many of whom were immigrants and are presented in an unflattering light.

579. Pascoe, Peggy A. "The Search for Female Moral Authority: Protestant Women and Rescue Homes in the American West, 1874-1939." Unpublished Ph.D. Dissertation, Stanford University, 1986. Order Number DA 86819803.

Donaldina Cameron's Chinese Mission House for Chinese prostitutes is one of the missions described.

580. Passero, Rosara L. "Ethnicity in the Men's Ready-Made Clothing Industry, 1880-1950: The Italian Experience in Philadelphia." Unpublished Ph.D. Dissertation, University of Pennsylvania, 1978. Order Number 7816342.

Some attention to women, especially as homeworkers and finishers of garments.

581. Penczer, Lynne O. "Resources and Family Power: Portuguese Adolescents in a New England City." Unpublished Ph.D. Dissertation, Yale University, 1986. Order Number DA8701070.

Wage earning increased boys' but not girls' autonomy; the reasons are explored.

582. Perez, Lisandro. "Immigrant Economic Adjustment and Family Organization: The Cuban Success Story Reexamined." *International Migration Review* 20 (1986): 4-20.

Cuban women's high rates of employment were the key to their families' high income.

583. Pernicone, Carol G. "The Bloody Ould Sixth: A Social Analysis of a New York City Working-class Community in the Mid-Nineteenth Century." Unpublished Ph.D. Dissertation, University of Rochester, 1973. Order Number 73-25,842.

Focus on family as economic and social unit, including analysis of Irish and German immigrant women as wage earners.

584. Pessar, Patricia R. "The Linkage Between the Household and Workplace of Dominican Women in the U.S." *International Migration Review* 18 (Winter 1984): 1188-1211.

Working for wages improved domestic social relations, but "beliefs about immigration and work which are rooted in the family, and the immigration goals that are realized through household cooperation, militate against working class identification and organized resistance in the workplace."

585. Pessar, Patricia. "The Dominicans: Women in the Household and the Garment Industry." Pp. 103-129 <u>New Immigrants in New York</u>. Ed. Nancy Foner. New York: Columbia University Press, 1987.

Women from lower-middle-class backgrounds thought of themselves as middle-class in U.S. (because they could afford more consumer goods); most, however, worked in poorly paid garment-industry jobs. Increased participation in family decision-making accompanied labor for wages and led to reluctance to return.

586. Pessar, Patricia. "The Role of Gender in Dominican Settlement in the United States." Pp. 273-294 <u>Women and Change in Latin America</u>. Ed. June Nash and Helen Safa. South Hadley, Mass.: Bergin and Garvey Publishers, 1986.

Women acquired more power within family as migrants and as wage-earners.

587. Pleck, Elizabeth H. "A Mother's Wages: Income Earning Among Married Italian and Black Women, 1896-1911." Pp. 367-392 <u>The American Family in Social Historical Perspective</u>. Ed. Michael Gordon. 2nd Ed., New York: St. Martin's, 1978.

Cultural barriers against Italian wives working were low fences rather than high stone walls.

588. Poston, Dudley L. et al. "Income and Occupational Attainment Patterns of Mexican Immigrants and Nonimmigrants." Pp. 100-119 <u>Mexican Immigrants and the Mexican American Community: An Evolving Relationship</u>. Ed. R. de la Garza and H. Browning. Austin: The University of Texas Press, 1985.

Includes data on women's earnings and work patterns, but finds ethnicity of more influence than gender.

589. Prieto, Yolanda. "Cuban Women and Work in the United States: A New Jersey Case Study." Pp. 95-112 <u>International Migration, The Female Experience</u>. Ed. Rita J. Simon and Caroline B. Bretell. Totowa, N.J.: Rowman & Allanheld, 1985.

The middle-class values of this group encouraged high labor-force participation among women.

590. Ranney, Susan and Sherrie A. Kossoudji. "The Labor Market Experience of Female Migrants: The Case of Temporary Mexican Migration to the U.S." <u>International Migration Review</u> 18(1984): 1120-1132.

591. Reimers, Cordelia W. "A Comparative Analysis of the Wages of Hispanics, Blacks, and Non-Hispanic Whites." Pp. 27-75 Hispanics in the U.S. Economy. Ed. Marta Tienda and Georges Borjas. Orlando and New York: Academic Press, 1985.

Compares Mexican, Cuban, Central American, and South American women. Education did not always lead to higher wages; presence of children in household lowered earnings of Mexican women. Several groups earned wages equal to or higher than those of non-Hispanic white women.

592. Rios-Bustamente, Antonio J., ed. Mexican Immigrant Workers in the United States. Los Angeles: Chicano Studies Center, University of California, 1981.

Includes a section on women workers.

593. Robbins, Jane E. "The Bohemian Women in New York." Charities and the Commons 13 (1904).

Many worked as cigar makers.

594. Romero, Mary. "Domestic Service in Transition from Rural to Urban Life: The Case of La Chicana." Women's Studies 13, 3 (1987): 199-222.

A common employment, especially for undocumented Mexican women.

595. Rosen, Ellen I. Bitter Choices: Blue-Collar Women in and Out of Work. Chicago: University of Chicago Press, 1987.

Contains interview materials with Portuguese women.

596. Ruiz, Vicki L. "A Promise Fulfilled: Mexican Cannery Workers in Southern California." Pacific Historian 30 (1986): 50-61.

Women were not passive or submissive on the job.

597. Ruiz, Vicki L. "By the Day or Week: Mexican Domestic Workers in El Paso." Pp. 269-283 "To Toil the Livelong Day;" America's Women at Work, 1780-1980. Ed. Carol Groneman and Mary Beth Norton. Ithaca and London: Cornell University Press, 1987.

598. Ruiz, Vicki L. Cannery Women, Cannery Lives: Mexican Women, Unionization, and the California Food Processing Industry, 1930-1950. Albuquerque: University of New Mexico Press, 1987.

Both the wage work and labor activism of cannery women contradicted stereotypes of home-bound and submissive Mexican women.

92   IMMIGRANT WOMEN IN THE U.S.

599. Safa, Helen I.   "The Differential Incorporation of Hispanic Women Migrants in to the U.S. Labor Force." Pp. 235-266 Female Immigrants to the United States: Caribbean, Latin American and African Experiences. Ed. Delores Mortimer and Roy Bryce-Laporte. Washington, D.C.: Research Institute on Immigration and Ethnic Studies, Smithsonian Institute, 1981.

Compares work patterns of Cubans and Puerto Ricans.

600. Salmon, Lucy M. Domestic Service. New York: MacMillan, 1901.

Includes some information on Irish and German women who commonly worked as servants.

601. Sarsfield, Nancy C. "An Acculturation Study of the Filipino Nurse into New Jersey Hospitals." Unpublished Ph.D. Dissertation, New York University, 1973.

602. Schneider, Dorothee. "'For Whom are All the Good Things in Life?' German American Housewives Discuss their Budgets." Pp. 145-162 German Workers in Industrial Chicago, 1850-1910. Ed. Hartmut Keil and John B. Jentz. DeKalb, Ill.: Northern Illinois University Press, 1983.

Most women mentioned that they ate better than in the homeland, but they were nevertheless not satisfying their own expectations for improvements in the U.S.

603. Segura, Denise A. "Chicanas and Mexican Immigrant Women in the Labor Market: A Study of Occupational Mobility and Stratification." Unpublished Ph.D. Dissertation, University of California, Berkeley, 1987. Order Number DA 8718154.

Twenty women of each group were studied. Even those who took low-status jobs believed they had experienced mobility.

604. Segura, Denise A. "Labor Market Stratification: The Chicana Experience." Berkeley Journal of Sociology 29 (1984): 57-80.

605. Shepherd, C. "Chinese Girl Slavery in America." Missionary Review 46 (1923): 893-898.

The sale and contracting of women was linked to prostitution.

606. Simon, Rita J. and Julian L. Simon. "Social and Economic Adjustment." Pp. 13-42 New Lives, The Adjustment of Soviet Jewish Immigrants in the United States and Israel. Ed. Rita J. Simon. Lexington, Mass.: Lexington Books, D.C. Heath, 1985.

Includes data on women's employment among Soviet Jewish refugees.

607. Simon, Rita J. and Margo C. DeLey "The Work Experience of Undocumented Mexican Women Migrants in Los Angeles." <u>International Migration Review</u> 18 (Winter 1984): 1212-1229.

Authors argue that studies of apprehended undocumented immigrants underestimated female representation.

608. Simon, Rita J. and Margo C. DeLey. "Undocumented Mexican Women: Their Work and Personal Experiences." Pp. 113-132 <u>International Migration, The Female Experience</u>. Ed. Rita J. Simon and Caroline B. Bretell. Totowa, N.J.: Rowman & Allanheld, 1985.

Undocumented Mexican women were less likely to speak the English language and work in factories as laborers; most intended to stay in the U.S.

609. Simon, Rita J. et al. "The Social and Economic Adjustment of Soviet Jewish Women in the United States." Pp. 76-94 <u>International Migration, The Female Experience</u>. Ed. Rita J. Simon and Caroline B. Bretell. Totowa, N.J.: Rowman & Allanheld, 1985.

Most of these refugee women worked in professions and skilled occupations and enjoyed a relatively easy and positive adjustment.

610. Smith, Carol J. "Work and Use of Government Benefits: A Case Study of Hispanic Women Workers in New York's Garment Industry." Unpublished D.S.W. Dissertation, Adelphi University School of Social Work, 1980. Order Number 8018637.

Compares eight Puerto Rican and twelve Dominican women, focusing on family and work. Their wages could not support children, and they encouraged migration of other family members to help them care for children.

611. Stansell, Christine. "The Origins of the Sweatshop: Women and Early Industrialization in New York City." Pp. 78-103 <u>Working-Class America: Essays in Labor, Community and American Society</u>. Ed. Michael H. Frisch and Daniel J. Walkowitz. Urbana: University of Illinois Press, 1983.

Although many of these workers were Irish and German women, this is not a central theme. The sweatshop became popular because it replicated gender relations of traditional families.

612. Stein, Leon. <u>The Triangle Fire</u>. Philadelphia: Lippincott, 1962.

Most of the women studied were immigrants or daughters of Italian and Eastern European Jews. The book is a chronology rather than an interpretation.

613. Steinberg, Stephen. _The Ethnic Myth: Race, Ethnicity and Class in America_. Boston: Beacon Press, 1981.

See especially Chapter 6, "Why Irish Became Domestics and Italians and Jews Did Not." When the Irish arrived there were no alternatives to domestic work; by the time the Jews and Italians arrived, factory doors had opened to women.

614. Sullivan, Teresa A. "The Occupational Prestige of Women Immigrants: A Comparison of Cubans and Mexicans." _International Migration Review_ 18 (Winter 1984): 1045-1062.

Women's social mobility differed from men's, largely because women were restricted to pink-collar jobs of nominally higher status but low in income.

615. Tarbox, Mary P. "The Origins of Nursing by the Sisters of Mercy in the United States: 1843-1910." Unpublished Ph.D. Dissertation, Columbia University Teachers College, 1986. Order Number DA 8704315.

The early nurse sisters of Pittsburgh were Irish nuns.

616. Taylor, Paul S. "Mexican Women in Los Angeles Industry in 1928." _Aztlán_ 11 (Spring 1980): 99-131.

Based on research undertaken in the 1920s. Most women were from the lower class, and 67 percent worked because of poverty; 5 percent were the sole supports of families; 10 percent, usually middle-class, worked to advance family ambitions; few lived apart from their families.

617. Tentler, Leslie. _Wage-Earning Women; Industrial Work and Family Life in the United States, 1900-1930_. New York: Oxford University Press, 1979.

Gives some attention to the fact that most of the women studied were immigrants and daughters. The emphasis, however, is on patterns shared by all of the working class.

618. Tienda, Marta and Patricia A. Guhleman. "The Occupational Position of Employed Hispanic Females." Pp. 243-276 _Hispanics in the U.S. Economy_. Ed. Marta Tienda and Georges Borjas. Orlando and New York: Academic Press, 1985.

Compares Mexicans, Puerto Ricans, Central Americans, and South Americans, controlling for time since arrival.

619. Tienda, Marta et al. "Immigration, Gender and the Process of Occupational Change in the United States, 1970-80." _International Migration Review_ 18 (Winter 1984): 1021-1044.

Compares Latin American, Caribbean, Asian, Filipino, and Cuban women. Immigrant women were moving into two jobs (laborers and farm laborers) that were being vacated by native-born workers.

620. Van Kleeck, Mary. Artificial Flower Makers. New York: Survey Associates, 1913.

Most workers were Italians and Eastern European Jews. Contains good pictures by Lewis Hines.

621. Van Kleeck, Mary. Women in the Bookbinding Trades. New York: Russell Sage Foundation, 1913.

Most workers were second-generation Irish and Germans. Good pictures.

622. Waldinger, Roger. "Immigration and Industrial Change in the New York Apparel Industry." Pp. 323-350 Hispanics in the U.S. Economy. Ed. Marta Tienda and Georges Borjas. Orlando and New York: Academic Press, 1985.

Since many of the small factories and shops are owned by immigrants, recruitment of women workers was done informally.

623. Waldinger, Roger. Immigrants in the New York City Garment Industry. Cambridge, Mass.: Joint Center for Urban Studies of MIT and Harvard University, 1982.

This industry remains a major employer of Chinese, other Asian, Caribbean, and Central and South American women immigrants.

624. Weber, Heidi. "The Mining Town Boarding House: A Surrogate Family for the Immigrant." Pennsylvania Ethnic Studies Newsletter (1985): 1-4.

A child's paper, this work based on oral history nevertheless contains useful information on women's work as keepers of boarders.

625. Weinberg, Sydney S. "Working Daughters." Lilith 8 (1981): 2-23.

Based on oral history, the article contains ample material from the author's interviews with Eastern European Jewish women.

626. Wertheimer, Barbara. We Were There: The Story of Working Women in America. New York: Pantheon Books, 1977.

Although the focus is working-class women, the book gives good special attention to the foreign-born, especially around the turn of the century.

627. Wilber, George L. Spanish Americans and Indians in the Labor Market. Lexington: University of Kentucky, 1974.

Distinguishes Mexicans and Cubans, with some attention to women's wage-earning and income.

628. Willett, Mabel H. Employment of Women in the Clothing Trades. New York: Columbia University, 1902.

Study of Eastern European Jewish and Italian workers in factories, and Italian wives doing homework.

629. Wong, Joyce M. "Prostitution: San Francisco Chinatown, Mid-and Late Nineteenth-Century." Bridge 6 (Winter 1978/79): 23-29.

Includes several good pictures.

630. Wong, Morrison G. "Chinese Sweatshops in the United States: A Look at the Garment Industry." Pp. 357-379 Research in the Sociology of Work, A Research Annual. Ed. Ida Harper Simpson and Richard L. Simpson. Greenwich, Conn.: JAI Press, 1983.

The San Francisco industry employed Chinese from its earliest days; Chinese were one-third to one-half of all workers before 1900. After World War I, men left the industry, but Chinese women remained. Today, subcontracting and low wages still prevail.

631. Wong, Morrison G. and Charles Hirschman. "Labor Participation and Socioeconomic Attainment of Asian-American Women." Sociological Perspectives 26 (1983); 423-446.

Japanese, Chinese, and Filipino women had higher-than-average rates of labor-force participation and wages, but recent immigrants were segregated in low-wage jobs. Contrasts first and second generation.

632. Woo, Deborah. "The Socioeconomic Status of Asian American Women in the Labor Force: An Alternative View." Sociological Perspectives 28 (July 1985): 307-338.

Offers a reinterpretation of Asian women's high labor-force participation rates as a product of economic necessity. Contrasts foreign- and native-born Asians. Both had high levels of education, but education did not translate into better jobs; instead, overeducated clericals were common.

633. Yamanaka, Keiko. "Labor Force Participation of Asian American Women: Ethnicity, Work and the Family." Unpublished Ph.D. Dissertation, Cornell University, 1987. Order Number DA 87 25833.

Compares the labor-force participation rates of native- and foreign-born Japanese, Chinese, Filipino, Korean, and Asian Indian women.

634. Yans-McLaughlin, Virginia. "Patterns of Work and Family Organization: Buffalo's Italians." Journal of Interdisciplinary History 2 (Autumn, 1971): 299-314.

Women contributed to family income by doing homework, since leaving the home was not culturally sanctioned.

635. Zavella, Patricia. "Abnormal Intimacy: The Varying Networks of Chicana Cannery Workers." *Feminist Studies* 11 (1985): 541-557.

Friendship on the job humanized the workplace but may also have blunted women's criticism of employers. Friendship ties could be a potent organizing tool in period of labor strife. Some workers are second-generation, although this is not an important point in article.

6

Working Together

INTRODUCTION

As women, as immigrants, as workers, as citizens, and as members of ethnic and minority groups, immigrant women work together with others outside their families to enrich their lives and to accomplish a wide variety of goals. This chapter surveys research on women as reformers, radicals, and feminists and as religious, community, political, or labor activists. The reader is also advised to turn to biography and autobiography; the lives of individual activists, many of whom achieved respect and even fame for their outstanding work with others, provide important insights into the collective activities described in this chapter.

Existing research suggests that immigrant women were far more likely to participate in ethnic and religious community organizations than they were to participate in unions or other types of U.S. workers' movements. Still, a growing literature documents immigrant women's strengths as strikers and the difficulties they faced as women in a movement dominated by men. Within their ethnic and religious communities, women's and men's activities also tended to be segregated by sex. Research on sisterhoods and women's communities within the Catholic Church makes this point in particularly vivid form. Women's community activism sometimes originated in their family responsibilities for caring and nurture; at other times women took men's fraternals as their model of community organization. "Female fraternals" seem to have been more common than women's auxiliaries to men's groups, for example.

Immigrant women, like men of similar background, rarely worked together toward common goals with native-born Americans, although they sometimes collaborated with other immigrant or working-class groups, especially within the labor movement. Surprisingly few immigrant women became involved in feminist or in general women's organizations. And political activism remained unusual even in the second generation.

100   IMMIGRANT WOMEN IN THE U.S.

Most of the research cited in this chapter examines the immigrants of the past. We still know almost nothing about initiatives among today's foreign-born females.

CITATIONS

636. Birnbaum, Lucia C. "Earthmothers, Godmothers, and Radicals: The Inheritance of Sicilian American Women." Marxist Perspectives 3 (Spring 1980): 128-141.

Contrasts the political passivity of Sicilian women in the U.S. to their past and present activism in Italy.

637. Blumfeld, Hanita F. "Jewish Women Sew the Union Label: A Study of Sexism and Feminism in the Emerging Unionization of the Garment Industry, New York City." Humanity and Society 6 (February 1982): 33-45.

638. Boone, Gladys. The Women's Trade Union League of Great Britain and the United States of America. New York: Columbia University Press, 1942.

See especially a chapter on the 1909 garment strike in New York, and on immigrant women's work with native-born women in the Women's Trade Union League.

639. Bristow, Edward J. Prostitution and Prejudice: The Jewish Fight Against White Slavery, 1870-1939. New York: Schocken Books, 1983.

Focus is on Eastern European Jews. See especially chapter 2 on Jewish prostitution in Eastern Europe and chapter 5 on the U.S.

640. Brown, Mary E. "The Making of Italian-American Catholics: Jesuit Work on the Lower East Side, New York, 1890-1950s." Catholic Historical Review 73 (April 1987): 285-303.

Includes some information on women's religious sodalities, popular among second-generation women.

641. Buhle, Mari Jo. "The Socialist Women and the 'Girl Strikers,' Chicago, 1910." SIGNS 1 (Summer 1976): 1039-1051.

Documents and commentary show that most workers were Jewish and that the most ardent strikers were unskilled and foreign-born women.

642. Buhle, Mari Jo. Women and American Socialism, 1870-1920. Urbana: University of Illinois Press, 1980.

Includes considerable information on well- and less-well known German and Irish activists of the first and second generations. Some attention is given to the relations of foreign-born and native-born radicals.

643. Burachinska, Lydia et al. Woman of Ukraine; Her Part on the Scene of History, in Literature, Arts and Struggle for Freedom. Philadelphia, Ukrainian National Women's League of America, 1955.

Although mainly about the homeland, also includes biographies of activists in the Ukrainian National Women's League of America.

644. Burton, Katherine. Cry Jubilee!. Allegheny, N.Y.: Sisters of St. Francis of the Third Order Regular, 1960.

The sisterhood was founded by an Italian priest and an Irish nun.

645. Burton, Katherine. The Bernardines. Villanova, Pa: Maryview Press, 1964.

The Bernardine Sisterhood was founded in 1894 by Polish immigrant women.

646. Butler, Mary P. The American Foundation of the Sisters of Notre Dame de Namur. Philadelphia: Dolphin Press, 1928.

The order was founded in the U.S. by Belgian sisters.

647. Callan, Louise. The Society of the Sacred Heart in North America. London: Longmans, Green & Co., 1937.

The order was founded by French sisters, including Rose Philippine Duchesne in 1818 in St. Louis. The book includes many lengthy excerpts from Duchesne's diaries and letters.

648. Cameron, Ardis. "Bread and Roses Revisited: Women's Culture and Working-Class Activism in the Lawrence Strike of 1912." Pp. 42-61 Women's Work and Protest: A Century of U.S. Women's Labor History. Ed. Ruth Milkman. Boston: Routledge and Kegan Paul, 1985.

Emphasizes the importance of neighborhood and female culture in supporting labor militancy; main groups studied are Italians, Syrians, and French-Canadians.

649. Casillas, Mike. "The Cananea Strike of 1906." Southwest Economy and Society 3 (1977-78): 18-32.

Many strikers were Mexican women food processors.

650. Chen, Diana et al. "A Study of Political Attitudes of Chinese and Puerto Rican Women." International Journal of Group Tensions 11, 1-4 (1981): 59-80.

Compares foreign-born and native-born of each group. Nativity did not influence voting patterns but political participation was lower for foreign-born women.

651. Chow, Esther N. "The Development of Feminist Consciousness among Asian American Women." Gender and Society 1 (September 1987): 284-299.

Considers past and present to explain their low level of participation in the U.S. feminist movement.

652. Clarissa, Sister, O.S.F. and Mary Olivia, O.S.F. With the Poverello--History of the Sisters of Saint Francis, Oldenburg, Indiana. New York: Kennedy and Sons, 1948.

The order was founded in the U. S. by Sister Theresa Hackelmeier, an Austrian immigrant from the mother convent in Vienna.

653. Cotera, Marta. "Feminism: The Chicana and Anglo Versions, a Historical Analysis." Pp. 217-234 Twice A Minority, Mexican American Women. Ed. Margarita B. Melville. Saint Louis: The C.V. Mosby Company, 1980.

Emphasizes the differing meanings of feminism for Mexican women.

654. Croxdale, Richard. "The 1938 San Antonio Pecan Shellers' Strike." Women in the Texas Workforce: Yesterday and Today. Ed. Richard Croxdale and Melissa Hield. Austin: People's History in Texas, 1979.

Many strikers were Mexican women.

655. Curran, Mary D. ""My Mother and Politics." The Massachusetts Review 13 (1972): 147-51.

Account of the author's second-generation Irish mother's career in politics.

656. D'Andrea, Vaneeta-Marie. "The Women of Survivance: A Case Study of Ethnic Persistence among the Members of Franco-American Women's Groups in New England, 1950-Present." Unpublished Ph.D. Dissertation, University of Connecticut, 1986. Order Number DA 86 29918.

A case study of the Fédération Féminine Franco-Americaine, a language maintenance organization for immigrant and second-generation women.

657. Davis, Allen. "The Women's Trade Union League: Origins and Organization." Labor History 5 (Winter 1964): 3-17.

Contains some information on the Irish labor activist Mary Kenney O'Sullivan, and her work in Chicago with Jane Addams.

658. Dehy, Elinor T. *Religious Orders of Women in the United States, Catholic, Accounts of their Origin, Works and Most Important Institutions, Interwoven with Histories of Many Famous Foundresses.* Hammond, Ind.: W.B. Conkey Co., 1930.

Many orders and foundresses were foreign-born, most frequently French-Canadian, French, Irish, or Eastern European.

659. Doughtery, D.M. et al. *Sisters of Saint Joseph of Carondelet.* St. Louis: Herder Book Co., 1966.

The order was founded in the U.S. by French nuns.

660. Dye, Nancy S. "Creating a Feminist Alliance: Sisterhood and Class Conflict in the New York Women's Trade Union League." *Feminist Studies* 2, 2/3 (1975): 24-38.

Emphasizes the high level of conflict within the league; interprets this mainly as a result of class differences, but mentions the influence of ethnicity, especially for Eastern European Jewish activists.

661. Dye, Nancy S. *As Equals and as Sisters: Feminism, Unionism, and the Women's Trade Union League of New York.* Columbia: University of Missouri Press, 1980.

Good attention to the organization of immigrant women in the garment industry and on relations between native- and foreign-born women in the Women's Trade Union League.

662. Elwell, Ellen Sue L. "The Founding and Early Programs of the National Council of Jewish Women: Study and Practice as Jewish Women's Religious Expression." Unpublished Ph.D. Dissertation, Indiana University, 1982. Order Number DA 8301060.

Many of the founders were second-generation German Jewish women. Initially the purpose of the group was Jewish education, but eventually women turned their efforts more exclusively toward philanthropy.

663. Evans, Mary E. *The Spirit is Mercy: The Story of the Sisters of Mercy in the Archdiocese of Cincinnati, 1858-1958.* Maryland: Newman Press, 1959.

The early work was done by Irish women sent from the mother house.

664. Ewens, Mary. "The Leadership of Nuns in Immigrant Catholicism." Pp. 101-149 Women and Religion in America. Vol. 1: *The Nineteenth Century: A Documentary History*. Ed. Rosemary R. Ruether and Rosemary S. Keller. New York: Harper and Row, 1981.

Most of the nuns discussed were Irish, French, and German.

IMMIGRANT WOMEN IN THE U.S.

665. Ewens, Mary. <u>The Role of the Nun in 19th Century America, Variations on the International Theme</u>. New York: Arno Press, 1978.

Most foundresses of orders were Irish, German, French, and French-Canadians; many worked within immigrant communities.

666. Frank, Dana. "Housewives, Socialists, and the Politics of Food: The 1917 New York Cost-of-Living Protests." <u>Feminist Studies</u> 11 (Summer 1985): 255-285.

Communally based market protests of Jewish Eastern European women did not easily fit the concepts and organizing approaches of male Socialists.

667. Fritschel, Herman L. <u>A Story of One Hundred Years of Deaconess Service</u>. Milwaukee: Lutheran Deaconess Motherhouse, 1949.

The group was founded and operated in its early years by German and second-generation women.

668. Gavit, John P. <u>Americans by Choice</u>. New York: Harper and Brothers, 1922.

See "The Foreign-born Woman, Her Home and Her Children, in American Politics." Many women were derivative citizens (through their husbands) and thus are considered derivative voters.

669. Golomb, Deborah G. "The 1893 Congress of Jewish Women: Evolution or Revolution in American Jewish Women's History?" <u>American Jewish History</u> 70 (1980): 68-90.

Founded by German Jewish women of the second generation; the focus is on the complex and evolving relations of the group to other Jewish community institutions.

670. Hanousek, Mary E. <u>A New Assisi: The First Hundred Years of the Sisters of St. Francis of Assisi, Milwaukee, Wisconsin, 1849-1949</u>. Milwaukee: Bruce, 1948.

The order was founded by German nuns from Bavaria.

671. Henry, Alice. <u>The Trade Union Woman</u>. New York: Burt Franklin, 1973. Orig. Pub. 1915.

Written by the Australian labor activist, the book contains some information on immigrant women active in a number of unions.

672. Henry, Alice. <u>Women and the Labor Movement</u>. New York: George H. Doran Co., 1923.

Written by the Australian labor reformer, it contains biographies of some women activists as well as attention to the national backgrounds of women working in many female trades and labor unions.

673. Herron, Sister Mary E. *The Sisters of Mercy in the United States, 1843-1928*. New York: The MacMillan Co., 1929.

The early work in most dioceses was done by sisters from Ireland. Many who entered the order in U.S. were also foreign-born or second-generation Irish women.

674. Holloway, Marcella M. "The Sisters of St. Joseph of Carondelet: 150 Years of Good Works in America." *Gateway Heritage* 7 (Fall 1986): 24-31.

The order was started in St. Louis by nuns from the French motherhouse; their specialty was education of the deaf.

675. Hurley, Sister Helen A. "The Sisters of St. Joseph and the Minnesota Frontier." *Minnesota History* 30 (March 1949): 1-13.

The first sisters to the St. Paul mission included French and Creole sisters from St. Louis; their work included opening and running a female academy.

676. Hurley, Sister Helen A. *On Good Ground: THe Story of the Sisters of St. Joseph in St. Paul*. Minneapolis: University of Minnesota Press, 1951.

The sisterhood was founded from St. Louis by several French, Creole and second-generation Irish sisters. Information about the early years is included.

677. Hyman, Colette A. "Labor Organizing and Female Institution-Building: The Chicago Women's Trade Union League, 1904-24." Pp. 22-41 *Women's Work and Protest: A Century of U.S. Women's Labor History*. Ed. Ruth Milkman. Boston: Routledge and Kegan Paul, 1985.

Most immigrants involved were Italians and Eastern European Jews; some activities were more labor oriented, others more feminist. Immigrant women served as labor organizers. Special projects included education and the teaching of English to women in their homes.

678. Hyman, Paula. "Immigrant Women and Consumer Protest: New York City Kosher Women's Meat Boycott of 1902." *American Jewish History* 70 (1980): 91-105.

Eastern European Jewish women organized one of the best-known food riots in U.S. history.

679. Infante, Isa M. "Politicalization of Immigrant Women from Puerto Rico and the Dominican Republic." Unpublished Ph.D. Dissertation, University of California, Riverside, 1977. Order Number 77-27,129.

Women who became feminists had already deviated from tradition in other ways, usually by earning wages or questioning church authority. The women studied participated only in autonomous women's organizations.

680. Jacoby, Robin M. "The Women's Trade Union League and American Feminism." *Feminist Studies* 3 (Fall 1975): 126-140.

By bringing together native-born and foreign-born women, the Women's Trade Union League helped broaden the suffrage movement prior to World War I.

681. Jensen, Joan M. "The Great Uprising in Rochester." Pp. 94-113 *A Needle, A Bobbin, A Strike; Women Needleworkers in America.* Ed. Joan M. Jensen and Sue Davidson. Philadelphia: Temple University Press, 1984.

Emphasizes the surprising militancy of all garment workers, including Italian, Eastern European Jewish, and Polish women.

682. Jurma, Mall et al. *Baltic Women's Council: 25 Years of Friendship and Cooperation, 1947-1972.* New York: Baltic Women's Council, 1972.

Focus is on the activists who founded this group in Germany, and then transplanted it to the U.S.

683. Keith, Henry. "The Black Political Tradition in New York: A Conjunction of Political Cultures." *Journal of Black Studies* 7 (June 1977): 455-484.

Notes a female mob tradition in the Caribbean homelands; women immigrants had lower feminist consciousness and lower levels of political activism than native-born Afro-American women. Documents immigrant females' participation in the Garvey movement and their rapid emancipation in New York City.

684. Kish, M. Olha, ed. *My Soul Doth Magnify the Lord*. Narberth, Pa.: Privately Printed, 1961.

Celebrates the fiftieth anniversary of the American foundation of the Order of the Sisters of St. Basil, and gives history of the Philadelphia Province of this Ukrainian order.

685. Klehr, Harvey. "Female Leadership in the Communist Party of the United States of America." *Studies in Comparative Communism* 10 (Winter 1977): 394-402.

Includes a statistical analysis of the backgrounds of women on the Party's Central Committee: ten were Jewish, six Catholic, and six Afro-American. Of the Catholics, one each was Italian, Ukrainian, Polish, Mexican, and Lithuanian, mainly foreign-born. Notes the absence of Scandinavian women, although men from those groups made up 10 percent of the male leadership.

686. Kohler, Mary H. *Rooted in Hope: The Story of the Dominican Sisters of Racine, Wisconsin.* Milwaukee: Bruce Publishing Co., 1962.

The early history of a congregation of Dominican sisters founded from the mother house in Holland.

687. Kohut, Rebecca. "Jewish Women's Organizations." *American Jewish Yearbook* 33 (1931-1932): 165-201.

688. Kryszak, Mary O. "Polish Women's Alliance of America, Reminiscences." Pp. 154-159 *Poles of Chicago, 1837-1937, A History of One Century of Polish Contribution to the City of Chicago, Illinois.* Chicago: Polish Pageant, 1937.

Tells of the foundation of a female fraternal for Polish women in 1898.

689. Kutscher, Carol B. "The Early Years of Hadassah, 1912-1921." Unpublished Ph.D. Dissertation, Brandeis University, 1976. Order Number 76-25,313.

Includes a biography of Henrietta Szold, who founded the organization.

690. Kuzmack, Linda G. "The Emergence of the Jewish Women's Movement in England and the United States, 1881-1933: A Comparative Study." Unpublished Ph. D. Dissertation, George Washington University, 1986. Order Number DA 8615758.

Focuses on how second- and later-generation German Jewish women organized to provide social service, especially for those of Eastern European backgrounds.

691. Lamphere, Louise. "On the Shop Floor: Multi-Ethnic Unity against the Conglomerate." Pp. 247-63 *My Troubles are Going to Have Trouble with Me: Everyday Trials and Triumphs of Women Workers.* Ed. Karen B. Sacks and Dorothy Remy. New Brunswick, N.J.: Rutgers University Press, 1984.

Explores how Portuguese workers were socialized to productivity during training, and then resocialized by fellow workers afterward. Notes efforts made to humanize workplace through break and lunch groups, parties, etc.

692. Lasker, Bruno. "The Food Riots." *The Survey* (1917): 638-641.

Jewish women on the Lower East Side organized these protests as the cost of food rose during World War I.

108   IMMIGRANT WOMEN IN THE U.S.

693. Lawson, Ronald, ed., with Mark Naison. <u>The Tenant Movement in New York City, 1904-1984</u>. New Brunswick: Rutgers University Press, 1986.

Describes neighborhood protests and organizations (rent strikes, etc.) in which Jewish immigrant women played a vital role. See especially Jenna W. Joselit, "The Landlord as Czar, Pre-World War I Tenant Activity," pp. 39-50 and Joseph A. Spencer, "New York City Tenant Organizations and the Post-World War I Housing Crisis," pp. 51-93.

694. Lee, Sirkka T. "The Finns". <u>Cultural Correspondence</u> 6 (Spring 1978): 41-49.

The reminiscence of a Finnish labor radical describes IWW (Industrial Workers of the World) halls as family groups. Women's committees ran schools; children called all the women of the community "aunties". Within this family model, women were relegated to kitchen work.

695. Lerner, Elinor. "American Feminism and the Jewish Question, 1890-1940." Pp. 305-328 <u>Anti-Semitism in American History</u>. Ed. David Gerber. Urbana: University of Illinois Press, 1985.

Emphasizes the considerable participation of individual Jewish women and Jewish women's organizations in the women's movement of the U.S., especially the suffrage movement. Lower East Side Jewish men were important supporters of the 1917 New York State Suffrage campaign.

696. Lerner, Elinor. "Jewish Involvement in the New York City Woman Suffrage Movement." <u>American Jewish History</u> 70 (June 1981): 442-461.

Jewish women workers participated in the Wage-earners' League.

697. Levin, Marvin. <u>Balm in Gilead: The Story of Hadassah</u>. New York: Schocken, 1973.

The story of the women's Zionist organization founded by Henrietta Szold, a second-generation Hungarian, and attracting membership from second and subsequent generations of Jewish women.

698. Levine, Susan. "Honor Each Noble Maid: Women Workers and the Yonkers Carpet Weavers' Strike of 1885." <u>New York History</u> 62 (1981): 153-176.

Most of the strikers studied were second-generation Irish and Germans, with foreign-born women the second largest group.

699. Long, Priscilla. "The Women of the Colorado Fuel and Iron Strike, 1913-14." Pp. 62-85 Women's Work and Protest: A Century of U.S. Women's Labor History. Ed. Ruth Milkman. Boston: Routledge and Kegan Paul, 1985.

Women of twenty different nationality groups participated in the strike, not as union members but as wives.

700. Loo, Chalsa and Paul Ong. "Slaying Demons with a Sewing Needle: Feminist Issues for Chinatown's Women." Berkeley Journal of Sociology 27 (1982): 77-87.

Focus is on the importance of workplace exploitation as a feminist issue for working Chinese women in California.

701. Madrigal, Reyes R. "La Chicana and the Movement: Ideology and Identity." Unpublished Ph.D. Dissertation, Claremont Graduate School, 1977. Order Number 7722487.

No attention to generation, but did find that middle- and upper-class women were most likely to support Chicanismo and its political agenda.

702. Mason, Karen M. ""Feeling the Pinch: The Kalamazoo Corsetmakers' Strike of 1912." Pp. 141-160 "To Toil the Livelong Day;" America's Women at Work, 1780-1980. Ed. Carol Groneman and Mary Beth Norton. Ithaca and London: Cornell University Press, 1987).

Focuses on the work of Pauline Newman, a Russian Jewish labor organizer sent to Kalamazoo.

703. McCarthy, T.P. Guide to Catholic Sisterhoods in the United States. Washington, D.C.: Catholic University of America, 1964.

Includes some information on the formation of sisterhoods by immigrant women in the nineteenth century.

704. McCreesh, Carolyn D. Women in the Campaign to Organize Garment Workers, 1880-1917. New York: Garland Publishing, 1985.

Many immigrant and second-generation Irish and Eastern European Jews were activists, often within the Women's Trade Union League. Tells the stories of some rank-and-file women who rose temporarily to prominence during garment strikes.

705. McHale, M. Jerome. On the Wing: The Story of the Pittsburgh Sisters of Mercy, 1843-1968. New York: Seabury Press, 1980.

The sisterhood was founded by Irish women and continued to recruit them during its early years.

110   IMMIGRANT WOMEN IN THE U.S.

706. Meyer, Ruth F. <u>Women on a Mission</u>. St. Louis: Concordia Publishing House, 1967.

The history of the Lutheran Women's Missionary League; most of early women activists were German and Scandinavian women of the first and second generations. Also includes information on men's reactions to the women's activism.

707. Meyerowitz, Ruth. "Organizing the United Automobile Workers': Women Workers at the Ternstedt General Motors Parts Plant." Pp. 235-258 <u>Women's Work and Protest: A Century of U.S. Women's Labor History</u>. Ed. Ruth Milkman. Boston: Routledge and Kegan Paul, 1985.

Many activists were second-generation Poles; notes their tendency to drop out after an initial period of activism.

708. Mora, Magdalena. "The Tolteca Strike: Mexican Women and the Struggle for Union Representation." Pp. 111-117 <u>Mexican Immigrant Workers in the U.S.</u> Ed. Antonio Rios-Bustamente. Los Angeles: Chicano Studies Research Center Publications, UCLA, 1981.

709. Morehouse, William M. "The Speaking of Margaret Sanger in the Birth Control Movement from 1916 to 1937." Unpublished Ph.D. Dissertation, Purdue University, 1968. Order Number 68-12,590.

Includes some material from an interview; focuses on impact of her speaking on the birth-control movement.

710. Novak, Michael. <u>The Guns of Lattimer, The True Story of a Massacre and a Trial, August 1897-March 1898</u>. New York: Basic Books, 1978.

On Eastern European women's participation in this strike and riot, see pp. 49-55.

711. Novickis, Biruté. <u>The Lithuanian Woman</u>. Brooklyn: Federation of Lithuanian Women's Clubs, 1968.

Information on women as exiles and emigrants, including foundation of the Baltic Women's Council and the Federation of Lithuanian Women's Clubs.

712. Palisi, Bartolomeo J. "Patterns of Social Participation in a Two-Generation Sample of Italian Americans." <u>Sociological Quarterly</u> 7 (Spring 1966): 167-178.

Women were less involved in voluntary associations than were men.

713. Peterson, Susan C. and Courtney A. Vaughn-Robertson. <u>Women with Vision, The Presentation Sisters of South Dakota, 1880-1985</u>. Champaign: The University of Illinois Press, 1988.

Tells of the early arrival of Irish nuns to begin the missionary work of their order.

714. Peterson, Susan. "A Widening Horizon: Catholic Sisterhoods on the Northern Plains, 1874-1910." <u>Great Plains Quarterly</u> 5 (Spring 1985): 125-32.

715. Peterson, Susan. "From Paradise to Prairie: The Presentation Sisters in Dakota, 1880-1896." <u>South Dakota History</u> 10 (Summer 1980): 210-222.

The first of the order to arrive in Dakota were Irish nuns who became parochial school and hospital builders.

716. Pickle, Linda S. "German and Swiss Nuns in Nineteenth-Century Missouri and Southern Illinois: Some Comparisons with Secular Women." <u>Yearbook of German-American Studies</u> 20 (1985): 61-81.

The American frontier offered nuns opportunities for autonomy that were closing in Europe.

717. Pickle, Linda S. "Women of the Saxon Immigration and Their Church." <u>Concordia Historical Institute Quarterly</u> 57 (1984).

718. Pienkos, Angela T. <u>A Brief History of Polanki: Polish Women's Cultural Club of Milwaukee, 1953-1973</u>. Milwaukee: The Author, 1973.

719. Plattner, Elissa M. "How Beautiful upon the Mountains: The Sisters of Divine Providence and their Mission to Kentucky Appalachia." Unpublished Ph.D. Dissertation, University of Cincinnati, 1987. Order Number DA 8722068.

The mission was founded by French sisters who came to Kentucky in 1889.

720. Pratt, Norma F. "Culture and Radical Politics: Yiddish Women Writers in America, 1890-1940." <u>American Jewish History</u> (September 1980): 68-90.

A good introduction to the lives of Eastern European Jewish women radicals and intellectuals.

721. Pratt, Norma F. "Transitions in Judaism: The Jewish American Woman through the 1930s." <u>American Quarterly</u> 30 (1978): 681-702.

Focus is on the changing patterns of community activism and radicalism among first- and second-generation Sephardic, German Reform, and Orthodox women. Some attention is also given to women writers.

112 IMMIGRANT WOMEN IN THE U.S.

722. Priesand, Sally. *Judaism and the New Woman*. New York: Behrman House, 1975.

Includes a chapter of biographies (Golda Meir and Ernestine Rose). Another chapter focuses on early Jewish women's organizations.

723. Quinn, Jane. "Nuns in Ybor City: The Sisters of St. Joseph and the Immigrant Community." *Tampa Bay History* 5 (Spring/Summer 1983): 24-41.

The first sisters came from France in 1866 to work with freed slaves; new recruits came from Florida, Canada, and Britain. They mainly worked as educators of Cuban children.

724. Rabinowitz, Benjamin. "The Young Men's Hebrew Associations (1854-1913)." *Publications of the American Jewish Historical Society* 37 (1947): 221-326.

Includes a section on the women's and juniors' sections; most founders were second-generation German Jews.

725. Radzialowski, Thaddeus. "'Let Us Join Hands': The Polish Women's Alliance." *Review Journal of Philosophy and Social Science* 2: 183-203. Reprinted in Maxine Seller, ed. *Immigrant Women* (Philadelphia: Temple University Press, 1981), pp. 174-180.

Describes a female fraternal which provided mutual aid and sociability for Polish women.

726. Rafael, Ruth K. "The YMHA and the YWHA in San Francisco." *Western States Jewish History* 19 (April 1987): 208-216.

The women's group organized shortly after the men's in San Francisco, by second-generation German Jews.

727. Reishus, Martha. *Hearts and Hands Uplifted, A History of the Women's Missionary Federation of the Evangelical Lutheran Church*. Minneapolis: Augsburg Publishing House, 1958.

Focuses on the work of the early pioneer women in the Norwegian church, including the formation of the first ladies aid, and the Women's Federation in 1917.

728. Riddell, Adalijiza S. "Chicanas and el Movimiento." *Aztlán* 5 (Spring/Fall 1974): 155-65.

Includes some information on the activism of Mexican women.

729. Roboff, Sari. *Boston's Labor Movement: An Oral History of Work and Union Organizing*. Boston: Boston 200 Corporation, 1977.

Briefly considers Irish women labor activists and the Women's Trade Union League. Includes some good pictures of immigrant working women.

730. Ross, Carl. "Servant Girls: Community Leaders, Finnish American Women in Transition." Pp. 41-54 Women Who Dared: The History of Finnish American Women. Ed. Carl Ross and K. Marianne Wargelin Brown. St. Paul, Minnesota: Immigration History Research Center, 1986.

Notes that Eastern communities of Finns were female-dominated because of the number of domestic servants who settled there; these women organized self-help societies.

731. Ross, Carl. "The Feminist Dilemma in the Finnish Immigrant Community." Finnish Americana 1 (1978): 71-83.

Describes a struggle waged after 1909, not against the status of women in American society, but against oppressive conditions (carryovers from old country) within the immigrant community itself.

732. Ryan, Mary P. Amid the Alien Corn. Saint Charles, Ill.: Jones Wood Press, 1967.

The story of German nuns who founded a congregation of Sisters of the Most Holy Rosary in 1853.

733. Savage, Sister Mary Lucia. The Congregation of St. Joseph of Carondelet. St. Louis: B. Herder, 1923.

The sisterhood was founded by immigrant women from France in 1834 in St. Louis.

734. Schatz, Ronald. "Union Pioneers: The Founders of Local Unions at General Electric and Westinghouse, 1933-1937." Journal of American History 66 (1979): 586-602.

Includes some information on women activists, many of whom were of second generation.

735. Schrode, Georg. "Mary Zuk and the Detroit Meat Strike of 1935." Polish American Studies 48 (Autumn 1986): 5-39.

This second-generation woman led a multiethnic and multiracial food boycott.

736. Schulman, Sarah. "When We Were Young: Walking Tour Through Radical Jewish Women's History on the Lower East Side, 1879-1919." Pp. 232-253 The Tribe of Dina: A Jewish Women's Anthology. Ed. Melanie Kaye/Kantrowitz and Irena Klepfisz. Montpelier, Vt.: Sinister Wisdom Books, 1986.

Describes key events and places of the Eastern European Jewish garment workers' unionization drives.

737. Seller, Maxine S. "The Uprising of the Twenty Thousand: Sex, Class and Ethnicity in the Shirtwaist Makers Strike of 1909." Pp. 280-303 Struggle a Hard Battle--Working-Class Immigrants. Ed. Dirk Hoerder. DeKalb, Ill.: University of Northern Illinois Press, 1986.

Focus is on the Eastern European Jewish activists.

738. Sevier, Christine. From Ratisbon Cloisters. Farmingdale, N.Y.: Nazareth Trade School Press, 1917.

The congregation was founded by Dominican sisters from Germany in 1853.

739. Shapiro-Perl, Nina. "Resistance Strategies: The Routine Struggle for Bread and Roses." Pp. 193-208 My Troubles are Going to Have Trouble with Me: Everyday Trials and Triumphs of Women Workers. Ed. Karen B. Sacks and Dorothy Remy. New Brunswick, N.J.: Rutgers University Press, 1984.

Workers discussed were mainly Portuguese immigrants; their struggles were over wages, cleaning requirements, and unwritten rules.

740. Shapiro-Perl, Nina. "The Piece Rate: Class Struggle on the Shop Floor: Evidence from the Costume Jewelry Industry in Providence, Rhode Island." Pp. 277-298 Case Studies in the Labor Process. Ed. Andrew Zimbalist. New York: Monthly Review Press, 1977.

The workers discussed are Portuguese immigrants.

741. Smith, Gary L. "The International Ladies Garment Workers' Union 'Labor Stage': A Propagandistic Venture." Unpublished Ph.D. Dissertation, Kent State University, 1975. Order Number 76-4945.

Tells mainly of the successful production of "Pins and Needles." Although the author does not focus on the fact, most were immigrant and second-generation Jewish and Italian men and women.

742. Snyder, Robert E. "Women, Wobblies, and Workers' Rights: The 1912 Textile Strike in Little Falls, New York." New York History 60 (January 1979): 29-57.

Polish, Slav, Austrian and Italian women were the most prominent strikers and activists.

743. Sochen, June. "Some Observations on the Role of Jewish Women as Communal Volunteers." American Jewish History 70 (1980): 23-34.

Some attention to immigrant and second-generation women in Jewish community institutions.

744. Sochen, June. <u>Consecrate Every Day: The Public Lives of Jewish American Women, 1880-1890</u>. Albany: State University of New York Press, 1981.

On immigrant and second-generation women, see especially chapters on women workers and radical and volunteer activists before World War II.

745. Solomon, Barbara M. <u>Pioneers in Service: A History of the Associated Jewish Philanthropies of Boston</u>. Boston: Associated Jewish Philanthropies, 1956.

Includes some information on second-generation German Jewish women who did considerable charity work with newly arrived Eastern European Jews through these agencies.

746. Sorin, Gerald. <u>The Prophetic Minority, American Jewish Immigrant Radicals, 1880-1920</u>. Bloomington: Indiana University Press, 1985.

Focus is on Eastern European Jews; see especially chapter 6, "The Women: World of Our Mothers and Others."

747. Stjänstedt, Ritta. "Finnish Women in the North American Labour Movement." Pp. 257-276 <u>Finnish Diaspora II: The United States</u>. Ed. Michael G. Karni. Toronto: The Multicultural History Society of Ontario, 1981.

748. Strong, Miriam. <u>Of Fish and Freedom: The Story of the Cuban Refugees</u>. Miami: Centro Hispano Catolico, 1964.

Tells story of the Cuban Dominican sisters who settled in Pennsylvania after leaving Cuba in 1962.

749. Szymczak, Robert. "An Act of Devotion: The Polish Gray Samaritans and the Relief Effort in Poland, 1919-1921." <u>Polish American Studies</u> 43 (Spring 1986): 13-36.

Study of an organization formed by second-generation women to aid the newly independent homeland.

750. Tax, Meredith. <u>The Rising of the Women; Feminist Solidarity and Class Conflict, 1880-1917</u>. New York and London: Monthly Review Press, 1980.

The emphasis is on cross-class alliances between middle-class feminists and working-class, largely immigrant women laborers, in a variety of organizations, including the Women's Trade Union Leagues in New York and Chicago.

751. Thomas, Trudelle H. "Daybooks and Deathbooks--the Writings of the Brown County Ursulines: A Rhetorical and Literary Analysis." Unpublished Ph.D. Dissertation, University of Cincinnati, 1987. Order Number DA 8729264.

The sisterhood was founded by French women in 1845; includes a biography of the foundress.

752. Turbin, Carole. "And We Are Nothing but Women." Pp. 203-222 Women of America. Ed. Carol Ruth Berkin and Mary Beth Norton. Boston: Houghton Mifflin, 1979.

Explores the conditions under which Irish women in Troy, N.Y. organized a successful union.

753. Turbin, Carole. "Beyond Conventional Wisdom: Women's Wage Work, Household Economic Contribution, and Labor Activism in a Mid-Nineteenth-Century Working-Class Community." Pp. 47-67 "To Toil the Livelong Day;" America's Women at Work, 1780-1980. Ed. Carol Groneman and Mary Beth Norton. Ithaca and London: Cornell University Press, 1987.

Family status supports different forms of labor activism, as shown by the Irish women of Troy.

754. Turbin, Carole. "Reconceptualizing Family, Work and Labor Organizing: Working Women in Troy, 1860-1890." Review of Radical Political Economics 16 (1984): 1-16.

Most of the women discussed are Irish; emphasizes that family relations could support as well as undermine activism.

755. Turbin, Carole. "Woman's Work and Woman's Rights--A Comparative Study of the Woman's Trade Union Movement and the Woman Suffrage Movement in the Mid-Nineteenth Century." Unpublished Ph.D. Dissertation, New School for Social Research, 1978.

Compares the Irish women in Troy's Collar Laundry union and native-born feminists of the same era.

756. Uyeunten, Sandra. "Filling the Gap in the Labor History of Japanese-American Women." Berkeley Women of Color Newsletter 1,1 (1983): 8-9.

757. Van Raaphorst, Donna L. Union Maids not Wanted: Organizing Domestic Workers, 1870-1940. New York: Praeger, 1988.

Domestic service was the work of Afro-American women, and in the nineteenth century of many foreign-born women in the North.

758. Vazquez, Mario F. "The Election Day Immigration Raid at Lilli Diamond Originals and the Response of the ILGWU." Pp. 145-148 Mexican Women in the United States: Struggles Past and Present. Ed. Magdalena Mora and Adelaida R. Del Castillo. Los Angeles: University of California, Chicano Studies Research Center Publications, 1980.

Many of the women apprehended were Mexicans, some working illegally.

759. Waldinger, Roger. "Another Look at the International Ladies' Garment Workers' Union: Women, Industry Structure and Collective Action." Pp. 86-109 Women's Work and Protest: A Century of U.S. Women's Labor History. Ed. Ruth Milkman. Boston: Routledge and Kegan Paul, 1985.

Focuses on conditions under which Eastern European Jewish and Italian women became union activists.

760. Walsh, Sister Marie. The Sisters of Charity of New York: 1809-1959. 2 Vol. New York: Fordham University Press, 1960.

This order of Irish women was especially active in education and care of poor children in the nineteenth century.

761. Wargelin Brown, K. Marianne. "A Closer Look at Finnish American Women's Issues." Pp. 213-238 Finnish Diaspora II: United States. Ed. Michael G. Karni. Toronto: The Multicultural History Society of Ontario, 1981.

Focus is on women as community activists, radicals, and labor activists.

762. Webb, Carol P. "The Lowell Mule Spinners' Strike of 1875." Pp. 11-20 Surviving Hard Times: The Working People of Lowell. Ed. Mary H. Blewett. Lowell, Mass.: Lowell Museum, 1982.

Shows how the English and Irish men and women strikers maintained solidarity during strike.

763. Weiler, N. Sue. "Walkout: The Chicago Men's Garment Workers' Strike: 1910-1911." Chicago History 8 (Winter, 1979-1980): 238-249.

Fifty percent of the work force was female, both foreign-born and second-generation; the main groups of strikers were Poles and Bohemians, with some Italians and Jews.

764. Weiser, Frederick S. Love's Response. Philadelphia: United Lutheran Publishers, 1962.

Explores religious groups founded by German women, and in early years involving mainly immigrants and second-generation Germans in the U.S.

765. Wilson, Tracey M. "The 1911 Hartford Garment Workers Strike." Connecticut Historical Society Bulletin 50 (Winter 1984): 23-47.

766. Woroby, Maria. "Ukrainian Radicals and Women." Cultural Correspondence 6 (Spring 1968): 50-56.

General information, including an account of the creation of women's agitation committees (circa 1897) and of the Sisterhood of Saint Olga.

767. Yu, Eui-Young. "The Activities of Women in South California Korean Community Organizations." Pp. 249-299 Korean Women in Transition: At Home and Abroad. Ed. Eui-Young Yu and Earl H. Phillips. Los Angeles: Center for Korean-American and Korean Studies, California State University, 1987.

7

Body

INTRODUCTION

Cited in this chapter are studies of health and aging, sexuality, and fertility. Of these three themes, the last has received by far the greatest attention.

Indeed, the fertility and childbearing patterns of immigrant women have been the subject of quite an extraordinary amount of research. Both in the past and today foreign-born women on average bear more children than do native-born women. Studies of fertility thus document the significant amount of time and bodily energy that foreign-born women invested in pregnancy; in that sense they do tell us something about immigrant women's lives.

Still, studies of fertility seem to reveal as much or more about perceptions of immigrant women than they tell us about the women themselves. The very size of this literature hints at the uneasiness with which native-born residents of the United States have confronted each new wave of child-bearing immigrant women, and the degree to which they have linked women and reproduction with nativist fears about racial, ethnic, and demographic change. Predictions of "race suicide" obviously fueled the earliest studies of immigrant fertility; these were followed by studies debunking earlier forecasts. Contemporary anxiety about a "browning" of the U.S. population also seems to have motivated social scientists to study the fertility of Mexican and Spanish-speaking peoples; Asian immigrants, by contrast, have been the focus of less scrutiny.

Changing fertility is sometimes used as a measure of women's cultural change and adaptation to life in the United States. Studies of the past do reveal rapid fertility declines in the second generation, while studies of contemporary immigrant women document considerable variation even within the foreign-born group. The effects of education, residence, employment, and minority status on fertility have all been explored.

CITATIONS

768. Abbott, Grace. "The Midwife in Chicago." American Journal of Sociology 20 (March 1915): 685-699.

Almost all midwives were foreign-born and had a foreign-born clientele. One-third had European certification while the remainder had "ridiculously inadequate" training.

769. Abramson, Paul R. and John Imai-Marquez. "The Japanese-American: A Cross-Cultural, Cross-Sectional Study of Sex Guilt." Journal of Research in Personality 16 (June 1982): 227-237.

A study of three generations. Although the group as a whole was highly acculturated generally, women's sex guilt was nevertheless higher in all generations than among native-born. Sex guilt did decline from generation to generation, however.

770. Alegria, Daniel et al. "El Hospital Invisibel: A Study of Curanderismo." Archives of General Psychiatry 34 (November 1977): 1354-1357.

Based on interviews with several Mexican-American women healers.

771. Alvirez, D. "The Effects of Formal Church Affiliation and Religiosity on the Fertility of American Catholics." Demography 10 (1973): 19-36.

Religious belief had no impact on desired family size and birth intervals among Mexican women.

772. Arafat, Ibtahaj S. "Trends in Family Planning: The American Egyptians' Case." International Migration Review 6, 4 (1972): 393-401.

773. Arkoff, Abe and H. Weaver. "Body Image and Body Dissatisfaction in Japanese-Americans." Journal of Social Psychology 68 (April 1966): 323-330.

No breakdown by generation provided, but does show that Japanese-American women were less satisfied than either men of their own group or Caucasian women. They would like to be taller.

774. Aviaro, H. "Latina Attitudes towards Abortion." Nuestro 5 (Aug/Sept 1981): 43-44.

Interviews with 120 Mexican women in Los Angeles showed variation from complete support to unwavering opposition to pro-choice stand.

775. Bachu, Amara and Martin O'Connell. "Developing Current Fertility Indicators for Foreign-Born Women from the Current Population Survey." <u>Review of Public Data Use</u> 12 (October 1984): 185-95.

Ranks the fertility levels of many groups. Latin-American, especially Mexican women had the highest fertility rates; Asian women, intermediate levels; and Europeans, the lowest rates.

776. Bean, Frank D. and C. H. Wood. "Ethnic Variations in the Relationship between Income and Fertility." <u>Demography</u> 11 (1974): 629-640.

Unlike Asians, income and fertility were negatively related among Mexican Americans.

777. Bean, Frank D. and Gary Swicegood. "Generation, Female Education and Mexican-American Fertility." <u>Social Science Quarterly</u> 63 (1982): 1311-1344.

Finds that education reduced women's fertility, especially in the second and later generations.

778. Bean, Frank D. and Gary Swicegood. <u>Mexican American Fertility Patterns</u>. Austin: University of Texas Press, 1985.

Contains good bibliography. Argues that high fertility--not immigration--explained most recent growth in the U.S. Mexican-American population. Examines the impact of generation, women's employment, and education on fertility.

779. Bean, Frank D. and John P. Marcum. "Differential Fertility and the Minority Status Hypothesis: An Assessment and Review." Pp. 189-212 <u>The Demography of Racial and Ethnic Groups</u>. Ed. Frank D. Bean and W. P. Frisbie. New York: Academic Press, 1978.

Mexicans had the highest fertility and Cubans the lowest.

780. Bean, Frank D. et al. "Generational Differences in Fertility among Mexican Americans: Implications for Assessing Immigration Effects." <u>Social Science Quarterly</u> 65 (June 1984): 573-582.

Fertility declined with time in the U.S., but migration from Mexico also disrupted fertility for immigrant women.

781. Bean Frank D. et al. "Role Incompatibility and the Relationship between Fertility and Labor Supply among Hispanic American Women." Pp. 221-242 <u>Hispanics in the U.S. Economy</u>. Ed. Georges Borjas and Marta Tienda. Orlando and New York: Academic Press, 1985.

Compares Mexicans, Puerto Ricans, and Cubans.

782. Becerra, Rosina M. and Diane De Anda. "Pregnancy and Motherhood among Mexican American Adolescents." Health and Social Work 9 (Spring 1984): 106-23.

The least acculturated girls were the most likely to marry upon pregnancy.

783. Becerra, Rosina M. and E. Fielder. "Adolescent Attitudes and Behavior." Institute for Social Science Research Quarterly 1 (Nov 1985):

Sexually active Mexican daughters were from the most acculturated and English-speaking families.

784. Berry, Gwendolyn H. Idleness and the Health of a Neighborhood. A Social Study of the Mulberry District. New York: Association for Improving the Condition of the Poor, 1933.

A study of Italians, which includes information on unemployment and employment by sex and generation, sickness rates by sex, and maternity rates.

785. Bradshaw, Benjamin S. and Frank D. Bean. "Some Aspects of the Fertility of Mexican-Americans." Pp. 143-164 Demographic and Social Aspects of Population Growth. Ed. Charles F. Westoff and Robert Parke, Jr. Washington, D.C.: Government Printing Office, 1972.

786. Briggs, John W. "Fertility and Cultural Change Among Families in Italy and America." American Historical Review 91 (December 1986): 1129-1145.

A comparative study of Italy and the U.S. finds lower fertility than expected in Europe, and roughly comparable rates in Rochester, N.Y. Notes that earlier studies measured immigrant women's assimilation through changing fertility patterns.

787. Buechley, Robert W., et al. "Excess Lung Cancer Mortality Rates Among Mexican Women in California." Cancer 10 (1957): 63-66.

788. Buell, Philip, et al. "Cancer of the Lung Among Mexican Immigrant Women in California." Cancer 22, 1 (1968): 186-192.

Foreign-born Mexican women started smoking earlier than native-born Mexican-Americans.

789. Calhoun, Arthur W. A Social History of the American Family from Colonial Times to the Present. 3 Vol. Cleveland: Arthur H. Clark, 1917-1919.

Includes scattered references to immigrant women; see especially the discussion in Vol. III of "Race Sterility and Suicide."

790. Card, Josefina J. "Differences in the Antecedents and Consequences of the Motivation for Fertility Control Among Filipino Migrants and Caucasian Controls." Journal of Population 2, 2 (1979): 140-161.

The relationship between motivation to control fertility and actual fertility was weakest for Filipino wives.

791. Card, Josefina J. "The Malleability of Fertility-Related Attitudes and Behavior in a Filipino Migrant Sample." Demography 15, 4 (1978): 459-476.

Filipinos used the less effective contraceptive techniques; women's desire to control their fertility was justified by the difficulty they experienced finding child care in the U.S.

792. Castro, Felipe G. et al. "The Health Beliefs of Mexican, Mexican American and Anglo American Women." Hispanic Journal of Behavioral Sciences 6 (December 1984): 365-383.

Notes women's dual system of beliefs which weakened with acculturation but did not disappear.

793. Castro, Rafaela. "Mexican Women's Sexual Jokes." Aztlán 13 (Spring and Fall 1982): 275-294.

Although the main source was a native-born woman, the article contrasts jokes told by immigrant and native women, noting the popularity of jokes about nuns in both groups.

794. Chavez, Leo R. et al. "Utilization of Health Services by Mexican Immigrant Women in San Diego." Women and Health 11 (Summer 1986): 3-20.

Contrasts legal and undocumented immigrants; both underutilized health services, but undocumented women were especially reluctant to use them.

795. Chavira, Alicia. "Women, Migration, and Health: Conditions and Strategies of a Mexican Migrant Population in the Midwest." Unpublished Ph.D. Dissertation, University of California at Los Angeles, 1987. Order Number DA 8803646.

Study of undocumented immigrants. Women oversaw the family's use of health care; they also influenced migration decisions of family.

796. Chavkin, Wendy et al. "Reproductive Health: Caribbean Women in New York City, 1980-1984." International Migration Review 21 (Fall 1987): 609-625.

Distinguishes among Puerto Rican, Hispanic Caribbean, and Non-Hispanic Caribbean women.

124 IMMIGRANT WOMEN IN THE U.S.

797. Cohen, Lucy M. <u>Culture, Disease and Stress among Latino Immigrants</u>. Washington, D.C.: Research Institute on Immigration and Ethnic Studies, Smithsonian Institution, 1979.

Based on interviews with men and women, this study includes good information on women in work and migration chapters, but surprisingly little in chapters on health. A chapter on self-control examines parent/child and male/female conflicts.

798. Cohen, Lucy. "Latino Adversity: Culture, Disease, and Stress Among Latin American Immigrants--A Summary." <u>Exploratory Fieldwork on Latino Migrants and Indochinese Refugees</u>. Ed. Roy S. Bryce-Laporte and Stephen R. Couch. Washington, D.C.: Smithsonian Institution Research Institute on Immigration and Ethnic Studies, 1977.

Most of the women studied had already started families, and thus worked as migrants to facilitate migration of other family members.

799. Davis, C. C. et al. "Hispanics: Changing the Face of America." <u>Population Bulletin</u> 38 (June 1983): 1-44.

Summarizes general demographic trends among Mexican and Cuban populations with attention to fertility.

800. Davis, Michael M. <u>Immigrant Health and the Community</u>. New York: Harper and Brothers, 1920.

See chapters "Birth Rates and Maternity Customs," "The Midwife," "Adequate Maternity Care."

801. de la Torre, Adela and Lynda Rush. "The Determinants of Breastfeeding for Mexican Migrant Women." <u>International Migration Review</u> 21 (Fall 1987): 728-744.

802. Declercq, Eugene and Richard Lacroix. "The Immigrant Midwives of Lawrence: The Conflict Between Law and Culture in Early Twentieth-Century Massachusetts." <u>Bulletin of the History of Medicine</u> 59 (1985): 232-246.

Most of the women studied were Irish, Italian, and Eastern Europeans.

803. Doty, Richard L. et al. "Sex Differences in Odor Identification Ability: A Cross-Cultural Analysis." <u>Neuropsychologia</u> 23, 5 (1985): 667-672.

Korean-American and Japanese-American women (like women in other groups) outperformed men.

804. Dye, Nancy S. "Modern Obstetrics and Working-Class Women: The New York Midwifery Dispensary, 1890-1920." <u>Journal of Social History</u> 20 (1987): 549-564.

Eastern European Jews were more likely to use the dispensary than other neighborhood groups--Italian, German, and Irish women.

805. Espin, Oliva. "Cultural and Historical Influences on Sexuality in Hispanic/Latin Women." Pp. 272-284 All American Women; Lines that Divide, Ties that Bind. Ed. Johnetta B. Cole. New York and London: The Free Press and Collier Macmillan Publishers, 1986.

Contains some information on immigrants. Many women felt that becoming American meant becoming sexually promiscuous.

806. Falasco, Dee and David M. Heer. "Economic and Fertility Differences Between Legal and Undocumented Migrant Mexican Families: Possible Effects of Immigration Policy Changes." Social Science Quarterly 65 (June 1984): 494-504.

Legal status had no effect on women's fertility.

807. Falasco, Dee. "Economic and Fertility Differences Between Legal and Illegal Migrant Mexican Families: The Potential Effects of Immigration Policy Changes." Unpublished Ph.D. Dissertation, University of Southern California, 1982. Dissertation Abstracts 43: 1701A. No Order Number given.

Existing evidence suggests that legalization would have no significant impact on fertility.

808. Fernald, Mabel R. A Study of Women Delinquents in New York State. New York: The Century, 1920.

Contrasts native- and foreign-born women in prison. Foreign-born women generally were underrepresented; Austrians, Russians, and Irish were the largest groups in the foreign-born category. Foreign-born women were relatively more likely to be incarcerated for crimes against property, although crimes against chastity were the most common charge.

809. Fischer, Gloria J. "Hispanic and Majority Student Attitudes toward Forcible Date Rape as a Function of Differences in Attitudes Toward Women." Sex Roles 17 (July 1987): 93-101.

Distinguishes bicultural Mexicans by birthplace of grandparents. Bicultural women, but not men, were more likely to blame women for date rape than either Hispanics or women generally.

810. Fischer, Nancy A. and John P. Marcum. "Ethnic Integration, Socioeconomic Status and Fertility Among Mexican Americans." Social Science Quarterly 65 (June 1984): 583-593.

Fertility was higher among women living in predominately Mexican-American neighborhoods. The data are also analyzed by generation.

811. Fleming, Margaret E. "White Ethnic Fertility in the U.S.: Convergence: 1890-1975." Unpublished Ph.D. Dissertation, Princeton University, 1980. Order Number 8022724.

Includes separate discussion of foreign-born women.

812. Ford, Kathleen. "Declining Fertility Rates of Immigrants to the United States (with some Exceptions)." Sociology and Social Research 70,1 (1985): 68-70.

Mexican women had higher rates than other foreign-born women, but rates for all groups were declining.

813. Ford, Kathleen. "Fertility of Caribbean, Central and South American Immigrants to the United States." Sociology and Social Research 70 (July 1986): 281-283.

Compares immigrant women to those in homeland and to U.S. native-born women. In all cases, immigrant women's fertility was lower than women's in the homeland, but also (with the exception of Cubans) higher than the U.S. average.

814. Freier, Michelle C. "Psychosocial and Physiological Influences on Birth Outcomes among Women of Mexican Origin or Descent." Unpublished Ph.D. Dissertation, University of California at Los Angeles, 1987. Order Number DA 8725996.

High anxiety led to longer labors.

815. Fruchter, Rachel G. et al. "Cervical Cancer in Immigrant Caribbean Women." American Journal of Public Health 76 (1986): 797-99.

Haitian and English-speaking Jamaican women delayed going to physicians, even after onset of symptoms.

816. Fruchter, Rachel G. et al. "Invasive Cancer of the Cervix: Failure in Prevention: Previous Pap Smear Tests and Opportunities for Screening." New York State Journal of Medicine 80 (1980): 740-745.

Haitian and English-speaking Caribbean women were less likely to get Pap smears than native-born women.

817. Gaviria, Moises et al. "Sociocultural Factors and Perinatal Health in a Mexican-American Community." Journal of the National Medical Association 74, 10 (1982): 983-989.

Long-term migrants from Mexico went earlier for prenatal care than did either native-born Mexican-Americans or the most recently arrived Mexican women.

818. Gebhart, John C. *The Growth and Development of Italian Children in New York City.* New York: New York Association for Improving the Condition of the Poor, 1924.

Compares the heights and weights, and other health conditions, of Italian boys and girls, mainly second-generation.

819. Gebhart, John C. *The Health of a Neighborhood: A Social Study of the Mulberry District.* New York: Association for Improving the Condition of the Poor, 1924.

Some attention to the wage-earning of Italian women, as well as to their illness rates from childbirth and other causes.

820. Goldschieder, Calvin. "Fertility of the Jews." Pp. 15-32 *Ethnic Groups of America: Their Morbidity, Mortality and Behavior Disorders.* Vol. 1: The Jews. Ed. Ailon Shiloh and Ida C. Selavan. Springfield, Ill.: Charles C. Thomas, 1973.

In the immigrant generation, women's fertility varied inversely with socioeconomic status; this was not true of later generations.

821. Goldschieder, Calvin. "Ideological Factors in Jewish Fertility Differentials." *The Jewish Journal of Sociology* 7, 1 (1965): 92-105.

In the first generation Orthodox Jewish women had higher-than-average fertility; differences diminished in the second generation.

822. Goldschieder, Calvin. "Nativity, Generation, and Jewish Fertility." *Sociological Analysis* 26 (Fall 1965): 137-147.

Jewish women's fertility converged with that of the general American population over time; differences between native-born and foreign-born Jews were greater in early twentieth century than they are today.

823. Gonzalez, Diana H. "Cuban Women, Sex Role Conflicts, and the Use of Prescription Drugs." *Journal of Psychoactive Drugs* 13 (January-March 1981): 47-51.

Both new wage-earning responsibilities and the loss of socioeconomic status were sources of stress for the women studied; many medicated themselves, following homeland traditions.

824. González, Nancie L. "Giving Birth in America: The Immigrant's Dilemma." Pp. 241-253 International Migration, The Female Experience. Ed. Rita J. Simon and Caroline B. Brettell. Totowa, N.J.: Rowman & Allanheld, 1985.

Compares two cases of childbirth--one a Dominican woman, one a Garifuna Guatemalan. Although midwives were commonly used in their homelands, both women expressed strong preference for hospital birth in the U.S. Giving birth to a child in the U.S. substantiated a woman's status as migrant in the eyes of her group.

825. Gordon, L.W. "New Data on the Fertility of Southeast Asian Refugees in the United States." Research Review 2 (Jan 1983): 3-6.

Examines Laotian, Vietnamese and Kampuchean women; all had higher-than-average fertility.

826. Guest, Avery. "Fertility Variation Among the U.S. Foreign Stock Population in 1900." International Migration Review 16 (Fall 1982): 577-596.

Culture did not influence rates of adaptation to U.S. fertility patterns, but urban immigrant women adjusted more quickly to lower rates typical of this country.

827. Gurak, Douglas T. "Assimilation and Fertility: A Comparison of Mexican American and Japanese American Women." Hispanic Journal of Behavioral Sciences 2 (September 1980): 219-239.

828. Gurak, Douglas T. "Sources of Ethnic Fertility Differences: An Examination of Five Minority Groups." Social Science Quarterly 59 (September 1978): 296-310.

Compares Puerto Ricans, Mexicans, Cubans, and Japanese. Neither minority status nor social characteristics explained all their differences in fertility. Identifies both low- and high-fertility groups within Hispanic population.

829. Haines, Michael. "Fertility, Marriage and Occupation in Pennsylvania Anthracite Region, 1850-1880." Journal of Family History 1 (Spring 1977): 28-55.

Compares fertility of native- and foreign-born in mining towns; miners' wives had lower fertility than expected.

830. Hamburger, Sonia. "Profile of Curanderos: A Study of Mexican Folk Practitioners." International Journal of Social Psychiatry 24 (Spring 1978): 19-25.

Women outnumbered men, but most worked at healing only part time. Few had much schooling.

831. Harbison, Sarah F. and Marjorie E. Weishaar. "Samoan Migrant Fertility: Adaptation and Selection." Human Organization 40 (Fall 1981): 268-273.

Samoan women in Hawaii had higher-than-average fertility.

832. Hareven, Tamara and Maris A. Vinovskis. "Patterns of Childbearing in Late Nineteenth-Century America: The Determinants of Marital Fertility in Five Massachusetts Towns in 1880." Pp. 85-125 Family and Population in Nineteenth-Century America. Ed Tamara K. Hareven and Maris A. Vinovskis. Princeton: Princeton University Press, 1978.

Compares all foreign-born to native-born, and provides some breakdowns for Irish and Canadian women of the immigrant and second generations.

833. Hareven, Tamara K. and Maris A. Vinovskis. "Marital Fertility, Ethnicity and Occupation in Urban Families: An Analysis of South Boston and South End in 1880." Journal of Social History 8 (Spring 1975): 69-93.

Compares an Irish ward to a mixed one, distinguishing foreign-born (mainly Irish) by generation. Both foreign-born and second-generation women had higher-than-average fertility.

834. Harris, Rachel et al. "Attitudes and Perceptions of Perinatal Concepts During Pregnancy in Women From Three Cultures." Journal of Clinical Psychology 37 (July 1981): 455-483.

Contrasts Cubans, Afro-Americans, and Anglos. Cubans had the most positive attitudes toward pregnancy. Marital status influenced attitudes, with married women having the most positive ones. Cuban women did not notice changes in level of baby's activity during pregnancy.

835. Hernandez-Peck, Maria C. "Frail Elderly Cubans: Decision Making for their Long-Term Care." Unpublished Ph.D. Dissertation, University of Denver, 1980. Order Number 8103837.

Found that the elderly of families including working wives with children were the most likely to be institutionalized.

836. Hopkins, David D. and Nancy G. Clarke. "Indochinese Refugee Fertility Rates and Pregnancy Risk Factors: Oregon." American Journal of Public Health 73 (November 1983): 1307-1309.

Women's fertility rate was 1.8 times the overall U.S. rate. Maternal and infant health risks were high, especially among the Hmong. Prenatal care improved with time in U.S.

837. Hunter, Kathleen et al. "Minority Women's Attitudes About Aging." <u>Experimental Aging Research</u> 5 (April 1979): 95-108.

Cuban and Chicano women were compared to other middle-aged women. Religious beliefs and family dynamics influenced their attitudes toward old age.

838. Hunter, Kathleen et al. "Sterilization among American Indian and Chicano Mothers. <u>International Quarterly of Community Health Education</u> 4,4 (1983-84): 343-52.

Miami Mexican mothers of five children or more were less likely to be surgically sterilized than either Indians or the general white population.

839. Ibrahim, I.B. et al. "Ethnicity and Suicide in Hawaii." <u>Social Biology</u> 24 (Spring 1977): 10-16.

Suicide rates of Japanese women were decreasing; they remained unchanged for Filipino women.

840. Jacques, Karen N. "Perceptions and Coping Behaviors of Anglo-American and Mexican Immigrant Battered Women: A Comparative Study." Unpublished Ph.D. Dissertation, United States International University, 1981. Order Number DA 8211072.

Both groups sought help. Mexican women were more likely to believe that violence against wives was widespread. Mexican women also believed that violence against women was sometimes justified (although never in their own cases).

841. Jaffe, A. J. et al. "The Changing Demography of Spanish Americans." <u>Studies in Population</u>. New York: Academic Press, 1980.

Tabular materials compare Mexican, Cuban, Central American and South American women's earnings, number of children, and rates of labor force participation.

842. Johnson, Carmen A. "Breast-feeding and Social Class Mobility: The Case of Mexican Migrant Mothers in Houston, Texas." Pp. 66-82 <u>Twice a Minority, Mexican American Women</u>. Ed. Margarita B. Melville. St. Louis: The C.V. Mosby Company, 1980.

Migrant women often abruptly changed their feeding practices.

843. Johnson, Nan E. and Suewen Lean. "Relative Income, Race, and Fertility." <u>Population Studies</u> 39 (March 1985): 99-112.

Compares Chinese, Japanese, and Blacks in California and in Hawaii.

844. Jordan, Rosan A. "The Vaginal Serpent and Other Themes from Mexican-American Women's Lore." Pp. 26-44 Women's Folklore, Women's Culture. Ed. Rosan A. Jordan and Susan J. Kalcik. Philadelphia: University of Pennsylvania.

Summarizes myths collected from native-born Mexican women in Texas. Similar myths were widespread among Mexicans, too. Myths about impregnation by animals expressed women's resentments against culturally required submissiveness.

845. Jurczak, Chester A. "Ethnicity, Status, and Generational Positioning: A Study of Health Practices among Polonians in Five Ethnic Islands." Unpublished Ph.D. Dissertation, University of Pittsburgh, 1964. Order Number 65-7020.

Based on interviews with Polish immigrant mothers and second-generation daughters.

846. Kaku, Kanae and Y. Scott Matsumoto. "Influence of a Folk Superstition on Fertility of Japanese in California and Hawaii, 1966." American Journal of Public Health 65 (February 1975): 17-174.

Because the Japanese believed that women born in 1966 would be bad-tempered, there was a sharp drop in fertility in Japan that year, and smaller declines among Japanese women in California and in Hawaii.

847. Kendall, Laurel. "Cold Wombs in Balmy Honolulu: Ethnogynecology among Korean Immigrants." Social Science & Medicine 25, 4 (1987): 367-76.

Studies Korean women's belief in "naeng" (chill of the uterus), which leads to vaginal discharge and infertility. Koreans in Honolulu saw this belief as reflecting old-fashioned ideas. Some women Americanized the concept to vaginitis. Others felt they had been mishandled by American medical personnel because the latter used different terminology and concepts to diagnose condition.

848. Kritz, Mary M. and Douglas T. Gurak. "Ethnicity and Fertility in the U.S.: Analysis of 1970 Public Use Sample Data." Review of Public Data Use 4 (May 1976): 12-23.

Compares 25 groups. Fertility varied enormously. Cubans, Japanese, French, Chinese, Korean, and Greek women had the lowest fertility.

849. Leonetti, Donna L. "Fertility in Transition: An Analysis of the Reproductive Experience of an Urban Japanese-American Population." Unpublished Ph.D. Dissertation, University of Washington, 1976. Order Number DA 76-20,720.

Examines second-generation Japanese women, concentrating on interaction of biological and cultural factors.

132   IMMIGRANT WOMEN IN THE U.S.

850. Leonetti, Donna L. "The Biocultural Pattern of Japanese-American Fertility." Social Biology 25 (Spring 1978): 38-51.

Study compares second-generation women to Japanese and to other native-born American women. Japanese women exhibited a late peak fertility pattern into the second generation.

851. Leonetti, Donna L. and Laura Newell-Morris. "Lifetime Patterns of Child-bearing and Employment: A Study of Second-Generation Japanese American Women." Journal of Biosocial Science 14 (January 1982): 81-97.

Although this group as a whole had high rates of labor-force participation, the homemakers among them had the highest fertility.

852. Levy, Julius. "The Maternal and Infant Mortality in Midwifery Practice in Newark, New Jersey." American Journal of Obstetrics and the Diseases of Women and Children 77 (1913): 41-53.

Most midwives and their clients in this study were Italian.

853. Lewin, Ellen. "Nobility of Suffering: Illness and Misfortune Among Latin American Immigrant Women." Anthropological Quarterly 52 (July 1979): 152-158.

A study of Mexican and Central American women. Women were intensely concerned with and repeatedly discussed their illnesses. Interprets this as ventilation of other tensions. Sickness was the only socially acceptable mode of self-involvement for the women.

854. Lindemann, Constance and Wilbur Scott. "The Fertility Related Behavior of Mexican American Adolescents." Journal of Early Adolescence 2 (Spring, 1982): 31-38.

Emphasizes that second-generation girls learned new attitudes toward childbearing from more acculturated Mexican-Americans, not from Anglo culture.

855. Linn, Margaret W. et al. "Differences by Sex and Ethnicity in the Psychosocial Adjustment of the Elderly." Journal of Health and Social Behavior 20 (1979): 273-81.

Although there were no differences by sex, Cuban men and women showed the most negative adjustment, perhaps because they remained cultural outsiders.

856. Linn, Margaret W. et al. "Fertility Related Attitudes of Minority Mothers with Large and Small Families." Journal of Applied Social Psychology 8 (January-March 1978): 1-14.

Compares Cubans and migrant Chicanos to native-born groups. Chicano women's negative attitudes toward birth control must have led them to avoid using it, since it was difficult to find any Chicano women with small families.

857. Marcum, John P. and Frank D. Bean. "Minority Group Status as a Factor in the Relationship between Mobility and Fertility: The Mexican American Case." Social Forces 55 (September 1976): 135-148.

The third generation had lower than expected average fertility. The study supports a minority group model for fertility behavior. Mobility also influenced the incidence of unintended fertility.

858. Maril, Robert L. and Anthony N. Zavaleta. "Drinking Patterns of Low-Income Mexican American Women." Journal for Studies on Alcohol 40 (May 1979): 480-484.

No attention to generation. Most women abstained completely.

859. Marshall, Harvey H., Jr. and Robert M. Jiobu. "An Alternate Test of the Minority Status and Fertility Relation," Pacific Sociological Review 21 (April 1978): 221-237.

A comparison of Chinese, Japanese, and Filipinos in Hawaii and California.

860. McIntosh, Karyl. "Folk Obstetrics, Gynecology, and Pediatrics in Utica, New York." New York Folklore 4 (Summer/Winter 1978): 49-59.

A list of beliefs collected from women of Polish and Italian descent, probably second-generation.

861. Mohr, James C. Abortion in America. New York: Oxford University Press, 1978.

Notes the widespread availability of abortion (often via midwives) in nineteenth-century German-language community.

862. Montero, Darrel. "The Elderly Japanese American: Aging among the First Generation Immigrants." Genetic Psychology Monographs 101 (February 1980): 99-118.

Gender is considered; older women's withdrawal from participation in voluntary organizations paralleled men's.

863. Myers, Vincent. "Drug-Related Sentiments among Minority Youth." Journal of Drug Education 8 (1978): 327-335.

Caribbean-born men and women were the most disapproving of drug use.

864. Namerow, Pearlina B. and J. E. Jones. "Ethnic Variation in Adolescent Use of a Contraceptive Service." Journal of Adolescent Health Care 3 (1982): 165-72.

Compares contraceptive patterns among Cuban and Puerto Rican visitors to a clinic.

134   IMMIGRANT WOMEN IN THE U.S.

865. Nassau, Mabel L. *Old Age Poverty in Greenwich Village: A Neighborhood Study.* New York: Fleming H. Revell, 1915.

Two-thirds of the women studied were foreign-born, mainly Irish. Many case studies include discussion of nativity and ethnic background.

866. Newman, Jacqueline M. "Chinese Immigrant Food Habits: A Study of the Nature and Direction of Change." Unpublished Ph.D. Dissertation, New York University, 1980. Order Number 811067.

Based on interviews with Chinese mothers living in Chinatown and in Queens, NY. Women adapted diets for first five years, but reversed adaptation thereafter as they recognized a link between food and ethnic heritage.

867. Ortiz, Silvia M. "An Analysis of the Relationship between the Values of Sexual Regulation, Male Dominance, and Motherhood, and Mexican-American Women's Attitudes, Knowledge and Usage of Birth Control." Unpublished Ph.D. Dissertation University of California, Santa Barbara 1987. Order Number DA 8803875.

Study of unacculturated Mexican-Americans.

868. Osako, Masako M. and William T. Liu. "Intergenerational Relations and the Aged among Japanese Americans." *Research on Aging* 8 (March 1986): 128-155.

A study of 100 pairs of immigrant mothers and second-generation daughters, emphasizing intragenerational cohesion.

869. Pavich, Emma G. "A Chicana Perspective on Mexican Culture and Sexuality." *Journal of Social Work and Human Sexuality* 4 (Spring 1986): 47-65.

Contrasts traditional, bicultural, and acculturated attitudes toward sexuality and sex roles.

870. Ragucci, Antoinette T. "Generational Continuity and Change in Concepts of Health, Curing Practices, and Ritual Expressions of the Women of an Italian-American Enclave." Unpublished Ph.D. Dissertation, Boston University, 1971. Order Number DA 71-26,465.

871. Rey, Kitty H. *The Haitian Family: Implications for the Sex Education of Haitian Children in the United States.* New York: Community Society of New York, 1970.

872. Rich, B. Ruby and Lourdes Arguelles. "Homosexuality, Homophobia and Revolution: Notes toward an Understanding of the Cuban Lesbian and Gay Male Experience, Part II." SIGNS 11 (Autumn 1985): 120-136

An earlier article focused on Cuba, both prior to the revolution and afterwards. In the U.S., greater tolerance developed and lesbians and gay men were more likely to "come out."

873. Rindfuss, R. R. and J.A. Sweet. Postwar Fertility Trends and Differentials in the United States. New York: Academic Press, 1977.

Low Asian-American fertility was the result of late marriage.

874. Rosenhouse-Persson, Sandra and Georges Sabagh. "Attitudes toward Abortion among Catholic Mexican American Women: The Effects of Religiosity and Education." Demography 20 (Feb 1983): 87-98.

Education liberalized attitudes but only for those brought up in Mexico; surprisingly, education had the reverse effect on the most devout women.

875. Rosenwaike, Ira. "Two Generations of Italians in America: Their Fertility Experience." International Migration Review 7 (Fall 1973): 271-280.

Change from large to small families was rapid for women of second generation, largely a product of urban residence.

876. Ruben, G. Rumbaut and John R. Weeks. "Fertility and Adaptation: Indochinese Refugees in the United States." International Migration Review 20 (1986): 428-465.

Distinguishes among Vietnamese, Laotian, Hmong, and Khmer. The fertility of all was much higher than among the U.S. average. A result was frequent welfare dependency.

877. Sabagh, Georges and David Lopez. "Religiosity and Fertility: The Case of Chicanas." Social Forces 59, 2 (1980): 431-439.

Catholic beliefs influenced the fertility of women reared in U.S. but not of those reared in Mexico.

878. Sabagh, Georges and Dorothy S. Thomas. "Changing Patterns of Fertility and Survival Among the Japanese on the Pacific Coast." American Sociological Review 10 (October 1945): 651-658.

Compares several generations. Fertility declined rapidly after 1920. Earlier fears of a demographic dragon were not realized.

879. Sargent, Carolyn and John Marcucci. "Aspects of Khmer Medicine among Refugees in Urban America." *Medical Anthropology Quarterly* 16 (November 1984): 7-9.

Investigates pre- and postnatal medical assistance and Khmer birth practices.

880. Selby, Maija L. "Infant Mortality in the Mexican American Community: An Analysis of Differentials in Infant, Neonatal, and Postneonatal Mortality by Ethnicity and Parental Nativity, 1974-75 Single Live Birth Cohort, Harris County Texas." Unpublished Dr. P.H. Dissertation, University of Texas Health Science Center at Houston School of Public Health, 1982. Order Number 8308257.

Immigrant Mexican mothers had lower rates of infant death than Anglos.

881. Seltzer, Mildred. "Jewish-American Grandmothers." Pp. 157-161 *A Woman's Guide to the Problems and Joys of Growing Older*. Ed. Lillian E. Troll et al. Englewood Cliffs, N.J.: Prentice Hall, 1977.

Aging among Eastern European Jews.

882. Shai, Donna and Ira Rosenwaike. "Violent Deaths among Mexican-, Puerto Rican- and Cuban-born Migrants in the United States." *Social Science and Medicine* 26, 2 (1988): 269-276.

Analysis offers breakdowns by sex. Although the focus is on men's elevated risks, women's risks were also higher than U.S. averages.

883. Siegel, Martha K. "A Jewish Aging Experience: A Description of the Role of Religion in Response to Physical Dysfunction in a Sample of Jewish Women 65 to 83 Years of Age." Unpublished Ph. D. Dissertation, Harvard University, 1976. Order Number 77-16,694.

No attention to generation, but the age of the women suggests that most were first- and second-generation. Women had few health-related beliefs which originated in religious belief.

884. Slesinger, Doris P. and Yoshitaka Okada. "Fertility Patterns of Hispanic Migrant Farm Women: Testing the Effect of Assimilation." *Rural Sociology* 49 (Fall 1984): 430-440.

Age, education, and ability to speak English lowered Mexican women's fertility.

885. Stern, Mark J. *Society and Family Strategy: Erie County, New York, 1850-1920*. Albany: State University of New York Press, 1987.

Includes some analysis of immigrant patterns.

886. Stern, Phyllis N. et al. "Culturally Induced Stress During Childbearing: The Filipino-American Experience." Health Care for Women International 6, 1-3 (1985): 105-121.

887. Swenson, Ingrid et al. "Contraceptive Practices and Fertility Among Southeast Asian, Black and White Mothers Attending a Maternal Infant Care Program." Social Biology 34 (Spring/Summer 1987): 47-56.

Distinguishes Hmong and other Southeast Asians. Both had higher age at first birth than Afro-American and native-born whites; both also had lower rates of breastfeeding and very low rates of contraceptive usage.

888. Swenson, Ingrid. "Birth Weight, Apgar Scores, Labor and Delivery Complications and Prenatal Characteristics of Southeast Asian Adolescents and Older Mothers." Adolescence 21 (Fall 1986): 711-722.

Compares Hmong and other Southeast Asian groups to native-born Afro-Americans and whites. Southeast Asian groups had favorable pregnancy outcomes because of low alcohol and tobacco use.

889. Swicegood, Gary. Language, Opportunity Costs and Mexican American Fertility. Austin: University of Texas, 1982.

Attention to the foreign-born subpopulation of women.

890. Thomas, Dorothy S. "Some Social Aspects of Japanese-American Demography." Proceedings of the American Philosophical Society 94 (1950): 459-480.

Emphasizes the decline in fertility during the second generation.

891. Uhlenberg, Peter. "Fertility Patterns Within the Mexican American Population." Social Biology 20 (1973): 30-39.

Study compares Mexican-born to other foreign-born women in 1919, 1940, and 1960.

892. Urdaneta, Maria L. "Chicana Use of Abortion: The Case of Alcala." Pp. 33-51 Twice a Minority, Mexican American Women. Ed. Margarita B. Melville. St. Louis: The C.V. Mosby Company, 1980.

Includes materials from interviews with Mexican women.

138   IMMIGRANT WOMEN IN THE U.S.

893. Valanis, Barbara M. and David Rush. "Partial Explanation of Superior Birth Weights Among Foreign-Born Women." Social Biology 26 (Fall 1979): 198-210.

Nonwhite women from the Caribbean, South America, and Africa had babies with higher birth weights than native-born Afro-American. Foreign-born women had more positive health behavior, perhaps as a consequence of their relatively high status in homeland.

894. Valanis, Barbara. "Relative Contribution of Maternal Social and Biological Characteristics to Birth Weight and Gestation Among Mothers of Different Childhood Socioeconomic Status." Social Biology 26 (Fall 1979): 211-225,.

Nonwhite Caribbean women had fewer low-birth-weight babies than native-born Afro-Americans. The higher childhood social status of Caribbean migrants was of more significance in explaining this outcome than were physiological factors.

895. Vázsonyi, Andrew. "The Cicisbeo and the Magnificent Cuckold: Boardinghouse Life and Lore in Immigrant Communities." Journal of American Folklore 91 (April-June 1978): 641-656.

Topic is the Hungarian star boarder (a man sexually involved with his married landlady). Most sources were men, but one woman quoted suggested that the relationship provided women with some leverage against their husbands. The article also contains some information on prostitution.

896. Ventura, S. J. and S. M. Taftel. "Childbearing Characteristics of United States and Foreign born Hispanic Mothers. Public Health Reports 100 (Nov/Dec 1985): 647-52.

Foreign-born Cuban and Mexican mothers were older, and less likely to smoke during pregnancy.

897. Vogel, Suzanne. "Toward Understanding the Adjustment Problems of Foreign Families in the College Community: The Case of Japanese Wives at the Harvard University Health Services." Journal of American College Health 34 (June 1986): 274-279.

898. William, Ronald L. et al. "Pregnancy Outcomes among Spanish Surnamed Women in California." American Journal of Public Health 76 (April 1986): 387-91.

Compares foreign- and native-born Mexican women for low-birth-weight children and infant death.

8

Mind

INTRODUCTION

Cited in this chapter are a small group of studies that in some way address immigrant women's subjectivity. As the length of this chapter reveals, the internal world of the immigrant woman remains unexplored territory. Historians, in particular, have found it difficult to address these topics, although studies of cultural change and Americanization (see Chapter 9) sometimes contain some information on the world view of the foreign-born female.

Education and religious belief have received the greatest attention. Many studies of the education of contemporary women immigrants are policy-oriented. Leisure, identity, and culturally specific ideas about women's place, "the woman question," or feminism in particular groups still need further study, as does the mental health of immigrant women adjusting to life in a new country. On all these points, the biographies, autobiographies, oral histories, and works of fiction cited in Chapters 10 through 12 should suggest valuable directions for future study.

CITATIONS

899. Abonyi, Malvina H. "The Role of Ethnic Church Schools in the History of Education in the United States: The Detroit Experience, 1850-1920." Unpublished Ph.D. Dissertation, Wayne State University, 1987. Order Number DA 87 14526.

Includes information on the role of the Felician Sisters, a Polish teaching order.

140   IMMIGRANT WOMEN IN THE U.S.

900. Amara Singham, Lorna R. "Patterns of Friendship among South Asian Women." Pp. 313-317 The Sourcebook on the New Immigration: Implications for the United States and the International Community. Ed. Roy S. Bryce-Laporte. New Brunswick, N.J.: Transaction Books, 1980.

Indian and Sri Lanka women in Boston and New York described friendship as a refuge from the family and their friends as more like family than family.

901. Anonymous. "Note on the Slovene Immigrant Women's Press." P. 279 The Press of Labor Migrants in Europe and North America, 1880s to 1930s. Ed. Christiane Harzig and Dirk Hoerder. Bremen: Publications of the Labor Newspaper Preservation Project, 1985.

Some description of women's reading materials.

902. Arellano, Margarita M. "A Study of the Problems of Latin American Students at the University of Texas at Austin and the Possible Effects of these Problems on Academic Achievement." Unpublished Ph.D. Dissertation, The University of Texas at Austin, 1987. Order Number DA 8717359.

Women did significantly better as undergraduates than men, but there was no comparable difference among graduate students.

903. Arkoff, Abe. "Deference-East, West, Mid-Pacific: Observations Concerning Japanese, American and Japanese-American Women." Psychologia 7 (December 1964): 159-164.

The three groups of women were quite similar; all were more deferent than the men of their group.

904. Babcock, Charlotte G. and Mark J. Gehrie. "The Japanese American Experience: An Approach through Psychoanalysis and Follow-Up." Journal of Psychoanalytic Anthropology 9 (Summer 1986): 373-390.

The case study of an immigrant woman social worker, tracing thirty years of her life in the U.S., and the shift in cultural ideals away from family dependency.

905. Balancio, Dorothy M. "The Making and Unmaking of a Myth: Italian American Women and their Community." Unpublished Ph. D. Dissertation, City University of New York, 1985. Order Number DA 8515606.

Based on oral histories with three generations of women; ranges broadly over many topics, but the main theme is women's changing identities.

906. Birnbaum, Lucia C. "Education for Conformity: The Case of Sicilian American Women Professionals." Pp. 243-252 <u>Italian Americans in the Professions</u>. Ed. Remigio U. Pane. New York: American Italian Historical Association, 1983.

Sicilian immigrant women lost independence and strength as they were educated toward individualism and professionalism.

907. Boulette, Teresa R. "Assertive Training with Low Income Mexican American Women." <u>Spanish Speaking Mental Health Research Center Monograph Series</u> no. 3 (1976): 67-71.

Argues that Mexican women particularly need training since they normally respond to abuse by crying and pleading.

908. Boulette-Ramirez, Teresa R. <u>Determining Needs and Appropriate Counseling Approaches for Mexican-American Women: A Comparison of Therapeutic Listening and Behavioral Research</u>. San Francisco: R and E Research Associates, 1976.

909. Braude, Ann D. "Jewish Women in the Twentieth Century: Building a Life in America." Pp. 131-174 <u>Women and Religion in America</u>. vol. 3: 1900-1968. Ed. Rosemary R. Ruether and Rosemary S. Keller. San Francisco: Harper and Row, 1986.

Includes some information on the lives of Harriet Szold, Julia Richman, Lillian Wald, Emma Goldman, Rose Pastor Stokes, Clara Lemlich, and Theresa Malkiel, focusing on their creative, religious, and secular thought. Eastern European Jewish women were sometimes uncomfortable with the requirements and restrictions of Judaism.

910. Braun, Jean S. and Hilda M. Chao. "Attitudes Toward Women: A Comparison of Asian-Born Chinese and American Caucasians." <u>Psychology of Women Quarterly</u> 2 (Spring 1978): 195-201.

Caucasian males and Asian-born women had the most conservative attitudes about freedom, independence, dating, courting etiquette, drinking, swearing, and telling jokes.

911. Bremer, Edith. "Education for 'Immigrant Women': What is It?" <u>Educational Foundations</u> 28 (January 1916): 289-298.

English classes did not generally appeal to foreign-born women, although their daughters made heavy use of night classes; some women's ethnic societies engaged in educational work.

912. Brewer, Eileen M. Nuns and the Education of American Catholic Women, 1860-1920. Chicago: Loyola University Press, 1987.

Includes information both about European-born nuns as teachers and about the immigrant and second-generation girls they educated.

913. Burdick, Susan E. "Gender, Culture and Classroom Interactions." Unpublished Ph.D. Dissertation, Michigan State University, 1987. Order Number DA 8714309.

Studied girls and boys in three settings, including a special bilingual class for refugees and an eighth-grade class of non-English speakers. Girls were generally more passive in the classroom, probably because of notions of appropriate gender behavior. Girls also occupied less classroom space than boys.

914. Burton, Katherine. Bells on Two Rivers: The History of the Sisters of the Visitation of Rock Island, Illinois. Milwaukee: Bruce Publishing, 1965.

The order was begun by Irish women to train teachers for girls' schools.

915. Calhoun, George et al. "An Ethnic Comparison of Self-Esteem in Portuguese-, Mexican-, and Anglo-American Pupils." Journal of Psychology 98 (January 1978): 11-14.

Portuguese boy students, but not girls, had higher self-esteem than the other groups."

916. Carreiro, Manuel C. "The Participation of the Portuguese Immigrant Female in Higher Education." Unpublished Ph.D. Dissertation, Boston College, 1980. Order Number 8017832.

Based on interviews with high school juniors and seniors. Many complex factors influenced their educational decisions.

917. Castellano, Vianne M. "The Effects of Early Father Absence and the Level of Anti-Social Behavior on the Development of Social Egocentrism in Adolescent Mexican American Girls." Unpublished Ph.D. Dissertation, University of California, Los Angeles, 1978. Dissertation Abstracts 39: 2825A. No Order Number given.

While not specified, the girls studied seem to be second-generation. Girls with antisocial behavior were more egocentric if their fathers were also absent.

918. Cervantes, Carmen M. "Catholic Education for Ministry among Hispanics." Unpublished Ph.D. Dissertation, University of the Pacific, 1987. Order Number DA 8713695.

Most teachers in the California program studied (CEMH) were bilingual lay women born in Latin American countries; the students were also mainly women and spoke only Spanish.

919. Chai, Alice. "Korean Women in Hawaii, 1903-1945, The Role of Methodism in Their Liberation and Their Participation in the Korean Independence Movement." Pp. 328-344 Women in New Worlds, Historical Perspectives on the Wesleyan Tradition. Ed. Hilah F. Thomas and Rosemary S. Keller. Nashville: Abingdon, 1981.

Although a wide range of topics are covered (work, picture brides, and the importance of the mother in passing on Korean identity to children), the focus is on women's religious beliefs. Many were Christians before leaving Korea. Women's church organizations contributed to the growing independence movement there.

920. Christy, Lai Chu T. "Culture and Control Orientation: A Study of Internal-External Locus of Control in Chinese and American-Chinese Women." Unpublished Ph.D. Dissertation, University of California, Berkeley, 1977. Order Number 78126520.

Chinese women in Hong Kong had a higher degree of internalized control mechanisms than those living in the U.S.

921. Cohen, Miriam. "Changing Education Strategies Among Immigrant Generations: New York Italians in Comparative Perspective." Journal of Social History 15 (1982): 443-466.

Compares the schooling patterns of second-generation Italians and Eastern European Jews. By the end of the 1930s the educational patterns of girls were increasingly similar.

922. Cohler, Bertram J. and Marvin Lieberman. "Personality Change across the Second Half of Life: Findings from a Study of Irish, Italian and Polish Women." Ethnicity and Aging. Ed. Donald Gelfand and A. Kutzik. New York: Springer, 1979.

923. Cortese, Margaret. "Self-Disclosure by Mexican-American Women: The Effects of Acculturation and Language of Therapy." Unpublished Ph.D. Dissertation, North Texas State University, 1979. Order Number 8013350.

Immigrant, less acculturated women had language problems which hindered self-disclosure. Proposes that women would be more likely to seek help if therapy were available in Spanish.

924. Crago, Florence. "Cultural Influences which Inhibit Academic Aspiration of the Chicana." Unpublished Ph.D. Dissertation, Claremont Graduate School, 1975. Order Number 76-15,752.

Compared Mexicans, Mexican-Americans, and Anglos in Mexico and California. Measured the impact of machismo. Mexican-American girls had lower educational aspirations than Anglos, but there was also evidence of role confusion in all groups.

144   IMMIGRANT WOMEN IN THE U.S.

925. Cuffaro, Sara T. "A Discriminant Analysis of Sociocultural Motivation and Personality Differences among Black, Anglo, and Chicana Female Drug Abusers in a Medium Security Prison." Unpublished Ph.D. Dissertation, United States International University, 1978. Order Number 7906217.

There were significant differences among the three groups; identifies variables that predicted for drug use.

926. Dane, Nancy A. "Social Environment and Psychological Stress in Latin American Immigrant Women." Unpublished Ph.D. Dissertation, California School of Professional Psychology, Berkeley, 1980. Order Number 8110173.

Women interviewed were mainly from El Salvador, Nicaragua, and Guatemala; for most women the existence of an interpersonal network was an important factor in avoiding stress.

927. Davis, Donna J. "The Effect of Homework Activities on English Proficiency of Foreign Student Wives Participating in a Conversational English Program." Unpublished Ph.D. Dissertation, Kansas State University, 1982. Order Number DA 8221830.

928. de Colon Rivera, Maria M. "Familial-Cultural Influences on Participation of U.S. Spanish-Speaking Women in Adult Education." Unpublished Ed.D. Dissertation, Michigan State University, 1978. Order Number 7907322.

Background was not identified, but most were probably Mexican. Culture, not just poverty, affected women's participation in education programs; women preferred classes for basic education and for improving communication skills.

929. Dunkas, N. and G. Nikelly. "The Persephone Syndrome: A Study of Conflict in the Adaptive Process of Married Greek Female Immigrants in the U.S.A." Social Psychiatry 7 (December 1972): 211-216.

The source of the mental health problem was a strong and unresolved attachment to the mother.

930. Dympna, Sister. Mother Caroline and the School Sisters of Notre Dame in North America. 2 Vols. St. Louis: Woodward and Tiernan, 1928.

This French-born daughter of a German father founded sisterhoods in Baltimore and Milwaukee.

931. Education Committee for Non-English-Speaking Women. A New Country and Women from the Old World. New York: Education Committee for Non-English-Speaking Women, 1925.

Includes pictures of home classes with mothers and children; pictures of classes of women in settlements and social welfare agencies, often with children present; information on handicraft exhibits which were used to attract and involve foreign-born mothers in education classes.

932. Eisenstein, Sarah. Give Us Bread But Give Us Roses: Working Women's Consciousness in the United States, 1890 to the First World War. London: Routledge and Kegan Paul, 1983.

Since the author's emphasis is on class and class-consciousness, she pays little attention to the nationality of the largely immigrant women she studied. Includes generous quotes from specific immigrant women.

933. El-Banyan, Abdullah S. "Cross-Cultural Education and Attitude Change: A Study of Saudi Arabian Students in the United States." Unpublished Ph.D. Dissertation, North Carolina State University at Raleigh, 1974. Order Number 75-5359.

Life in the U.S. did not change male foreign students' attitudes toward either women or family relations.

934. Espin, Oliva M. and B. Warner. "Attitudes Towards the Role of Women in Cuban Women Attending a Community College." Journal of Psychology 28 (Autumn 1982): 233-239.

935. Ghahreman, Mahin. "A Comparative Study of Life Satisfaction and Self-Confidence among American and Iranian Women in the United States." Unpublished Ph.D. Dissertation, United States International University, 1982. Order Number DA 8215510.

Iranian women had lower rates of self-acceptance than American women generally.

936. Gray, Donna. "The Impact of Higher Education and Feminism on Women in the Brain Drain." Pp. 122-127 The Brain Drain from the West Indies and Africa. Ed. Norma Niles and Trevor G. Gordon. East Lansing, Mich.: Michigan State University West Indian Students Association, 1977.

937. Greenberg, Harvey R. and Rima D. "'A Bintel Brief': The Editor as Compleat Therapist." Psychiatric Quarterly 52 (Fall 1980): 222-230.

Analyzes the famous Yiddish-language newspaper advice column; most of those seeking advice about personal and family concerns were Eastern European Jewish women.

938. Habers, Christopher G. "The Universal Minority: A Study of the Female Brain Drain of Students from Three Developing Countries." Unpublished Ph.D. Dissertation, Columbia University, 1972.

939. Hardy-Fanta, Carol and Priscila Montana. "The Hispanic Female Adolescent: A Group Therapy Model." *International Journal of Group Psychotherapy* 32 (July 1982): 351-366.

Study of six second-generation girls who were impulsively aggressive or depressed. Describes origins of problems and the course of therapy.

940. Heller, Rita R. "The Women of Summer: The Bryn Mawr Summer School for Women Workers: 1921-1938." Unpublished Ph.D. Dissertation, Rutgers University, 1986. Order Number DA 86 20038.

Includes follow-up study of three percent of the students, many of whom were second-generation Southern and Eastern Europeans; the impact of schooling on their subsequent lives is emphasized.

941. Hynes, Kathleen and Jorge Werbin. "Group Psychotherapy for Spanish-Speaking Women." *Psychiatric Annals* 7 (December 1977): 52-63.

Mexican-American, Nicaraguan, and Salvadoran women were studied. Women were extremely distressed about the care of their children, and they expressed that stress through somatic symptoms.

942. Irwin, Elizabeth A. *Truancy: A Study of the Mental, Physical, and Social Factors of the Problem of Non-Attendance at School*. New York: Public Education Association of the City of New York, 1915.

Main groups studied were second-generation Irish and Germans, with some Eastern European Jews and Italians. Contrasts boys and girls who showed differing patterns of truancy.

943. Isasi-Diaz, Ada and Yolanda Tarango. *Hispanic Women: Prophetic Voice in the Church*. San Francisco: Harper and Row, 1988.

Several Mexican and Cuban women discuss their religious faith and how it influenced their lives.

944. Johnson, Ronald C. "Age and Cohort Effects on Personality Factor Scores across Sexes and Racial/Ethnic Groups." *Personality and Individual Differences* 4, 6 (1983): 709-13.

A study of Japanese and Chinese in Hawaii; significant personality differences by generation, sex, and ethnic group were found.

945. Johnston, Maxene and Merrell E. Sarty. "Maternal Beliefs about Vitamin Efficacy in Four U.S. Subcultures." Journal of Cross-Cultural Psychology 9 (September 1978): 327-338.

No generation given, but the study compares English- and Spanish-speaking Mexican mothers. Spanish-speakers who were the mothers of daughters expressed more magical beliefs about vitamins.

946. Jun, Suk-ho. "Communication Patterns among Young Korean Immigrants." International Journal of Intercultural Relations 8, 4 (1984): 373-389.

Women read fewer American newspapers than men, but rates of reading increased with time in the U.S.

947. Kelly, Gail P. "Adult Education for Vietnamese Refugees: Commentary on Pluralism in America." Journal of Ethnic Studies 5 (Winter 1978): 55-64.

Women were taught appropriate sex roles through the teaching of the English language.

948. Kelly, Gail P. "Schooling, Gender and the Reshaping of Occupational and Social Expectations: The Case of Vietnamese Immigrants in the United States." International Journal of Women's Studies 1 (July/August 1978): 323-335.

Materials used in programs for educating women offered no positive examples of what women might be in the U.S.; women were sometimes discouraged from taking language classes at all, while men were prepared mainly for menial jobs.

949. Kelly, Gail P. "The Schooling of Vietnamese Immigrants; Internal Colonialism and Its Impact on Women". Pp. 276-296 Comparative Perspectives of Third World Women: The Impact of Sex, Race and Class. Ed. Beverly Lindsay. New York: Praeger Publishers, 1980.

Refugee women were introduced to U.S. sex roles as they were taught English language.

950. Kim, Sil Dong. "Interracially Married Korean Women Immigrants: A Study in Marginality." Unpublished Ph.D. Dissertation, University of Washington, 1979. Order Number 7927816.

Women developed immunity to failure through emphasizing conformity to outside norms.

951. Krause, Corinne A. "Ethnic Culture, Religion, and the Mental Health of Slavic-American Women." Journal of Religion and Health 18 (1979): 298-307.

148   IMMIGRANT WOMEN IN THE U.S.

952. Krause, Corinne A.   Grandmothers, Mothers and Daughters: an Oral History Study of Ethnicity, Mental Health, and Continuity of Three Generations of Jewish, Italian, and Slavic-American Women. New York: American Jewish Committee Institute on Pluralism and Group Identity, 1978.

Although many topics are covered, the general focus is on mental health and cultural change.

953. Kunnu, Felix B. "The Relationship of Ego Development and Career Maturity in Nigerian Male and Female College Students." Unpublished Ph.D. Dissertation, George Peabody College for Teachers of Vanderbilt University, 1987. Order Number DA 8723891.

Includes analysis of 30 women students in the U.S., but found few differences by sex.

954. Kuznicki, Sister Ellen M.   "An Ethnic School in American Education: A Study of the Origin, Development and Merits of the Educational System of the Felician Sisters in the Polish American Catholic Schools of Western New York." Unpublished Ph.D. Dissertation, Kansas State University, 1973.

The foundresses of this school were Polish nuns, and many of the students were of the second generation.

955. Lam-Phoon, Sally C.   "A Comparative Study of the Learning Styles of Southeast Asian and American Caucasian College Students on Two Seventh-Day Adventist Campuses." Unpublished Ph.D. Dissertation, Andrews University, 1987. Order Number DA 8724214.

Both background and gender influenced styles of learning.

956. Lape, Esther. "Americanizing Our New Women Citizens." Life and Labor 8 (1918): 96-98.

957. Lerner, Elinor.   "Immigrant and Working-Class Involvement in the New York City Woman Suffrage Movement, 1905-1917: A Study in Progressive Era Politics." Unpublished Ph.D. Dissertation, University of California, Berkeley, 1981. Order Number DA 8212009.

Attitudes of Jewish, Irish, and Italian immigrants towards women's suffrage varied, with Jews most supportive.

958. Li, Lillian.   "Two Chinese Ghosts."   California Folklore Quarterly 4 (July 1945): 278-280.

Recounts a story told by a Chinese woman in California.

959. Lindström-Best, Varpu and Allen Seager. "Toveritar and Finnish Canadian Women, 1900-1930." Pp. 243-264 The Press of Labor Migrants in Europe and North America, 1880s to 1930s. Ed. Christiane Harzig and Dirk Hoerder. Bremen: Publications of the Labor Newspaper Preservation Project, 1985.

This newspaper, its editors (Helmi Mattson, Hulda Anderson, and Selma Jokela-McCone), and many of its readers were actually in the U. S.

960. Lipner, Nira H. "The Subjective Experience of Israeli Immigrant Women: An Interpretive Approach." Unpublished Ph.D. Dissertation, The George Washington University, 1987. Order Number DA 8708356.

Focuses on the development of identity in the new homeland.

961. Loo, Chalsa. "Chinatown's Wellness: An Enclave of Problems." Journal of the Asian American Psychological Association 7, 1 (1982): 13-18.

No attention to generation, but the women studied lived in Chinatown, and many were probably immigrants. Many suffered from low self-esteem and expressed dissatisfaction with traditional marriages.

962. Lord, Carmen B. "The Relationship of Maternal Employment and Ethnic Origin to the Sex Role Perception of Cuban-American and Anglo-American Female Adolescents." Unpublished Ph.D. Dissertation, University of Miami, 1980. Order Number 8022887.

Daughters of employed Cuban mothers were less liberal in sex-role attitudes than Anglo daughters, but Cuban daughters expected to combine work, marriage, and mothering while Anglo girls wanted to quit work when they had children.

963. Manansala, Erlinda. "Differences in Style of Coping with Stress among Male and Female International Students at an Urban University." Unpublished Ph.D. Dissertation, Boston University School of Education, 1976. Order Number 77-4071.

Women foreign students experienced more stress than men while living in the U.S.

964. Markides, Kyriakos and Janice Farrell. "Marital Status and Depression among Mexican Americans." Social Psychiatry 20, 2 (1985): 86-91.

A study of three generations. Women generally and the unmarried of both sexes had the highest levels of depression. Marital status had no significance in the first generation, and divorce no significance in the third generation (where rates of divorce were rising).

965. Markides, Kyriakos and Sally W. Vernon. "Aging, Sex-Role Orientation, and Adjustment: A Three Generations Study of Mexican Americans." *Journal of Gerontology* 39 (September 1984): 586-591.

Older women with traditional sex-role attitudes were the most likely to be depressed.

966. McDannell, Colleen. *The Christian Home in Victorian America, 1840-1900*. Bloomington: Indiana University Press, 1986.

See the chapter on Catholic domesticity which includes some information on Irish women and their religious faith.

967. McDonald, Sister Grace. "Pioneer Teachers: The Benedictine Sisters of St. Cloud." *Minnesota History* 35 (June 1957): 263-271.

German nuns founded the academy after a short stay in Pennsylvania; they worked initially with the children of German Catholic immigrants.

968. Meloni, Christine F. "A Comparison of Characteristics and Problems of Male and Female Students from Japan and South Korea Studying in EFL Programs in 11 Selected Universities in the United States." Unpublished Ph.D. Dissertation, The George Washington University, 1987. Order Number DA 87 25266.

Korean women suffered particularly from homesickness.

969. Miranda, Manuel R. et al. "Mexican American Dropouts in Psychotherapy as Related to Level of Acculturation." *Spanish Speaking Mental Health Research Center Monograph Series* no. 3 (1976): 35-50.

The level of acculturation was not related to continuation of therapy.

970. Montenegro, Raquel. "Educational Implications of Cultural Values and Attitudes of Mexican-American Women." Unpublished Ph.D. Dissertation, Claremont Graduate School, 1973.

Both native-born and foreign-born were loyal to their families and proud of their heritage, but all rejected the dominant role of authoritarian husbands. None identified with the women's movement, but many supported its goals.

971. Oates, Mary J. "Organized Volunteerism: The Catholic Sisters of Massachusetts, 1870-1940." *Women in American Religion*. Ed. Janet W. James. Philadelphia: University of Pennsylvania Press, 1980.

Some attention to the teaching work of the French-Canadian sisters, the Grey Nuns of the Cross.

972. Orsi, Robert A. The Madonna of 115th Street: Faith and Community in Italian Harlem, 1880-1950. New Haven: Yale University Press, 1985.

See a general section on women in Italian Harlem and another section that focuses on the special religious devotions of women.

973. Palacios, Maria and Juan N. Franco. "Counseling Mexican-American Women." Journal of Multi-Cultural Counseling and Development 14 (July 1986): 124-131.

Focuses on sources of stress: language, poverty, acculturation, and immigration difficulties. Troubled women underused mental health facilities.

974. Rigg, Pat. "Petra: Learning to Read at 45." Journal of Education, Boston 167, 1 (1985): 129-139.

Explains why a Mexican migrant woman had remained illiterate and notes the effects of tutoring on her.

975. Salgado de Snyder, Velia N. "Mexican Immigrant Women: The Relationship of Ethnic Loyalty, Self-Esteem, Social Support and Satisfaction to Acculturative Stress and Depressive Symptomatology." Unpublished Ph.D. Dissertation, University of California, 1986. Order Number DA 8621129.

A study of women who migrated after age fourteen; most were satisfied and expected to remain, but those who came here involuntarily suffered more depression.

976. Scatena, Maria. "Educational Movements that have Influenced the Sister Teacher Education Program of the Congregation of the Sisters of Providence: 1840-1940." Unpublished Ph.D. Dissertation, Loyola University of Chicago, 1987. Order Number DA 8718294.

The order was founded by missionary sisters from France. Included are notes on the life of Mother Theodore Guérin, the French mother superior. The focus is on the educational work of the order.

977. Scelsa, Joseph V. "Italian-American Women: Their Families and American Education, Systems in Conflict." Pp. 169-171 The Family and Community Life of Italian Americans. Ed. Richard N. Juliani. Staten Island: The Italian American Historical Association, 1981.

Emphasizes the conflicts between family values and educational aspirations.

978. Schneider, Florence H. Patterns of Workers' Education: the Story of the Bryn Mawr Summer School. Washington, D.C.: American Council on Public Affairs, 1941.

Many of those attending the school were second-generation women.

979. Seller, Maxine. "Defining Socialist Womanhood: The Women's Page of the Jewish Daily Forward in 1919." American Jewish History 76 (June 1987): 416-38.

Good information on how a newspaper shaped new ideals of womanhood.

980. Seller, Maxine. "The Education of Immigrant Children in Buffalo, New York, 1890-1916." New York History 57 (April 1976): 183-200.

Girls' vocational training was limited to domestic service and sewing.

981. Seller, Maxine. "The Education of the Immigrant Women: 1900-1935." Journal of Urban History 4 (1978): 307-330.

982. Sharlip, William and Albert A. Owens. Adult Immigrant Education: Its Scope, Content and Methods. New York: MacMillan, 1925.

See the chapter on women's classes which emphasizes differences between foreign-born women, who are hesitant to attend, and their daughters, the second-generation, who eagerly attend night classes. Men and women had to be separated if programs were to succeed. Teaching materials for women emphasized the care of home and children.

983. Simonielli, Katina. "On Investigating the Attitudes Toward Achievement and Success in Eight Professional U.S. Mexican Women." Aztlán 12 (Spring 1981): 121-137.

Based on interviews with middle-class women, several of whom seem to be second-generation.

984. Sluzki, Carlos E. "The Sounds of Silence: Two Cases of Elective Mutism in Bilingual Families." Family Therapy Collections 6 (1983): 68-77.

Two cases of bilingual families (Mexican-American; Salvadoran) where girls refused to talk, perhaps because choice of language was associated with alliances within the family.

985. Smith, Doris. "American-Irish Women in Education." Recorder (Bulletin of the American Irish Historical Society) 34 (1973): 33-39.

Brief mention of several second-generation women educators.

986. Sue, Stanley and James K. Morishima. The Mental Health of Asian Americans; Contemporary Issues in Identifying and Treating Mental Problems. San Francisco: Jossey-Bass Publishers, 1982.

See a section on appropriate sex roles among Chinese, Japanese, and Filipinos.

987. Taves, Ann. The Household of Faith, Roman Catholic Devotions in Mid-Nineteenth-Century America. South Bend, Indiana: University of Notre Dame Press, 1986.

Irish women formed most Catholic devotional organizations, and two-thirds of these societies limited membership to women.

988. Thomas, Deborah. "An Indian Student Community: Segregation of the Sexes and the Effects of Education." International Journal of Sociology of the Family 18 (Spring 1988): 97-111.

Education expanded women's occupational opportunities, but had no effect on segregation.

989. Toai, Ton That. "Adult Authority Figure, Grade, Sex and Moral Judgment in Vietnamese Immigrant Children." Unpublished Ph.D. Dissertation, Columbia University, 1978. Order Number 7819454.

Because sexual dichotomies were common in Vietnamese culture, the author was surprised to find no differences between the boys and girls studied.

990. Turner, Kay F. "Mexican American Home Altars: Towards Their Interpretation." Aztlán 13 (Spring/Fall 1982): 309-326.

The erection of an altar was a female tradition. The study focuses on women as folk artists.

991. Turner, Kay. "La Vela Prendida: Mexican-American Women's Home Altars." Folklore Women's Communication 25 (1981): 5-6.

An important folk handicraft.

992. Van Kleeck, Mary. Working Girls in Evening Schools. New York: Survey Associates for the Russell Sage Foundation, 1914.

Three-quarters of the girls studied were foreign-born or second-generation, with many Jews and Germans among them. Most attended in the hopes of finding better jobs.

993. Van Tran, Thanh and Lauretta Byars. "Sources of Subjective Well-Being among Vietnamese Women in the United States." Free Inquiry in Creative Sociology 15 (November 1987): 195-198.

English capabilities, education, length of time in the U.S., social support, and income all affected women's sense of well-being.

154   IMMIGRANT WOMEN IN THE U.S.

994. Vega, William A. et al. "Depressive Symptoms and their Correlates among Immigrant Mexican Women in the United States." Social Science and Medicine 22, 6 (1986): 645-652.

Found extraordinarily high rates of depressive symptoms among immigrant women from Mexico. Those here less than five years, and socially isolated were particularly at risk.

995. Vega, William A. et al. "Migration and Mental Health: An Empirical Test of Depression Risk Factors among Immigrant Mexican Women." International Migration Review 21 (Fall 1987): 512-529.

California women studied; loss of interpersonal ties and level of perceived work opportunities influenced rates of depression.

996. Vega, William A. et al. "The Relationship of Marital Status, Confidant Support, and Depression among Mexican Immigrant Women." Journal of Marriage and the Family 48 (August 1986): 597-605.

Disrupted marriages produced higher level symptoms; never-married women had the lowest levels. Confidants significantly altered the impact of depression.

997. Weinberg, Sydney S. "The World of our Mothers: Family, Work and Education in the Lives of Jewish Immigrant Women." Frontiers 7 (1983): 71-79.

Based on oral histories, this study includes particularly good information on women's education.

998. Williams, Harvey. "Social Isolation and the Elderly Immigrant Woman." Pacific Historian 26 (Summer, 1982): 15-24.

Women were not particularly isolated.

999. Wong, Kay S. "Chinese American Women: A Phenomenological Study of Self-Concept." Unpublished Ph.D. Dissertation, The Wright Institute, 1983. Order Number DA 8317774.

A Study of the lives of five women born in China.

1000. Woodward, Elizabeth A. "Educational Opportunities for Women from Other Lands." University of the State of New York Bulletin no. 718 (September 15, 1920).

The foreign-born woman was the last in the family to obtain education, and thus an impediment in the family's assimilation.

1001. Yanagida, Evelyn and Anthony J. Marsella. "The Relationship between Depression and Self-Concept Discrepancy among Different Generations of Japanese-American women." Journal of Clinical Psychology 34 (July 1978): 654-659.

Study of women in Hawaii. Self-concept discrepancy and depression were positively related in some generations; in studies of Western psychology, they are always linked.

1002. Zapata, Vincente S. "Family Size and Mexican-American Teenagers: A Study of Desired Number of Children and Selected Family Characteristics in Teenage Mexican-American Girls." Unpublished Ph.D. Dissertation, University of California, Los Angeles, 1976. Order Number 76-28,587.

Most studied were second-generation. They believed the ideal age for marriage was twenty. Most communicated little with their mothers about sexuality. The family size they desired varied considerably.

1003. Zinn, Maxine B. "Employment and Education of Mexican-American Women: the Interplay of Modernity and Ethnicity in Eight Families." Harvard Educational Review 50,1 (1980): 47-62.

Although generation is not considered, focus is on cultural change. Economic restraints were more important than culture in determining level of education. Modern patterns were not simply substituted for traditional ones, but interacted with them.

9

Cultural Change

INTRODUCTION

Only a few scholars have attempted to outline the dimensions of assimilation, acculturation, and culture change for immigrant women or the ways in which women's and men's patterns of adjustment overlapped or differed. A few recent studies by historians have focused on immigrant women's perceptions of American womanhood, often as filtered through the lens of public school teachers or popular culture. It seems obvious that, for many immigrant women in this century, the broad American ideals of individualism, independence, and (later) sexual fulfillment represented sharp challenges to traditional notions of appropriate female behavior. Studies of contemporary immigrant women, by contrast, emphasize mainly the overwhelming importance of learning English in easing the adaptation of the foreign-born.

Much of the information currently available about cultural change comes from studies of the second generation. (Only rarely do studies address subsequent generations, largely because few systematic sources identify nativity beyond that point; rather, they substitute broad definitions of ethnic identity for national origin.) Overall, these studies point to the rapidity of change within this generation, and the likelihood of conflict between American-born daughters and foreign-born mothers and fathers as a result.

Also cited in this chapter are a small number of studies which focus on immigrant women's contacts with the native-born. These contacts cannot be easily summarized, although it seems likely that personal contacts were more often the exception than the rule, especially in the past.

CITATIONS

1004. Addams, Jane. <u>The Spirit of Youth and the City Streets</u>. New York: The MacMillan Co., 1909.

Information on cultural change in "The Wrecked Foundations of Domesticity;" on the second generation, see sections on dance halls and morality problems.

1005. Anthony-Welch, Lillian D. "A Comparative Analysis of the Black Woman as Transmitter of Black Values, Based on Case Studies of Families in Ghana and among Jamaicans and Afro-Americans in Hartford, Connecticut." Unpublished Ed. D. Dissertation, University of Massachusetts, 1976. Order Number 77-6371.

Women were the primary transmitters of culture in all three cases.

1006. Barton, H. Arnold. "Scandinavian Immigrant Women's Encounter with America." <u>Swedish Pioneer Historical Quarterly</u> 25 (January 1974): 37-42.

Swedish single women domestic workers were particularly enthusiastic about the U.S.; the better educated showed some interest in the American feminist movement.

1007. Berrol, Selma C. "Class or Ethnicity: The Americanized German Jewish Woman and Her Middle Class Sisters." <u>Jewish Social Studies</u> 47 (Winter 1985): 21-32.

The second generation had concerns similar to those treated in native-born and middle-class women's magazines of the period.

1008. Blicksilver, Edith. "The <u>Bintl Briv</u> Woman Writer: Torn Between European Traditions and the American Life Style." <u>Studies in American Jewish Literature</u> 3 (Winter 1977-78): 36-49.

Classifies the problems that motivated Eastern European Jewish women to write letters to this advice column.

1009. Boone, Margaret S. "The Uses of Traditional Concepts in the Development of New Urban Roles: Cuban Women in the United States." Pp. 235-270 <u>World of Women: Anthropological Studies of Women in the Societies of the World</u>. Ed. Erika Bourguignon, et al. New York: Praeger, 1980.

Women were defined in sexual terms. Second-generation women resented the tradition of chaperoning during courtship. Wives provided leadership within the extended family.

1010. Breckinridge, Sophonisba P. and Edith Abbott. <u>The Delinquent Child and the Home: A Study of the Delinquent Wards of the Juvenile Court of Chicago</u>. New York: The Russell Sage Foundation, 1917.

See especially the chapter "The Child of Immigrants," which gives breakdowns by sex and particular nationality groups. Large numbers of the girls studied were German, Polish, and Irish.

1011. Cernius, V.J. "The Acculturation of a Group of Lithuanian Women: A Follow-Up Study." <u>Journal of Baltic Studies</u> 11 (1980): 254-64.

Traces the lives of 24 women beginning in 1957.

1012. Chang, Lydia L. "Acculturation and Emotional Adjustment of Chinese Women Immigrants." Unpublished D.S.W. Dissertation, Columbia University, 1980. Order Number 8023486.

Young migrants acculturated most quickly; acculturated women had more egalitarian marriages; physically healthy women were the best adjusted emotionally but few troubled women sought mental health care.

1013. Chin, A.S. "Adaptive Role of Chinese Women in the United States." <u>Chinese Society of America Bulletin</u> 14 (1979): 183-196.

1014. Connor, John W. "Acculturation and Family Continuities in Three Generations of Japanese Americans." <u>Journal of Marriage and the Family</u> 36, 1 (1974): 159-168.

Some attention to changing sex roles.

1015. Connor, John W. <u>Tradition and Change in Three Generations of Japanese Americans</u>. Chicago: Nelson-Hall, 1977.

The focus is on personality and psychology of the individual across three generations; good attention to gender throughout.

1016. Crandall, Jo Ann et al. "Existing Programs for Orientation of Women Refugees and Migrants," <u>Migration Today</u> 10 (1982): 33-42.

Describes programs aimed at aiding women's adjustment during their first weeks in the U.S.

1017. Daniels, John. <u>America Via the Neighborhood</u>. New York: Harper and Brothers, 1920.

See the chapter on women and Americanization in schools and social settlements.

1018. Davison, Lani. "Women Refugees: Special Needs and Programs." <u>Journal of Refugee Resettlement</u> 1 (1981): 16-26.

Focuses on the special adjustment problems of Vietnamese, Hmong, and Indochinese refugee women, including sexual abuse, impact of poor nutrition on reproduction, and levels of education (which were lower then men's). The article also documents women's superior ability to cope and to adapt.

1019. Deutsch, Phyllis. "Theater of Mating: Jewish Summer Camps and Cultural Transformation." <u>American Jewish History</u> 75 (1986): 307-321.

The focus is on dating and leisure customs among second-generation Eastern European Jews.

1020. di Leonardo, Micaela. <u>The Varieties of Ethnic Experience; Kinship, Class, and Gender among California Italian-Americans</u>. Ithaca and London: Cornell University Press, 1984.

Mainly a study of second-generation or later generations. See especially, "'I Think God Helps Us': Women, Work, Ethnicity, and Ideology." Emphasizes the work that women do to maintain the kinship network.

1021. Dominguez, Virginia. "The Nature of Change: Cuban Women in the United States." <u>Women and Change: The Cuban Case</u>. Ed., Maria Cristina Herrera. Institute of Cuban Studies, 1981.

1022. Ellis, Pearl I. <u>Americanization Through Homemaking</u>. Los Angeles: Wetzel Publishing, 1929.

The focus is immigrant Mexican women in California.

1023. Embree, John F. <u>Acculturation among the Japanese of Kona, Hawaii</u>. New York: Krauss Reprint, 1969.

See especially the section on "Birth and Marriage."

1024. Ewen, Elizabeth. "City Lights; Immigrant Women and the Rise of the Movies." <u>SIGNS</u> 5 (1980): 545-565.

The theme is the impact of popular culture and Americanization on the second generation's efforts to become American women.

1025. Ewens, Mary. "Removing the Veil: The Liberated American Nun." Pp. 255-278 <u>Women of Spirit: Female Leadership in the Jewish and Christian Tradition.</u> Ed. Rosemary Ruether and Eleanor McLaughlin. New York: Simon & Schuster, 1979.

Sisterhoods changed rules in response to the new American environment; also includes the biography of Mother Caroline Friess, a Paris-born nun of Bavarian parents who worked among German immigrants in Pennsylvania and Wisconsin.

1026. Fong, Stanley L.M. "Assimilation and Changing Roles of Chinese Americans." <u>Journal of Social Issues</u> 29, 2 (1973): 115-127.

Focus is on changing sex roles of females in the second generation; as a result, their relations to their parents and to the men of their own generation changed.

1027. Fong, Stanley L.M. and Harvey Peskin. "Sex-Role Strain and Personality Adjustment of China-Born Students in America: A Pilot Study." <u>Journal of Abnormal Psychology</u> 74 (October 1969): 563-567.

Since students were traditionally male in China, it was assumed that women would feel more strain when they became students in the U.S. Actually, women with student visas rejected typical Chinese female characteristics which were more widely accepted by naturalized Chinese women and women with permanent residence in the U.S.

1028. Fox, Geoffrey. "Honor, Shame and Women's Liberation in Cuba: Views of Working-Class Emigré Men." Pp. 273-290 <u>Female and Male in Latin America.</u> Ed. Ann Pescatello. Pittsburgh: University of Pittsburgh Press, 1973.

Contrasts changing attitudes toward women and their proper roles among recently arrived male and female Cuban refugees in Chicago.

1029. Frank, Blanche B. "The American Orthodox Jewish Housewife: A Generational Study in Ethnic Survival." Unpublished Ph.D. Dissertation, City University of New York, 1975. Order Number 76-3818.

The theme is change over three generations. Immigrants initially Americanized, but then revitalization of orthodox practices began in the second generation.

1030. Grinstein, Alexander. "Profile of a 'Doll'--A Female Character Type." Pp 79-94 <u>The Psychodynamics of American Jewish Life.</u> Ed. Norman Kiell. New York: Twayne Publishing Co., 1967.

Describes second-generation daughters of Eastern European Jews in psychoanalytic (and very unflattering) terms. Their lives were focused on clothing, fashion, and remaining physically attractive.

162   IMMIGRANT WOMEN IN THE U.S.

1031. Hernandez, Cibeles. "Acculturation of Cuban Mothers and Children's Adjustment." Unpublished Ph.D. Dissertation, Hofstra University, 1982. Order Number DA8310239.

Teachers perceived children of less-assimilated Cuban mothers as less well-adjusted.

1032. Ho, Yuet-fung. "Women and Creating a Chinese American Culture." Bu Gao Ban Winter/Spring, 1985.

1033. Hung, Lucy. "Dating and Courtship Innovations of Chinese Students in America." Marriage and Family Living 18 (February 1956): 25-29.

Group dating, go-betweens, self-introductions, and cooking parties substituted for traditional courtship customs.

1034. Kelly, Gail P. From Vietnam to America: A Chronicle of the Vietnamese Immigration to the United States. Boulder: Westview Press, 1977.

Refugees were 45 percent female; case studies include some information on them. Teaching English to women included the teaching of proper sex roles; feminists also taught sessions on "Women in America."

1035. Khouzam, Nevine N. "The Adjustment Process of Hispanic Students at the University of Florida, 1985-1986." Unpublished Ph.D. Dissertation, The University of Florida, 1986. Order Number DA8704180.

Among students from Latin American countries, women adjusted to American culture more slowly than men.

1036. Kibria, Nazli. "Patterns of Adaptation and Survival among Vietnamese in an Urban Setting: A Study of Family and Gender." Unpublished Ph.D. Dissertation, University of Pennsylvania, 1986. Order Number DA8703226.

Traditional gender ideals retained significance for both men and women; women's interaction with outside institutions often reinforced rather than challenged these traditions.

1037. Kim, Chong O. "Korean Immigrant Mothers in the United States: Patterns of Assimilation in Relation to the Perception of their Children's Behavior." Unpublished D.S.W. Dissertation, Adelphi University, 1983. Order Number DA 8322266.

A study of 125 mothers' perceptions of their children's behavioral problems; no variation in children's problems by level of mother's assimilation was found.

1038. Kranau, Edgar J. et al. "Acculturation and the Hispanic Woman: Attitudes toward Women, Sex-Role Attribution, Sex-Role Behavior and Demographics." Hispanics Journal of Behavioral Sciences 4 (March 1982): 21-40.

Contrasts Cuban, Peruvian, Bolivian, Puerto Rican, and Mexican-American women, ranking individuals by acculturation. "Feminine household behaviors" declined with acculturation. Education and age were positively associated with acculturation.

1039. Krause, Corinne A. "Urbanization Without Breakdown: Italian, Jewish and Slavic Women in Pittsburgh, 1900 to 1945." Journal of Urban History 4 (May 1978): 291-305.

Based on oral histories, this study emphasizes the successful mental adjustment of most women. Still, all the women interviewed knew others who lost their health, committed suicide, or were otherwise unable to adjust.

1040. Lalli, Michael. "The Italian-American Family: Assimilation and Change, 1900-1965." The Family Coordinator 18 (January 1969): 44-48.

Courtship patterns changed in the second generation.

1041. Lee, Dorothy. "Folklore of the Greeks in America." Folk-Lore 47 (1936): 294-310.

Greek women were preservers of old traditions.

1042. Marshall, Catherine A. et al. "Value Conflict: A Cross-Cultural Assessment Paradigm." Journal of Applied Rehabilitation Counseling 14 (Spring 1983): 74-78.

Case study of counseling of a young Japanese woman, focusing on problems that originated in cultural differences.

1043. Matthews, Ellen. Culture Clash. Chicago: Intercultural Press, 1982.

This diary kept by a sponsor of Vietnamese refugees includes valuable descriptions of the gradual adaptation of women and family ties to a new environment.

1044. Maxson, Charles H. Citizenship. New York: Oxford University Press, 1930.

See pp. 107-111, which describe naturalization by marriage and the impact of the Cable Act on foreign-born women.

1045. Melville, Margarita B. "Mexican Women Adapt to Migration." International Migration Review 12 (Summer 1978): 225-235.

The mental stress of acculturation in Houston was especially severe for undocumented migrants.

164   IMMIGRANT WOMEN IN THE U.S.

1046. Meredith, William and B.J. Tweten, eds. Compiled Proceedings: Helping Indochinese Families in Transition, Conference May 11-12, 1981. Lincoln: Nebraska University, College of Home Economics, 1981.

Includes materials on the counseling of Vietnamese women.

1047. Meredith, William M. and George P. Roue. "Changes in Lao Hmong Marital Attitudes after Immigrating to the United States." Journal of Comparative Family Studies 17 (Spring 1986): 117-126.

The Hmong were a polygamous society; women remained more traditional in attitudes toward marriage than men.

1048. Murai, Eiko. "The Enhancement of the Alien's Adjustment through Interpersonal Relationships within the Ethnic Group toward the Socialization into the Host Society: Japanese Women's Case." Unpublished Ph.D. Dissertation, University of Michigan, 1972. Order Number DA 72-29157.

Contact with native-born Americans facilitated adjustment.

1049. Noisuwan, Samran. "Acculturation of Young Children in Mixed Thai-American Marriages in Urban and University Communities." Unpublished Ph.D. Dissertation, University of Oregon, 1979. Order Number 7927266.

All families studied had Thai mothers and American fathers; children were most interested in American culture and all spoke English exclusively. Only in food preferences was the mother's influence visible.

1050. Osei, Gabriel K. "Caribbean Women at Home and Abroad." Pp. 117-128 Caribbean Women: Their History and Habits. Ed. G. K. Osei. London: The African Publication Society, 1979.

Emphasizes and criticizes the tendency of migrant women to adopt white culture, which the author believes leads to the abandonment of home and religion. Some attention to the U.S.

1051. Park, Seong H. "The Identification of Factors Related to Childrearing Expectations of Korean-American Immigrant Parents of Preschool Children." Unpublished Ph.D. Dissertation, North Texas State University, 1983. Order Number DA 8327055.

Mothers had more positive attitudes toward play--and played with their children more--than did fathers. Parental play increased with assimilation.

1052. Peiss, Kathy. "Gender Relations and Working-Class Leisure: New York City, 1880-1920." Pp. 98-111 "To Toil the Livelong Day;" America's Women at Work, 1780-1980. Ed. Carol Groneman and Mary Beth Norton. Ithaca and London: Cornell University Press, 1987.

Most of the women studied are immigrant and second-generation; emphasis is on Americanization in response to American popular culture.

1053. Peiss, Kathy. Cheap Amusements; Working Women and Leisure in Turn-of-the-Century New York. Philadelphia: Temple University Press, 1986.

Little attention to national backgrounds or generation, but most women discussed are immigrants and second-generation. Focus is on popular culture transforming notions of womanliness.

1054. Penti, Marsha. "Piikajutut: Stories Finnish Maids Told." Pp. 55-71 Women Who Dared: The History of Finnish American Women. Ed. Carl Ross and K. Marianne Wargelin Brown. St. Paul, Minnesota: Immigration History Research Center, 1986.

Reports on stories collected from women returners who had worked many years, or all their lives, as domestic servants in the U.S.

1055. Penti, Marsha. "The Role of Ethnic Folklore Among Finnish American Returnees." Unpublished Ph.D. Dissertation, Indiana University, 1983. Order Number DA 8406836.

Based on interviews, many with returned female immigrants who had worked as domestic servants in the U.S. Provides a different perspective on the cultural change that occurs as a result of this type of work.

1056. Peterson, Susan. "Religious Communities of Women in the West: The Presentation Sisters' Adaptation to the Northern Plains Frontier." Journal of the West 21 (April 1982): 65-70.

Irish sisters abandoned the cloister and switched from teaching Sioux Indians to teaching local Catholic children in Fargo, as well as making many other adjustments to a new environment.

1057. Reed, Dorothy. "Leisure Time of Girls in a 'Little Italy': A Comparative Study of the Leisure Interests of Adolescent Girls of Foreign Parentage, Living in a Metropolitan Community, to Determine the Presence or Absence of Interest Differences in Relation to Behavior." Unpublished Ph.D. Dissertation, Columbia University, 1932.

The Italian second generation.

1058. Roberts, Marjorie. "Italian Girls on American Soil." Mental Hygiene 13 (October 1929): 757-768.

Emphasizes the second generation's conflicts with parents over wages, socializing and courtship.

1059. Ryan, Christine E. "Indochinese Refugees in the U.S.: Background Characteristics, Initial Adjustment Patterns, and the Role of Policy." Unpublished Ph.D. Dissertation, Brown University, 1987. Order Number DA 8715554.

Patterns of adjustment differed by sex.

1060. Seller, Maxine. "The 'Women's Interest Page' of the Jewish Daily Forward: Socialism, Feminism and Americanization in 1919." Pp. 221-242 The Press of Labor Migrants in Europe and North America, 1880s to 1930s. Ed. Christiane Harzig and Dirk Hoerder. Bremen: Publications of the Labor Newspaper Preservation Project, 1985.

Assumes that this was important source of information for Eastern European Jewish women seeking to adjust to American life. The column provided no fashion or beauty advice, but much information on education, child psychology, love, marriage and family life.

1061. Sewell-Coker, Beverly et al. "Social Work Practice with West Indian Immigrants." Social Casework 66 (November 1985): 563-568.

Girls attempting to acquire the freedoms of their native-born friends were regarded as rebellious and referred to social agencies.

1062. Simon, Rita J. "Refugee Families' Adjustment and Aspirations: A Comparison of Soviet Jewish and Vietnamese Immigrants." Ethnic and Racial Studies 6 (October 1983): 492-504.

Based in part on interviews with mothers and daughters. Adolescents of both groups were quite similar. Among parents, mothers of two groups exhibited the strongest differences. Both generations and groups had high educational and mobility expectations.

1063. Szapocznik, Jose et al. "Theory and Measurement of Acculturation." Inter-American Journal of Psychology 12 (1978): 113-30.

Acculturation rates varied with both age and sex.

1064. Tait, Joseph. Some Aspects of the Effect of the Dominant American Culture Upon Children of Italian-Born Parents. Clifton, N.J.: Augustus M. Kelley, 1972.

Second-generation girls had lower inferiority feelings and overall better adjustment and more emotional stability than boys.

1065. Tharp, Roland G. et al. "Changes in Marriage Roles Accompanying the Acculturation of the Mexican American Wife." Journal of Marriage and the Family 30 (August 1980): 404-412.

Based on a survey of women's attitudes; contrasts less acculturated (Spanish -speaking) and more acculturated (English-speaking) attitudes toward family authority, sex, and familism.

1066. True, Ruth S. The Neglected Girl. West Side Studies. New York: Russell Sage Foundation, Survey Associates, 1914.

Most of the girls studied are second-generation Irish and German.

1067. Tsegga, Asaye. "The Effects of Sex, Socioeconomic Status, and Generation on the Acculturation of Chinese-American Students." Unpublished Ed.D. Dissertation, University of Southern California, 1983. Dissertation Abstracts 44: 1413A. No Order Number given.

Sex had little effect on acculturation, but generation did.

1068. Vega, William A. et al. "Marital Strain, Coping, and Depression among Mexican-American Women." Journal of Marriage and the Family 50 (May 1988): 391-403.

Compares women of several levels of acculturation.

1069. Walter, I. "One Year after Arrival: The Adjustment of Indochinese Women in the United States (1979-1980)." International Migration 19 (1981): 129-152.

Most were refugees.

1070. Webster, Janice R. "Domestication and Americanization: Scandinavian Women in Seattle, 1888 to 1900." Journal of Urban History 4 (1978): 275-290.

Contacts between domestic servants and native-born women employers in Seattle encouraged rapid Americanization.

1071. Wong, Anna. "A Study of the Initial Adjustment to the American Society of Six Chinese Immigrant Females in High School." Unpublished Ph.D. Dissertation, The Wright Institute, 1980. Order Number 8104798.

Based on interviews with three women born in China and three born in Vietnam. The family lives of the two groups differed. The biggest difficulty for both was the lack of English language abilities, which isolated them in school and in the community.

1072. Yanigasako, Sylvia J. *Transforming the Past, Tradition and Kinship Among Japanese Americans*. Stanford: Stanford University Press, 1985.

Includes much information on changing marriage, filial, sibling, and kinship relationships in immigrant and second generation. Good attention to women's work.

1073. Yeung, Wing Hon and Michael A. Schwartz. "Emotional Disturbance in Chinese Obstetrical Patients: A Pilot Study." *General Hospital Psychiatry* 8 (July 1986): 258-62.

Study of 126 immigrant women emphasizes the emotional stresses of acculturation.

1074. Yu, Lucy C. "Acculturation and Stress within Chinese American Families." *Journal of Comparative Family Studies* 15 (Spring 1984): 77-94.

No attention to generation, but compares more and less-acculturated individuals. Men's stress declined more rapidly with acculturation than did women's. Both the least and the most acculturated women seemed most worried about supporting elderly parents financially.

1075. Zayas, Luis H. "Toward an Understanding of Suicide Risks in Young Hispanic Females." *Journal of Adolescent Research* 2 (Spring 1987): 1-11.

Compares first and second generation women, focusing on gender-role socialization and inter-generational conflict.

10

Biography

INTRODUCTION

The lives of individual immigrant women have not been ignored; most biographical studies are of women considered notable in some way. The contributions of immigrants and women to American life were also an early concern of both women's studies and immigration history.

The increased use of oral history in recent years has also begun to broaden our understanding of individual biography, providing information about the average and ordinary rather than the outstanding woman. This chapter cites both formal biographies and oral histories which focus on individual lives.

Given the extent of immigrant women's activism in the labor movement and ethnic and religious communities, it is probably appropriate that a considerable number of biographies have been dedicated to women activists in these arenas. A very few women--Emma Goldman, Mary "Mother" Jones, Anzia Yezierska, and Henrietta Szold--have, however, drawn a disproportionate share of biographers' attention.

Biographies also reveal the surprising accomplishments of immigrant women in other fields, particularly in the creative and performing arts. English and Irish actresses, and opera singers from a broader range of backgrounds, have long been attracted to the United States for professional reasons. Some of these women settled permanently in the United States, while others pursued trans-Atlantic careers for much of their lives. They thus provide a very interesting counterpoint to the family- or community-oriented women whose lives are documented in non-biographical works.

CITATIONS

1076. Abrams, Jeanne. "Unsere Leite ('Our People'): Anna Hillkowitz and the Development of the East European Jewish Woman Professional in America." American Jewish Archives 37 (1985): 275-289.

Second-generation German Jewish fundraiser for the Denver Jewish Consumptives' Relief Society.

1077. Altman, Addie R. and Bertha R. Proskauer. Julia Richman, Two Biographical Appreciations of the Great Educator. New York: The Julia Richman High School Association, 1916.

Life of the second-generation German Jewish educator, by her sisters.

1078. Andrews-Coryta, Stepanka. "Dr. Olga Stastny, Her Service to Nebraska and the World." Nebraska History 68 (Spring 1987): 20-27.

A Czech physician in Nebraska.

1079. Anonymous. Madame Restell: An Account of Her Life and Horrible Practices, Together with Prostitution in New York, its Causes, and Effects upon Society. New York: Published by the Proprietor, and sold by all dealers in Cheap Books, 1847.

An infamous English abortionist, Anna Trow Lohman.

1080. Apodaca, Maria L. "The Chicana Woman: An Historical Materialist Perspective." Latin American Perspectives 4 (Winter and Spring 1977): 70-89.

Includes an excerpt from a student's "Biographical Sketch of an Immigrant Woman," as well as some analysis of Mexican immigrant women.

1081. Armstrong, Margaret. Fanny Kemble, A Passionate Victorian. New York: The MacMillan Co., 1938.

An English actress.

1082. Asher, Nina L. "Dorothy Jacobs Bellanca: Feminist Trade Unionist, 1894-1946." Unpublished Ph.D. Dissertation, University of New York at Binghamton, 1982. Order Number DA8223493.

A Latvian Jewish labor activist.

1083. Asher, Nina L. "Dorothy Jacobs Bellanca: Women Clothing Workers and the Runaway Shops." Pp. 195-226 A Needle, A Bobbin, A Strike. Ed. Joan Jensen and Sue Davison. Philadelphia: Temple University Press, 1984.

A Latvian Jewish labor activist in the Amalgamated Clothing Workers.

1084. Askowith, Dora. <u>Three Outstanding Women</u>. New York: Bloch Publishing Co., 1941.

Includes the life of Rebekah Kohut, a Hungarian Jewish community activist.

1085. Bainbridge, Lucy S. <u>Helping the Helpless in Lower New York</u>. New York: Fleming H. Revell, 1917.

Case studies from a mission case worker, many of which focus on immigrant and second-generation women of German and Irish backgrounds.

1086. Baker, Houston A., Jr., ed. <u>Three American Literatures: Essays in Chicano, Native American, and Asian-American Literature for Teachers of American Literature</u>. New York: Modern Language Association of America, 1982.

See especially Jeffrey Paul Chan et al., "An Introduction to Chinese-American and Japanese-American Literatures," pp. 197-228; and Fusao Inada Lawson, "Of Place and Displacement: The Range of Japanese-American Literature," pp. 254-265; both include notes on the lives of female writers of fiction.

1087. Baker, Racel. <u>The First Woman Doctor; The Story of Elizabeth Blackwell, M.D.</u> London: G. G. Harrap, 1947.

The English-born physician.

1088. Balakian, Nona. <u>A New Accent in American Fiction, The Armenian-American Writer</u>. New York: Armenian Benevolent Union of America, 1958.

Contains a biography and discusses the work of Marjorie Housepian.

1089. Baldwin, Charles C. <u>Martha Ostenso: Daughter of the Vikings</u>. New York: 1930.

Life of the Norwegian novelist.

1090. Banks, Ann, ed. <u>First-Person America</u>. New York: Alfred A. Knopf, 1980.

Although there are no women's oral histories in the chapter on immigrants, see the stories in "Monumental Stone" (two Italian widows); the chapter on women at work includes the oral history of a second-generation Irish woman.

1091. Barborka, Geoffrey A. <u>H.P. Blavatsky, Tibet and Tulku</u>. Madras: Theosophical Publishing House, 1966.

The Russian-born spiritualist lived and worked in both the U.S. and Europe.

1092. Barker, Barbara M. "The American Careers of Rita Sangalli, Giuseppina Morlacchi and Maria Bonfanti: Nineteenth Century Ballerinas." Unpublished Ph.D. Dissertation, New York University, 1981. Order number 81-27890.

Sangalli returned to Italy; the others married and remained to perform in the U.S.

1093. Barnard, Charles. <u>Camilla: A Tale of a Violin</u>. Boston: Loring, 1874.

Camilla Urso was an Italian musician.

1094. Barolini, Helen. <u>The Dream Book, an Anthology of Writings by Italian American Women</u>. New York: Schocken Books, 1985.

Includes some notes on the lives and writings of immigrant and second-generation Italian women writers.

1095. Barry, John D. <u>Julia Marlowe</u>. Boston: E.H. Beacon, 1907.

An English actress.

1096. Bartlett, Elizabeth A. "Liberty, Equality, Sorority: Origins and Interpretations of American Feminist Thought: Frances Wright, Margaret Fuller, and Sarah Grimke". Unpublished Ph.D. Dissertation, University of Minnesota, 1981. Order Number DA 8206325.

Wright was a Scottish-born radical and writer who lived many years in the U.S.

1097. Bates, Helen M. <u>Lotta's Last Season</u>. Brattleboro, Vt.: Private Printing, E. L. Hildreth & Co., 1940.

The life of Lotta Crabtree, a second-generation English actress.

1098. Baxandall, Rosalyn F. "Elizabeth Gurley Flynn: The Early Years." <u>Radical America</u> 8 (1975): 90-102.

A second-generation Irish labor activist and radical.

1099. Baxandall, Rosalyn F. <u>Words on Fire: The Life and Writing of Elizabeth Gurley Flynn</u>. New Brunswick, N.J.: Rutgers University Press, 1987.

This collection of the writings of the second-generation Irish radical and labor activist also contains a biographical introduction.

1100. Beeton, Beverly. "'I Am an American Woman': Charlotte Ives Cobb Godbe Kirby." <u>Journal of the West</u> 27 (April 1988): 13-19.

An English-born woman.

BIOGRAPHY   173

1101. Belonzi, Arthur A. "Margaret M. Heckler: Student Legislator to Ambassador." Pp. 53-64 Women Leaders in Contemporary U.S. Politics. Ed. Frank P. LeVeness and Jane P. Sweeney. Boulder, Co.: Lynne Rienner, 1987.

A second-generation Irish political activist.

1102. Benedictine of Stanbrook Abbey. Frances Xavier Cabrini, The Saint of the Emigrants. London: Burns, Oates & Washbourne, 1944.

Italian nun, saint, and missionary.

1103. Bennett, Helen C. American Women in Civic Work. New York: Dodd, Mead & Co., 1915.

Contains a chapter on the life of Anna Howard Shaw, English minister and feminist.

1104. Berkman, Ted. The Lady and the Law: The Remarkable Life of Fanny Holtzman. Boston: Little, Brown, 1976.

A second-generation child of Austrian Jews and early Hollywood lawyer.

1105. Berrol, Selma C. "Julia Richman and the German Jewish Establishment: Passion, Arrogance, and the Americanization of the Ostjuden." American Jewish Archives 38 (November 1986): 137-177.

A second-generation German Jewish educator and community activist.

1106. Berrol, Selma C. "When Uptown Met Downtown: Julia Richman's Work in the Jewish Community of New York, 1880-1912." American Jewish History 70 (September 1985): 35-67.

A second-generation German Jewish reformer and educator in New York City's public schools.

1107. Besant, Annie W. H.P Blavatsky and the Masters of the Wisdom. London: Theosophical Publishing House, 1922.

A life of the Russian-born spiritualist.

1108. Bethune, Joanna. The Life of Mrs. Isabella Graham. New York: J.S. Taylor, 1839.

A Scottish charity worker.

1109. Binns, Archie in collaboration with Olive Kooken. Mrs. Fiske and the American Theatre. New York: Crown Publishers, 1955.

An English actress.

174   IMMIGRANT WOMEN IN THE U.S.

1110. Bird, Stewart et al. <u>Solidarity Forever: An Oral History of the IWW</u>. Chicago: Lake View Press, 1985.

Of 29 oral history interviews, four were with women. See especially "Women in Textiles" which includes lives of second-generation Jews and Italians in Paterson, New Jersey and the story of a Slovenian woman in a mining town.

1111. Blicksilver, Edith. "Monica Krawcyzk's Polish Pride." <u>Turn-of-the Century Women</u> 1 (1984): 42-44.

Life of a Polish writer.

1112. Bloch, Irvin. <u>Neighbor to the World</u>. New York: World, 1969.

The life of Lillian Wald, a second-generation German Jew, nurse and founder of the Henry Street Settlement House.

1113. Boardman, Anne C. <u>Such Love Is Seldom: A Biography of Mother Mary Walsh, O.P.</u> New York: Harper, 1950.

The Irish founder of the Dominican Sisters of the Sick Poor in New York.

1114. Bobbé, Dorothie. <u>Fanny Kemble</u>. New York: Minton, Balch & Co., 1931.

An English actress.

1115. Bolek, Francis, ed. <u>Who's Who in Polish America</u>. New York: Harbinger House, 1943.

Brief entries for Polish and second-generation women prominent in the church, the Felician sisters, ethnic societies, and public and private education.

1116. Borden, Lucille P. <u>Francesca Cabrini. Without Staff or Script</u>. New York: MacMillan, 1945.

The Italian nun who specialized in work among immigrants.

1117. Boydston, Jo Ann. <u>The Poems of John Dewey</u>. Carbondale: Southern Illinois University Press, 1977.

The introduction tells of his relationship with Anzia Yezierska, for whom some of his poems were probably written.

1118. Britt, Roberta H. "The Role of Turkish and Rhodes Sephardic Women in the Seattle Sephardic Community." Unpublished Ph.D. Dissertation, The Union for Experimenting Colleges and Universities, 1981. Order Number DA 8209936.

An oral history of three generations of Jewish women.

1119. Brizzolara, Andrew. "Profile: Elise Warenskjold." <u>Migration Today</u> 7 (April 1979): 39.

A Norwegian writer in Texas.

1120. Brooks, Van Wyck. The Confident Years, 1885-1915. New York: Dutton, 1952.

Includes biographical material on Emma Goldman.

1121. Browder, Clifford. Madame Restell, the Abortionist: The Wickedest Woman in New York. Hamden, Conn.: Archon Books, 1988.

The life of Anna Trow Lohman, born in England.

1122. Brown, Olympia, ed. Democratic Ideals; A Memorial Sketch of Clara B. Colby. n.p.: The Federal Suffrage Association, 1917.

The prominent English-born feminist and suffragist.

1123. Brownmiller, Susan. Shirley Chisholm: A Biography. New York: Doubleday and Co., 1971.

The life of the second-generation Barbadian born in Brooklyn. She became the first Afro-American woman to serve in Congress.

1124. Bruchac, Joseph, ed. Breaking Silence: An Anthology of Contemporary Asian American Poets. New York: Greenfield Review Press, 1983.

Includes short biographies and writings of Chinese, Japanese, Filipino, and second-generation poets.

1125. Bruns, Roger A. The Damndest Radical; The Life and World of Ben Reitman, Chicago's Celebrated Social Reformer, Hobo King, and Whorehouse Physician. Urbana and Chicago: University of Illinois Press, 1987.

Includes a detailed account of Reitman's romantic and political involvement with Emma Goldman.

1126. Bryce-Laporte, Roy S. "Obituary to a Female Immigrant and Scholar: Lourdes Casal." Pp. 349-355 Female Immigrants to the United States: Caribbean, Latin American and African Experiences. Ed. Delores Mortimer and Roy Bryce-Laporte. Washington, D.C.: Research Institute on Immigration and Ethnic Studies, Smithsonian Institute, 1981.

A short life of the Cuban professional.

1127. Buchanan, Susan H. "Profile of a Haitian Migrant Woman." Pp. 112-142 Female Immigrants to the United States. Ed. Delores M. Mortimer and Roy S. Bryce-Laporte. Washington, D.C.: Smithsonian Institution, Research Institute for Ethnic Studies, 1981.

1128. Buckley, Joan N. "Martha Ostenso: A Critical Study of Her Novels." Unpublished Ph.D. Dissertation, University of Iowa, 1976. Order Number 77-3718.

A biography and analysis of the novels of the second-generation Norwegian author of O River Remember and other works.

1129. Buckley, Joan N. "Martha Ostenso: Norwegian-American Immigrant Novelist." Norwegian-American Studies 28 (1979): 69-81.

This Norwegian author migrated first to Canada; she wrote mainly in English.

1130. Bularzik, Mary J. "The Bonds of Belonging: Leonora O'Reilly and Social Reform." Labor History 24 (1983): 60-84.

A second-generation Irish labor activist and feminist who worked with the Women's Trade Union League.

1131. Burnett, Vivian. The Romantick Lady, The Life Story of an Imagination. New York and London: C. Scribner's Sons, 1927.

An adulatory account of Frances Burnett, English author, by her child.

1132. Burton, Katherine. Mother Butler of Marymount. New York and Toronto: Longmans, Green & Co., 1944.

This Irish nun founded the Marymount schools and colleges.

1133. Butt, G. Baseden. Madame Blavatsky. London: Rider & Co., 1926.

The Russian-born spiritualist.

1134. Caddell, G. Lincoln. Barbara Heck: Pioneer Methodist. Cleveland, Tenn.: Pathway Press, 1961.

An early missionary born in Ireland of German parents.

1135. Callan, Louise. Phillipine Duchesne: Frontier Missionary of the Sacred Heart. Westminster, Maryland: Newman Press, 1957.

This French nun brought her order to U.S.

1136. Cameron, Allan G. Helen Hopekirk, A Critical and Biographical Sketch. N. p.:1885.

A Scottish musician.

1137. Cantarow, Ellen. Moving the Mountain: Women Working for Social Change. Old Westbury, N.Y.: The Feminist Press, 1980.

Includes the story of Jessie Lopez de la Cruz, a second-generation Mexican community activist.

1138. Carruth, Reba and Vivian J. Nelsen. "Shirley Chisholm: Woman of Complexity, Conscience and Compassion." Pp. 9-20 Women Leaders in Contemporary U.S. Politics. Ed. Frank P. LeVeness and Jane P. Sweeney. Boulder, Co.: Lynne Rienner, 1987.

The second-generation Barbadian/Guyanan political activist and feminist.

1139. Chai, Alice. "A Picture Bride from Korea: The Life History of a Korean American Woman in Hawaii." Bridge: An American Perspective 6 (Winter 1978): 37-42.

An oral history with a Korean.

1140. Chambers, Peggy. A Doctor Alone; A Biography of Elizabeth Blackwell, the First Woman Doctor, 1821-1910. London: Bodley Head, 1956.

The English-born physician.

1141. Char, Tin-Yuke. The Sandalwood Mountains. Honolulu: The University Press of Hawaii, 1975.

Includes the life histories of several immigrant women.

1142. Chun-Hoon, Lowell. "Jade Snow Wong and the Fate of Chinese-American Identity." Pp. 125-135 Asian Americans: Psychological Perspectives. Ed. Stanley Sue and Nathaniel N. Wagner. Ben Lomond, Cal.: Science and Behavior Books, 1973.

Biography and literary analysis of the second-generation author.

1143. Clark, Vévé et al. The Legend of Maya Deren: A Documentary Biography and Collected Works. New York: Anthology Film Archives/Film Culture, 1988.

An account of the Russian filmmaker's life also includes scripts, correspondence, and interviews.

1144. Clum, John P. "Nellie Cashman." Arizona Historical Review 3 (1931): 9-34.

An Irish adventuress and gold-rush businesswoman.

1145. Code, Reverend Joseph B. Great American Foundresses. New York: Macmillan, 1929.

Many who founded American Catholic sisterhoods were Irish, French, Canadian, and German.

1146. Cohen, Ricki C. "Fannia Cohn and the International Ladies' Garment Workers Union." Unpublished Ph.D. Dissertation, University of Southern California, 1976. Dissertation Abstracts 37, 4 (1976): 2380-A. No Order Number given.

Biography of the Russian-born ILGWU leader, focusing on her work in the education department.

1147. Coleman, Arthur P. and Marian M. Wanderers Twain: Modjeska and Sienkiewicz: A View from California. Cheshire, Conn.: Cherry Hill Books, 1964.

A Polish actress.

1148. Coleman, Marian M. Fair Rosalind: The American Career of Helen Modieska. Cheshire, Conn.: Cherry Hill Books, 1969.

A Polish actress.

1149. Comer, Irene F. "Little Nell and the Marchioness: Milestone in the Development of American Musical Comedy." Unpublished Ph.D. Dissertation, Tufts University, 1979. Order Number 7920519.

Includes information on Lotta Crabtree, the second-generation English actress who first starred in the role.

1150. Conklin, Margaret M. An American Teresa. 2nd ed. n.p., 1947.

A second-generation Carpatho-Ruthenian nun, Teresa Demjanovich.

1151. Coogan, M. Jane. Mary Frances Clarke. Dubuque: Mt. Carmel Press, 1977.

The Irish nun who brought the Sisters of Charity of the Blessed Virgin Mary to U.S.

1152. Cook, Blanche W. "Female Support Networks and Political Activism: Lillian Wald, Crystal Eastman, Emma Goldman." Chrysalis 3 (1977): 44-61.

Wald was a second-generation German Jew and social reformer; Goldman a Russian-born Jewish anarchist and radical.

1153. Corcoran, Mary L. The Seal of Simplicity: Life of Mother Emilie. Privately Printed, 1958.

The life of Emilie Kemen, a French nun of the Sisters of Saint Mary of Namur in Lockport, New York.

1154. Cordova, Dorothy L. "Pinays--Pilipinos in America." Pp. 113-122 Gathering Ground: New Writing and Art by Northwest Women of Color. Ed. Jo Cochran et al. Seattle: Seal Press, 1984.

Includes three biographies of Pilipina women. Most of the volume consists of poetry and fiction.

1155. Corwin, Margaret. "Minna Schmidt: Businesswoman, Feminist and Fairy Godmother to Chicago." Chicago History 7 (Winter 1978-79): 226-235.

This German domestic servant eventually built a prosperous business as a maker of costumes and dolls.

1156. Coser, Lewis A. Refugee Scholars in America; Their Impact and Experiences. New Haven and London: Yale University Press, 1984.

The German and German Jewish exiles studied include Charlotte Buehler, Karen Horney, and Hannah Arendt.

1157. Courtney, Marguerite. Laurette. New York: Rinehart, 1955.

The second-generation Irish actress Laurette Taylor.

1158. Cox, Richard W. "Wanda Gág: The Bite of the Picture Book." Minnesota History 44 (Fall 1975): 238-54.

This second-generation Czech artist and illustrator is best known for her children's books.

1159. Crawford, Anne Fears and Crystal S. Ragsdale. Women in Texas. Burnet, Tex.: Eakin Press, 1982.

Contains a short account of the life of Elisabet Ney, German sculptress.

1160. Creahan, John. The Life of Laura Keene, Actress, Artist, Manager and Scholar. Philadelphia: The Rodgers Publishing C., 1897.

A rambling account of the English actress's life.

1161. Curry, Peggy S. "A Transplanted Britisher." Pp. 28-42 The Women Who Made the West. Ed. The Western Writers of America. Garden City, N.Y.: Doubleday, 1980.

An English lady-in-waiting for a wealthy traveler remained in the U.S. after marrying a cowboy.

1162. Cutrer, Emily F. The Art of the Woman, The Life and Work of Elisabet Ney. Lincoln: University of Nebraska Press, 1988.

A German sculptress who settled in Texas.

1163. D'Auvergne, Edmund B. *Lola Montez, An Adventuress of the Forties*. London: T.W. Laurie, 1909.

She was Irish-born.

1164. Dakin, Susanna B. *Perennial Adventure: A Tribute to Alice Eastwood, 1859-1953*. San Francisco: California Academy of Sciences, 1954.

A Canadian botanist.

1165. Dalmazzo, G.M. *Adelina Patti's Life*. London: Cooper Brothers & Attwood, 1877.

An opera singer born in Spain of Italian parents.

1166. Daly, Sister John Marie. "Mary Anderson, Pioneer Labor Leader." Unpublished Ph.D. Dissertation, Georgetown University, 1968. Order Number 69-2703.

Swedish labor activist and first head of the Women's Bureau.

1167. Dance, Daryl C. *Fifty Caribbean Writers: A Bio-bibliographical Critical Sourcebook*. Westport, Conn.: Greenwood Press, 1986.

Brief lives of several Jamaican and Antiguan women writers in the U.S.

1168. Daniels, Doris G. "Lillian D. Wald: The Progressive Woman and Feminism." Unpublished Ph.D. Dissertation, City University of New York, 1977. Order Number 77-11,171.

This second-generation German Jew was social reformer, nurse, and settlement house foundress.

1169. Dannett, Sylvia G. L. *She Rode with the Generals, The True and Incredible Story of Sarah Emma Edmonds alias Franklin Thompson*. New York: T. Nelson, 1960.

Sarah Edmonds was a Canadian male impersonator and soldier in the Civil War.

1170. Dash, Joan. *A Life of One's Own: Three Gifted Women and the Men They Married: Margaret Sanger, Edna St. Vincent Millay, Maria Goeppert-Mayer*. New York; Harper & Row, 1973.

Sanger, the birth-control activist, was second-generation Irish; Goeppert-Mayer was a German Nobel prize-winning physicist.

1171. Dash, Joan. *Summoned to Jerusalem: The Life of Henrietta Szold*. New York: Harper & Row, 1979.

The second-generation Hungarian Jew who founded Hadassah and became an important Zionist activist.

BIOGRAPHY   181

1172. Dearborn, Mary V. Love in the Promised Land, The Story of Anzia Yezierska and John Dewey. New York: The Free Press, 1988.

The Polish Jewish writer of novels and short stories about immigrant life.

1173. Delatte, Carolyn E. "An American Odyssey: A Biography of Lucy Bakewell Audubon." Unpublished Ph. D. Dissertation, Louisiana State University, 1979. Order Number 7927522.

The English-born wife of Audubon came with her family to the U.S. in the early 1800s.

1174. Dempsey, David, and Raymond P. Baldwin. The Triumphs and Trials of Lotta Crabtree. New York: W. Morrow, 1968.

A second-generation English actress.

1175. DiDonato, Pietro. Immigrant Saint: The Life of Mother Cabrini. New York: McGraw Hill, 1960.

The Italian missionary and nun.

1176. Donelin, Mary C. "American Irish Women Firsts." Journal of the American Historical Society 24 (1925): 215-221.

Brief lives of notable Irish women in education and community.

1177. Drinnon, Richard. Rebel in Paradise: A Biography of Emma Goldman. Chicago: University of Chicago Press, 1961.

The well-known Russian Jewish radical and anarchist.

1178. Driver, Leota S. Fanny Kemble. Chapel Hill: The University of North Carolina Press, 1933.

An English actress.

1179. Duffus, Robert L. Lillian Wald, Neighbor and Crusader. New York: MacMillan, 1938.

This second-generation German Jewish nurse started the Henry Street Settlement.

1180. Duncan, Hannibal G. Immigration and Assimilation. Boston: D.C. Heath, 1933.

Book II contains life histories of first- and second-generation women of many backgrounds.

1181. Dunn, Georgia. *Towers of Montauer*. Derby, N.Y.: Saint Paul's Publications, 1971.

The life of Mary Hannappel, the Dutch foundress of the Sisters of Saint Francis of Penance and Christian Charity in the U.S.

1182. Duus, Masayo. *Tokyo Rose: Orphan of the Pacific*. Trans. Peter Duus. New York: Kodansha International, 1979.

A second-generation Japanese woman falsely accused of being the infamous World War II traitor.

1183. Dworkin, Susan. "Henrietta Szold--Liberated Woman." Pp. 164-170 *The Jewish Woman: An Anthology*. Ed. Elizabeth Koltun. New York: Schocken Books, 1976.

The Hungarian Jewish Zionist.

1184. Eckhardt, Celia M. *Fanny Wright; Rebel in America*. Cambridge, Mass.: Harvard University Press, 1984.

A Scottish writer who advocated a variety of radical causes in the U.S.

1185. Endelman, Gary E. "Solidarity Forever: Rose Schneiderman and the Women's Trade Union League." Unpublished Ph.D. Dissertation, University of Delaware, 1978. Order Number 7800123.

The life of the Polish Jewish labor activist.

1186. Epstein, Helen. *Children of the Holocaust: Conversations with Sons and Daughters of Survivors*. New York: G.P. Putnam's Sons, 1979.

The second-generation author's efforts to unravel her family's secrets; also contains reminiscences of other children about their immigrant parents. Contains bibliography.

1187. Ericsson, Mary K. *A Ragusan Bride: Dubrovnik to San Francisco*. Palo Alto, Cal: Ragusan Press, 1981.

The life of a Croatian woman as told by her daughter.

1188. Fabe, Maxine. *Beauty Millionaire; the Life of Helena Rubinstein*. New York: Crowell, 1972.

The Polish beauty entrepreneur.

1189. Falk, Candace. *Love, Anarchy and Emma Goldman*. New York: Holt, Rinehart, and Winston, 1984.

A life of the Russian Jewish anarchist, emphasizing the linkage between her personal life and political beliefs, with much information on her relationship to Ben Reitman.

1190. Fancourt, M. St. J. *They Dared to be Doctors: Elizabeth Blackwell and Elizabeth Garrett Anderson.* London: Longmans, 1965.

Blackwell was English-born.

1191. Feeley, Dianne. "Antoinette Konikow: Marxist and Feminist." *International Socialist Review* 33 (1972): 42-46.

An Eastern European Jewish radical.

1192. Fetherling, Dale. *Mother Jones, the Miners' Angel: A Portrait.* Carbondale: Southern Illinois University Press, 1974.

The well-known Irish labor agitator and radical.

1193. Fife, Dale. *Weddings in the Family.* New York: Farrar, 1956.

The story of an Alsatian couple in Toledo, Ohio, the author's grandparents.

1194. Fineman, Irving. *Woman of Valor--Life of Henrietta Szold.* New York: Simon and Schuster, 1961.

A second-generation Hungarian Jew, Szold founded Hadassah.

1195. Fink, Deborah. "Anna Oleson: Rural Family and Community in Iowa, 1880-1920." *Annals of Iowa* 48 (Summer/Fall 1987): 251-263.

The life of an ordinary Norwegian farm woman.

1196. Fink, Gary M. *Biographical Dictionary of American Labor Leaders.* Westport, Conn.: Greenwood Press, 1984.

Short entries on immigrant and second-generation labor activists Mary Anderson, Dorothy Bellanca, Elisabeth Christman, Fannia Cohn, Elizabeth Gurley Flynn, Alice Henry, Mother Mary Harris Jones, Pauline Newman, Margaret Dreier Robins, Rose Schneiderman, Rose Pastor Stokes, and Maud O'Farrell Swartz.

1197. Fisher, Dexter, ed. *The Third Woman: Minority Women Writers of the U.S.* New York: Houghton Mifflin, 1980.

Short biographies of a small number of foreign-born and second-generation Mexican and Asian women writers.

1198. Fitzgerald, Mary P. *Beacon on the Plains.* Leavenworth, Kan.: St. Mary College, 1939.

Life of the Irish missionary to Indians, Mother Hayden.

184   IMMIGRANT WOMEN IN THE U.S.

1199. Follis, Jane T. "Frances Wright: Feminism and Literature in Antebellum America." Unpublished Ph.D. Dissertation, The University of Wisconsin, Madison, 1982. Order Number DA8304265.

A Scottish radical and writer.

1200. Foner, Philip S., ed. Mother Jones Speaks, Collected Writings and Speeches. New York: Monad Press, 1983.

Besides her writings, includes an assessment of her life.

1201. Ford, D. M. "Anna Howard Shaw: Physician and Pioneer." Englishwoman 47 (1920): 210-218.

A prominent English feminist and minister.

1202. Fortune, James and Jean Burton. Elizabeth Ney. New York: Alfred A. Knopf, 1943.

A German sculptress in Texas.

1203. Ganguli, B.N. Emma Goldman: A Portrait of a Rebel Woman. New Delhi: R.N. Sachder at Allied Publisher, 1979.

A brief life of the Russian Jewish radical and anarchist.

1204. Gannon, Joseph A. "Lillian D. Wald: A Study of Education at the Henry Street Settlement Based on her Writings and Papers." Unpublished Ph. D. Dissertation, Fordham University, 1979. Order Number 7911204.

Wald was a second-generation German Jew whose work as a nurse led her to found the Henry Street Settlement.

1205. Garcia, Mario T. "Chicano History; An Oral History Approach." The Journal of San Diego History 23 (Winter 1977): 46-54.

Includes several oral histories with Mexican and second-generation women.

1206. Garland, Anne W. Women Activists, Challenging the Abuse of Power. New York: The Feminist Press and the City University of New York, 1988.

Short accounts of the lives of several second-generation (Polish, Austro-Hungarian) community activists.

1207. Garrison, Dee. "Karen Horney and Feminism." SIGNS 6 (Summer 1981): 672-69.

An intellectual biography of the German psychologist.

1208. Gehle, Frederick W. *Our Dubbledam Journey: An Account of How a Family Came to America, 1891-1941.* New York: Frederick W. Gehle, 1941.

A memoir which focuses on his English mother and her journey to the U.S. on a Dutch ship.

1209. Gerber, David A. "The First African Woman Graduate of an American University." *Negro History Bulletin* 36 (April 1973): 84-85.

A Christian South African woman received a degree from Wilberforce University in Ohio; she returned to her homeland after graduation.

1210. Gibbs, Henry. *Affectionately Yours, Fanny: Fanny Kemble and the Theatre.* London and New York: Jarrolds, 1947.

An English actress.

1211. Gil, Carlos. "Lydia Mendoza: Houstonian and First Lady of Mexican American Song." *The Houston Review* 3 (Summer 1981): 249-260.

Mendoza was a popular singer of the 1930s and 1940s, born in Mexico and performing first in the border region and later nationwide.

1212. Glass, Beaumont. *Lotte Lehmann, A Life in Opera & Song.* Santa Barbara: Capra Press, 1988.

A German singer with a substantial career in the U.S.

1213. Goar, Marjory. *Marble Dust: A Biography of Elisabet Ney.* Austin: Eakin Press, 1984.

A German sculptress in Texas.

1214. Goldberg, Isaac. *Queen of Hearts, The Passionate Pilgrimage of Lola Montez.* New York: The John Day Co., 1936.

An Irish adventuress and actress.

1215. Goldsmith, Margaret. *Seven Women Against the World.* London: Methuen, 1935.

Includes a section on Russian Jewish anarchist Emma Goldman.

1216. Gornick, Vivian. *Fierce Attachments, A Memoir.* New York: Farrar Straus Giroux, 1987.

Life with the author's second-generation Russian Jewish mother.

186   IMMIGRANT WOMEN IN THE U.S.

1217. Gornick, Vivian. *The Romance of American Communism*. New York: Basic Books, 1977.

Includes short accounts of the lives of several Eastern European Jewish radicals, mainly of the second generation.

1218. Graham, Mrs. Isabella. *The Power of Faith: Exemplified in the Life and Writings of the Late Mrs. Isabella Graham, of New-York*. New York: Kink & Mercein, William A. Mercein, Printer, 1819; orig. publ. 1816.

An early Scottish welfare worker.

1219. Granowicz, Antoni. *Modjeska, Her Life and Loves*. New York: T. Yoseloff, 1956.

A Polish actress.

1220. Graves, William W. *Life and Times of Mother Bridget Hayden*. St. Paul, Kansas: Journal Press, 1938.

She was an Irish missionary to the Indians.

1221. Green, Archie. "The Death of Mother Jones." *Labor History* 1 (1960): 68-80.

The Irish labor activist and radical.

1222. Greenbaum, Lenora. "Two Families, Three Generations: One Story." Pp. 69-89 *New Lives, The Adjustment of Soviet Jewish Immigrants in the United States and Israel*. Ed. Rita J. Simon. Lexington, Mass.: Lexington Books, D.C. Heath, 1985.

Based on interviews (some with women) of Soviet Jewish refugees to Israel and the U.S.

1223. Gross, David C. *Pride of our People: The Stories of One Hundred Outstanding Jewish Men and Women*. Garden City, N.Y.: Doubleday, 1979.

Includes a biography of Golda Meir, a Russian-born woman, raised in Milwaukee, who became leader of Israel.

1224. Grossinger, Tani. *Growing Up at Grossinger's*. New York: D. McKay C., 1975.

Biographical materials on Jennie Grossinger, the Austrian Jewish businesswoman and manager of a large Catskill resort.

1225. Gunn, Rex. *They Called her Tokyo Rose*. San Francisco: Japanese American Citizens League, 1977.

Japanese-American woman accused of treason.

1226. Harper, Jacob C. *Ellen Browning Scripps*. La Jolla: n.p., 1936.

The life of an English newspaper writer and publisher.

1227. Harris, Frank. *Contemporary Portraits, Fourth Series*. New York: Brentano's, 1923.

Includes a short life of Emma Goldman.

1228. Healy, Kathleen. *Frances Warde, American Foundress of the Sisters of Mercy*. New York: Seabury Press, 1973.

Life of an Irish nun.

1229. Heifetz, Julie. *Oral History and the Holocaust: A Collection of Poems from Interviews with Survivors of the Holocaust*. New York: Pergamon, 1985.

Women outnumber men in this oral history collection from St. Louis Holocaust survivors.

1230. Helen Louise, Sister. *Sister Julia (Susan McGroarty), Sister of Notre Dame de Namur*. New York: Benziger Brothers, 1928.

An Irish nun and educator.

1231. Henderson, Janet K. "Four Nineteenth-Century Professional Women." Unpublished Ed. D. Dissertation, Rutgers University, 1982. Order Number DA 8218323.

Includes the life of Elizabeth Blackwell, the English-born physician.

1232. Henney, Nella B. *Anne Sullivan Macy, The Story Behind Helen Keller*. Garden City, N.Y.: Doubleday, Doran & Co., 1933.

She was a second-generation Irish teacher of the blind.

1233. Henriksen, Louise L. *Anzia Yezierska, A Writer's Life*. New Brunswick and London: Rutgers University Press, 1988.

An account of the Polish Jewish writer's life by her daughter, based on memories and letters.

1234. Hepokoski, Carol. "Milma Lappala: Unitarian Minister and Humanist." Pp. 158-164 *Women Who Dared: The History of Finnish American Women*. Ed. Carl Ross and K. Marianne Wargelin Brown. St. Paul, Minnesota: Immigration History Research Center, 1986.

A Finnish religious leader.

1235. Hoehling, Mary. *Girl Soldier and Spy: Sarah Emma Edmonds*. New York: Messner, 1959.

A somewhat fictionalized account of the Canadian nurse and male impersonator.

1236. Holden, William C. *Teresita*. Owings Mill, Md.: Stemmer House, 1978.

The life of Teresa Urrea, a Mexican folk healer who attracted a popular following in the southwestern U.S.

1237. Hsu, Vivian. "Maxine Hong Kingston as Psycho-Autobiographer and Ethnographer." *International Journal of Women's Studies* 6 (November/December 1983): 429-442.

Relates Kingston's personal psychic development to common traits in first-generation Chinese.

1238. Hughes, Arthur J. and Frank P. LeVeness. "Congresswoman Geraldine A. Ferraro: An American Legacy." Pp. 35-52 *Women Leaders in Contemporary U.S. Politics*. Ed. Frank P. LeVeness and Jane P. Sweeney. Boulder, Co.: Lynne Rienner, 1987.

The second-generation Italian Congresswoman and vice-presidential candidate.

1239. International Committee for World Peace Prize Award. *Rosika Schwimmer, World Patriot, A Biographical Sketch*. New York: International Committee for World Peace Prize Award to Rosika Schwimmer, 1937.

Schwimmer was a Hungarian Jewish feminist and pacifist.

1240. Ireland, Joseph N. *Mrs. Duff*. Boston: J. R. Osgood, 1882.

An English-born actress.

1241. Ishill, Joseph. *Emma Goldman: A Challenging Rebel*. Transl. Herman Frank. Berkeley Heights, N.J.: Oriole Press, 1957.

The Russian Jewish radical and anarchist.

1242. James, Edward and Janet, eds. *Notable American Women*. 3 Vol. Cambridge, Mass.: Harvard University Press, 1971.

Short biographies of over 100 immigrant and second-generation women of many backgrounds and accomplishments.

1243. Jean, Sister Patricia. *Only One Heart: The Story of a Pioneer Nun in America*. New York: Doubleday, 1963.

An Irish nun's story.

1244. Jennings, Rosa S. "A Scrap of Americana." *Annals of Iowa* 3rd Series 29 (April 1948): 290-297.

The story of her Dutch parents' settlement in Iowa.

1245. Johnston, Malcolm S. *Elizabeth Blackwell and her Alma Mater: The Story in the Documents*. Geneva, N.Y.: Humphrey, 1947.

The education of the English-born physician.

1246. Jones, Kay F. "Ana Frohmiller: Watchdog of the Arizona Treasury". *Journal of Arizona History* 25 (Winter 1984): 349-368.

The first female state treasurer, a second-generation Irish woman.

1247. Kahn, Lisa. "American Women Who Write in German." *MELUS, The Journal of the Society for the Study of the Multi-Ethnic Literature of the United States* 5,4 (Winter 1978): 63-70.

Refers to the lives of Austrian and German women, many who migrated after 1930.

1248. Karabatsos, Lewis T. "Yvonne Hoar: Mill Worker, Union Organizer, Shop Steward." Pp. 125-40 *Surviving Hard Times: The Working People of Lowell*. Ed. Mary H. Blewett. Lowell, Mass.: Lowell Museum, 1982.

An oral history with a second-generation French-Canadian labor activist in Lowell, Mass.

1249. Karvonen, Hilda. "Three Proponents of Woman's Rights in the Finnish-American Labor Movement from 1910-1930: Selma Jokela McCone, Maiju Nurmi and Helmi Mattson." Pp. 123-135 *Women Who Dared: The History of Finnish American Women*. Ed. Carl Ross and K. Marianne Wargelin Brown. St. Paul, Minnesota: Immigration History Research Center, 1986.

The lives of feminists and labor activists.

1250. Katkov, Norman. *The Fabulous Fanny, The Story of Fanny Brice*. New York: S.S. Knopf, 1953.

A second-generation Austrian and Alsatian comedienne. The work contains some errors, but also material from her unpublished autobiography.

1251. Keller, Helen. *Teacher: Anne Sullivan Macy; A Tribute by the Foster-Child of her Mind*. Garden City, N.Y.: Doubleday, 1955.

A famous second-generation Irish teacher.

1252. Kelman, Harold. *Helping People: Karen Horney's Psychoanalytic Approach*. New York: Science House, 1971.

The life and thought of the German psychoanalyst.

1253. Keppel, Ruth. *Trees to Tulips; Authentic Tales of the Pioneers of Holland, Michigan.* Holland, Michigan: n.p., 1947.

Pioneer Dutch women, including the story of the author's family's arrival.

1254. Kessler-Harris, Alice. "Organizing the Unorganizable: Three Jewish Women and their Union." *Labor History* 17 (1976): 5-23.

The lives of Eastern European Jewish labor activists Fannia Cohn, Rose Schneiderman, and Rose Pesotta.

1255. Kessner, Thomas and Betty B. Caroli. *Today's Immigrants: Their Stories. A New Look at the Newest Americans.* New York: Oxford University Press, 1981.

Ample excerpts from oral histories with Peruvian, West Indian, Chinese, Irish, and Honduran women.

1256. Kikumura, Akemi. *Through Harsh Winters; The Life of a Japanese Immigrant Woman.* Novato, Cal.: Chandler & Sharp Publishers, 1981.

An excellent life history and discussion of the author's mother. Important themes are the woman's relations to her husband and children.

1257. Klein, Gerda W. *A Passion for Sharing, the Life of Edith Rosenwald Stern.* Chappaqua, N.Y.: Rossel Books, 1984.

A second-generation German Jewish woman who was a community activist and philanthropist.

1258. Klein, Herman. *The Reign of Patti.* New York: The Century Co., 1920.

An operatic soprano, born in Spain of Italian parents.

1259. Kodama-Nishimotot, Michi et al., ed. *Hanahana: An Oral History Anthology of Hawaii's Working People.* Honolulu: Ethnic Studies Oral History Project, University of Hawaii at Manoa, 1984.

Oral histories with immigrant and second-generation Filipino, Chinese, and Japanese women.

1260. Kohler, Mary H. *Life and Work of Mother Benedicta Bauer.* Milwaukee: Bruce Publishing Co., 1937.

She was the Dutch foundress of the Dominican sisters in Racine, Wisconsin.

1261. Kramer, Sydelle and Jenny Masur, eds. *Jewish Grandmothers.* Boston: Beacon Press, 1976.

Oral histories with ten Russian Jewish women.

1262. Kranitz-Sanders, Lillian. **Twelve Who Survived: An Oral History of the Jews of Lodz, Poland, 1930-1954.** New York: Irvington Publishers, 1984.

Half are with women; one section describes the decision to go to America or Israel and the adjustment in U.S., but the main focus is on homeland experiences.

1263. Kransdorf, Martha. "Julia Richman's Years in the New York City Public Schools: 1872-1912." Unpublished Ph.D. Dissertation, University of Michigan, 1979. Order Number 7926461.

This second-generation German Jewish teacher was an educator who pioneered new school programs for handicapped students and the children of immigrants. The study tells of her frequent clashes with the Eastern European Jewish community on the Lower East Side.

1264. Lagemann, Ellen. **A Generation of Women: Education in the Lives of Progressive Reformers.** Cambridge, Mass.: Harvard University Press, 1979.

Information on the family background and education of the second-generation German Jewish Lillian Wald and Russian Jewish Rose Cohen.

1265. LaGumina, Salvatore. **The Immigrants Speak; Italian Americans Tell Their Story.** New York: Center for Migration Studies, 1979.

Of 13 oral histories, five are with women, including a miner's wife, an Italian Welfare League activist, and a second-generation school teacher.

1266. Landau, Penny M. "The Career of Mary Ann Duff, The American Dissons, 1810-1839." Unpublished Ph.D. Dissertation, Bowling Green State University, 1979. Order Number 7926461.

An English-born actress.

1267. Landau, Saul and Paul Jacobs. **To Serve the Devil.** New York: Vintage Books, 1971.

See especially volume 2, "Story of Wong Ah So: Prostitute."

1268. Lang, Barbara. **The Process of Immigration in German-American Literature from 1850-1900.** American Studies, A Monograph Series. Vol. 64. Munich: Fink Verlag, 1988.

Includes information on German immigrant women writers.

1269. Larsen, Karen. **Ingeborg Astrup Larsen: Her Family and Her Girlhood in Norway.** Northfield, Minn.: Norwegian-American Historical Association, 1958.

The life of the author's mother.

1270. Lauw, Louisa. *Fourteen Years with Adelina Patti; Reminiscences of Louisa Lauw.* Transl. Jeremiah Loder. New York: N.L. Munro, 1884.

An opera singer born in Spain of Italian parents.

1271. Leahy, J. Kenneth. *As the Eagle; The Spiritual Writings of Mother Butler.* New York: P.J. Kenedy, 1954.

Includes the biography of the Irish-born nun and founder of Marymount schools and colleges.

1272. Lebeson, Anita L. *Recall to Life--The Jewish Woman in America.* South Brunswick: Thomas Yoseloff, 1970.

Includes biographical material on some prominent women like Mary Antin, Ernestine Rose, Rebekah Kohut, Henrietta Szold, Rosa Sonneschein, Hannah Solomon, and others.

1273. Leeder, Elaine J. "The Gentle Warrior: Rose Pesotta, Anarchist and Labor Organizer." Unpublished Ph.D. Dissertation, Cornell University, 1985. Order Number DA 8516940.

Russian-born Jewish labor activist in the International Ladies Garment Workers' Union.

1274. Lenk, Edward A. "Mother Marianne Cope (1838-1918): The Syracuse Franciscan Community and Molokai Lepers." Unpublished Ph.D. Dissertation, Syracuse University, 1986. Order Number DA 8716935.

This German woman and her sisterhood worked primarily in Hawaii.

1275. Levin, Alexandra L. "Henrietta Szold and the Russian Immigrant School," *Maryland History Magazine* 57 (March 1962): 1-15.

Second-generation Hungarian Jewish community activist and Zionist; describes her efforts for education of recently arrived Russian immigrants.

1276. Levin, Alexandra L. *The Szolds of Lombard Street: A Baltimore Family, 1850-1909.* Philadelphia: Jewish Publication Society of America, 1960.

Background on Henrietta Szold, the second-generation Hungarian Jewish community activist, foundress of Hadassah.

1277. Levinger, Elma E. *Fighting Angel: The Story of Henrietta Szold.* New York: Behrman House, 1946.

Hungarian Jewish Zionist and community activist, foundress of Hadassah.

1278. Lewandowski, Monica A. "A Credible Candidate: The Campaign Oratory of Geraldine A. Ferraro." Unpublished Ph.D. Dissertation, Indiana University, 1987. Order Number DA 8717804.

The second-generation Italian Congresswoman portrayed herself as an assertive but traditional woman.

1279. Lewis, Oscar. Lola Montez: The Mid-Victorian Bad Girl in California. San Francisco: The Colt Press, 1938.

An Irish-born adventuress.

1280. Lindborg, Kristina and Carlos J. Ovando. Five Mexican-American Women in Transition: A Case Study of Migrants in the Midwest. San Francisco: L R & E Associates, 1977.

Includes oral histories with women who grew up in Mexico; all were part of migrant labor families; much information on family roles and identities.

1281. Lindewall, Arvo. Rosalia. Yonkers: National Sponsoring Committee, 1942.

Finnish labor activist Rosa Lemberg.

1282. Ling, Amy. "Edith Eaton: Pioneer Chinamerican Writer and Feminist." American Literary Realism, 1870-1910 16 (August 1983): 287-298.

She was English-born of an English father and a Chinese mother; her younger sister (Winifred) took a Japanese pen name to write.

1283. Ling, Amy. "Writer in the Hyphenated Condition: Diana Chang." MELUS 7 (Winter 1980): 69-83.

Although the article focuses mainly on her fiction, it also includes some biography of this bicultural writer: she was born in U.S. of a Chinese father and Eurasian mother, but raised in China.

1284. Linkugel, Wilmer and Kim Giffin. "The Distinguished War Service of Dr. Anna Howard Shaw." Pennsylvania History 28 (October 1961): 372-385.

The English feminist and minister.

1285. Lippard, Lucy R. Eva Hesse. New York: New York University Press, 1976.

A German Jewish sculptress; includes excerpts from her diaries.

1286. Litwin-Grinberg, Ruth R. "Lives in Retrospect: A Qualitative Analysis of Oral Reminiscence as Applied to Elderly Jewish Women." Unpublished D.S.W. Dissertation, University of California, Berkeley, 1982.

Eight women were interviewed, all born Jewish in Eastern Europe. Each identified a "point of conversion" in her life.

1287. Llanes, José. Cuban Americans: Masters of Survival. Cambridge, Mass.: Abt Books, 1982.

Based on interviews with Cubans, about one-third with women.

1288. Logan, Herschel C. Buckskin and Satin. Harrisburg, Pa.: Stackpole Co., 1954.

The life of Giuseppina Morlacchi, the Italian dancer.

1289. Logan, Lorna. Ventures in Mission: The Cameron House Story. Wilson Creek, Wash.: Crawford Hobby Print Shop, 1976.

Explores Donaldina Cameron's "rescue" work with Chinese prostitutes; she was born in New Zealand of Scottish parents.

1290. Loggins, Vernon. Two Romantics and Their Ideal Life. New York: Odyssey, 1946.

Some biographical material on Elisabet Ney, the German sculptress.

1291. Long, Priscilla. Mother Jones, Woman Organizer. Cambridge, Mass.: Red Sun Press, 1976.

The famous Irish radical and labor agitator.

1292. Lorit, Sergio C. Frances Cabrini. New York: New York City Press, 1970.

An Italian nun and missionary.

1293. Lowenthal, Marvin. Henrietta Szold: Life and Letters. New York: Viking Press, 1942.

The second-generation Hungarian Jewish community activist who founded Hadassah.

1294. Lynch, Alice C. The Kennedy Clan and Tierra Redonda. San Francisco: Marnell & Co., 1935.

Includes the story of Kate Kennedy, an Irish teacher and reformer in San Francisco.

1295. Madison, Charles A. "Emma Goldman: Biographical Sketch." <u>Critics and Crusaders</u>. New York: Fredrick Ungar Publishing Co., 1947.

A short account of the life of the Russian Jewish radical and anarchist.

1296. Malak, Henry M. <u>Theresa of Chicago</u>. Trans. Ann K. Dudzik. Lemont, Ill.: League of the Servant of God Mother Mary Theresa, 1975.

The life of Polish Mary Theresa Dudzik, who founded the Franciscan sisters of Chicago in 1894.

1297. Marie Therese, Sister. <u>Cornelia Connelly</u>. Westminster, Md.: Newman Press, 1961.

An English nun who founded the Society of the Holy Child Jesus in England and in Pennsylvania.

1298. Marinacci, Barbara. <u>They Came from Italy</u>. New York: Dodd, Mead, 1967.

Includes information on Francesca Cabrini, Italian missionary.

1299. Marsh, Margaret. <u>Anarchist Women, 1870-1920</u>. Philadelphia: Temple University Press, 1981.

Includes the lives of English-born Helena Born and Russian Jewish Marie Ganz and Mollie Steiner.

1300. Martin, Mildred C. <u>Chinatown's Angry Angel: The Story of Donaldina Cameron</u>. Palo Alto, Cal.: Pacific Books, 1977.

New Zealand-born (of Scottish parents), she became a missionary worker with Chinese prostitutes.

1301. Martindale, Cyril C. <u>Life of Mother Francesca Saverio Cabrini, Foundress of the Missionary Sisters of the Sacred Heart</u>. London: Burns, Oates, and Washburne, 1931.

An Italian nun.

1302. Mathias, Elizabeth and Richard Raspa. <u>Italian Folktales in America; The Verbal Art of an Immigrant Woman</u>. Foreword by Roger D. Abrahams. Detroit: Wayne State University Press, 1985.

The life of a storyteller and a collection of her tales, written 44 years earlier by her daughter.

1303. Mavity, Nancy B. <u>Sister Aimee</u>. Garden City, N.Y.: Doubleday, Doran & Co., 1931.

A partial life of the Canadian evangelist Aimee Semple McPherson.

1304. Maynard, Theodore. The Better Part: The Life of Teresa Demjanovich. New York: Macmillan, 1952.

A second-generation Ruthenian Sister of Charity in New Jersey.

1305. Maynard, Theodore. Too Small a World: The Life of Francesca Cabrini. Milwaukee: The Bruce Publishing Co., 1945.

The Italian nun and missionary.

1306. McArdle, Sister Mary A. California's Pioneer Sister of Mercy: Mother Mary Baptist Russell, 1829-1898. Fresno: Academy Library Guild, 1954.

An Irish-born nun.

1307. McCrosson, Mary. The Bell and the River. Palo Alto, Calif: Pacific Books, 1956.

The story of Mother Joseph Pariseau, French foundress of the Sisters of Providence in the West.

1308. McCunn, Ruthanne L. Chinese American Portraits: Personal Histories 1828-1988. San Francisco: Chronicle Books, 1988.

Includes lives of Chinese women from several immigrant generations.

1309. McCunn, Ruthanne L. Thousand Pieces of Gold: A Biographical Novel. San Francisco: Design Enterprises of San Francisco, 1981.

The story of Lalu Nathoy (Polly Bemis), a Chinese slave, prostitute, and pioneer.

1310. McDonald, Dorothy R. and Katherine Newman. "Relocation and Dislocation: The Writings of Hisaye Yamamoto and Wakako Yamauchi." MELUS 7 (Fall 1980): 21-38.

Includes biographies of two second-generation Japanese women who wrote about internment.

1311. McDonald, Lucile. "Mother Joseph." Pp. 120-129 The Women Who Made the West. Ed. The Western Writers of America. Garden City, N.Y.: Doubleday, 1980.

This French-Canadian woman ran parochial schools in Tacoma, Washington.

1312. McFarland, C.K. "Crusade for Child Laborers: 'Mother' Jones and the March of the Mill Children." Pennsylvania History 38 (1971): 283-296.

Describes the Irish labor activist's march with Philadelphia factory children to publicize the evils of child labor.

1313. McGovern, James R.   "Anna Howard Shaw: New Approaches to Feminism."   Journal of Social History 3 (Winter 1969): 135-53.

Focuses on the English-born feminist's "emotional problems," which led to achievement and dedication to her cause.

1314. McLoughlin, William G.   "Aimee Semple McPherson: 'Your Sister in the King's Glad Service.'"   Journal of Popular Culture 1 (Winter 1967): 193-217.

The popular evangelist was born in Canada.

1315. Merriam, Eve, ed.   Growing Up Female in America, Ten Lives.   Garden City, N.Y.: Doubleday, 1971.

Includes chapters on the English feminist Dr. Anna Howard Shaw, Irish "Mother" Mary Jones, and second-generation German Jewish Elizabeth Gertrude Stern.

1316. Michelet, Maren.   Glimpses from Agnes Mathilde Wergeland's Life.   Minneapolis: Folkebladet Publishing, 1916.

A Norwegian.

1317. Milinowski, Marta.   Teresa Carreño, "By the Grace of God".   New Haven: Yale University Press, 1940.

A Venezuelan concert pianist.

1318. Miller, Sally M.   "From Sweatshop Worker to Labor Leader: Theresa Malkiel, a Case Study."   American Jewish History 68 (1978): 189-205.

An Eastern European Jewish labor activist.

1319. Miller, Sally M.   "Other Socialists; Native-Born and Immigrant Women in the Socialist Party of America, 1901-1917."   Labor History 24 (1983): 84-102.

Includes biographical materials on Theresa Malkiel, Meta Lilienthal, and Antoinette Konikow.

1320. Miller, Sally M. and Mary Wedegartner, eds.   "Experiences of Immigrant Women: We Also Built Stockton."   Pacific Historian: A Quarterly of Western History and Ideas 26 (Summer 1982): 1-65.

Reports on an oral history project with 60 women of many backgrounds, ages, and times of arrival.

1321. Molek, Mary.   Immigrant Woman.   Dover, Delaware: M. Molek, 1976.

A fictionalized account of her Slovenian mother's life.

198   IMMIGRANT WOMEN IN THE U.S.

1322. More, Hermon, et al. **Juliana Force and American Art**. New York: Whitney Museum of American Art, 1949.

This second-generation German was an art museum director.

1323. Morrison, Joan and Charlotte F. Zabusky. **American Mosaic; The Immigrant Experience in the Words of Those Who Lived It**. New York: E.P. Dutton, 1980.

Short oral histories and lives of immigrants from many backgrounds; of 138, fifty-three are with women.

1324. Namias, June. **First Generation: In the Words of Twentieth-Century American Immigrants**. Boston: Beacon Press, 1978.

Short oral histories with Jewish, Irish, Italian, Armenian, Japanese, Greek, Mexican, Guatemalan, Trinidadian, French, and Vietnamese women.

1325. National American Women's Suffrage Association. **Anna Howard Shaw; A Memorial**. New York: National Woman Suffrage Publishing Co., 1919.

The life of the English-born suffragist and minister.

1326. National Council of Jewish Women, Pittsburgh Section. **By Myself, I'm a Book! An Oral History of the Immigrant Jewish Experience in Pittsburgh**. Waltham, Mass.: American Jewish Historical Society, 1972.

1327. Nicoll, Bruce H. "Mari Sandoz, Nebraska Loner." **The American West** 2 (Spring 1965): 32-36.

The second-generation German and Swiss author of **Old Jule** and other novels.

1328. Nies, Judith. **Seven Women: Portraits from the American Radical Tradition**. New York: Viking Press, 1977.

Includes material on Mother Jones, the Irish labor agitator.

1329. Niethammer, Carolyn. "The Lure of Gold." Pp. 71-87 **The Women Who Made the West**. Ed. The Western Writers of America. Garden City, N.Y.: Doubleday, 1980.

The life of Nellie Cashman, an Irish gold-rush adventuress in Arizona and Alaska, who ran boarding houses and restaurants for miners.

1330. Nomura, Gail M. "Tsugiki, a Grafting: A History of a Japanese Pioneer Woman in Washington State." **Women's Studies Journal** 14 (1987).

1331. North, Nancy. "Sharing Good Times and Bad." Pp. 7-13 in Conversations with the Recent Past: Northeast Iowa Oral History Project. Ed. Luis Torres. Decorah, Iowa: Luther College Press, 1975.

Includes an oral history with a second-generation Norwegian farm woman.

1332. Norton, Minerva B. A True Teacher: Mary Mortimer, Memoir. New York: Fleming H. Revell Co., 1894.

An English teacher and founder of a girls' school.

1333. Nugent, Helen L. Sister Julia. New York: Benziger Brothers, 1928.

The life of Irish nun, Julia McGroarty.

1334. Nugent, Helen L. Sister Louise, American Foundress. New York: Benziger Brothers, 1931.

The life of Louise Van der Schrieck, a Belgian nun who brought the Sisters of Notre Dame de Namur to the U.S.

1335. O'Donovan-Rossa, Margaret. My Father and Mother were Irish. New York: Devin-Adair, 1939.

Life in a Fenian family, from a daughter's memories of her childhood.

1336. O'Farrell, M. Brigid and Lydia Kleiner. "Anna Sullivan, Trade Union Organizer." Frontiers 2 (1977): 29-36.

An Irish labor activist.

1337. O'Higgins, Patrick. Madame; An Intimate Biography of Helena Rubinstein. New York: Viking Press, 1971.

The Polish entrepreneur in the beauty industry.

1338. Owen, Harry G. An Outline of the Career of Mme. Marcella Sembrich. New York: Sembrich Memorial Association, 1945.

She was a Polish opera singer.

1339. Owens, Sister M. Lilliana. Loretto in Missouri. St. Louis: B. Herder, 1965.

The life of Irish nun and missionary, Mother Mary Bridget Hayden.

1340. Palmer, Phyllis M. "Frances Wright D'Arusmont: Case Study of a Reformer." Unpublished Ph.D. Dissertation, Ohio State University, 1973. Order Number 73-26,887.

Attention to the Scottish writer's years as a social reformer in the U.S.

1341. Papanikolas, Helen. *Emily--George*. Salt Lake City: University of Utah Press, 1987.

The lives of the author's Greek mother and father.

1342. Payne, Elizabeth. *Reform, Labor and Feminism; Margaret Dreier Robins and the Women's Trade Union League*. Urbana and Chicago: University of Illinois Press, 1988.

Life and times of Robins, a second-generation German labor activist; includes biographical material on other foreign-born women active in the Women's Trade Union League.

1343. Peragallo, Olga. *Italian-American Authors and Their Contributions to American Literature*. New York: S.F. Vanni, 1949.

Includes biographies of ten immigrant and second-generation women writers, some not well-known.

1344. Perkins, Alice J.G. and Theresa Wolfson. *Frances Wright, Free Enquirer, The Study of a Temperament*. Philadelphia: Porcupine Press, 1972; orig. publ. 1939.

The Scottish radical and writer.

1345. Perry, Elisabeth I. *Belle Moskowitz, Feminine Politics and the Exercise of Power in the Age of Alfred E. Smith*. New York: Oxford University Press, 1987.

A second-generation Eastern European Jewish political activist in the Democratic Party.

1346. Philipson, Ilene. *Ethel Rosenberg; Beyond the Myths*. New York: Franklin Watts, 1988.

The second-generation Eastern European Jew, accused and convicted of espionage.

1347. Poirier, Suzanne. "Emma Goldman, Ben Reitman, and Reitman's Wives: A Study in Relationships." *Women's Studies* 24 (Feb. 1988): 277-97.

The Russian Jewish anarchist and her lover.

1348. Pollack, Barbara. *The Collectors: Dr. Claribel and Miss Etta Cone*. Indianapolis: Bobbs-Merrill, 1962.

Two second-generation German Jewish sisters who both became art collectors of note.

1349. Pope-Hennessey, Una. *Three English Women in America*. London: E. Benn, 1929.

Includes the story of actress Fanny Kemble.

1350. Porter, Jack N. "Rosa Sonnenschein [sic] and The American Jewess: First Independent English Language Jewish Women's Journal in the United States." American Jewish History 68 (September 1978): 57-63.

A second-generation German Jewish activist who helped found the National Council of Jewish Women.

1351. Porter, Jack N. "Rosa Sonneschein and The American Jewess Revisited: New Historical Information on an Early American Zionist and Jewish Feminist." American Jewish Archives 32 (November 1980): 125-131.

Corrects early errors about the life of the second-generation German Jewish community activist in the National Council of Jewish women; includes reminiscence by a relative.

1352. Putnam, Frank B. "Teresa Urrea, 'The Saint of Cabara.'" Southern California Quarterly 45 (September 1963).

A Mexican folk healer with a strong following in the U.S. Southwest.

1353. Quinn, Susan. A Mind of Her Own, The Life of Karen Horney. New York: Summit Books, 1987.

A German psychoanalyst.

1354. Rabinovitz, Lauren H. "Radical Cinema: The Films and Film Practices of Maya Deren, Shirley Clarke and Joyce Wieland." Unpublished Ph.D. Dissertation, University of Texas at Austin, 1982. Order Number DA 8309189.

Maya Deren was a Russian-born filmmaker.

1355. Rabinowitz, Dorothy. New Lives: Survivors of the Holocaust Living in America. New York: Alfred A. Knopf, 1976.

Based on 108 interviews, many of them with women.

1356. Raider, Roberta A. "A Descriptive Study of the Acting of Marie Dressler." Unpublished Ph.D. Dissertation, University of Michigan, 1970. Order Number 71-15,276.

She was a Canadian-born comedienne.

1357. Ramos, Luis A. Angela de Hoyos: A Critical Look. Albuquerque: Pajaritos Publications, 1979.

Life and writings of a Mexican-born poetess.

1358. Rasmussen, Janet E.   "'The Best Place on Earth for Women': The American Experience of Aasta Hansteen." Norwegian-American Studies 31 (1986): 245-268.

A feminist, painter, and writer, Hansteen returned to Norway when language difficulties prevented her from participating as she wished in U.S.

1359. Reaver, J. Russell.   "Lithuanian Tales from Illinois." Southern Folklore Quarterly 12 (December 1948): 259-265 and 14 (September 1950): 160-168.

Life of a woman storyteller and her tales.

1360. Reichert, William O. Partisans of Freedom: A Study in American Anarchism. Bowling Green: Bowling Green University Popular Press, 1976.

Includes a chapter on the Russian Jewish anarchist Emma Goldman.

1361. Reifert, Gail and Eugene M. Dermody. Women Who Fought: An American History. Norwalk, Cal.: Cerritos College, 1978.

Includes a chapter on the Russian Jewish anarchist Emma Goldman, and brief notes on Irish labor activist Mother Jones.

1362. Reznick, Allen E.   "Lillian D. Wald: The Years at Henry Street." Unpublished Ph.D. Dissertation, University of Wisconsin, 1973. Order Number 74-9199.

A second-generation German Jewish nurse and settlement-house foundress.

1363. Richardson, James B. Mrs. James R. Vincent: A Memorial Address Delivered at a Meeting of the Managers of the Vincent Memorial Hospital. Cambridge, Mass.: The Riverside Press, 1911.

Life of an English actress.

1364. Ritter, Ellen.   "Elizabeth Morgan: Pioneer Female Labor Agitator." Central States Speech Journal 21 (1971): 242-251.

English labor activist in Chicago.

1365. Roberts, Carl E. The Mysterious Madame: Helena Petrovna Blavatsky; the Life & Work of the Founder of the Theosophical Society. New York: Brewer and Warren, 1931.

Russian mystic and foundress of Theosophy.

1366. Robins, Margaret D. *Margaret Dreier Robins: Her Life, Letters, and Work.* Ed. Mary E. Dreier. New York: Island Press Cooperative, 1950.

A second-generation German trade unionist, reformer, and feminist.

1367. Rodriguez, Richard and Gloria C. Rodriguez. "Teresa Urrea: Her Life as it Affected the Mexican-U.S. Frontier." *El Grito: Journal of Contemporary Mexican American Thought* 5 (Summer 1972): 48-68.

A folk healer born in Mexico but exiled to the U.S. in 1892.

1368. Rosicky, Rose, comp. *A History of Czechs (Bohemians) in Nebraska.* Omaha: Czech Historical Society of Nebraska, 1929.

Includes brief biographies of early Nebraska settlers, including women, and information on several women's religious and community groups.

1369. Ross, Ishbel. *Child of Destiny; The Life Story of the First Woman Doctor.* London: V. Gollancz, 1950.

English-born doctor Elizabeth Blackwell.

1370. Rothchild, Sylvia. *A Special Legacy: An Oral History of Soviet Jewish Emigrés in the United States.* New York: Simon and Schuster, 1985.

Based on 176 interviews made for the William E. Wiener Library of American Jewish Committee. Although no breakdown is given, women's experiences are well represented; much attention to homeland.

1371. Rothluebber, Francis B. *He Sent Two.* Milwaukee: Bruce Publishing, 1965.

The lives of two German foundresses of the School Sisters of Saint Francis in Milwaukee, Wisconsin.

1372. Rourke, Constance. *Troupers of the Gold Coast, or the Rise of Lotta Crabtree.* New York: Harcourt, Brace and Co., 1928.

A second-generation English actress.

1373. Rubinstein, Charlotte S. *American Women Artists: From Early Indian Times to the Present.* Boston: G.K. Hall, 1982.

Includes a short account of the life of Elisabet Ney, German sculptress.

1374. Rushmore, Robert. *Fanny Kemble.* New York: Crowell-Collier Press, 1970.

An English actress.

1375. Russell, Charles E. *Julia Marlow, Her Life and Art*. New York: Appleton, 1927.

An English actress.

1376. Russell, Matthew, S.J. *The Life of Mother Mary Baptist Russell, Sister of Mercy*. New York: The Apostleship of Prayer, 1901.

An Irish nun.

1377. Saarinen, Aline. *The Proud Possessors, The Lives, Times and Tastes of Some Adventurous American Art Collectors*. New York: Random House, 1958.

Includes a chapter on Katherine Robins, a second-generation German art patron and artist.

1378. Sahli, Nancy A. "Elizabeth Blackwell M.D. (1821-1910): A Biography." Unpublished Ph.D. Dissertation, University of Pennsylvania, 1974. Order Number 75-2774.

Born in England, the first woman physician eventually returned to her homeland.

1379. Salcido, Ramos M. "Undocumented Aliens: A Study of Mexican Families." *Social Work* 24 (July 1979): 306-311.

Includes excerpts from the personal histories of several undocumented women immigrants.

1380. Salvaneschi, Lenore. "Die Frau Pastor: The Life of a Missouri Synod Lutheran Pastor's Wife in the First Half of the Twentieth Century." *Palimpset* 67 (1986): 53-68.

1381. Sánchez, Marta E. *Contemporary Chicana Poetry; A Critical Approach to an Emerging Literature*. Berkeley: University of California Press, 1985.

Includes some notes on the lives of three Mexican and second-generation poets: Alma Villanueva, Lorna Dee Cervantes, and Lucha Corpi.

1382. Schappes, Morris U. "Three Women." *Jewish Currents* 29 (1975): 5-7.

Brief lives of the Polish Jewish feminist Ernestine Rose and the Russian Jewish labor activist Clara Lemlich.

1383. Scharman, Ralph. "Elizabeth Morgan, Crusader for Labor Reform". *Labor History* 14 (Summer 1973): 340-351.

An English labor activist.

1384. Scheier, Paula. "Clara Lemlich Shavelson." *Jewish Life* 8 (1954): 4-11.

An Eastern European Jewish labor activist, famous for her participation in New York's 1909 garment workers' strike.

1385. Schoen, Carol B. "Anzia Yezierska: New Light on the 'Sweatshop Cinderella.'" MELUS 7 (Fall 1980): 3-11.

Yezierska's biography is confused, and the writer cultivated uncertainty about her life. Much of her fiction is autobiographical in important elements.

1386. Schoen, Carol B. Anzia Yezierska. Boston: Twayne Publishers, 1982.

Although the focus is on her written work, the book includes notes on the life of the Polish Jewish writer.

1387. Schofield, Ann. "Mother Jones in Kansas: An Archival Note." Labor History 27 (1986): 431-42.

Some notes on the Irish labor agitator, and the text of a talk she gave to miners after the Ludlow massacre.

1388. Scholten, Pat C. "Militant Women for Economic Justice: The Persuasion of Mary Harris Jones, Ella Reeve Bloor, Rose Pastor Stokes, Rose Schneiderman, and Elizabeth Gurley Flynn." Unpublished Ph.D. Dissertation, Indiana University, 1979. Order Number 7916904.

Focus is on the rhetoric of these labor activists and charismatic leaders.

1389. Scholten, Pat C. "The Old Mother and Her Army: The Agitative Strategies of Mary Harris Jones." West Virginia History 40 (1979): 365-374.

The Irish labor activist's work among West Virginia miners.

1390. Scott, Alma. Wanda Gág: The Story of an Artist. Minneapolis: University of Minnesota Press, 1949.

A second-generation Czech artist and writer of children's books.

1391. Seaver, James E. Deh-he-wa-mis: or, A Narrative of the Life of Mrs. Mary Jemison. Batavia, N.Y.: W. Seaver and Son, 1842, orig. publ. 1824.

A popular account of a Canadian woman's Indian captivity; it appeared in over thirty editions.

1392. Seifer, Nancy. Nobody Speaks for Me: Self-Portraits of American Working Class Women. New York: Simon and Schuster, 1976.

Oral histories with activists, includes one with a second-generation Italian and one with a second-generation French woman.

1393. Selavan, Ida C. "Bobba Hannah, Midwife." American Journal of Nursing 73 (April 1973): 681-683.

The life and work of a Lithuanian Jewish midwife in Pittsburgh, Hannah Sandusky.

1394. Seller, Maxine. "Beyond the Stereotype: A New Look at the Immigrant Woman, 1880-1924." Journal of Ethnic Studies 3 (Spring 1975): 59-70.

The lives of nontraditional women, including Rose Pesotta, Jewish labor activist; Josephine Humjpel Zemen, Czech journalist; Antonietta Pisanelli Alessandro, Italian theater founder.

1395. Sharkey, Mary A. The New Jersey Sisters of Charity. New York: Longmans, 1933.

Vols. 1-2 summarize the lives of immigrant generations, mainly Irish women like Mary Xavier Mehegan who founded the community.

1396. Shulman, Alix K. "Emma Goldman: Anarchist Queen." Pp. 218-228 Feminist Theorists, Three Centuries of Key Women Thinkers. Ed. Dale Spender. New York Pantheon Books, 1983.

The Russian Jewish radical and anarchist.

1397. Shulman, Alix K. "Emma Goldman--Feminist and Anarchist." Women: A Journal of Liberation 1 (1970): 21-24.

Russian Jewish radical did not think of herself as feminist, but many modern feminists consider her one.

1398. Shulman, Alix K. To The Barricades: The Anarchist Life of Emma Goldman. Lexington, Mass.: D.C. Heath, 1970.

This life of the Russian Jewish radical emphasizes the liberated life she led.

1399. Sicherman, Barbara, et al. Notable American Women, The Modern Period. Cambridge and London: The Belknap Press of Harvard University Press, 1980.

Brief biographies of many immigrant and second-generation workers and activists in a wide variety of fields.

1400. Sickels, Eleanor M. Twelve Daughters of Democracy; True Stories of American Women, 1865-1930. New York: Viking Press, 1942.

Includes short lives of Mother Mary Jones, Mary Dahl (a Norwegian woman who settled on the Great Plains), and Sophie Irene Loeb, a Russian Jewish woman in Chicago.

1401. Sidel, Ruth. *Urban Survival; The World of Working-Class Women*. Boston: Beacon Press, 1978.

Notes on the lives of Latin-American community activists, as well as second-generation Italian, Irish, and Jewish women involved in grass-roots and neighborhood reform efforts.

1402. Silverman, Ely. "Margaret Webster's Theory and Practice of Shakespearean Production in the United States, 1937-1953." Unpublished Ph.D. Dissertation, New York University, 1969. Order Number DA 70-15,984.

She was an English stage director.

1403. Simkhovitch, Mary K. and Elizabeth Ogg. *Quicksand, the Way of Life in the Slums*. Evanston, Ill.: Row, Peterson, 1942.

Includes a case history of an Italian family in the 1930s, which contains good portraits of the wife and the daughter.

1404. Singer, Joy D. *My Mother, the Doctor*. New York: Dutton, 1970.

The life of the author's Russian mother.

1405. Sisters of Reparation of the Congregation of Mary. *Blessed Are the Merciful: The Life of Mother Mary Zita, 1844-1917*. New York: n.p., 1953.

An Irish nun.

1406. Solberg, S.E. "Sui Sin Far/Edith Eaton: First Chinese-American Fictionist." *MELUS* 8 (Spring 1981): 27-38.

This writer had a Chinese mother and an English father, and also lived and worked part of her life in Canada.

1407. Solomon, Martha. *Emma Goldman*. Boston: Twayne, G.K. Hall and Co., 1987.

Notes on the life of the Russian anarchist, along with a good bibliography and analysis of her writings.

1408. Sothern, E.H. *Julia Marlowe's Story*. Ed. Fairfax Downey. New York: Rinehart, 1954.

An English actress.

1409. Spencer, Ralph W. "Dr. Anna Howard Shaw: The Evangelical Feminist." Unpublished Ph.D. Dissertation, Boston University, 1972. Order Number DA 72-25,334.

This English-born minister was also an important leader of the suffrage movement.

1410. Stauffer, Helen W. *Mari Sandoz*. Boise, Idaho: Boise State University, 1984.

The life of the second-generation German and Swiss writer.

1411. Stauffer, Helen W. *Mari Sandoz; Story Catcher of the Plains*. Lincoln: University of Nebraska Press, 1982.

The second-generation Swiss and German author of novels about prairie life.

1412. Steel, Edward M. "Mother Jones in the Fairmont Field, 1901." *Journal of American History* 57 (1970): 290-307.

Describes an organizing trip the Irish labor agitator made to work with miners.

1413. Steel, Edward M., ed. *The Speeches and Writings of Mother Jones*. Pittsburgh: University of Pittsburgh Press, 1988.

The introduction summarizes the life and times of the Irish labor activist.

1414. Steiner, Dale R. *Of Thee We Sing: Immigrants and American History*. San Diego: Harcourt Brace Jovanovich, Publishers, 1987.

Chapters tell the lives of Gro Svendsen (Norwegian), Emma Goldman (Russian Jew) and Jamie Nguyen (Vietnamese).

1415. Steiner, Ruth. "The 'Girls' in Chicago." *American Jewish Archives* 26 (April 1974): 5-22.

A memoir that focuses on the lives of her father's aunts, two Bohemian Jewish immigrants who became a social worker and a nurse.

1416. Steinitz, Lucy Y. and David M. Szony. *Living after the Holocaust*. New York: Bloch, 1977.

Includes reminiscences and poetry by survivors, plus some scholarly articles on psychological issues.

1417. Stern, Peter and Jean Yarbrough. "Hannah Arendt." *American Scholar* 47 (Summer 1978): 371-381.

A reminiscence by former students of the German philosopher and political theorist focusing on her as a teacher.

1418. Stoll, Joseph. *The Lord is My Shepherd: The Life of Elizabeth Kemp Stutzman*. Aylmer, Ont.: Pathway, 1965.

A German-American church activist.

1419. Stone, William L. <u>Maria Monk and the Nunnery of the Hotel Dieu</u>. New York: Howe & Bates, 1836.

This Canadian woman purportedly authored the most popular anti-Catholic tract of her era.

1420. Stromvall, Phyllis. "The Family History of Sophie and Theresa." Pp. 149-169 <u>Surviving Hard Times: The Working People of Lowell</u>. Ed. Mary H. Blewett. Lowell, Mass.: Lowell Museum, 1982.

Oral histories with a Polish woman and her second-generation Italian daughter-in-law in Lowell.

1421. Stuecher, Dorothea D. "Double Jeopardy: Nineteenth Century German American Women Writers." Unpublished Ph.D. Dissertation, University of Minnesota, 1981. Order Number DA 8206427.

The lives and writings of Therese Robinson, Mathilde Franziska Anneke, and Kathinka Sutro-Schücking.

1422. Suhl, Yuri. <u>Ernestine Rose and the Battle for Human Rights</u>. New York: Reynal & Hitchcock, 1959.

An early Polish Jewish feminist.

1423. Sullivan, Mary L. "Mother Cabrini: Missionary to Italian Immigrants." <u>U.S. Catholic Historian</u> 6 (Fall 1987): 265-279.

The Italian nun and her mission work.

1424. Surawicz, Frida G. "The Woman Foreign Medical Graduate Psychiatrist." <u>Psychiatric Annals</u> 7 (April 1977): 184-189.

Includes four case studies.

1425. Swift, Fletcher H. <u>Emma Marwedel, 1818-1893. Pioneer of the Kindergarten in California</u>. Berkeley: University of California Press, 1931.

A German pioneer in kindergarten teaching.

1426. Symonds, John. <u>Blavatsky, Medium and Magician</u>. London: Odham's Press, 1959.

The Russian spiritualist who founded Theosophy.

1427. Tabor, Margaret E. <u>Elizabeth Blackwell; the First Medical Woman</u>. London: Sheldon Press, 1925.

The English physician.

210   IMMIGRANT WOMEN IN THE U.S.

1428. Talbot, Toby. *A Book about My Mother*. New York: Farrar Straus Giroux, 1980.

An account of her Yiddish-speaking Polish Jewish mother's life.

1429. Tamarkin, Stanley R. "Rose Pastor Stokes: The Portrait of a Radical Woman, 1905-1919." Unpublished Ph.D. Dissertation, Yale University, 1983. Order Number DA 84 12439.

An Eastern European Jewish radical, best known for her radical politics and marriage to a wealthy New Yorker.

1430. Tateishi, John. *And Justice for All: An Oral History of the Japanese American Detention Camps*. New York: Random House, 1984.

About one-third are oral histories with women.

1431. Taub, Harold J. *Waldorf-in-the-Catskills: The Grossinger Legend*. New York: Sterling Publishing Co., 1952.

Includes biographical material on Jennie Grossinger, Austrian Jewish hotel entrepreneur.

1432. Taylor, Bride N. *Elisabet Ney, Sculptor*. New York: The Devin-Adair Co., 1916.

A German migrant to Texas.

1433. Tenison, Eva M. *Louise Imogen Guiney, Her Life and Works, 1861-1920*. London: MacMillan and Co., Ltd., 1923.

An Irish poet and scholar.

1434. Terkel, Louis. *"The Good War": An Oral History of World War Two*. New York: Pantheon Books, 1984.

Includes stories of an interned second-generation Japanese, a Japanese and a German war bride, and a second-generation Spanish school teacher.

1435. Thoburn, James M. *Life of Isabella Thoburn*. New York: Eaton and Mains, 1903.

A second-generation Scottish missionary.

1436. Thomas, Lately (pseud). *The Vanishing Evangelist*. New York: Viking Press, 1959.

The case of Canadian evangelist Aimee Semple McPherson's kidnapping.

1437. Tibbets, Joel W. "Women Who Were Called: A Study of the Contributions to American Christianity of Anna Lee, Jemima Wilkinson, Mary Baker Eddy, and Aimee Semple McPherson." Unpublished Ph.D. Dissertation, Vanderbilt University, 1976. Order Number 76-22,371.

McPherson was a Canadian-born evangelist; some attention is given to her kidnapping and aptitude for public relations.

1438. Tovar, Ines H. "Sara Estela Ramirez: The Early Twentieth Century Texas-Mexican Poet." Unpublished Ph.D. Dissertation, University of Houston, 1984. Order Number DA 8428105.

She was also a Mexican revolutionary, feminist, and labor activist in Texas.

1439. Tyler, Parker. Florine Stettheimer: A Life in Art. New York: Farrar, Straus, 1963.

A second-generation German Jewish painter.

1440. von Hassell, Malve. "Issei Women between Two Worlds, 1875-1985." Unpublished Ph.D. Dissertation, New School for Social Research, 1987. Order Number DA 8715863.

Their life histories show considerable alienation from their own lives.

1441. Wagenknecht, Edward C. Daughters of the Covenant: Portraits of Six Jewish Women. Amherst: The University of Massachusetts Press, 1983.

Brief sketches of Lillian D. Wald, Emma Goldman, and Henrietta Szold.

1442. Wagner, Maria. "Mathilde Anneke's Stories of Slavery in the German-American Press." MELUS 6 (Winter 1979): 9-16.

Some biographical information on this German-born journalist and author.

1443. Ward, David A. "The Unending War of Iva Ikuko Toguri D'Aquino: The Trial and Conviction of 'Tokyo Rose.'" Amerasia Journal 1 (July 1971): 26-35.

A second-generation Japanese woman charged and convicted of treason for wartime English-language broadcasts from Japan.

1444. Wargelin Brown, K. Marianne. "Three 'Founding Mothers' of Finnish America." Pp. 136-157 Women Who Dared: The History of Finnish American Women. Ed. Carl Ross and K. Marianne Wargelin Brown. St. Paul, Minnesota: Immigration History Research Center, 1986.

Brief sketches of Finnish community activists Ida Pasanen, Thyra Rautalahti, and Maggie Walz (Margareeta Niranen).

1445. Waterman, William R. Frances Wright. New York: Columbia University Press, 1924.

A Scottish radical and writer.

1446. Waterston, Anna C. Adelaid Phillipps: A Record. Boston: Cupples, Upham & Co., 1883.

An English actress and opera singer.

1447. Webb, Mary G. and E.L. Webb, eds. Famous Living Americans. Greencastle, Ind.: C. Webb & Co.., 1915.

Includes a chapter on Anna Howard Shaw, English feminist and minister.

1448. Werstein, Irving. Labor's Defiant Lady: The Story of Mother Jones. New York: Thomas Y. Crowell, 1969.

The Irish labor agitator.

1449. Westcott, Marcia. The Feminist Legacy of Karen Horney. New Haven and London: Yale University Press, 1986.

The life and work of the German psychoanalyst.

1450. Wexler, Alice. Emma Goldman in America. Boston: Beacon Press 1986.

The U.S. years of the Russian Jewish radical and anarchist.

1451. Wexler, Alice. Emma Goldman: An Intimate Life. New York: Pantheon, 1984.

The personal life behind the activism of this Russian Jewish radical and anarchist.

1452. Williams, Gertrude. Priestess of the Occult, Madame Blavatsky. New York: A.A. Knopf, 1946.

She was a Russian spiritualist and founder of Theosophy.

1453. Wilson, Carol G. Alice Eastwood's Wonderland: The Adventures of a Botanist. San Francisco: California Academy of Sciences, 1955.

An official biography of a Canadian botanist.

1454. Wilson, Carol G. Chinatown Quest: The Life Adventures of Donaldina Cameron. Stanford: Stanford University Press, 1932.

Born of Scottish parents in New Zealand, she became a missionary worker with prostitutes in San Francisco's Chinatown.

1455. Wilson, Dorothy C. *Lone Woman, the Story of Elizabeth Blackwell, the First Woman Doctor.* Boston: Little, Brown, 1970.

The English-born physician.

1456. Wilson, Philip W. *Gen. Evangeline Booth of the Salvation Army.* New York: C. Scribner's Sons, 1948.

An authorized account of the English religious leader, who came to direct the U.S. Army.

1457. Winter, William. *Ada Rehan, a Study.* London and New York: Private Printing A. Daly, 1891.

An Irish actress.

1458. Wise, James W. *Legend of Louise: The Life Story of Mrs. Stephen S. Wise.* New York: Jewish Opinion Publishing Co., 1949.

The German Jewish wife of a well-known reform rabbi.

1459. Worland, Elizabeth C. "American Catholic Women and the Church, to 1920." Unpublished Ph.D. Dissertation, St. Louis University, 1982. Order Number DA 8223752.

Includes notes on the life of Mary Kenney O'Sullivan, a second-generation Irish labor organizer and factory inspector.

1460. Wyndham, Horace. *The Magnificent Montez, from Courtesan to Convert.* London: Hutchinson & Company, 1935.

Irish actress and adventuress Lola Montez.

1461. Young-Bruehl, Elisabeth. *Hannah Arendt, For Love of the World.* New Haven: Yale University Press, 1982.

The life of the German political theorist, and her contributions to philosophy and the study of politics.

1462. Zeitlin, Rose. *Henrietta Szold: Record of a Life.* New York: Dial Press, 1952.

This second-generation Hungarian Jewish woman founded Hadassah.

11

Autobiography

INTRODUCTION

It is probably significant that there is no neat correspondence between the list of immigrant women whom biographers have chosen to write about and the immigrant women who chose to document and explain their own lives. Autobiographers have not always been the "notable women." Thus autobiographies can be compared with the oral histories cited in the previous chapter. Because they also reveal what immigrant women wanted to tell of their lives, I have included in this chapter some published collections of letters and diaries written by foreign-born females.

Not all autobiographies by foreign-born women focus on their life in the United States. Many memoirs by Holocaust survivors tell the story of lives prior to migration, and this pattern can be observed in other autobiographies as well. In some cases, women writers seem to assume that it is their exotic homeland that makes their stories worth telling. Other autobiographers reveal almost no interest in their own status as immigrant or second-generation American at all, but recount the details of family and professional life, a spiritual odyssey, or unusual experiences without reference to nativity or ethnicity. This, too, is probably significant.

Besides autobiographical accounts, this chapter cites a limited number of literary studies which shed light on the lives of autobiographers or immigrant women generally.

CITATIONS

1463. Adler, Polly. *A House is Not a Home*. New York: Rinehart, 1953.

The notorious madam of house of prostitution and Russian Jew.

1464. Aladjem, Henrietta. *The Sun is My Enemy: One Woman's Victory Over a Mysterious and Dreaded Disease*. Englewood Cliffs, N.J.: Prentice-Hall, 1972.

Focus on a Bulgarian's disease.

1465. Allilueva, Svetlana. *Twenty Letters to a Friend*. Trans. Priscilla Johnson McMillan. New York: Harper & Row, 1967.

Stalin's Russian daughter's reactions to her life in the U.S.

1466. Anderson, Mary. *Woman at Work: The Autobiography of Mary Anderson*. Minneapolis: University of Minnesota Press, 1951.

A second-generation Swedish labor leader and first head of women's bureau.

1467. Andres, Chaya R. *Years Have Sped By: My Life Story*. Ed. Jeanett Cohen. Dallas: The Author, 1981.

The life of an ordinary Eastern European Jew.

1468. Antin, Mary. *At School in the Promised Land, or the Story of a Little Immigrant*. Boston: Houghton Mifflin, 1912.

Heavily autobiographical account by a Russian Jewish writer.

1469. Antin, Mary. *From Plotzk to Boston*. Boston: W.B. Clarke & Co., 1899.

Russian Jewish writer.

1470. Antin, Mary. *The Promised Land*. Boston and New York: Houghton Mifflin, 1912.

Russian Jewish writer.

1471. Armaghanian, Arsha L. *Arsha's World and Yours*. New York: Vantage Press, 1977.

The diary of an Armenian girl including a section on her migration.

1472. Athas, Daphne. *Greece by Prejudice*. Philadelphia: Lippincott, 1962.

A second-generation Greek returns to the homeland.

1473. Barker-Nunn, Jeanne. "Telling the Mother's Story: History and Connection in the Autobiographies of Maxine Hong Kingston and Kim Chernin." *Women's Studies* 14 (1987): 55-63.

1474. Barr, Amelia Huddleston. *All the Days of My Life*. New York: Appleton, 1913.

An English-born novelist, settling in Texas.

1475. Barr, Amelia Huddleston. *Three Score and Ten; A Book for the Aged*. New York and London: Appleton, 1915.

English-born novelist.

1476. Barschak, Erna. *My American Adventure*. New York: Ives Washburn, 1945.

The life of a German Jewish refugee, a psychologist and university professor, and her adjustment to the American environment.

1477. Barton, H. Arnold, ed. *Letters from the Promised Land: Swedes in America, 1840-1914*. Minneapolis: University of Minnesota Press, 1975.

Letters by Swedish men and women include their reactions to the position of women in U.S.

1478. Baum, Vicki. *It Was All Quite Different: The Memoirs of Vicki Baum*. New York: Funk & Wagnalls, 1964.

An Austrian Jewish screenwriter from Vienna.

1479. Beaumont, Betty Bentley. *Twelve Years of My Life: An Autobiography*. Philadelphia: T.B. Peterson, 1887.

An English-born woman who lived in Mississippi keeping a small store.

1480. Beh, Siew Hua. "Growing Up with Legends of the Chinese Swordswomen." Pp. 121-126 *The Politics of Women's Spirituality: Essays on the Rise of Spiritual Power within the Feminist Movement*. Ed. Charlene Spretnak. Garden City: Doubleday, 1982.

Provides insight into Malaysian religious myths.

1481. Belmont, Eleanor Robson. *Fabric of Memory*. New York: Farrar, Straus and Cudahy, 1957.

An English actress, daughter and granddaughter of actresses.

1482. Bengis, Ingrid. *Combat in the Erogenous Zone*. New York: A.A. Knopf, 1972.

A second-generation Russian Jew.

1483. Bengis, Ingrid. *I Have Come Here to be Alone*. New York: Simon and Schuster, 1976.

A Russian Jew of the second generation.

1484. Bentlage, Mary K. *My Name Was Kay*. New York: Exposition, 1965.

A second-generation German growing up in rural Iowa.

1485. Berg, Gertrude with Cherney Berg. *Molly and Me*. New York: McGraw-Hill, 1961.

The second-generation Russian Jewish actress.

1486. Berg, Rebecca Himber. "Childhood in Lithuania." Pp. 269-82 *Memoirs of My People*. Ed. Leo Schwartz. Philadelphia: Jewish Publication Society of America, 1943.

1487. Berkowitz, Sarah Bick. *Where are My Brothers?* New York: Helios Books, 1965.

A Polish Jew who migrated after the Holocaust.

1488. Bethune, George W. *Memoirs of Mrs. Joanna Bethune*. New York: Harper and Brothers, 1863.

An early Canadian charitable worker; the book contains extracts of her writings and some biographical materials.

1489. Bingle, Alice. *A Woman's Diary*. New York: Vantage, 1958.

An English nurse.

1490. Bingle, Alice. *The Best Years*. n.p. 1961.

English nurse.

1491. Bjorn, Thyra Ferre. *Mama's Way*. New York: Rinehart, 1958.

A Swedish novelist.

1492. Bjorn, Thyra Ferre. *This is My Life*. New York: Holt, Rinehart, and Winston, 1966.

Swedish novelist.

1493. Blackwell, Elizabeth. *Pioneer Work in Opening the Medical Profession to Women; Autobiographical Sketches*. London: Longmans, Green, and Co., 1895.

An English woman who became the first American doctor

1494. Blegen, Theodore C. "Guri Endreson, Frontier Heroine." *Minnesota History* 10 (December 1929): 425-430.

A reprinted letter and the biography of a Norwegian heroine of the Sioux uprising of 1862.

1495. Blegen, Theodore C., trans. and ed. "Immigrant Women and the American Frontier: Three Early 'American Letters.'" <u>Norwegian-American Historical Association Studies and Records</u> 5 (1930): 14-25.

Letters and some biography of Norwegians Jannicke Saehle, Henrietta Jessen, and Guri Endreson.

1496. Blicksilver, Edith. <u>The Ethnic American Woman, Problems, Protests, Lifestyle</u>. Dubuque, Iowa: Kendall/Hunt Publishing Co., 1978.

Includes many short autobiographical selections.

1497. Blinde, Patricia Lin. "Icicle in the Desert: Form and Perspective in the Works of Two Chinese-American Writers." <u>MELUS</u> 6 (Fall 1979): 51-72.

An analysis of the autobiographical writings of Maxine Hong Kingston and Jade Snow Wong.

1498. Blum, Elsa Proehl. <u>They Pleased World Stars; A Memoir of My Parents</u>. New York: Vantage, 1960.

A second-generation German composer.

1499. Boulding, Elise Bior-Hansen. <u>Born Remembering</u>. Wallingford, Pennsylvania: Pendle Hill, 1975.

A second-generation Scandinavian sociologist and pacifist.

1500. Bowen, Ralph H., ed. and trans. <u>A Frontier Family in Minnesota; Letters of Theodore and Sophie Best, 1851-1920</u>. Minneapolis: University of Minnesota Press, 1981.

A Swiss family, with letters by both.

1501. Bowyer, Edith Nicholl. <u>Observations</u>. New York: MacMillan, 1898.

An English woman who lived on a New Mexico farm.

1502. Braggiotti, Gloria. <u>Born in a Crowd</u>. New York: Crowell, 1957.

A second-generation Italian returns to her parents' homeland.

1503. Brand, Sandra. <u>I Dare to Live</u>. New York: Shengold Publishers, n.d.

A Polish Jewish Holocaust survivor's account, covering mainly the war years. The book ends with her migration to the U.S.

1504. Brauer, Mrs. Oscar P., trans. "As Thou Leadest Me." *Concordia Historical Institute Quarterly* 28 (Winter 1956): 166-177.

Includes the biography and letters of Emilie Lohmann Koenig, a German Lutheran pastor's wife who wrote letters home in the 1850s.

1505. Briggs, Margaret Yang. *Daughter of the Khans*. New York: Norton, 1955.

An independent Chinese girl.

1506. Britten, Emma Hardinge. *Autobiography*. London: John Heywood, 1900.

An English spiritualist prior to and during the Civil War.

1507. Burch, Connie B. "Women's Voices, Women's Visions: Contemporary American-Jewish Women Writers." Unpublished Ph.D. Dissertation, Purdue University, 1987. Order Number DA 8729722

An historical section analyzes the autobiographies of Mary Antin, Emma Goldman, and Anzia Yezierska.

1508. Burke, Billie with Cameron Shipp. *With a Feather in my Nose*. New York: Appleton-Century-Crofts, 1949.

A English actress

1509. Burland, Rebecca and Edward Burland. *A True Picture of Emigration. Or 14 years in the interior of North America, Being a full and impartial account of the various difficulties and ultimate success of an English family who emigrated from Barwick-In-Elmet, near Leeds, in the year 1821*. New York: Citadel Pres, 1968, orig. publ. 1848.

Includes a long description of the woman's trip to settle in Illinois.

1510. Burnett, Frances Hodgson. *The One I Knew Best of All*. London: Frederick Warnes and Co., 1893.

The childhood and youth on the English writer of children's books.

1511. Burr, Charles C. *The Lectures of Lola Montez, With a Full and Complete Autobiography of her Life*. Philadelphia: T.B. Peterson & Brothers, 1958.

An Irish actress and adventuress; unreliable.

1512. Burton, Naomi. *More than Sentinels*. Garden City: Doubleday, 1964.

An English woman converts to Catholicism.

1513. Cade, Winifred, ed. I Think Back: Being the Memoirs of Grandma Gruen. San Antonio: Private Printing, 1937.

The memories of a German pioneer in Texas.

1514. Cassini, Marguerite. Never a Dull Moment: Memoirs of Countess Marguerite Cassini. New York: Harper, 1956.

Russian exile and anti-Communist.

1515. Chao, Buwei Yang. Autobiography of a Chinese Woman. New York: John Day Publishing Company, 1947.

A Chinese cookbook writer who arrived during World War II.

1516. Chavchavadze, Paul. Marie Avinov, Pilgrimage Through Hell. Englewood Cliffs, N.J.: Prentice-Hall, 1968.

A Russian aristocrat, her various tribulations in U.S.S.R. and her journey out via Nazi Germany.

1517. Chennault, Anna. The Education of Anna. New York: Times Books, 1980.

This Chinese woman married a U.S. general and became a political activist.

1518. Chin, Louise. "I'm an American." The Record of the Girls' Friendly Society of the U.S.A. 43 (January 1935): 20.

A short early account by a Chinese girl.

1519. Chisholm, Shirley. The Good Fight. New York: Harper and Row, 1973.

Second-generation, her father was from British Guyana, and her mother from Barbados. Tells the story of this political activist's and Congresswoman's run for the U.S. presidency.

1520. Chisholm, Shirley. Unbought and Unbossed. Boston: Houghton Mifflin Co., 1970.

Second-generation Congresswoman. Her father was from British Guyana, and her mother from Barbados. Describes her childhood with her grandmother in Barbados. One chapter on feminism is called "Women and their Liberation".

1521. Chou, Cynthia L. My Life in the United States. North Quincy, Mass.: Christopher, 1970.

The story of a Chinese woman.

222   IMMIGRANT WOMEN IN THE U.S.

1522. Christian, Barbara T. "Black, Female and Foreign-Born: A Statement." Pp. 177-176 Female Immigrants to the United States: Caribbean, Latin American and African Experiences. Ed. Delores Mortimer and Roy Bryce-Laporte. Washington, D.C.: Research Institute on Immigration and Ethnic Studies, Smithsonian Institute, 1981.

A short life of a student from the Virgin Islands.

1523. Cisneros, Evangelina. The Story of Evangelina Cisneros. New York: Continental Publishing Co., 1898.

A Cuban revolutionary who was rescued by an American journalist and brought to the U.S.

1524. Clausen, C.A., ed. The Lady with the Pen: Elise Waerenskjold in Texas. Northfield, Minn.: Norwegian-American Historical Association, 1961.

Letters from a Norwegian woman in Texas, and a biographical introduction to her life.

1525. Cohen, Rose Gallup. Out of the Shadow. New York: George H. Doran Co., 1918.

A Russian Jew.

1526. Coleman, Ann Thomas. Victorian Lady on the Texas Frontier: The Journal of Ann Raney Coleman. Ed. C. Richard King. Norman, Okla: University of Oklahoma Press, 1971.

An English pioneer.

1527. Connolly, Olga Fikotova. The Rings of Destiny. New York: McKay, 1968.

A Czech athlete who met and married a U.S. athlete; love triumphed.

1528. Cornaby, Hannah Hollingsworth. Autobiography and Poems. Salt Lake City: J.C. Graham & Co., 1881.

An English Mormon who moved to Utah.

1529. Cumming, Kate. A Journal of Hospital Life in the Confederate Army of Tennessee, From the Battle of Shiloh to the end of the War with Sketches of Life and Character, and Brief Notices of Current Events During the Period. Louisville: J.P. Morton & Co., 1866.

She was a Scottish hospital administrator for the Confederacy.

1530. Curwell, Laura E. Whither Shall I Wander? An Autobiography. New York: Vantage, 1958.

An English migrant to Canada and later the U.S. circa World War I.

1531. Cusack, May. *Nun of Kenmare; An Autobiography*. Boston: Ticknor, 1888.

The Irish-born Mother Superior converted to the Baptist faith in New York.

1532. Daché, Lilly. *Talking Through My Hats*. Ed. Dorothy Roe Lewis. New York: Coward-McCann, 1946.

A French milliner.

1533. Dahl, Borghild M. *Finding My Way*. New York: Dutton, 1962.

The life of a blind second-generation Norwegian novelist.

1534. Dahl, Borghild M. *I Wanted to See*. New York: Macmillan, 1944.

Tells of this second-generation Norwegian novelist's victory over eye disease.

1535. Davies, Mrs. Eliza. *The Story of an Earnest Life*. Cincinnati: Central Book Concern, 1881.

A Scottish missionary who worked in Australia, Virginia, and Kentucky.

1536. De Hueck, Catherine. *Friendship House*. New York: Sheed and Ward, 1946.

A Russian who migrated to Canada and later became a Catholic activist.

1537. De Hueck, Catherine. *My Russian Yesterdays*. Milwaukee: Bruce, 1951.

More of the story of a Russian Catholic activist.

1538. de Wolfe, Elsie. *After All*. New York and London: Harper & Brothers, 1935.

A second-generation Canadian interior decorator.

1539. Del Mar, Marcia. *A Cuban Story*. Winston-Salem: John F. Blair Publishers, 1979.

The story of a woman refugee; her father had fled the Spanish Civil War to Cuba in the 1930s.

1540. Demirturk, Emine Lale. "The Female Identity in Cross-Cultural Perspective: Immigrant Women's Autobiographies." Unpublished Ph.D. Dissertation, The University of Iowa, 1986. Order Number DA 8622761.

Analyzes the works of Yezierska, Wong, Kingston and Antin. Finds distinctive themes, especially the effort to erase patriarchal definitions of being female.

224   IMMIGRANT WOMEN IN THE U.S.

1541. Dennis, Peggy. "Memories from the Twenties." Cultural Correspondence 6 (1978); 84-86.

A second-generation Eastern European Jew and Communist Party activist.

1542. Dennis, Peggy. The Autobiography of an American Communist: A Personal View of a Political Life, 1925-1975. Westport, Conn.: Lawrence Hill, 1977.

A second-generation Eastern European Jew and radical.

1543. Dessler, Julia Shapiro. Eyes on the Goal. New York: Vantage, 1954.

Life of a Lithuanian woman.

1544. Deutsch, Helene. Confrontations with Myself: An Epilogue. New York: Norton, 1973.

A Polish Jewish psychoanalyst.

1545. Dodd, Bella Visono. School of Darkness. New York: P.J. Kenedy, 1954.

An Italian lawyer, Communist activist and later Catholic activist.

1546. Doering, Bertha-Charlotte. Romance of a Heavenly Princess. Los Angeles: The "Trust in God" Publishing House, 1921.

The life of the Swedish foundress of a missionary society in California.

1547. Dreier, Mary E. Margaret Dreier Robins, Her life, Letters and Work. New York: Island Press Cooperative, 1950.

This second-generation German became a labor activist and feminist.

1548. Dressler, Marie. My Own Story, as Told to Mildred Harrington. Boston, Little Brown, 1934.

The Canadian-born actress was of German descent.

1549. Dressler, Marie. The Eminent American Comedienne Marie Dressler in the Life Story of an Ugly Duckling; An Autobiographical Fragment in Seven Parts. New York: Robert M. McBride, 1924.

A Canadian actress of German descent.

1550. Drew, Louisa Lane. Autobiographical Sketch of Mrs. John Drew. New York: Scribner, 1899.

An English actress who often worked in the U.S.

1551. Eaton, Evelyn. **Every Month Was May**. New York: Harper & Brothers, 1946.

A Canadian who moved first to France, and later to the U.S.

1552. Eaton, Evelyn. **The Trees and Fields Went the Other Way**. New York: Harcourt Brace Jovanovich, 1974.

A Canadian writer.

1553. Eaton, Winnifred. **ME**. New York: The Century, 1915.

English-born writer, daughter of Chinese mother and English father; she wrote under the Japanese pen name Onoto Watann and invented a Japanese past for herself.

1554. Edelman, Fannie. **The Mirror of Life: The Old Country and the New**. New York: Exposition Press, 1961.

1555. Edmonds, Jean S. **Leaves from a Nurse's Life's History**. Rochester: Press of the Democrat & The Chronicle, 1906.

A Canadian missionary nurse who served in Africa and (with U.S. troops) in the Spanish-American War.

1556. Edmonds, Sarah. **Nurse and Spy in the Union Army, Comprising the Adventures and Experiences of a Woman in Hospitals, Camps and Battlefields**. Hartford: W.S. Williams and Co., 1865. Later reprinted under other titles.

A Canadian nurse.

1557. Ellis, Christine. "People Who Cannot be Bought." Pp. 9-33 **Rank and File**. Ed. Alice Lynd and Staughton Lynd. Boston: Beacon Press, 1973.

A second-generation Polish radical and labor activist.

1558. Ets, Maria Hall. **Rosa: The Life of an Immigrant Woman**. Minneapolis: University of Minnesota Press, 1970.

Transcriptions of the life story of Rosa Cassiari as told to the author at a Chicago settlement house.

1559. Evosevick, Sarah Vukelich. **Sarah: her Life, her Restaurant, her Recipes**. Pittsburgh: Pittsburgh History & Landmarks Foundation, 1987.

The reminiscences of a Serbian woman.

1560. Farseth, Pauline and Theodore C. Blegen, eds. **Frontier Mother: The Letters of Gro Svendsen**. Northfield, Minn.: Norwegian American Historical Association, 1950.

Letters from a Norwegian farm woman; the introduction includes biographical materials.

226   IMMIGRANT WOMEN IN THE U.S.

1561. Fermi, Laura. **Atoms in the Family: My Life with Enrico Fermi**. Chicago: University of Chicago Press, 1954.

An Italian focuses on life with her famous husband.

1562. Fischer, Markoosha. **Reunion in Moscow; A Russian Revisits Her Country**. New York: Harper & Row, 1962.

A Russian woman flees but later returns to the U.S.S.R.

1563. Fisher, Florrie as told to Jean Davis and Todd Persons. **The Lonely Trip Back**. Garden City, N.Y.: Doubleday, 1971.

A second-generation Eastern European Jew tells of her problems with drugs and prostitution.

1564. Fisher, Minnie. **Born One Year Before the 20th Century: Minnie Fisher/An Oral History**. New York: Community Documentation Workshop, St. Mark's Church in the Bowery, 1976.

The life of an Eastern European Jewish woman and worker.

1565. Flynn, Elizabeth Gurley. **I Speak My Own Piece, Autobiography of the Rebel Girl**. New York: Masses & Mainstream, 1955, reissued as **The Rebel Girl**, 1973.

This second-generation Irish woman was a radical and labor activist.

1566. Flynn, Elizabeth Gurley. **The Alderson Story, My Life as a Political Prisoner**. New York: International Publishers, 1963, orig. publ. 1955.

The second-generation Irish radical and labor activist tells of imprisonment.

1567. Frankau, Pamela. **Pen to Paper; A Novelist's Notebook**. Garden City, N.Y.: Doubleday, 1962.

An English-born novelist.

1568. Gabor, Eva. **Orchids and Salami**. Garden City, N.Y.: Doubleday, 1954.

A Hungarian actress.

1569. Gabor, Jolie as told to Cindy Adams. **Jolie Gabor**. New York: Mason/Charter, 1975.

The Hungarian mother of the actress sisters.

1570. Gabor, Zsa Zsa with Gerold Frank. **Zsa Zsa Gabor, My Story**. Cleveland: World, 1960.

The Hungarian actress.

1571. Gág, Wanda. Growing Pains, Diaries and Drawing for the Years 1908-1917. New York: Coward McCann, 1940.

A second-generation Czech artist and writer.

1572. Gamble, Lillian M. Mor's New Land. New York: Exposition, 1951.

A second-generation Norwegian tells of her life, but focuses on her parents.

1573. Gamio, Manuel. The Mexican Immigrant: His Life Story. New York: Arno Press, 1969, orig. publ. 1931.

Includes seventeen women's lives.

1574. Ganz, Marie. Rebels: Into Anarchy--and Out Again. New York: Dodd, Mead, and Co., 1919.

A radical activist, anarchist and Austrian Jew.

1575. Garcia, Céline Frémaux. Céline: Remembering Louisiana 1850-1871. Ed. Patrick J. Geary. Athens: University of Georgia Press, 1988.

A second-generation middle-class southern girl growing up in a French immigrant family.

1576. Garden, Mary and Louis Biancolli. Mary Garden's Story. New York: Simon and Schuster, 1951.

The famous English opera singer.

1577. Geva, Tamara. Split Seconds; A Remembrance. New York: Harper & Row, 1972.

A Russian dancer who joined Balanchine.

1578. Gilbert, Anne Hartley. The Stage Reminiscences of Mrs. Gilbert. Ed. by Charlotte M. Martin. New York: Scribner's Sons, 1901.

An English dancer and actress.

1579. Gluck, Gemma La Guardia. My Story. Ed. S.L. Schneiderman. New York: McKay, 1961.

A second-generation Italian, and sister of the New York politician.

1580. Godoy, Mercedes. When I Was a Girl in Mexico. Boston: Lothrop, Lee, and Shepherd, 1919.

The daughter of a Mexican diplomat describes her life growing up in Mexico, Cuba, and the U.S.

1581. Goldman, Emma and Alexander Berkman. *Nowhere at Home: Letters from Exile of Emma Goldman and Alexander Berkman.* Ed. Richard and Anna Maria Drinnon. New York: Schocken Books, 1975.

The Russian Jewish radical and anarchist.

1582. Goldman, Emma. *Living my Life.* Ed. Richard and Anna Maria Drinnon. New York: New American Library, 1977.

The Russian Jewish radical and anarchist.

1583. Goldman, Emma. *My Disillusionment in Russia.* New York: Thomas Y. Crowell, 1970.

Russian Jewish radical tells of life after deportation from the U.S..

1584. Goldmark, Josephine. *Pilgrim of '48: One Man's Part in the Austrian Revolution of 1848 and a Family Migration to America.* New Haven: Yale University Press, 1930.

The second half of the book focuses on her migration from Austria along with parents and friends.

1585. Goritzina, Kyra. *Service Entrance: Memoirs of a Park Avenue Cook.* New York: Carrick & Evans, 1939.

A Russian aristocratic couple and their life and work as servants in New York.

1586. Graham, Isabella. *The Unpublished Letters and Correspondence of Mrs. Isabella Graham, from the Year 1767 to 1814, Exhibiting her Religious Character in the Different Relations of Life.* Selected and Arranged by her Daughter, Mrs. Bethune. New York: J. S. Taylor, 1838.

An early Scottish charitable worker.

1587. Graham, Sheilah with Gerold Frank. *Beloved Infidel; The Education of a Woman.* New York: Holt, 1958.

The English-born Hollywood columnist.

1588. Graham, Sheilah. *A State of Heat.* New York: Grosset & Dunlap, 1972.

The English Hollywood columnist.

1589. Graham, Sheilah. *Confessions of a Hollywood Columnist.* New York: Morrow, 1969.

The English Hollywood columnist.

1590. Graham, Sheilah. *The Rest of the Story.* New York: Coward-McCann, 1964.

The English Hollywood columnist.

AUTOBIOGRAPHY 229

1591. Greenburger, Ingrid. *A Private Treason; A German Memoir*. Boston: Little, Brown, 1973.

1592. Guiney, Louise. *Letters of Louise Imogen Guiney*. Ed. Grace Guiney. New York and London: Harper & Brothers, 1926.

A second-generation Irish poet and writer.

1593. Gull, Caroline. *The Story of My Life*. Philadelphia: n.p., 1935.

A Swiss nurse and physical therapist in Pennsylvania.

1594. Harding, Bertita Leonarz. *Mosaic in the Fountain*. Philadelphia: Lippincott, 1949.

A Hungarian writer.

1595. Hare, Catherine, comp. *Life and Letters of Elizabeth L. Comstock*. London: Headley Brothers, 1895.

English Quaker minister.

1596. Hart, Sara Liebenstein. *The Pleasure is Mine; An Autobiography*. Chicago: Valentine-Newman, 1947.

A second-generation German Jewish woman who was a reformer and activist in women's clubs and welfare work with Jane Addams in Chicago. Includes a chapter on her sisters.

1597. Hartman, May Weisser. *I Gave My Heart*. New York: Citadel, 1960.

Second-generation Russian Jew, work in orphanage.

1598. Hasanovitz, Elizabeth. *One of Them; Chapters from a Passionate Autobiography*. Boston and New York: Houghton Mifflin, 1918.

A Russian Jew who was a New York garment worker and active in the garment unions.

1599. Hatfield, Inge. *Life with the Real McCoy*. New York: Vantage, 1965.

A German woman's life and marriage to an American.

1600. Henie, Sonja. *Wings on My Feet*. New York: Prentice-Hall, 1940.

The Norwegian skater.

1601. Henry, Alice. *Memoirs of Alice Henry*. Ed. Nettie Palmer. Melbourne: n.p., 1944.

An Australian labor activist.

1602. Higbee, Blanche. *The Autobiography of a Pioneer Woman*. Spokane: Knapp Book Store, 1935.

A French teacher in Illinois and Michigan; she married a farmer in Washington.

1603. Hilf, Mary as told to Barbara Bourns. *No Time for Tears*. New York: Yoseloff, 1964.

A Russian Jewish businesswoman in Milwaukee.

1604. Hobbs, Lisa. *Running Towards Life*. New York: McGraw-Hill, 1971.

An Australian writer of travel accounts.

1605. Holt, C. E. *An Autobiographical Sketch of a Teacher's Life, Including a Residence in the Northern and Southern States, California, Cuba and Peru*. Quebec: J. Carrel, 1875.

She was Canadian by birth.

1606. Hotchkiss, Christine Oppeln-Bronikowska. *Home to Poland*. New York: Farrar, Straus and, Cudahy, 1958.

A Polish writer returns to her homeland, working for *Reader's Digest*.

1607. Houston, Jean W. "Beyond Manzanar: A Personal View of Asian American Womanhood." In *Asian Americans: Social and Psychological Perspectives*. Ed. R. Endo, S. Sue, and N.N. Wagner. Palo Alto: Science and Behavior Books, 1980.

A Japanese woman remembers her internment during World War II.

1608. Houston, Jean W. and D. Houston. *Farewell to Manzanur: A True Story of Japanese American Experience During and After the World War II Internment*. Boston: Houghton Mifflin, 1973.

1609. Hua, Chuang. *Crossings*. Boston: Northeastern University Press, 1988.

A Chinese upper-class emigrée.

1610. Humula, Anna J. *Echoing Memories*. Boston: Christopher, 1963.

A Moravian woman's life.

1611. Ikeda-Spiegel, Motoko. "Concentration Camps in the U.S." *Heresies* 8 (1979): 90-97.

A Japanese memoir of interment during World War II.

AUTOBIOGRAPHY   231

1612.   Ileana,   Princess   of   Rumania.   I Live Again.   New York: Rinehart, 1951.

A Rumanian emigrée.

1613.   Isely,   Elise   Dubach   as   told   to   Bliss   Isely. Sunbonnet Days.   Caldwell, Idaho: Caxton, 1935.

A woman tells of her life as a Swiss pioneer on a farm in Kansas.

1614.   Jannopoulo, Helen P.   And Across Big Seas.   Caldwell, Idaho: Caxton Publishers, 1949.

A Greek woman recalls her migration and arrival in the U.S.

1615.   Jastrow, Marie.   A Time to Remember: Growing Up in New York Before the Great War.   New York: Norton, 1979.

A Serbian Jew and her family.

1616.   Jastrow, Marie.   Looking Back: The American Dream through Immigrant Eyes.   New York: W.W. Norton, 1986.

The life of an Austrian Serbian Jew, including many pictures and a detailed portrayal of her father.

1617.   Jennings, Rosa Schreurs.   "A Scrap of Americana." Annals of Iowa   3rd Series 29 (April 1949):   589-598.

Experiences of the Dutch second generation, including her own reminiscences.

1618.   Jeritza, Maria.   Sunlight and Song.   New York and London: Appleton, 1924.

An Austrian opera singer in New York.

1619.   Jex, Eliza Goodson.   In Memoriam.   Spanish Fork, Utah: Spanish Fork Press, 1921.

An English convert to Mormonism, her migration to Utah, and her participation in a plural marriage.

1620.   Joe, Jeanne.   Ying-Ying: Pieces of a Childhood.   San Francisco: East/West Publishing Co., 1982.

Reminiscences of growing up in Chicago's Chinatown.

1621.   Jones, Mary (Mother).   The Autobiography of Mother Jones.   Ed. Mary Field Parton.   Chicago: Charles H. Kerr, 1925.

An Irish labor activist, orator, and radical.

IMMIGRANT WOMEN IN THE U.S.

1622. Juhasz, Suzanne. "Towards a Theory of Form in Feminist Autobiography: Kate Millett's *Flying* and *Sita*; Maxine Hong Kingston's *The Woman Warrior*." Pp. 221-237 *Women's Autobiography: Essays in Criticism*. Ed. Estelle C. Jelinek. Bloomington and London: Indiana University Press, 1980.

An analysis of the second-generation Chinese writer's autobiography.

1623. Kahn, Frida. *Generation in Turmoil*. Great Neck, N.Y.: Channel Press, 1960.

A Ukrainian Jewish woman who traveled to Germany, France, and finally to the U.S. just before World War II.

1624. Kelly, Fanny. *Narrative of My Captivity among the Sioux Indians*. Chicago: Donnelley, Gassette & Loyd, 1880, orig. publ. 1871.

A Canadian woman.

1625. Kemble, Fanny. *A Year of Consolation*. New York: Wiley & Putnam, 1847.

The English actress tells of her year in Rome.

1626. Kemble, Fanny. *Further Records, 1848-1883*. New York: H. Holt and Co., 1891.

The English actress.

1627. Kemble, Fanny. *Journal of a Residence in America*. Brussels: A. Wahlen, 1835.

The English actress.

1628. Kemble, Fanny. *Journal of a Residence on a Georgian Plantation in 1829-1839*. New York: Harper & Bros., 1863.

The English actress.

1629. Kemble, Fanny. *Records of a Girlhood*. New York: Henry Holt, 1879.

The early career of the English actress.

1630. Kemble, Fanny. *Records of Later Life*. New York: H. Holt and Co., 1882.

The English actress.

1631. Kenny, Elizabeth. *And They Shall Walk*. New York: Dodd, Mead, 1943.

An Australian nurse, who worked with paralysis.

AUTOBIOGRAPHY 233

1632. Kinel, Lola. *This is My Affair*. Boston: Little, Brown, and Co., 1937.

A Pole who lived in Russia; she worked as Isadora Duncan's secretary, and migrated to Hollywood in the 1920s.

1633. Kingston, Maxine Hong. *The Woman Warrior: Memoir of a Girlhood Among Ghosts*. New York: Random House, 1976.

A second-generation Chinese writer, focusing on her early years, and writing in a fantastical manner.

1634. Klein, Gerda Weissmann. *All But My Life*. New York: Hill and Wang, 1957.

A Polish Jew, Holocaust survivor and war bride.

1635. Knauff, Ellen Raphael. *The Ellen Knauff Story*. New York: W.W. Norton, 1952.

A war bride who, because of her complex past (German by birth, Czech through marriage, living in England) became a civil-rights case in the U.S., saved only at the last moment from deportation.

1636. Knef, Hildegard. *The Gift Horse*. Trans. David A. Palastanga. New York: Dell Publishing Company, 1972.

A German actress and singer.

1637. Knef, Hildegard. *The Verdict*. New York: Ballantine Books, 1977. Trans. David A. Palastanga.

A German actress and singer who worked in Hollywood for many years before marrying an Englishman and leaving for England.

1638. Kohut, Rebecca Bettelheim. *More Yesterdays: An Autobiography (1925-1949): A Sequel to My Portion*. New York: Bloch Publishing, 1950.

A Hungarian Jewish community activist.

1639. Kohut, Rebecca Bettelheim. *My Portion: An Autobiography*. New York: Thomas Seltzer, 1925.

A Hungarian Jewish community activist and welfare worker.

1640. Koren, Else Hysing. *The Diary of Elisabeth Koren, 1853-1855*. Trans. and ed. by David T. Nelson. Northfield, Minn.: Norwegian-American Historical Association, 1955.

A Norwegian who lived on an Iowa farm; the introduction includes biographical notes.

1641. La Roe, Else Kienle. *Woman Surgeon: The Autobiography of Else K. La Roe, M.D.* New York: The Dial Press, 1957.

A German-born plastic surgeon.

1642. LaLonde, Leona M. *Belgium was My Home*. Portland, Oregon: Binfords & Mort, 1944.

A Belgian tells of her childhood on farm.

1643. Lamarr, Hedy. *Ecstasy and Me; My Life as a Woman*. New York: Bartholomew House, 1966.

An Austrian actress.

1644. Lang, Lucy Fox Robins. *Tomorrow is Beautiful*. New York: Macmillan, 1948.

A Russian Jew.

1645. Langseth-Christensen, Lillian. *Voyage Gastronomique; A Culinary Autobiography*. New York: Hawthorn, 1973.

A second-generation Austrian who continued the transcontinental life-style of her father.

1646. Langtry, Lillie. *The Days I Knew*. New York: Doran, 1924.

An English actress who also worked in the U.S.

1647. Lawrence, Gertrude. *A Star Danced*. Garden City, NY: Doubleday, Doran, 1945.

An English actress and musical comedy star in the U.S.

1648. Lawson, Josephine. *Reminiscences from a Simple Life*. Oakland: Messiah's Advocate, 1920.

A Swedish worker with the Adventists.

1649. Lawton, Mary. *Schumann-Heink, The Last of the Titans*. New York: MacMillan Co., 1928.

The German singer's U.S. career; autobiographical in format.

1650. Le Gallienne, Eva. *At 33*. New York and Toronto: Longmans, Green, 1934.

A French-born Broadway star.

1651. Le Gallienne, Eva. *With a Quiet Heart*. New York: Viking, 1953.

A French-born actress and translator; much of her career was in the U.S.

1652. Lehmann, Lilli. *My Faith Through Life*. New York: Putnam, 1914.

A German opera singer in the U.S.

1653. Lehmann, Lotte. *Midway in My Song*. Trans. Margaret Ludwig. New York: Books for Libraries Press, 1970, orig. publ. 1938.

A German-born opera singer.

1654. Lehmann, Lotte. *Wings of Song, an Autobiography*. London: Kegan Paul, Trench, Trübner & Co., 1938.

A German opera singer, includes information on her U.S. career.

1655. Leitner, Isabella with Irving Leitner. *Saving the Fragments: From Auschwitz to New York*. New York: New American Library, 1985.

The spare memories of a Hungarian Jewish woman from the liberation of Auschwitz until her arrival in New York.

1656. Lenihan, Mina Ward. *Betwixt the Here and There*. Philadelphia: Dorrance, 1953.

A musician from New Zealand who lived twelve years in the U.S.

1657. Levorsen, Barbara. "Early Years in Dakota." *Norwegian-American Studies* 21 (1962): 158-197.

A second-generation Norwegian, who moved with her foster parents to North Dakota.

1658. Levy, Harriet Lane. *920 O'Farrell Street*. New York: Doubleday, 1947.

A second-generation German Jew remembering her San Francisco neighborhood.

1659. Lewis, Anna, ed. "Diary of a Missionary to the Choctaws, 1860-1861." *Chronicles of Oklahoma* 17 (Dec. 1939): 428-447.

Scottish religious worker Sue McBeth.

1660. Lewis, Anna, ed. "Letters Regarding Choctaw Missions and Missionaries." *Chronicles of Oklahoma* 17 (December 1939): 275-285.

Sue McBeth, a Scottish missionary.

1661. Lewis, Anna, ed. "The Diary of Sue McBeth--A Missionary to the Choctaws, 1860-1861." *Chronicles of Oklahoma* 21 (June 1943): 186-195.

A Scottish religious activist.

1662. Lilienthal, Meta. *Dear Remembered World: Childhood Memories of an Old New Yorker*. New York: Richard R. Smith, 1947.

A second-generation German community activist.

1663. Lin, Alice. *Grandmother Had No Name*. San Francisco: China Books, 1988.

A memoir of a Chinese woman who came to the U.S. as a student in the 1960s; also tells the lives of many of her female relatives in China.

1664. Lin, Mao-chu. "Identity and Chinese-American Experience: A Study of Chinatown American Literature since World War II." Unpublished Ph.D. Dissertation, University of Minnesota, 1987. Order Number DA 8727423.

Discusses "romantic stereotypical autobiographies" like Jade Snow Wong's and Virginia Lee's. Considers Maxine Hong Kingston's autobiography as unique because of the warm reception it received.

1665. Lindheim, Irma Levy. *Parallel Quest, a Search of a Person and a People*. New York: T. Yoseloff, 1962.

A second-generation middle-class German Jewish woman who became a Zionist activist working in Palestine.

1666. Lips, Eva. *Rebirth in Liberty*. New York: Flamingo, 1942.

The Americanization of a German intellectual.

1667. Lips, Eva. *Savage Symphony, A Personal Record of the Third Reich*. Transl. Dorothy Thompson. New York: Random House, 1938.

The author left Germany with her anthropologist husband to live in New York.

1668. Lixl-Purcell, Andreas, ed. *Women of Exile: German-Jewish Autobiographies Since 1933*. Westport, Conn.: Greenwood Press, 1988.

1669. Logan, Milla Zenovich. *Bring Along Laughter*. New York: Random House, 1947.

A second-generation Serbian girl growing up in San Francisco.

1670. Logan, Milla Zenovich. *Cousins and Commissars; An Intimate Visit to Tito's Yugoslavia*. New York: Scribner, 1949.

A second-generation Serbian who returned to the homeland.

1671. Loucks, Jennie Erickson. Oklahoma Was Young and So Was I. San Antonio: Naylor, 1964.

A second-generation Finn.

1672. MacLean, Annie M. "I Become American." Sociology and Social Research 16 (May-June 1932): 427-433.

A Canadian-born woman tells of her migration and her easy adjustment, as well as the small cultural differences.

1673. Maeder, Clara Fisher. Autobiography. Ed. by Douglas Taylor. New York: The Dunlap Society, 1897.

An English actress and singer.

1674. Mander, Anica Vesel with Sarika Finci Hofbauer. Blood Ties; A Woman's History. New York: Random House, 1976.

A German Jew who traveled to Italy and later to the U.S.

1675. Manning, Marie (writing as Beatrice Fairfax). Ladies Now and Then. New York: E.P. Dutton & Co., 1944.

This second-generation English journalist wrote a love-lorn column.

1676. Markham, Pauline. Life of Pauline Markham. New York: n.p., 1871.

An English actress on the U.S. stage.

1677. Marshall, Mrs. Anne James. The Autobiography. Pine Bluff, Ark.: Adams-Wilson, 1897.

An English teacher in Arkansas and her marriage to a clergyman.

1678. Massing, Hede. This Deception. New York: Duell, Sloan, and Pearce, 1951.

An Austrian Jew from Vienna became a Soviet agent but later denounced Communism.

1679. Matsui, Haru. Restless Wave: My Life in Two Worlds. New York: Modern Age Books, 1940.

A Japanese political activist and daughter of a prominent family migrated and then returned.

1680. McCormack, Lily Foley. I Hear You Calling Me. Milwaukee: Bruce, 1949.

An Irish singer.

238   IMMIGRANT WOMEN IN THE U.S.

1681. McPherson, Aimee Semple. *Give Me My Own God*. New York: H.C. Kinsey & Co., 1936.

A Canadian evangelist.

1682. McPherson, Aimee Semple. *In the Service of the King: The Story of My Life*. New York: Boni and Liveright, 1927.

The Canadian evangelist's life; it was probably ghost written.

1683. McPherson, Aimee Semple. *The Story of My Life*. Ed. Raymond W. Becker. Los Angeles: Echo Park Evangelistic Association, 1951.

The Canadian evangelist; mainly excerpts of her writings.

1684. McPherson, Aimee Semple. *This is That: Personal Experiences, Sermons and Writings*. Los Angeles: The Bridal Call Publishing Co., 1919. Rev. 1923.

The Canadian evangelist; it includes some autobiographical materials.

1685. Meir, Golda. *My Life*. New York: G.P. Putnam's Sons, 1975.

Stateswoman, Socialist and Russian Jew tells of growing up in Milwaukee and Denver before moving to Palestine in 1921.

1686. Meyer, Agnes Ernst. *Out of These Roots, The Autobiography of an American Woman*. Boston: Little, Brown, 1953.

A second-generation German woman who became a journalist.

1687. Michel, Auguste Marie. *A Mutilated Life Story, Strange Fragments of an Autobiography*. Chicago: The Author, 1911.

French nurse and doctor in an African hospital and in the western U.S.

1688. Millberg, Karen Schwencke. *Fight Against the Wind*. New York: Odyssey Press, 1947.

A Danish woman.

1689. Modjeska, Helen. *Letters to Emilia, Record of a Friendship*. Ed. Marion Moore Coleman. Cheshire, Conn.: Cherry Hill Books, 1967.

A Polish actress.

1690. Modjeska, Helena. *Memories and Impressions of Helena Modjeska; An Autobiography*. New York: The MacMillan Co., 1910.

A Polish actress.

1691. Moise, Penina. Secular and Religious Works of Penina Moise, with a Brief Sketch of Her Life. Charleston: N. G. Duffy Printer, 1911.

A second-generation German and West Indian Jewish hymnist and religious writer.

1692. Morris, Edita. Straitjacket: Autobiography. New York: Crown Publishers, 1978.

A Swedish novelist who escaped her family "straitjacket" with an American man.

1693. Mueller, Amelia. There Have to Be Six; A True Story About Pioneering in the Midwest. Scottdale, Pa.: Herald Press, 1966.

A second-generation German Mennonite, growing up in a farm family in Kansas and Texas.

1694. Mulder, Arnold. "Grootmoeder's Hundred Years." Knickerbocker Weekly 10 (January, 1944): 18-24.

Early life as recalled by the author's Dutch grandmother.

1695. Murphy, Patricia. Glow of Candlelight: The Story of Patricia Murphy. Englewood Cliffs, N.J.: Prentice-Hall, 1961.

A Canadian operator of a fishing business and, in New York, a restaurant.

1696. Negri, Pola. Memoirs of a Star. Garden City, N.Y.: Doubleday, 1970.

A Polish actress in Germany and Hollywood.

1697. Nelson, David T., ed. and trans. The Diary of Elisabeth Koren 1853-1855. Northfield, Minn.: Norwegian-American Historical Association, 1955.

A Norwegian woman tells of her migration and settlement in Iowa.

1698. Nelson, Teresa Leopando Lucero. White Cap And Prayer. New York: Vantage, 1955.

A Filipino nurse.

1699. Newby, Elizabeth. A Migrant with Hope. Nashville: Broadman Press, 1977.

A child of Spanish-speaking Mexican migrant laborers whose home base was in south Texas

240   IMMIGRANT WOMEN IN THE U.S.

1700. Newman, Judith Sternberg. *In the Hell of Auschwitz; The Wartime Memories of Judith Sternberg Newman.* New York: Exposition, 1963.

A German Jewish Holocaust survivor.

1701. Nin, Anais. *Paris Revisited*. Santa Barbara: Capra Press, 1972.

The French writer.

1702. Nin, Anais. *The Diary of Anais Nin, 1931-34*. New York: Harcourt, Brace, and World, 1966.

1703. Nin, Anais. *The Diary of Anais Nin, 1934-39*. New York: Harcourt, Brace & World, 1967.

1704. Nin, Anais. *The Diary of Anais Nin, 1939-44*. New York: Harcourt Brace Jovanovich, 1969.

1705. Nin, Anais. *The Diary of Anais Nin, 1944-47*. New York: Harcourt Brace Jovanovich, 1971.

1706. Nin, Anais. *The Diary of Anais Nin, 1947-55*. New York: Harcourt Brace Jovanovich, 1974.

1707. Nin, Anais. *The Diary of Anais Nin, 1955-66*. New York: Harcourt Brace Jovanovich, 1976.

1708. Norton, Minerva Brace. *A True Teacher: Mary Mortimer, Memoir*. New York: Fleming H. Revell Co., 1894.

An English teacher and head of a Milwaukee school.

1709. Nowicki, Stella. "Back of the Yards." Pp. 67-88 *Rank and File*. Ed. Alice Lynd and Staughton Lynd. Boston: Beacon Press, 1973.

An oral history with a second-generation Polish radical in Chicago.

1710. O'Neal, Mary T. *These Damn Foreigners*. Hollywood, Cal.: Minerva Printing & Publishing Co., 1971.

A Welsh woman tells of the strike in Ludlow, where she had gone to find her deserter husband; she recounts the massacre of workers there.

1711. Ohori, Fumiye. "American or Japanese?" *The Record of the Girls' Friendly Society of the U.S.A.* 43 (January 1935): 12-13.

1712. Okubo, Miné. *Citizen 13660*. New York: Columbia University Press, 1946.

A second-generation Japanese woman was traveling in Europe when war broke out; she writes of her subsequent internment.

1713. Okumara, Taki. Seventy Years of Divine Blessings. Japan: n.p., 1934.

A Japanese Methodist missionary worker in Hawaii.

1714. Olsson, Anna. "I'm Scairt": Childhood Days on the Prairie. Rock Island: Augustana Book Concern, 1927. Repr. as A Child of the Prairie.

The Swedish author was president of Augustana College; written in "baby talk", the book nevertheless includes interesting perspective on childhood in an immigrant family.

1715. Orpen, Mrs. Memories of the Old Emigrant Days in Kansas, 1862-1865. Edinburgh and London: William Blackwood and Sons, 1926.

An English child on a Kansas farm.

1716. Packer, Mrs. Jane Knight. Life and Spiritual Experiences of Mrs. Dr. Jane B. Packer, Clairvoyant Physician. Taunton: Sweet, 1892.

A Canadian spiritualist in New England.

1717. Padow, Mollie Potter. A Saga of Eighty Years of Living. Philadelphia: Dorrance, 1971.

A second-generation Lithuanian Jewish labor activist.

1718. Papashvily, George and Helen. Anything Can Happen. New York: Harper & Bros., 1944.

The lives of a Russian couple.

1719. Paul, Almira. The Surprising Adventures of Almira Paul, a Young Woman, who, Garbed as a Male, has...Actually Served as a Common Sailor on Board of English and American Armed Vessels without a Discovery of her Sex Being Made. Boston: N. Coverly, Jr., 1916.

A Canadian male impersonator from Nova Scotia, who sailed with the Americans in the War of 1812.

1720. Pauli, Hertha E. Break of Time. New York: Hawthorn Books, 1972.

A Jew who left Vienna just before World War II.

1721. Pawlowicz, Sala Kaminska with Kevin Klose. I Will Survive. New York: Norton, 1962.

A Polish Jew who survived a concentration camp to migrate to the U.S.

1722. Penzik, Irena. Ashes to the Taste. New York: University Publishers, 1961.

A Polish Jew and disillusioned Communist Party activist.

242   IMMIGRANT WOMEN IN THE U.S.

1723. Pesotta, Rose. Bread Upon the Waters. New York: Dodd, Mead, and Co., 1945.

A Russian Jewish labor activist.

1724. Pesotta, Rose. Days of Our Lives. Boston: Excelsior, 1958.

A Russian Jewish labor activist; inclues much on her Ukrainian homeland and childhood.

1725. Petrova, Olga. Butter with My Bread. Indianapolis: The Bobbs-Merrill, Co., 1942.

An Eastern European stage and screen star, and writer.

1726. Petrovskaya, Kyra. Kyra. Englewood Cliffs, N.J.: Prentice-Hall, 1959.

A Russian emigrée who came to the U.S. after World War I.

1727. Petterson, Lucille, ed. "Ephraim is my Home Now: Letters of Anna and Anders Petterson, 1884-1889. Part I." Wisconsin Magazine of History 69 (1986): 187-210.

1728. Pickford, Mary. Sunshine and Shadow. Garden City, N.Y.: Doubleday, 1955.

The Canadian actress.

1729. Picon, Molly. So Laugh a Little. New York: Messner, 1962.

A second-generation Russian Jewish actress, includes the story of her immigrant parents and grandparents.

1730. Plotkin, Sara. Full-Time Active: Sara Plotkin, An Oral History. Ed. Arthur Tobier. New York: Community Documentation Workshop, 1980.

A Jewish community activist.

1731. Polasek, Emily M.K. A Bohemian Girl in America. Ed. Edward Hayes. n.p.: Rollins Press, 1982.

1732. Polykoff, Shirley. Does She...Or Doesn't She? And How She Did It. Garden City, N.Y.: Doubleday, 1975.

A second-generation Eastern European Jewish advertising genius.

1733. Preus, Caroline Dorothea Margarethe (Keyser). Linka's Diary on Land and Sea 1845-1864. Trans and ed. Johan Carl Keyser Preus and his wife Diderikke Margrethe, nee Brandt. Minneapolis: Augsburg, 1952.

Tale of journey and life in U.S. by a Norwegian woman.

AUTOBIOGRAPHY   243

1734. Prisland,   Marie.   From   Slovenia--to America,
Recollections   and   Collections.   Chicago: The Slovenian
Women's Union of America, 1968.

Includes considerable information on community work and
notable women, but also her autobiography.

1735. Raaen, Aagot. Grass of the Earth: Immigrant Life in
the Dakota Country. Northfield, Minn.: Norwegian-American
Historical Association, 1950.

A Norwegian child growing up on a Dakota farm.

1736. Raaen, Aagot. Measure of My Days.   Fargo, N.D.:
North Dakota Institute for Regional Studies, 1953.

Sequel to Grass of the Earth: a Norwegian woman's college
years, trip to Europe and return to the U.S.

1737. Racowitza, Elena von Dönniges. Princess Helene von
Racowitza, an Autobiography. New York: Macmillan, 1910.

A German actress who made a long tour in California.

1738. Radziwill, Ekaterina Rzewuska. It Really Happened.
New York: Dial Press, 1932.

A Russian refugee's struggle to survive in New York.

1739. Randall, Isabelle. A Lady's Ranch Life in Montana.
London: W.H. Allen, 1887.

An Englishwoman in rural Montana.

1740. Rasmussen, Anne-Marie. There Was Once a Time. New
York: Harcourt Brace Jovanovich, 1975.

A Norwegian domestic servant who worked for the Rockefeller
family.

1741. Reiss, Johanna. The Upstairs Room.   New York:
Thomas Y. Crowell, 1972.

A Dutch Jew recounts her experiences during World War II.

1742. Resnick, Rose. Dare To Dream, The Rose Resnick
Story. San Francisco: Strawberry Hill Press, 1988.

The second-generation daughter of Russian Jews, this blind
woman became a musician and organizer of a summer camp for
blind children.

1743. Reznikoff, Sara.   "Early History of a Seamstress."
Family Chronicle. New York: Universe Books, 1971.

A Russian Jew.

1744. Richards, Marilee, ed. "Life Anew for Czech Immigrants: The Letters of Marie and Vavrin Strítecky 1913-1934." South Dakota History 11 (Fall/Winter 1981): 253-304.

The letters were written jointly by this Czech couple.

1745. Richardson, Mary Walsham Few. Scenes in the Eventful Life of Mrs. Mary Richardson. Columbus: W.G. Hubbard & Co., 1894.

An English milliner in New Hampshire and her temperance work.

1746. Ritter, Darlene M. "The Letters of Louise Ritter from 1893 to 1925: A Swiss-German Immigrant Woman to Antelope County, Nebraska." Unpublished Ph. D. Dissertation, University of Nebraska, Lincoln, 1979. Order Number 8008326.

Focus is on her autobiography and letters, and the disruptive shock of migration.

1747. Robins, Elizabeth. Raymond and I. New York: Macmillan, 1956.

An English actress remembers her Alaska years.

1748. Rodzinski, Halina. Our Two Lives. New York: Scribner, 1976.

A Pole of a musical family tells of her marriage to a conductor.

1749. Rogers, Clara K. The Story of Two Live, Memories of a Musical Career. Norwood: Plimpton Press, 1932.

An English singer's life, focusing on her marrige in the U.S.

1750. Roisdal, Agnes (pseud.). Defend My Mother. New York: Vantage, 1951.

A second-generation Norwegian, her New York childhood and her life with relatives on a Norwegian farm.

1751. Rosen, Ruth and Sue Davidson, eds. The Maimie Papers. Old Westbury, N.Y.: The Feminist Press, 1977.

A second-generation Jewish prostitute.

1752. Rosenberg, Ethel Greenglass. The Rosenberg Letters. London: Dennis Dobson, 1953.

The second-generation Eastern European Jew who was convicted of espionage.

1753. Rosenthal, Jean and Lael Wertenbaker. The Magic of Light; The Craft and Career of Jean Rosenthal, Pioneer in Lighting for the Modern Stage. Boston: Little, Brown, 1972.

A second-generation Rumanian Jew who worked as a lighting designer.

1754. Rosler, Martha. "Tijuana Maid." Heresies 1 (January 1977): 8-13.

The story of a Mexican domestic servant.

1755. Ross, Dorothy. Stranger to the Desert. New York: Wilfred Funk, 1959.

An English woman who abruptly married a Texas cattle rancher.

1756. Rostenberg, Leona and Madeleine B. Stern. Old and Rare: Thirty Years in the Book Business. New York: Abner Schram, 1974.

Two second-generation German Jews, their studies in Germany and their book business in New York.

1757. Royce, Sarah. A Frontier Lady, Recollection of the Gold Rush and Early California. New Haven: Yale University Press, 1932.

An English pioneer, includes a biographical sketch by her daughter-in-law.

1758. Rubin, Steven. "Ethnic Autobiography: A Comparative Approach." Journal of Ethnic Studies 9 (Spring 1981): 75-80.

Includes some analysis of Mary Antin, whose work is compared to that of other Jews and of Afro-Americans.

1759. Rubinstein, Helena. My Life for Beauty. New York: Simon and Schuster, 1966.

The Polish businesswoman and cosmetician.

1760. Rudolph, Marguerita. The Great Hope. New York: John Day, 1948.

A Ukrainian.

1761. Ruskay, Sophie. Horsecars and Cobblestones. New York: Beechhurst Press, 1948.

A second-generation Russian Jewish childhood, focusing on her mother's business and family life in New York.

1762. Rybacki, Stella. *Thrills, Chills and Sorrow*. New York: Exposition, 1954.

An Eastern European girl growing up in the Pennsylvania coal fields.

1763. Salz, Helen A. *Sketches of an Improbable Ninety Years*. Berkeley: Bancroft Library, Regional Oral History Office, University of California/Berkeley, 1975.

Transcript of an oral history interview with the second-generation German Jewish poetess and civil liberties activist. Also contains descriptions of her many immigrant domestic servants.

1764. Sandberg, Sara. *Mama Made Minks*. Garden City, N.Y.: Doubleday, 1964.

A second-generation Austrian Jew tells of her childhood, focusing on her mother who ran a Harlem fur store.

1765. Sandberg, Sara. *My Sister Goldie*. Garden City, N.Y.: Doubleday, 1968.

A second-generation Austrian Jew describes her family's move to Riverside Drive and to middle- class life.

1766. Sandoz, Mari. *Sandhill Sundays and Other Recollections*. Lincoln: University of Nebraska Press, 1970; orig. publ. 1927.

The second-generation German and Swiss novelist.

1767. Sandoz, Mari. *The Christmas of Phonograph Records: A Recollection*. Lincoln: University of Nebraska Press, 1966.

The second-generation German and Swiss novelist recalls details of her prairie childhood.

1768. Sanger, Margaret Higgins. *Margaret Sanger, an Autobiography*. New York: W.W. Norton, 1938.

The second-generation Irish birth-control reformer.

1769. Sanger, Margaret Higgins. *My Fight for Birth Control*. New York: Farrar & Rinehart, 1931.

The second-generation Irish birth-control activist.

1770. Saroff, Sophie. *Stealing the State: An Oral History*. New York: Community Documentation Workshop, 1983.

A Russian Jew.

1771. Schechter, Hope M. Hope Mendoza Schechter--Activist in the Labor Movement, the Democratic Party, and the Mexican-American Community: An Interview. Berkeley, Cal.: Regional Oral History Office, Bancroft Library, University of California, Berkeley, 1980.

An oral history with this second-generation Mexican labor activist in the garment industry.

1772. Schelbert, Leo. "On Interpreting Immigrant Letters: The Case of Johann Caspar and Wilhelmina Honegger-Hanhart." Yearbook of German-American Studies 16 (1981): 141-152.

A German man's and woman's views of migration and early settlement contrasted sharply.

1773. Schenck, Lucy Reissig. Seven, Eight--Shut the Gate! The Heartwarming Story of an American Family. New York: Greenwich Book Publishers, 1958.

A second-generation German girl growing up in her minister father's home.

1774. Schneider, Aili Gronlund. The Finnish Bakers' Daughters. Ontario: The Multicultural History Society of Ontario, 1986.

A second-generation Finn born in Canada, migrated several times between the two countries with her family.

1775. Schneiderman, Rose with Lucy Goldthwaite. All for One: Chapters from a Passionate Autobiography. Boston: Houghton Mifflin, 1918.

A Russian Jewish labor activist.

1776. Schneiderman, Rose. "A Cap Maker's Story." The Independent 58 (1905): 935-938.

A Russian Jewish labor activist.

1777. Schroeder, Adolf E. and Carla Schulz-Geisberg, ed. Hold Dear, As Always; Jette, a German Immigrant Life in Letters. Columbia, Mo.: University of Missouri Press, 1988.

Letters written to family members in Germany from 1836 to 1897.

1778. Schroeter, Elizabeth A. From Here to the Pinnacles: Memories of Mennonite Life in the Ukraine and in America. New York: Exposition, 1956.

A Ukrainian from a Mennonite family who acquired a Ph.D.

248   IMMIGRANT WOMEN IN THE U.S.

1779. Seckar, Alvena V. "Slovak Wedding Customs." <u>New York Folklore Quarterly</u> 3 (Autumn 1947): 189-205.

A memoir of her experience as a flower girl in a West Virginia mining-camp wedding; good description of the bride, music and food.

1780. Segal, Lore Groszmann. <u>Other People's Houses</u>. New York: Harcourt, Brace & World, 1958.

An Austrian Jew sent to England during World War II, went to the Dominican Republic before migrating to the U.S.

1781. Segale, Rose M. <u>At the End of the Santa Fé Trail</u>. Columbus: Columbian Press, 1932.

An Italian-born nun who worked in New Mexico.

1782. Seklow, Edna. <u>So Talently My Children</u>. Cleveland: World, 1966.

A second-generation Eastern European Jewish playwright tells of her New York depression childhood and family.

1783. Sermolino, Maria. <u>Papa's Table d'Hote</u>. Philadelphia: Lippincott, 1952.

A second-generation Italian journalist tells of growing up in and around her parents' Greenwich Village restaurant.

1784. Shand, Margaret Clark with Ora M. Shand. <u>The Summit and Beyond</u>. Caldwell, Idaho: Caxton, 1959.

A Scottish adventuress in California and Alaska, where she operated roadhouses.

1785. Shaw, Anna H. <u>The Story of a Pioneer</u>. New York: Harper, 1915.

The English suffragist and minister who worked in Michigan and Massachusetts.

1786. Sher, Eva Goldstein. <u>Life with Father Goldstein</u>. New York: Funk & Wagnalls, 1967.

A second-generation Russian Jew growing up on a New Jersey farm.

1787. Shick, Maete Gordon. <u>The Burden and the Trophy; An Autobiography</u>. Trans. Mary J. Reuben. New York: Pageant, 1957.

A Lithuanian Jew followed her husband to a dairy business and poverty in the U.S.

1788. Siegal, Aranka. *Grace in the Wilderness: After the Liberation, 1945-1948.* New York: Farrar, Straus & Giroux, 1985.

A Hungarian Jewish Holocaust survivor's experiences in Sweden, prior to migration to U.S.

1789. Siegal, Aranka. *Upon the Head of the Goat: A Childhood in Hungary, 1939-1944.* New York: Farrar, Straus & Giroux, 1981.

The Hungarian childhood of a Holocaust survivor.

1790. Simon, Kate. *A Wider World, Portraits of a Adolescence.* New York: Harper and Row, 1986.

An Eastern European Jew. The book is a sequel to *Bronx Primitive.*

1791. Simon, Kate. *Bronx Primitive: Portraits in a Childhood.* New York: Viking Press, 1982.

An Eastern European Jewish memoir of childhood.

1792. Simonian, Leonie B. *Shadow of Destiny.* Whittier: Western Printing Corporation, 1933.

A French singer who settled in California.

1793. Siwundhla, Alice (Princess Msumba). *Alice Princess-- An Autobiography.* Mountain View, Cal.: Pacific Press, 1965.

This African woman became a U.S. college student with missionary support.

1794. Siwundhla, Alice (Princess Msumba). *My Two Worlds.* Mountain View, Cal.: Pacific Press, 1971.

African, a sequel to *Alice Princess.*

1795. Slater, Lisa A. *The Rape of Berlin.* Brooklyn: Pageant-Poseidon Ltd., 1972.

A German born in Berlin writes of her anti-Communist reactions to occupation of the city.

1796. Snow, Carmel White with Mary Louise White Aswell. *The World of Carmel Snow.* New York: McGraw-Hill, 1962.

An Irish editor for *Vogue* and *Harper's Bazaar.*

1797. Soldene, Emily. *My Theatrical and Musical Recollections.* London: Downey, 1897.

An English actress and singer's U.S. career.

250   IMMIGRANT WOMEN IN THE U.S.

1798. Solomon, Hannah G. *Fabric of My Life, the Autobiography of Hannah G. Solomon*. New York: Bloch Publishing Co. for the National Council of Jewish Women, 1946.

A second-generation German Jewish community activist and foundress of the National Council of Jewish women.

1799. Sone, Monica Itoi. *Nisei Daughter*. Boston: Little, Brown, 1953.

A second-generation Japanese and her hotel-owning Seattle family; includes account of their internment during World War II.

1800. Soong, Irma Tam. *Chinese-American Refugee: A World War II Memoir*. Honolulu: Hawaii Chinese History Center, 1984.

1801. Soregi, Priscilla Varga. *Come Back, My Son, Come Back*. New York: Comet Press, 1959.

A Hungarian writes of homestead life in Oklahoma.

1802. Spacks, Patricia Meyer. "Selves in Hiding." Pp. 112-132 *Women's Autobiography*. Ed. Estelle C. Jelinek. Bloomington: Indiana University Press, 1980.

Includes some analysis of the autobiographies of Emma Goldman and Golda Meir.

1803. Sponland, Ingeborg. *My Reasonable Service*. Minneapolis: Augsburg Publishing House, 1938.

A Norwegian Lutheran deaconess and nurse.

1804. Stan, Anisoara. *They Crossed Mountains and Oceans*. New York: William-Frederick, 1947.

A Rumanian exhibitor and importer of folk art and crafts.

1805. Stanley, Ilse Davidsohn. *The Unforgotten*. Boston: Beacon, 1957.

A German Jewish woman who migrated with her son to relatives during the 1930s.

1806. Steel, Edward M., ed. *The Correspondence of Mother Jones*. Pittsburgh: University of Pittsburgh Press, 1985.

Letters dated 1900-1930 describe her life; includes a biographical note.

1807. Stenhouse, Fanny. *Expose of Polygamy in Utah. A Lady's Life among the Mormons...as One of the Wives of a Mormon Elder During a Period of More than Twenty Years*. New York: American News Co., 1872.

An English Mormon who became a wife in a plural marriage.

AUTOBIOGRAPHY   251

1808. Stern, Elizabeth G. (writing as Leah Morton). I am a Woman--and a Jew. New York: J.H. Sears, 1926.

A second-generation German Jewish community activist.

1809. Stern, Elizabeth G. (writing as Leah Morton). When Love Comes to Woman. New York: J. H. Sears, 1929.

A second-generation Russian Jew, focusing on her case work with young unwed mothers.

1810. Stern, Elizabeth G. My Mother and I. New York: MacMillan, 1917.

A second-generation German Jewish community activist; includes biographical information about her German Jewish mother.

1811. Stokes, Rose Pastor. "The Little Breadwinner." Jewish Currents 12 (June 1958): 8-11.

Two chapters from the unpublished autobiography of this Russian Jewish radical.

1812. Stokes, Rose Pastor. "Voice from the Sweatshop." Lilith 8 (1981): 24-25.

Excerpts from an unpublished autobiography by a Eastern European Jewish radical.

1813. Stone, Goldie. My Caravan of Years. New York: Bloch Publishing Co., 1945.

The life of a Jewish girl from Lithuania, her marriage and life of community service in Chicago.

1814. Sugimoto, Etsu Inagaki. A Daughter of the Samurai. Garden City: Doubleday, Page, 1925.

Japanese university teacher.

1815. Suttilagsana, Supattra. "Recurrent Themes in Asian American Autobiographical Literature." Unpublished Ph.D. Dissertation, Bowling Green State University, 1986. Order Number DA 8705514.

Analyzes the works of Jade Snow Wong, Jeanne Wakatsuki Houston, Kathleen Tamagawa Eldridge, and Maxine Hong Kingston.

1816. Tamagawa, Kathleen. Holy Prayers in a Horse's Ear. New York: Ray Long & Smith, 1932.

She migrated with her Japanese father and Irish mother.

252   IMMIGRANT WOMEN IN THE U.S.

1817. Tapping, Minnie Ellingson. **Eighty Years at the Gopher Hole; The Saga of a Minnesota Pioneer (1867-1947)**. New York: Exposition, 1958.

A second-generation Norwegian describes frontier life in Minnesota.

1818. Taylor, Elizabeth R. **Elizabeth Taylor; An Informal Memoir**. New York: Harper & Row, 1965.

The English actress.

1819. Taylor, Elizabeth R. **Nibbles and Me**. New York: Duell, Sloan, and Pearce, 1946.

The English child actress recounts, at age 13, her life with her pet chipmunk.

1820. Tetrazzini, Luisa. **My Life of Song**. London: Cassell, 1921.

An Italian opera singer, including information on her U.S. career.

1821. Thomas, William J. and Florian Znaniecki. **The Polish Peasant in Europe and America**. Ed. Eli Zaretsky. Champaign: University of Illinois Press, 1985.

Includes letters by Polish women in the section "Correspondence between Husbands and Wives."

1822. Thompson, Ariadne. **The Octagonal Heart**. Indianapolis: Bobbs-Merrill, 1956.

A second-generation Greek daughter of a businessman and consul in St. Louis.

1823. Thompson, Goldianne Guyer. **Pioneer Living with Mama; The Autobiography of Goldianne Guyer Thompson**. Denver: Publishers Press, 1971.

A second-generation German's childhood in Missouri and Texas.

1824. Thomson, Gladys Scott. **A Pioneer Family: The Birkbecks in Illinois 1818-1827**. London: Jonathan Cape, 1953.

Farm life in Illinois as described in letters by the English-born Elizabeth Birkbeck.

1825. Tompkins, Leonara Brooke. **My Lovely Days**. New York: Carlton, 1966.

An Indian woman born in Britain became a war bride after World War II and settled in Vermont.

1826. Tucker, Sophie. Some of these Days. Garden City: Doubleday, Doran, 1945.

A Russian Jewish singer.

1827. Uchida, Yoshiko. Desert Exile; The Uprooting of a Japanese American Family. Seattle: University of Washington Press, 1982.

A Japanese girl's account of internment, with much anecdotal material on family relations, women's and men's roles, women's organizations, the Japanese Women's Christian Temperance Association, women students' club, etc.

1828. Utley, Freda. Lost Illusion. Philadelphia: Fireside, 1948.

An English wife of a Russian political prisoner; she fled to the U.S.

1829. Utley, Freda. Odyssey of a Libera; Memoirs. Washington, D.C. : Washington National Press, 1970.

An English woman married to a Russian husband imprisoned in U.S.S.R., with an anti-Communist theme. She eventually migrated to the U.S.

1830. Velazquez, Loreta J. The Woman in Battle; A Narrative of the Exploits, Adventures and Travels of Madame Loreta Janeta Velazquez, Otherwise known as Lieutenant Harry T. Buford, Confederate States Army. Hartford: T. Belknap, 1876.

A Cuban male impersonator and Confederate spy.

1831. Viertel, Salka. The Kindness of Strangers. New York: Holt, Rinehart, and Winston, 1969.

A Polish Jewish actress in Hollywood.

1832. von Mises, Margit. My Life with Ludwig von Mises. New Rochelle, N.Y.: Arlington, 1976.

A German actress traveled with her scientist husband to the U.S. just before World War II.

1833. von Trapp, Maria A. Around the Year with the Trapp Family. New York: Pantheon, 1955.

The Austrian ex-nun, singer, and musician.

1834. von Trapp, Maria A. Maria. Carol Stream, Ill: Creation House, 1972.

The Austrian ex-nun, singer, and musician.

1835. von Trapp, Maria A. *The Story of the Trapp Family Singers, Yesterday, Today, and Forever*. Philadelphia: Lippincott, 1949.

The Austrian ex-nun, singer, and musician.

1836. von Trapp, Maria A. with Ruth T. Murdoch. *A Family on Wheels; Further Adventures of the Trapp Family Singers*. Philadelphia: Lippincott, 1959.

The Austrian ex-nun, singer, and musician.

1837. Wagner, Friedelind. *Heritage of Fire*. New York: Harper, 1945.

Wagner's German granddaughter, and her life in England and the U.S.

1838. Wald, Lillian D. *The House on Henry Street*. New York: Henry Holt, 1915.

This second-generation German Jewish nurse founded the social settlement.

1839. Wald, Lillian D. *Windows on Henry Street*. Boston: Little, Brown, 1934.

A sequel to *The House on Henry Street*; a second-generation German Jew.

1840. Wallach, Erica. *Light at Midnight*. Garden City: Doubleday, 1967.

This German woman was a member of the Communist Party and a spy before marrying an American soldier; the book tells of her return to Germany and imprisonment there as a spy.

1841. Walska, Ganna. *Always Room at the Top*. New York: R.R. Smith, 1943.

A Polish opera singer.

1842. Walther, Anna H. *A Pilgrimage with a Milliner's Needle*. New York: Frederick A. Stokes, 1917.

A Danish milliner in New York.

1843. Ward, Maisie. *To & Fro on the Earth: The Sequel to an Autobiography*. New York: Sheed and Ward, 1973.

An English biographer and Catholic activist.

1844. Ward, Maisie. *Unfinished Business*. New York: Sheed and Ward, 1964.

An English biographer and Catholic worker activist.

AUTOBIOGRAPHY   255

1845. Webster, Margaret. Don't Put Your Daughter on the Stage. New York: Alfred A. Knopf, 1972.

An English director, actress, and writer.

1846. Wheeler, Thomas C., ed. The Immigrant Experience; The Anguish of Becoming American. New York: Dial Press, 1971.

Includes Jade Snow Wong, "Puritans of the Orient," the account of a second-generation Chinese.

1847. Whiffen, Blanche Gaston. Keeping off the Shelf. New York: E.P. Dutton, 1928.

An English actress and her career on both sides of Atlantic.

1848. Wildenhain, Marguerite. The Invisible Core; A Potter's Life and Thoughts. Palo Alto, Cal.: Pacific, 1973.

A German girl, raised in France, who founded a craftsmen's colony in California.

1849. Wiley, Irena. Around the Globe in Twenty Years. New York: David McKay, 1962.

A Polish sculptress, married to an American diplomat.

1850. Williams, Katherine. Where Else but America?: Vignettes on American Life by a West Indian Female Immigrant. Annapolis: Fishergate Publishing, 1977.

1851. Winslow, Catherine Reignolds. Readings from the Old English Dramatists. Boston: Lee and Shephard, 1895.

An English actress.

1852. Winslow, Catherine Reignolds. Yesterdays with Actors. Boston: Cupples and Hurd, 1887.

An English actress.

1853. Wojciechowska, Maia. Till the Break of Day: Memories, 1939-1942. New York: Harcourt Brace Jovanovich, 1972.

A Polish woman who fled with her family to France and then to Washington.

1854. Wong, Diane Yen-Mei. Making Waves, An Anthology of Writings by and about Asian American Women. Boston: Beacon Press, 1988.

Besides autobiographical writings, this book contains short stories, poetry, and essays.

IMMIGRANT WOMEN IN THE U.S.

1855. Wong, Jade Snow. *Fifth Chinese Daughter*. New York: Harper & Row, 1950.

A second-generation Chinese, she wrote in the third person--a mode she found more appropriate for Chinese sensibilities.

1856. Wong, Jade Snow. *No Chinese Stranger*. New York: Harper & Row, 1975.

A sequel to *Fifth Chinese Daughter*, with heavy emphasis on her father's influence.

1857. Wong, Lorraine. "Chinese All American Girl." *The Record of the Girls' Friendly Society of the U.S.A.* 43 (January 1935): 22.

1858. Wormeley, Katharine. *The Other Side of the War; With the Army of the Potomac*. Boston: Ticknor & Co., 1889.

An English hospital and relief worker in Civil War.

1859. Woytinsky, Emma Shadkhan. *Two Lives in One*. New York: Praeger, 1965.

A Russian Jew who followed her diplomat husband to French, German, and finally U.S. posts.

1860. Xan, Erna Oleson as told to Thurine Oleson. *Wisconsin My Home*. Madison: University of Wisconsin Press, 1950.

A second-generation Norwegian's pioneer life on a Wisconsin farm.

1861. Yezierska, Anzia. *Red Ribbon on a White Horse*. New York: Scribners, 1950.

The Polish Jewish writer.

1862. Young, Ella. *Flowering Dusk*. New York: Longmans, Green, 1945.

An Irish writer and poet.

1863. Yurka, Blanche. *Bohemian Girl: Blanche Yurka's Theatrical Life*. Athens, Ohio: Ohio University Press, 1970.

A second-generation Czech actress.

1864. Yzenbaard, John H., ed. "'America' Letters from Holland." *Michigan History* 32 (March 1948): 37-65.

Letters written home from Michigan by a Dutch brother and sister.

1865. Zaharias, Mildred (Babe) Didrikson as told to Harry Paxton. *This Life I've Led: My Autobiography*. New York: A.S. Barnes, 1955.

The second-generation Norwegian athlete and her family life in Texas.

1866. Zaimi, Nexhmie. *Daughter of an Eagle, The Autobiography of an Albanian Girl*. New York: Ives Washburn, 1937.

The preparations of an Albanian Moslem girl for migration to the U.S.

1867. Zakrzewska, Marie E. *A Memoir*. Boston: New England Hospital for Women and Children, 1903.

A Polish, German-trained woman physician in New York and Boston.

1868. Zakrzewska, Marie E. *A Woman's Quest*. Ed. Agnes C. Vietor. New York: Appleton, 1924.

A Polish physician and women's rights advocate born in Germany.

1869. Zassenhaus, Hiltgunt. *Walls: Resisting the Third Reich--One Woman's Story*. Boston: Beacon Press, 1974.

A German who aided political prisoners in Denmark and Norway; she became a physician in the U.S.

1870. Zelayeta, Elena E. *Elena*. Englewood Cliffs, N.J.: Prentice-Hall, 1960.

A Mexican, of immigrant Spanish parents, who found success in the U.S. as a restaurateur and cookbook author.

12

Fiction

INTRODUCTION

This chapter lists fictional works, mainly novels, about the immigrant experience. A sizable minority of these works were written by women. As the length of the chapter reveals, fiction should be an important source of information for students of immigrant women. Yet these works have not received wide attention. Historians and social scientists have rarely attempted to use fiction as a primary source. Scholars of literature have had other reasons for ignoring much of this fiction, since little of it meets the criteria for inclusion in new or old literary canons. For scholars in the interdisciplinary fields of American studies and women's studies, on the other hand, fictional works of the kind cited here should be a particularly rich find.

The family saga is an important genre in fiction about immigrants. Many of the books included here fall into this category. Almost any family saga tells something of the lives of women, but I have cited mainly those works of fiction with significant or well-developed female characters.

A possibly important distinction in studying fiction is between those works written by "insiders" and those by "outsiders." After some thought, I decided to cite both types. The works of outsiders reveal much about the stereotyping of immigrants or women, while those by insiders often provide us with a better introduction to the subjectivity of immigrant women than is readily available in any other kind of source, with the possible exception of autobiography. Where possible I have indicated those works most obviously written from the perspective of the outsider.

Aside from writings of fiction, this chapter also includes citations to a small group of literary studies which analyze fiction by or about immigrant women.

CITATIONS

1871. Abucewicz, John A. *Fool's White*. New York: Carlton Press, 1969.

A second-generation Polish girl in Lowell Mass. becomes a nun.

1872. Aldrich, Bess S. *A Lantern in Her Hand*. New York: D. Appleton, 1928.

The story of Abbie Deal, a second-generation Scottish and Irish pioneer woman in Nebraska.

1873. Algren, Nelson. *Never Come Morning*. New York: Harper, 1942.

The story of a near-gangster and his Polish girlfriend, who ends up in a Chicago brothel.

1874. Asch, Sholem. *The Mother*. New York: Liveright, 1930.

A Polish Jewish mother's struggles with her second-generation daughters.

1875. Atkins, Annette. "Women on the Farming Frontier: The View from Fiction." *The Midwest Review*, 2nd series 3 (Spring 1981): 1-10.

Analysis of a number of writers about immigrant women on frontier, emphasizing the importance of Beret in Rolvaag's *Giants in the Earth* as the prototype for many portrayals of them.

1876. Avery, Evelyn G. "In Limbo: Immigrant Children and the American Dream." *MELUS* 8 (Winter 1981): 25-32.

Includes analysis of women characters in works by Yezierska, Puzo, and others.

1877. Babson, Naomi L. *Look Down from Heaven*. New York: Reynal & Hitchcock, 1942.

The life of a second-generation Finnish girl in a New England seaport.

1878. Baker, Estelle. *The Rose Door*. Chicago: Charles H. Kerr, 1911.

The story of an Eastern European Jewish girl who becomes a prostitute.

1879. Ball, Walter. *Carmella Commands*. New York: Harper & Bros., 1929.

The Americanization of a second-generation Italian, daughter of peasants in New York.

1880. Baner, Skulda V. <u>Latchstring Out</u>. Boston: Houghton Mifflin, 1944.

The story of a second-generation Swedish girl in Michigan.

1881. Bankowsky, Richard. <u>After Pentecost</u>. New York: Random House, 1961.

A Polish woman moves to New Jersey, and tragically dies.

1882. Bankowsky, Richard. <u>One Dark Night (Three Canticles)</u>. New York: Random House, 1964.

A Polish woman in New Jersey marries an older man.

1883. Bannan, Helen M. "Warrior Women: Immigrant Mothers in the Works of Their Daughters." <u>Women's Studies</u> 6, 2 (1979): 165-177.

An analysis of many immigrant women's novels and autobiographies, focusing on portrayals of their mothers.

1884. Barolini, Helen. <u>Umbertina</u>. New York: Seaview Books, 1979.

An Italian immigrant to western New York State and her granddaughter.

1885. Battle, Lois. <u>War Brides</u>. New York: St. Martin's Press, 1982.

Story of an English war bride.

1886. Beckley, Zoe. <u>A Chance to Live</u>. New York: The MacMillan Co., 1918.

A second-generation Irish girl and a fire at the "Circle Waist Company."

1887. Bell, Thomas. <u>Out of this Furnace</u>. Boston: Little, Brown and Co., 1941.

The tale of a Slovak from Hungary, and the continuing story of his daughter and her children in Pittsburgh.

1888. Bilik, Dorothy S. <u>Immigrant-Survivors: Post Holocaust Consciousness in Recent Jewish American Fiction</u>. Middletown, Conn.: Wesleyan University Press, 1980.

Some analysis of Susan Schaefer's <u>Anya</u>, the account of an Eastern European Jewish woman who eventually migrates to the U.S.

1889. Bjorn, Thyra F. <u>A Trilogy: Papa's Wife, Papa's Daughter, Mama's Way</u>. New York: Holt, Rinehart, and Winston, 1961.

A fictionalized account of the author's Swedish family.

262   IMMIGRANT WOMEN IN THE U.S.

1890. Blake, Eleanor. *Seedtime and Harvest*. New York: G.P. Putnam's Sons, 1935.

A second-generation Norwegian girl grows up in Michigan.

1891. Blicksilver, Edith. "Monica Krawczyk: Chronicler of Polish-American Life." *MELUS* 7 (Fall 1980): 13-20.

Examines the male and female characters in this Polish writer's fiction, especially *If the Branch Blossoms*.

1892. Blicksilver, Edith. "The Japanese-American Woman, the Second World War and the Relocation Camp Experience." *Women's Studies International Forum* 5, 3/4 (1982): 351-353.

Analyzes the work by Janice Mirikitani.

1893. Blustein, Bryna L. "Beyond the Stereotype: A Study of Representative Short Stories of Selected Contemporary Jewish American Female Writers." Unpublished Ph.D. Dissertation, Saint Louis University, 1986. Order Number DA 8628756.

Analysis of the writings of Anzia Yezierska and second-generation writers, including Tilly Olsen.

1894. Brice-Finch, Jacqueline L. "The Caribbean Diaspora: Four Aspects, in Novels from 1971-1975." Unpublished Ph.D. Dissertations, University of Maryland, College Park, 1987. Order Number DA 8725503.

Analysis of female characters in migration and return, including attention to writings of Paule Marshall.

1895. Brinig, Myron. *May Flavin*. Toronto and New York: Farrar & Rinehart, 1938.

An Irish woman raises her family in the slums of New York.

1896. Bristol, Helen O. *Let the Blackbird Sing: A Novel in Verse*. New York: Exposition Press, 1952.

This novel in verse includes the story of a Polish woman of German descent.

1897. Brock, E. L. *Here Comes Kristie*. New York: Alfred A. Knopf, 1942.

A children's book about a Norwegian girl in Minnesota.

1898. Budd, Lillian. *April Harvest*. New York: Duell, Sloan, and Pearce, 1959.

A second-generation Swedish girl leaves Chicago to return to Europe.

1899. Budd, Lillian. *April Snow*. Philadelphia: J.B. Lippincott Co., 1951.

First of a trilogy about a Swedish Chicago family, with good portraits of the women.

1900. Budd, Lillian. *Land of Strangers*. Philadelphia: Lippincott, 1953.

A Swedish couple adjusts to Chicago.

1901. Bullard, Arthur. *Comrade Yetta*. New York: MacMillan, 1913.

A Jewish garment worker during the 1909 strike.

1902. Burns, John H. *The Gallery*. New York and London: Harper & Brothers Publishers, 1947.

Includes the story of some Italian war brides.

1903. Cahan, Abraham. *Yekl and the Imported Bridegroom, and Other Stories of the New York Ghetto*. New York: Dover Publications, 1970.

Stories about Eastern European Jews in New York, originally published in 1896 and 1898.

1904. Cannon, Cornelia J. *Heirs*. Boston: Little, Brown, 1930.

A Polish schoolteacher falls in love with a wealthy Yankee in New Hampshire.

1905. Cannon, Cornelia J. *Red Rust*. Boston: Little, Brown, 1928.

Swedish man succeeds in raising a new form of wheat in Minnesota only because of his wife's hard work; includes portraits also of the man's sister and step-daughter.

1906. Carr, Harriett H. *Borghild of Brooklyn*. New York: Ariel, 1955.

A child's story of a Norwegian girl in Brooklyn.

1907. Casey, Daniel J. and Robert E. Rhoades, eds. *Irish-American Fiction, Essays in Criticism*. New York: AMS Press, 1979.

See especially Bonnie Kimel Scott, "Women's Perspectives in Irish-American Fiction from Betty Smith to Mary McCarthy," pp. 87-104 and Maureen Murphy, "Elizabeth Cullinan: Yellow and Gold," pp. 139-172.

1908. Castle, William and Robert Joseph. *Hero's Oak*. New York: Reader's Press, 1945.

A Polish woman living on a Vermont farm from 1910 to 1936.

1909. Cather, Willa. "The Bohemian Girl." Pp. 13-42 *Willa Cather's Collected Short Fiction, 1892-1912*. Lincoln: University of Nebraska Press, 1970.

1910. Cather, Willa. *My Antonia*. Boston: Houghton Mifflin Co., 1918.

A Bohemian girl grows up on the prairies of Nebraska; also includes the stories of Scandinavian first- and second-generation women.

1911. Cather, Willa. *O Pioneers!* Boston: Houghton Mifflin Company, 1913.

The two main characters are a second-generation Swedish woman and a Bohemian girl of the prairies.

1912. Cather, Willa. *The Song of the Lark*. Boston: Houghton Mifflin, 1915.

A second-generation Swedish woman becomes an artist.

1913. Cautela, Giuseppe. *Moon Harvest*. New York: Dial Press, 1925.

A young Italian couple travels to America.

1914. Chase, Mary E. *Mary Christmas*. Boston: Little, Brown & Co., 1926.

The life of an Armenian woman living in New England.

1915. Christianson, J. R. "Literary Traditions of Norwegian-American Women." Pp. 92-110 *Makers of an American Immigrant Legacy: Essays in Honor of Kenneth O. Bjork*. Ed. Odd S. Lovoll. Northfield, Minn.: The Norwegian-American Historical Association, 1980.

1916. Christman, Elizabeth. *A Nice Italian Girl*. New York: Dodd, 1976.

Story of an unwed mother, a second-generation Italian.

1917. Chu, Louis. *Eat a Bowl of Tea*. New York: Lyle Stuart, 1961.

Includes the story of a Chinese war bride.

1918. Cohen, Lester. *Coming Home*. New York: Viking, 1945.

A World War II veteran returns home to the second-generation Polish girl he left behind.

1919. Cohen, Sarah B. "Mary Antin's *The Promised Land*: A Breach of Promise." *Studies in American Jewish Literature* 3 (Winter 1977-78): 28-35.

FICTION   265

1920. Colby, Frances B. *The Black Winds Blow*. New York: Harrison-Hilton Books, 1940.

An Irish girl marries into a wealthy Boston family.

1921. Conway, Brooks (pseud.). *The Loving are the Daring*. New York: Prentice-Hall, 1947.

A second-generation German widow raises six children in the midwest.

1922. Crane, Stephen. *Maggie: A Girl of the Streets*. New York: D. Appleton & Co., 1896.

The fall of a New York Irish girl.

1923. Crew, Helen C. *Alanna*. New York: Harper & Bros., 1929.

An Irish woman leaves her village to join an aunt and uncle in Baltimore.

1924. Cullinan, Elizabeth. *House of Gold*. Boston: Houghton Mifflin Co., 1970.

The theme is an Irish mother's pride in home ownership.

1925. Curran, Mary D. *The Parish and the Hill*. Boston: Houghton Mifflin, 1948.

The narrator of this family story is a third-generation Irish girl growing up in Holyoke, Mass.; contains portraits of her second-generation mother and immigrant grandparents.

1926. Dahl, Borghild. *Karen*. New York: Random House, 1947.

A Norwegian servant girl marries in Dakota.

1927. De Capite, Michael. *Maria*. New York: John Day Co., 1943.

The story of a second-generation Italian girl.

1928. Dearborn, Mary V. *Pocahontas's Daughters; Gender and Ethnicity in American Culture*. New York and Oxford: Oxford University Press, 1986.

Analysis of the writings and lives of Anzia Yezierska, Martha Ostenso, Elizabeth Stern, and Mary Antin.

1929. Deasy, Mary. *The Hour of Spring*. Boston: Little, Brown, 1948.

An Irish family saga which includes good portraits of second-generation women.

1930. Deighton, Len. *Goodbye, Mickey Mouse*. New York: Ballantine Books, 1982.

Includes the story of an English war bride.

1931. DeLespinasse, Cobie. *The Bells of Helmus*. Portland, Ore.: Metropolitan Press Publishers, 1934.

A 13-year-old girl becomes a Dutch community's "bad" woman.

1932. Di Donato, Pietro. *This Woman*. New York: Ballantine, 1958.

Continues the story of some of the characters in Di Donato's better-known novels, *Christ in Concrete* and *Three Circles of Light*, but with more attention to women.

1933. Dickens, Monica. *The Nightingales are Singing*. Boston: Little, Brown & Co., 1953.

The story of an English war bride.

1934. Dineen, Joseph F. *Queen Midas*. Boston: Little, Brown, 1958.

An Irish girl rises to wealth in Boston.

1935. Dooley, Roger. *Days Beyond Recall*. Milwaukee: Bruce, 1949.

The life of an Irish woman in Buffalo.

1936. Dreiser, Theodore. *Jennie Gerhardt*. New York: World Publishing, 1911.

A second-generation German girl falls in love with an Irish man.

1937. Driscoll, Paul. *My Felicia*. New York: MacMillan, 1945.

A second-generation Polish girl must choose between community and wealthy American love.

1938. Dunphy, Jack. *Nightmovers*. New York: Morrow, 1967.

The life of an Irish widow in Brooklyn.

1939. Dyrud, David L. "Varies of Marginality: The Treatment of the European Immigrant in the Middlewestern Frontier Novel." Unpublished Ph.D. Dissertation, Purdue University, 1979.

See especially the chapter "Familial Tensions."

1940. Fairbanks, Carol. "Lives of Girls and Women on the Canadian and American Prairies." <u>International Journal of Women's Studies</u> 2 (September/October 1979): 452-472.

Analysis of autobiographies and novels, some of which address the stories of immigrant women.

1941. Fairbanks, Carol. <u>Prairie Women: Images in American and Canadian Fiction</u>. New Haven, Conn.: Yale University Press, 1986.

Immigrant fiction writers from non-English-speaking countries did not so often portray women as reluctant pioneers or idealize their male characters as much as writers of other backgrounds.

1942. Fanning, Charles. "Elizabeth Cullinan's <u>House of Gold</u>: Culmination of an Irish-American Dream." <u>MELUS</u> 7 (Winter 1980): 31-48.

Subject of article is the powerful Irish mother who figures in Cullnan's works.

1943. Far, Sui Sin (pseud. Edith M. Eaton). <u>Mrs. Spring Fragrance</u>. Chicago: A.C. McClung, 1912.

A Chinese woman's life.

1944. Feld, Rose C. <u>Sophie Halenczik, American</u>. Boston: Little, Brown & Co., 1943.

The story of a Czech widow in Connecticut.

1945. Fenollosa, Mary. <u>Sunshine Beggars</u>. Boston: Little, Brown & Co., 1918.

An Italian family saga in New England seaport town, with good portrayals of women.

1946. Ferber, Edna. <u>Fanny Herself</u>. New York: A. Stokes Co., 1917.

The life of a Jewish immigrant.

1947. Ferber, Edna. <u>So Big</u>. New York: Fawcett, 1973, orig. publ. 1924.

Life of a Dutch widow and her son.

1948. Fernald, Helen C. <u>Plow the Dew Under</u>. New York: Longmans, Green, 1952.

The story of Russian German Mennonites in Kansas and an immigrant mother eager to Americanize.

1949. Field, Rachel. *All This, and Heaven Too*. New York: Macmillan, 1938.

The fictionalized life of French woman who became a New York hostess.

1950. Fine, David M. *The City, The Immigrant, and American Fiction, 1880-1920*. Metuchen: Scarecrow Press, 1977.

Some attention to the works of Mary Antin, Myra Kelly, Anzia Yezierska, and a number of lesser known women writers. Useful bibliography.

1951. Fisher, Jerilyn B. "The Minority Woman's Voice: A Cultural Study of Black and Chicana Fiction." Unpublished Ph.D. Dissertation, American University, 1978. Order Number 7817917.

No attention to generation; some analysis of work of Estela Portillo. Author found that, unlike men, minority women writers did not focus on racial clashes, but rather on "interracial struggles" between the sexes.

1952. Flack, Ambrose. *Family on the Hill*. New York: Thomas Y. Crowell Co., 1945.

A Czech family saga, with good portrait of the mother.

1953. Forbes, Kathryn. *Mamma's Bank Account*. New York: Harcourt, Brace & Co., 1943.

A Norwegian family in San Francisco, with special attention to the mother.

1954. Freitag, George. *The Lost Land*. New York: Coward, 1947.

A second-generation Irish girl marries a German-American man.

1955. French, Marilyn. *Her Mother's Daughter*. New York: Summit Books, 1987.

Three generations of women in a Polish family in New York.

1956. Frye, Joanne S. "The Woman Warrior: Claiming Narrative Power, Recreating Female Selfhood." *The Faith of a (Woman) Writer*. Ed. Alice Kessler-Harris and William McBrien. Westport, Conn.: Greenwood Press, 1988.

Analysis of the writings of Maxine Hong Kingston.

1957. Fuller, Margaret W. *Alma*. New York: William Morrow & Co., 1927.

The life of a Danish woman.

1958. Gamble, Lillian. *Mor's New Land*. New York: Exposition Press, 1951.

The tale of a Norwegian woman and her family.

1959. Gartner, Carol B. "A New Mirror for America: The Fiction of the Immigrant Ghetto, 1890-1930." Unpublished Ph.D. Dissertation, New York University, 1970. Order Number DA 70-18,999.

Discusses Anzia Yezierska and Myra Kelly (second-generation Irish teacher of East Side Jews) and their writings.

1960. Gidding, Joshua. *The Old Girl: A Novel*. New York: Holt, Rinehart & Winston, 1980.

The story of the author's Eastern European Jewish grandmother.

1961. Gold, Michael. *Jews without Money*. New York: Avon, 1973. Orig. publ. 1930.

Stories of Eastern European Jews, see especially "Did God Make Bedbugs?" and "The Gangster's Mother."

1962. Goldberg, Mark F. "The Representation of Love and Romance in American Fiction about East European Jews in New York City: 1894-1917." Unpublished Ph.D. Dissertation, New York University, 1970. Order Number DA 71-13,643.

1963. Goldstein, Ruth T. *The Heart is Half a Prophet*. New York: MacMillan, 1976.

A second-generation Hassidic girl growing up in Brooklyn in the 1930s.

1964. Gosselink, Sara E. *Roofs Over Strawtown*. Grand Rapids, Mich.: William B. Eerdmans Publishing Co., 1945.

The story of Pella, Iowa, a Dutch settlement, as narrated by an elderly woman to her grandson.

1965. Granowicz, Antoni. *An Orange Full of Dreams*. New York: Dodd, Mead, 1971.

A Polish actress retires in California.

1966. Granowicz, Antoni. *Bolek*. Edinburgh and New York: Thomas Nelson & Sons, 1942.

A second-generation Polish girl goes to Poland and brings Bolek back with her.

1967. Gringhuis, Richard H. *Hope Haven: A Tale of a Dutch Boy and Girl who Found a New Home in America*. Grand Rapids, Mich.: William B. Eerdmans Publishing Co., 1947.

A children's book.

270   IMMIGRANT WOMEN IN THE U.S.

1968. Gringhuis, Richard H. *Tulip Time*. Chicago: A. Whitman & Co., 1951.

A child's book about a second-generation boy and girl who help their Dutch uncle win a prize.

1969. Habe, Hans (pseud. Jean Bekessy). *Off Limits*. Trans. Ewald Osers. New York: Frederick Fell, Inc., 1957.

The story of a German war bride.

1970. Habe, Hans (pseud. Jean Bekessy). *Walk in Darkness*. Trans. Richard Hanser. New York: G.P. Putnam's Sons, 1948.

The story of a German war bride.

1971. Hagopian, Richard. *Faraway the Spring*. New York: C. Scribner's Sons, 1952.

The tale of a caring but unlovable Armenian mother.

1972. Hapgood, Hutchins. *An Anarchist Woman*. New York: Duffield, 1909.

The story of a second-generation radical of German and French parentage.

1973. Havighurst, Walter and Marion. *High Prairie*. New York: Farrar & Rinehart, 1944.

The life of a Norwegian boy and girl growing up in Wisconsin.

1974. Hobart, Alice T. *The Cup and the Sword*. Indianapolis: Bobbs-Merrill Co., 1942.

A half-French, half-English woman goes to live with her French grandparents in California.

1975. Hughes, Rupert. *Love Story*. New York: Harper and Brothers, 1934.

The story of a second-generation Polish opera singer in New York.

1976. Hughes, Rupert. *The Triumphant Clay*. Hollywood: House Warven, 1951.

The life of second-generation Polish woman in New York.

1977. Hurst, Fannie. *Lummox*. New York: Harper, 1923.

A second-generation servant girl of Swedish and Slav parents, living in New York.

1978. Ifkovic, Edward. *Anna Marinkovich*. New York: Maryland Books, 1980.

The story of a Croatian woman.

FICTION 271

1979. Inglehart, Babette. "Daughters of Loneliness: Anzia Yezierska and the Immigrant Woman Writer." Studies in American Jewish Literature 1 (Winter 1975).

The life and fiction of this Polish Jewish writer.

1980. Ishiguro, Kazuo. A Pale View of Hills. New York: Penguin Books, 1983.

The life of a Japanese war bride.

1981. Janney, Russell. The Miracle of the Bells. New York: Prentice Hall, 1948.

A second-generation Polish girl dies just as her Hollywood career is about to take off.

1982. Jessey, Cornelia. Teach the Angry Spirit. New York: Corwin Publishers, 1949.

A brother and sister growing up in Mexican Los Angeles during World War II.

1983. Jessey, Cornelia. The Growing Roots. New York: Crown Publishers, 1947.

The story of a Jewish family in Colorado in the 1890s, with special focus on the daughter.

1984. Jones, Elizabeth O. Maminka's Children. New York: MacMillan Co., 1940.

A child's book about a Czech mother and her children.

1985. Kelly, Myra. Little Aliens. New York: Grosset and Dunlap, 1910.

Stories by a second-generation Irish school teacher in Lower East Side schools; see especially "The Etiquette of Yetta," which focuses on a Eastern European Jewish girl.

1986. Kim, Elaine H. Asian American Literature, an Introduction to the Writings and their Social Context. Philadelphia: Temple University Press, 1982.

The authors analyzed include Maxine Hong Kingston and Jade Snow Wong, as well as several less well known writers of shorter fiction. See especially "Chinatown Cowboys and Warrior Women: Searching for a New Self-Image" and a section in the final chapter on "Asian American Women's Writings."

1987. Korfker, Dena. Ankie Comes to America. Grand Rapids, Mich.: Zondervan Publishing House, 1954.

A child's book about a little Dutch girl's journey.

1988. Krawczyk, Monica. *If the Branch Blossoms and Other Stories*. Minneapolis: Polonie, 1950.

Includes several stories about Polish women.

1989. Lacovia, R.M. "Migration and Transmutation in the Novels of McKay, Marshall, and Clarke." *Journal of Black Studies* 7 (June 1977): 437-454.

Some analysis of the writings of Paule Marshall as well as attention to women characters in novels by McKay and Clark.

1990. Larsson, Gösta. *Ships in the River*. New York: McGraw Hill Book Co., 1946.

A Norwegian woman marries a Czech in New York.

1991. Laufer, Pearl D. "Between Two Worlds: The Fiction of Anzia Yezierska." Unpublished Ph.D. Dissertation, University of Maryland, 1981. Order Number DA8202617.

Analyzes selected novels, emphasizing the author's modernity in comparison to native fiction writers of the period.

1992. Lederer, Charlotte. *Yanko in America*. New York: Thomas Y. Crowell Co., 1943.

A children's book about a Slovak brother and sister.

1993. Levenberg, Diane E. "Parents and their Children in the American-Jewish Novel of Immigration, 1912-1946." Unpublished Ph.D. Dissertation, New York University, 1987. Order Number DA 8801549.

Analyzes novels by Mary Antin, Anzia Yezierska and Beatrice Bisno.

1994. Levin, Meyer. *The Old Bunch*. New York: Citadel Press, 1946, orig. publ. 1937.

Cultural change among ten Eastern European Jewish boys and girls in Chicago in the 1920s and 1930s.

1995. Lewis, Janet. *Against a Darkening Sky*. New York: Doubleday, 1943.

A Scottish woman and her Swiss husband in Encina, California.

1996. Lewisohn, Ludwig. *Trumpet of Jubilee*. New York: Harper, 1937.

The widow of a German Jew murdered by Nazis goes to relatives in the U.S.

1997. Lin, Yu-Taug. *Chinatown Family, A Novel*. New York: J. Day Co., 1948.

Good characterizations of the mother and daughter of the family.

1998. Lindsay, Mela M. *Shuka Balan: The White Lamb*. Lincoln, Neb.: American Historical Society of Germans from Russia, 1976.

A German Russian peasant girl emigrates.

1999. Lion, Hortense. *The Grass Grows Green*. New York: Houghton Mifflin, 1935.

A Bavarian woman in New York during World War I.

2000. Lundeberg, Olav T. *The Song of Aino*. Minneapolis: Augsburg, 1942.

A Finnish-American girl living in North Minnesota.

2001. Mannin, Ethel. *Red Rose: A Novel Based on the Life of Emma Goldman*. London: Jarrolds, 1941.

A fictionalized account of the Russian Jewish anarchist's life.

2002. Marshall, Paule. "Black Immigrant Women in *Brown Girl, Brownstones*." Pp. 2-13 *Female Immigrants to the United States: Caribbean, Latin American and African Experiences*. Ed. Delores Mortimer and Roy Bryce-Laporte. Washington, D.C.: Research Institute on Immigration and Ethnic Studies, Smithsonian Institute, 1981.

Caribbean women are triply invisible--as women, as Afro-Americans, and as foreigners.

2003. Marshall, Paule. *Brown Girl, Brownstones*. New York: Random House, 1959.

A second-generation Barbadian girl growing up in Brooklyn.

2004. Matson, Norman H. *Day of Fortune*. New York: D. Appleton-Century Co., 1928.

A Norwegian family tale with good portraits of women.

2005. Mazow, Julia W. *The Woman who Lost Her Names: Selected Writings of American Jewish Women*. San Francisco: Harper & Row, 1980.

A number of the short stories focus on immigrant and second-generation women, and some are written by them as well.

2006. McAlpine, Dale. *Marie Naimska: A Saga of Chicago*. Philadelphia: Dorrance & Co., 1954.

A Chicago Polish family saga, with good portraits of the women.

2007. McDonald, Julie. *Amalie's Story*. New York: Simon & Schuster, 1970.

A Danish woman and her husband settle in Iowa.

2008. McSorley, Edward. *Kitty, I Hardly Knew You*. New York: Doubleday, 1959.

The story of two young Irish immigrants.

2009. Means, Florence. *The Moved Outers*. Boston: Houghton Mifflin, 1945.

The story of a Japanese family and its internment.

2010. Michel, Sonya. "Mothers and Daughters in American Jewish Literature: The Rotted Cord." Pp. 272-82 *The Jewish Woman: New Perspectives*. Ed. Elizabeth Koltun. New York: Schocken Books, 1976.

2011. Michener, James. *Sayonara*. New York: Random House, 1954.

The story of a Japanese war bride and her husband.

2012. Miller, Beth, ed. *Women in Hispanic Literature: Icons and Fallen Idols*. Berkeley: University of California Press, 1983.

See especially Elizabeth Ordonez, "Sexual Politics and the Theme of Sexuality in Chicana Poetry," pp. 316-339.

2013. Miller, Helen. *Kirsti*. New York: Doubleday, 1965.

A Finnish girl in Idaho defies her family for a boy of a different religion.

2014. Miniter, Edith. *Our Natupski Neighbors*. New York: Henry Holt, 1916.

A Polish family in New England, with good attention to the wife of the family.

2015. Morante, Elsa. *History: A Novel*. Trans Angus Davidson. New York: A. A. Knopf, 1977.

Includes the story of an Italian war bride.

2016. Mori, Toshio. *Woman from Hiroshima*. San Francisco: Isthmus Press, 1978.

A Japanese woman's life.

2017. Mori, Toshio. *Yokohama, California*. Caldwell, Idaho: Caxton, 1949.

See especially "The Woman Who Makes Swell Doughnuts," the portrait of a Japanese woman.

2018. Namioka, Lensey. *Who's Hu*. New York: The Vanguard Press, 1980.

A novel about growing up female and Chinese-American.

2019. Nathan, Robert. *The Sea-Gull Cry*. New York: Knopf, 1942.

A Polish refugee makes friends at Cape Cod.

2020. Nemic, Bozena. *The Grandmother*. Chicago: A.C. McClurg & Co, 1931.

The life of a Croatian woman.

2021. Nieh, Hualing. *Mulberry and Peach: Two Women of China*. Boston: Beacon Press, 1988.

A young woman in wartime China and her problems after emigrating.

2022. Ormonda, Czenzi. *Laughter from Downstairs*. New York: Farrar, Strauss, 1948.

A Czech family's story, written from the perspective of the nine-year-old daughter.

2023. Ornitz, Samuel. *Bride of the Sabbath*. New York: Rinehart & Company, 1951.

An account of Lower East Side Jewish life, with several important secondary female characters.

2024. Orton, Helen. *The Winding River: A Story of French Émigrés on the Susquehanna*. Philadelphia: J.B. Lippincott Co., 1944.

A French girl and her aunt travel to Pennsylvania in the 1790s.

2025. Ostenso, Martha. *O River Remember*. New York: Dodd, Mead & Co., 1943.

A Norwegian girl and her family.

2026. Pagano, Jo. *Golden Wedding*. New York: Random House, 1943.

An Italian family in Italy, Colorado, Utah, and California, with a good portrait of the mother.

276   IMMIGRANT WOMEN IN THE U.S.

2027. Pasquarelli, John. *The Temporary Wife*. New York: New Voices, 1954.

Italian lovers emigrate to the U.S.

2028. Perkins, Luch F. *Cornelia; The Story of a Benevolent Despot*. Boston: Houghton Mifflin Co., 1919.

The main character is the mischievous second-generation Dutch daughter of a minister.

2029. Petrakis, Harry M. *A Dream of Kings*. New York: David McKay, 1966.

Includes the story of a Greek widow who runs a pastry shop.

2030. Petrakis, Harry M. *In the Land of Mourning*. New York: David McKay, 1966.

Like many of his works, includes the story of a Greek widow.

2031. Petrakis, Harry M. *Pericles on 31st Street*. Chicago: Quadrangle Books, 1965.

Contains several stories about Greek widows.

2032. Petrakis, Harry M. *The Odyssey of Kostas Volakis*. New York: David McKay, 1963.

The story of a Greek and his wife in Chicago in the 1920s.

2033. Pine, Hester. *The Waltz is Over*. New York: Farrar & Rinehart, 1943.

A three-generation German family saga, with good attention to women.

2034. Puzo, Mario. *The Fortunate Pilgrim*. New York: Lancer Books, 1964.

A fictionalized account of the author's Italian mother.

2035. Rabine, Leslie W. "No Lost Paradise: Social Gender and Symbolic Gender in the Writings of Maxine Hong Kingston." *SIGNS: Journal of Women in Culture and Society* 12 (1987): 471-492.

Includes a good bibliography of Hong's writings.

2036. Ralph, Julian. *People We Pass, Stories of Life Among the Masses of New York City*. New York: Harper and Brothers, 1896.

Short stories tell of immigrant and second-generation Irish and German life in New York; some focus on women.

2037. Randolph, Vance. <u>Hedwig</u>. New York: Vanguard, 1935.

A German-Russian girl travels to Kansas, Oklahoma, and the Ozarks.

2038. Rischin, Moses, ed. <u>Grandma Never Lived in America, The New Journalism of Abraham Cahan</u>. Bloomington: Indiana University Press, 1985.

Contains selections of Cahan's writings, mainly from <u>New York Commercial Advertiser</u>, 1897-1903; information on immigrant women is scattered through the whole, but see especially "Love and Marriage," "Living in the Public Eye," "'Ach Wie Schoen': A Tenement House Empress," "The Only Married Woman in the House Who Understands Every English Word," and "Females and Feminists."

2039. Roisdal, Agnes. <u>Defend My Mother</u>. New York: Vantage Press, 1952.

A Norwegian family disintegrates in Brooklyn; good portrait of woman.

2040. Rolvaag, Ole E. <u>Giants in the Earth</u>. New York: Harper and Brothers, 1929.

A Norwegian family settles on the prairies, and the mother sinks into madness.

2041. Ronyoung, Kim. <u>Clay Walls</u>. Sag Harbor, N.Y.: Permanent Press, 1986.

Includes the story of a Korean domestic servant.

2042. Rosenberg, Joseph D. <u>Kosher Americans</u>. Atlantic City: Associated Publishing Co., 1929.

Eastern European Jewish life in New York, focusing on the immigrant mother and daughter.

2043. Rossiliano, Elly L. <u>My Sins</u>.

An autobiographical novel by a Polish singer.

2044. Rud, Anthony M. <u>The Second Generation</u>. Garden City: Doubleday, Page & Co., 1923.

A Scandinavian-American family with generational conflicts; contains good portraits of women.

2045. Ruddy, Anna C. (pseud. Christian McLeod). <u>The Heart of the Stranger: A Story of Little Italy</u>. New York: Fleming H. Revell, 1908.

Includes the tale of a woman healer, although most of the novel treats a social settlement's contacts with Italian boys.

2046. Ruud, Curtis D. "Beret and the Prairie in *Giants in the Earth*." *Norwegian American Studies* 28 (1979): 217-244.

An analysis of the most famous fictional woman in Norwegian-American literature.

2047. Salvatori, Mariolina. "Women's Work in Novels of Immigrant Life." *MELUS* 9 (Winter II 1982): 39-58.

Examines works by Rolvaag, di Donato, Yezierska, and Bell.

2048. Saroyan, William. *The Human Comedy*. New York: Harcourt, Brace & Co., 1945.

An Armenian mother alone raising her children.

2049. Schaeffer, Susan F. *Anya, a Novel*. New York: MacMillan, 1974.

A Polish Jewish woman and Holocaust victim who migrates to the U.S., with a focus on her European experiences.

2050. Schrag, Otto. *Sons of the Morning*. New York: Doubleday, 1945.

A French war bride settles in New England.

2051. Shank, Margarethe E. *The Coffee Train*. New York: Doubleday, 1953.

A three-generation Norwegian family, which focuses on the granddaughter and her German neighbors.

2052. Sheehan, Susan. *Kate Quinton's Days*. Boston: Houghton Mifflin, 1984.

The old age and decline of a second-generation Irish woman.

2053. Sinak, Maria. *Katka, A Novel*. Detroit: S. J. Bloch, 1946.

The story of an Eastern European girl.

2054. Sinclair, Upton. *King Coal*. New York: MacMillan, 1918.

An Irish woman strike leader and her love affair with a rich American.

2055. Smith, Betty. *Maggie-Now*. New York: Harper, 1958.

A second-generation daughter in a Brooklyn Irish family.

2056. Song, Cathy. *Picture Bride*. New Haven, Conn.: Yale University Press, 1983.

A Japanese bride travels to the U.S.

FICTION   279

2057. Sourian, Peter. <u>Miri</u>. New York: Pantheon, 1957.

An orphaned Greek girl is brought to the U.S. by her rich, autocratic uncle.

2058. Spitzer, Antoinette. <u>These are My Children</u>. New York: MacCauley, 1935.

Three generations of German and German-American women.

2059. Suckow, Ruth. <u>Cora</u>. New York: Alfred A. Knopf, 1929.

A German immigrant family in Iowa moves to factory town.

2060. Suckow, Ruth. <u>Country People</u>. New York: Alfred A. Knopf, 1924.

A family saga of Iowa's Germans, with some attention to the wife of the family.

2061. Sugimoto, Etsu. <u>A Daughter of the Narikan</u>. Garden City, N.Y.: Doubleday, 1932.

A Japanese woman.

2062. Sugimoto, Etsu. <u>A Daughter of the Nohfu</u>. Garden City, N.Y.: Doubleday, 1935.

A Japanese woman.

2063. Sugimoto, Etsu. <u>A Daughter of the Samurai</u>. Garden City, N.Y.: Doubleday/Page, 1925.

Tale of Japanese life in the U.S.

2064. Sugimoto, Etsu. <u>Grandmother O Kyo</u>. Garden City, N.Y.: Doubleday, 1940.

The story of a Japanese woman.

2065. Sykes, Hope L. <u>The Joppa Door</u>. New York: G.P. Putnam's Sons, 1935.

A German Russian family settles in the West; the focus is on the daughter.

2066. Sykes, Hope L. <u>The Second Hoeing</u>. New York: G.P. Putnam's Sons, 1935.

The story of the daughter of a German-Russian farmer in Colorado.

2067. Tax, Meredith. <u>Rivington Street</u>. New York: William Morrow and Co., 1982.

Eastern European Jewish life in New York through the lives of an immigrant woman and her daughters.

280   IMMIGRANT WOMEN IN THE U.S.

2068. Tobenkin, Elias. The House of Conrad. New York: Frederick A. Stokes Co., 1918.

A three-generation German family; the main character is man, but there are good portraits of several secondary female characters.

2069. Uchida, Yoshiko. Picture Bride: A Novel. Flagstaff, Ariz: Northland Press, 1987.

A Japanese woman's life in California, and her World War II internment.

2070. Uchida, Yoshiko. The Best Bad Thing. New York: Atheneum, 1983.

A second-generation Japanese girl and her family life.

2071. Vásquez, Richard. Chicano. New York: Doubleday and Co., 1970.

Four generations of the Sandoval family in California, including several strong Mexican female characters.

2072. Walden, Daniel, ed. Jewish Women Writers and Women in Jewish Literature. Albany: State University of New York Press, 1983.

Essays discuss women characters by women and by men authors.

2073. Wembridge, Eleanor. Other People's Daughters. Boston and New York: Houghton Mifflin, 1926.

See "The New House," the story of a Hungarian factory girl and her conflicts with parents.

2074. Wilentz, Gay A. "From Africa to America: Cultural Ties that Bind in the Works of Contemporary African and African-American Women Writers." Unpublished Ph.D. Dissertation, The University of Texas at Austin, 1986. Order Number DA 8700309.

Analysis of the fiction of Paule Marshall.

2075. Willette, Dorothy D. The Spear Penny. New York: Coward-McCann, 1949.

A Welsh woman settles in Ohio.

2076. Williams, Tennessee. Rose Tattoo. New York: New Directions, 1951.

A story of Gulf Coast Sicilians, an Italian woman and her deserting husband.

2077. Williams, William C. *The Build-Up*. New York: Random House, 1952.

A Norwegian woman married to German man in New Jersey during World War I.

2078. Williams, William C. *White Mule*. Connecticut: New Directions, 1937.

The life of an Alsatian and his Norwegian wife.

2079. Winston, Clara. *The Hours Together*. Philadelphia: J.B. Lippincott, 1961.

An elderly Austrian refugee couple adjusts to life in New York.

2080. Winther, Sophus K. *Mortgage Your Heart*. New York: MacMillan, 1937.

Part of a trilogy about Danish family life in Nebraska.

2081. Winther, Sophus K. *Take All to Nebraska*. New York: MacMillan, 1936.

Part of a trilogy about Danish family in Nebraska; attention is given to the mother of six sons.

2082. Xan, Erna O. *Home for Good*. New York: Ives Washburn, 1952.

A second-generation Norwegian girl's story of her family life.

2083. Yezierska, Anzia. *Bread Givers*. Garden City, N.Y.: Doubleday, 1927.

An Eastern European Jewish girl struggles to free herself from her family.

2084. Yezierska, Anzia. *Children of Loneliness: Stories of Immigrant Life in America*. New York: Funk & Wagnalls, 1923.

Many of the stories are fictionalized accounts of the author's experiences as a Polish Jewish woman.

2085. Yezierska, Anzia. *Salome of the Tenements*. New York: Bon, 1923.

A Jewish immigrant girl marries a gentile with unhappy results.

2086. Zastrow, Erika. *Broken Arcs*. New York: Henry Holt, 1932.

A German immigrant girl.

Indices

Author Index

Abbott, Edith, 429-430
Abbott, Grace, 56-57, 768
Ablon, Joan, 432
Abonyi, Malvina H., 899
Abrams, Jeanne, 1076
Abramson, Paul R, 769
Abucewicz, John A., 1871
Abyaneh, Parvin, 433
Adams, Paul L., 225
Addams, Jane, 58-59, 434, 1004
Addis, Patricia, 1
Adler, Peter, 226
Adler, Polly, 1463
Afoa, Ioane A., 227
Aguirre, Benigno E., 228-229
Ahern, Susan, 156
Aladjem, Henrietta, 1464
Alba, Richard D., 230
Albornoz, Jaime I., 231
Alcalay, Rina, 232
Alcantara, Ruben R., 157
Aldrich, Bess S., 1872
Aldrich, Mark, 435
Alegria, Daniel, 770
Algren, Nelson, 1873
Allilueva, Svetlana, 1465
Almquist, Elizabeth M., 60
Altman, Addie R., 1077
Alvarez, Robert R., Jr., 233
Alvirez, D., 771
Amara Singham, Lorna R., 900
Anderson, Mary, 1466
Andres, Chaya R., 1467
Andrews-Coryta, Stepanka, 1078
Anh, Nguyen Thi, 436
Anthony, Katharine, 437.

Anthony-Welch, Lillian D., 1005
Antin, Mary, 1468, 1469-1470
Apodaca, Maria L., 1080
Aquino, Belinda, 61
Arafat, Ibtahaj S., 772
Archdeacon, Thomas J., 158
Arellano, Margarita M., 902
Arkoff, Abe, 773, 903
Armaghanian, Arsha L., 1471
Armitage, Susan, 62
Armstrong, M. Jocelyn, 234
Armstrong, Margaret, 1081
Arrinaga, Esther K., 63
Asch, Sholem, 1874
Ashbury, Herbert, 438
Asher, Nina L., 1082-1083
Askowith, Dora, 1084
Athas, Daphne, 1472
Atkins, Annette, 1875
Auten, Nellie M., 439
Avery, Evelyn G., 1876
Aviaro, H., 774
Babcock, Charlotte G., 904
Babson, Naomi L., 1877
Baca, Reynaldo, 159
Bach, Robert L., 440
Bachu, Amara, 775
Badillo-Veiga, Amerigo, 441
Bainbridge, Lucy S., 1085
Baines, Dudley, 160
Baker, Estelle, 1878
Baker, Houston A., Jr., 1087
Baker, Racel, 1087
Bakke, E. Wight, 235
Balakian, Nona, 1088
Balancio, Dorothy M., 905

Balch, Emily, 64
Baldwin, Charles C., 1089
Ball, Walter, 1879
Baner, Skulda V., 1880
Bankowsky, Richard, 1881-1882
Banks, Ann, 1090
Bannan, Helen M., 1883
Barborka, Geoffrey A., 1091
Barkan, Elliott R., 161
Barker, Barbara M., 1092
Barker-Nunn, Jeanne, 1473
Barnard, Charles, 1093
Barolini, Helen, 1094, 1884
Barr, Amelia Huddleston, 1474-1475
Barron, Milton L., 236
Barry, John D., 1095
Barschak, Erna, 1476
Bartlett, Elizabeth A., 1096
Barton, H. Arnold, 1006, 1477
Bates, Helen M., 1097
Battle, Lois, 1885
Baum, Charlotte, 65, 442
Baum, Vicki, 1478
Baxandall, Rosalyn F., 1098-1099
Beale, Jenny, 162
Bean, Frank D. 163, 776-781
Beaumont, Betty Bentley, 1479
Becerra, Rosina M., 782-783
Beckley, Zoe, 1886
Beeton, Beverly, 1100
Beh, Siew Hua, 1480
Bell, Thomas, 1887
Belmont, Eleanor Robson, 1481
Belonzi, Arthur A., 1101
Benedictine of Stanbrook Abbey, 1102
Bengis, Ingrid, 1482-1483
Bennett, Helen C., 1103
Benoit, Virgil, 237
Benson, Paulette, 238
Bentlage, Mary K., 1484
Berg, Gertrude, 1485
Berg, Rebecca Himber, 1486
Berkman, Ted, 1104
Berkowitz, Sarah Bick, 1487
Berman, Louis, 239
Bernard, Richard N., 240
Berrol, Selma C., 1007, 1105-1106
Berry, Gwendolyn H., 784
Besant, Annie W., 1107
Bethune, George W., 1489
Bethune, Joanna, 1108

Beyers, Marjorie, 443
Bienstock, Beverly G., 241
Bilik, Dorothy S., 1888,
Bingle, Alice, 1489-1490
Binns, Archie, 1109
Bird, Stewart, 1110
Birnbaum, Lucia C., 636, 906
Bjorn, Thyra F., 1491-1492, 1889
Blackwelder, Julia K., 444-445
Blackwell, Elizabeth, 1493
Blake, Eleanor, 1890
Blake, Judith, 164
Blau, Zena S., 242
Blea, Irene I., 66
Blegen, Theodore C., 67, 1494-1495.
Blewett, Mary H., 446
Blicksilver, Edith, 1008, 1111, 1496, 1891-1892
Blinde, Patricia Lin, 1497
Bloch, Harriet, 243
Bloch, Irvin, 1112
Bloom, Florence T., 447
Blum, Elsa Proehl, 1498
Blumfeld, Hanita F., 637
Blustein, Bryna L., 1893
Boardman, Anne C., 1113
Bobbé, Dorothie, 1114
Bodnar, John, 68, 244, 448-449
Bogen, Elizabeth, 69
Bolek, Francis, 1115
Bolles, Lynn A., 165
Bonacich, Edna M., 450
Boone, Gladys, 638
Boone, Margaret S., 1009
Borah, Woodrow, 245
Borden, Lucille P., 1116
Boris, Eileen, 451
Bose, Christine E., 452
Boulding, Elise Bior-Hansen, 1499
Boulette, Teresa R., 907-908
Bowen, Ralph H., 1500
Bowyer, Edith Nicholl, 1501
Boyd, Carol J., 246
Boyd, Monica, 453
Boydston, Jo Ann, 1117
Bradshaw, Benjamin, 785
Braggiotti, Gloria, 1502
Brana-Shute, Rosemary, 3
Brand, Sandra, 1503
Brandt, Lillian, 247
Braude, Ann D., 909
Brauer, Mrs. Oscar P., 1504

AUTHORS

Braun, Jean S., 910
Breckinridge, Sophonisba P., 70, 166, 429, 1010
Bremer, Edith, 911
Bressler, Marvin., 248
Brewer, Eileen M., 912
Brice-Finch, Jacqueline L., 1894
Briggs, John W., 786
Briggs, Margaret Yang, 1505
Brinig, Myron, 1895
Briody, Elizabeth K., 454
Bristol, Helen O., 1896
Bristow, Edward J., 639
Britt, Roberta H., 1118
Britten, Emma Hardinge, 1506
Brizzolara, Andrew, 1119
Brock, E. L., 1897
Brody, Eugene B., 167
Brooks, Van Wyck, 1120
Browder, Clifford, 1121
Brown, Mary E., 640
Brown, Olympia, 1122
Browning, Harley L., 168
Brownmiller, Susan, 1123
Bruchac, Joseph, 1124
Bruns, Roger A., 1125
Bryan, Dorothy P., 249
Bryant, Carol A., 250
Bryce-Laporte, Roy S., 169, 1126
Buchanan, Susan H., 71, 1127
Buck, Rinker, 455
Buckley, Joan N., 1128-1129
Budd, Lillian, 1898-1900
Buechley, Robert W., 787
Buell, Philip, 788
Buhle, Mari Jo, 4, 641-642
Bukowczyk, John J., 72
Bularzik, Mary J., 1130
Bullard, Arthur, 1901
Burachinska, Lydia, 643
Burch, Connie Beth Saulmon, 1507
Burdick, Susan E., 913
Burgess, Judith, 170
Burke, Billie, 1508
Burki, Elizabeth A., 251
Burland, Rebecca, 1509
Burma, John H., 252-253
Burnett, Frances Hodgson, 1510
Burnett, Vivian, 1131
Burns, John H., 1902
Burr, Charles C., 1511
Burton, Katherine, 644-645, 914, 1132
Burton, Naomi, 1512
Butler, Elizabeth B., 456

Butler, Mary P., 646
Butt, G. Baseden, 1133
Byington, Margaret F., 254
Cabello-Argandona, Roberto, 5
Caddell, G. Lincoln, 1134
Cade, Winifred, 1513
Cahan, Abraham, 1903
Calhoun, Arthur W., 789
Calhoun, George, 915
Callan, Louise, 647, 1135
Cameron, Allan G., 1136
Cameron, Ardis, 648
Campbell, Helen S., 457
Candelaria, Cordelia, 6-7
Cannon, Cornelia J., 1904-1905
Cantarow, Ellen, 1137
Cantor, Aviva, 8
Cappozzoli, Mary J., 255
Card, Josefina J., 790-791
Cardenas, Gilbert, 458
Carliner, Geoffrey, 459
Caroli, Betty B., 9, 73
Carpenter, Margaret, 460
Carr, Harriett H., 1906
Carreiro, Manuel C., 916
Carruth, Reba, 1138
Cartwright, O. G., 461
Casal, Lourdes, 10, 462
Casas, J. Manuel, 256
Casey, Daniel J., 1907
Casgupta, Shamita D., 257
Casillas, Mike, 649
Cassini, Marguerite, 1514
Castellano, Vianne 258, 917
Castle, William, 1908
Castro, Felipe G., 463, 792
Castro, Mary G., 74, 464
Castro, Rafaela, 793
Catapusan, Benicio T., 259
Cather, Willa, 1909-1912
Cautela, Giuseppe, 916
Cavan, Ruth S., 260
Cernius, V. J., 1011
Cervantes, Carmen M., 918
Chai, Alice Y., 13, 261, 919, 1139
Chambers, Peggy, 1140
Chaney, Elsa M., 171
Chang, Lydia L., 1012
Chao, Buwei Yang, 1515
Char, Tin-Yuke, 1141
Char, Walter F., 262
Chase, Mary E., 1913
Chavchavadze, Paul, 1516
Chavez, John, 263
Chavez, Leo R., 794
Chavira, Alicia, 795

286   IMMIGRANT WOMEN IN THE U.S.

Chavkin, Wendy, 796
Chen, Diana, 650
Cheng, Lucie, 467
Chennault, Anna, 1517
Chih, Ginger, 76
Chin, A. S., 1013
Chin, Louise, 1518
Chisholm, Shirley, 1519-1520
Chiswick, Barry R., 468
Choi, Elizabeth S. C., 264
Chou, Cynthia L., 1521
Chow, Esther N., 651
Christian, Barbara T., 1522
Christianson, J.R., 1915
Christman, Elizabeth, 1916
Christy, Lai Chu T., 920
Chu, Louis, 1917
Chun-Hoon, Lowell, 1142
Chung, Hyo Jin, 469
Cisneros, Evangelina, 1523
Claghorn, Kate H., 265
Clarissa, Sister, 652
Clark, Sue A., 470
Clark, VéVé, 1143
Clausen, C. A., 1524
Clinton, Catherine, 78
Clum, John P., 1144
Code, Reverend Joseph B., 1145
Cohen, Jessica L., 266
Cohen, Lester, 1918
Cohen, Lizabeth A., 267
Cohen, Lucy M., 79, 172, 471, 797-798
Cohen, Miriam J., 472, 921
Cohen, Ricki C., 1146
Cohen, Rose Gallup, 1525
Cohen, Sarah B., 1919
Cohen Stuart, Bertie A., 14
Cohler, Bertram J., 922
Colby, Frances B., 1920
Colcord, Joanna C., 268
Cole, Johnnetta B., 80
Cole, Marie C., 81
Coleman, Ann Thomas, 1526
Coleman, Arthur P., 1147
Coleman, Marian M., 1148
Colen, Shellee, 473
Comer, Irene F., 1149
Conklin, Margaret M., 1150
Connolly, Olga Fikotova, 1527
Connor, John W., 269-270, 1014-1015
Conway, Brooks, 1921
Coogan, M. Jane, 1151
Cook, Blanche W., 1152
Cook, Patsy A., 15
Cook, Sherburne F., 271
Cooney, Rosemary S., 475-476

Corcoran, Mary L., 1153
Cordasco, Francesco, 16
Cordova, Dorothy L., 1154
Cornaby, Hannah Hollingsworth, 1528
Cortes, Carlos, 173
Cortese, Margaret, 923
Corwin, Margaret, 1155
Coser, Lewis A., 1156
Cotera, Marta, 17, 82-83, 653
Courtney, Marguerite, 1157
Cox, Richard W., 1158
Crago, Florence, 924
Crandall, Jo Ann, 1016
Crane, Stephen, 1922
Crawford, Anne Fears, 1159
Creahan, John, 1160
Crew, Helen C., 1923
Cromwell, Vicky L., 272
Cross, Gary, 477
Croxdale, Richard, 654
Cuddy, Dennis L., 174
Cuffaro, Sara T., 925
Cullinan, Elizabeth, 1924
Culp, Alice B., 478
Cumming, Kate, 1529
Curran, Mary D., 655, 1925
Curry, Peggy S., 1161
Curwell, Laura E., 1530
Cusack, May, 1531
Cutrer, Emily F., 1162
D'Andrea, Vaneeta-Marie, 18, 273, 656
D'Auvergne, Edmund B., 1163
Daché, Lilly, 1532
Dahl, Borghild M., 1533-1534, 1926
Dakin, Susanna B., 1164
Dalmazzo, G.M., 1165
Daly, Sister John Marie, 1166
Dance, Daryl C., 1167
Dane, Nancy A., 926
Daniel, Robert L., 84
Daniels, Doris G., 1168
Daniels, John, 1017
Dannett, Sylvia G. L., 1169
Darabi, Katherine F., 19
Dash, Joan, 1170-1171
Davies, Mrs. Eliza, 1535
Davis, Allen, 657
Davis, C. C., 799
Davis, Donna J., 927
Davis, Michael M., 800
Davis, Susan G., 479
Davison, Lani, 1018
De Capite, Michael, 1927
de Caro, Francis A., 20

de Colon Rivera, Maria M., 928
de Cubas, Mercedes M., 274
De Hueck, Catherine, 1536-1537
De Jong, Gordon F., 175
de la Torre, Adela, 801
de Wolfe, Elsie, 1538
Dearborn, Mary V., 1172, 1928
Deasy, Mary, 1929
Declercq, Eugene, 802
Dehy, Elinor T., 658
Deighton, Len, 1930
del Castillo, R. Griswold, 275
Del Mar, Marcia, 1539
Delatte, Carolyn E., 1173
DeLespinasse, Cobie, 1931
Demirturk, Emine Lale, 1540
Dempsey, David, 1174
Dennis, Peggy, 1541-1542
Dessler, Julia Shapiro, 1543
Deutsch, Helene, 1544
Deutsch, Phyllis, 1019
Di Donato, Pietro, 1932
di Leonardo, Micaela, 1020
Dickens, Monica, 1933
Dickinson, Joan Y., 480
DiDonato, Pietro, 1175
Dillon, Richard, 481
Dineen, Joseph F., 1934
Diner, Hasia R., 85
Ding, Barbara, 86
Dixon, Marlene, 482
Dodd, Bella Visono, 1545
Doering, Bertha-Charlotte, 1546
Doi, Mary L., 21
Dominguez, Virginia R., 176, 1021
Donato, Katharine, 177
Donelin, Mary C., 1176
Dooley, Roger, 1935
Doran, Terry, 87
Doty, Richard L., 803
Doughtery, D.M., 659
Dreier, Mary E., 1547
Dreiser, Theodore, 1936
Dressler, Marie, 1548-1549
Drew, Louisa Lane, 1550
Drinnon, Richard, 1177
Driscoll, Paul, 1937
Driver, Leota S., 1178
Dublin, Louis I., 483
Dubnoff, Steven J., 276
Dudden, Faye E., 484
Duffus, Robert L., 1179
Duffy, Susan, 22
Duncan, Hannibal G., 1180

Dunkas, N., 929
Dunn, Georgia, 1181
Dunphy, Jack, 1938
Duus, Masayo, 1182
Dworkin, Susan, 1183
Dye, Nancy S., 660-661, 804
Dympna, Sister, 930
Dyrud, David L., 1939
Early, Frances H., 485
Eaton, Evelyn, 1551-1552
Eaton, Winnifred, 1553
Eckhardt, Celia M., 1184
Edelheit, Martha, 486
Edelman, Fannie, 1554
Edmonds, Jean S., 1555
Edmonds, Sarah, 1556
Eisenbruch, Maurice, 277
Eisenstein, Sarah, 932
El-Banyan, Abdullah S., 933
Ellis, Christine, 1557
Ellis, Pearl I., 1022
Elwell, Ellen S., 23, 662
Embree, John F., 1023
Endelman, Gary E., 1185
Endo, Russell, 278
Epstein, Helen, 1186
Erickson, Charlotte, 88
Ericsson, Mary K., 1187
Escovar, Luis, 279
Esparza, Ricardo, 280
Espin, Oliva M., 805, 934
Ets, Maria Hall, 1558
Evans, Mary E., 663
Evosevick, Sarah Vukelich, 1559
Ewen, Elizabeth, 89, 1024
Ewens, Mary, 664-665, 1025
Fabe, Maxine, 1188
Fairbanks, Carol, 24, 1940-1941
Falasco, Dee, 806-807
Falk, Candace, 1189
Fancourt, M. St. J., 1190
Fanning, Charles, 1942
Far, Sui Sin, 1943
Farseth, Pauline, 1560
Feeley, Dianne, 1191
Feld, Rose C., 1944
Fenollosa, Mary, 1945
Ferber, Edna, 1946-1947
Fermi, Laura, 1561
Fernald, Helen C., 1948
Fernald, Mabel R., 808
Fernández-Kelly, M. Patricia, 487
Ferree, Myra M., 488
Fetherling, Dale, 1192
Field, Rachel, 1949
Fife, Dale, 1193

Fine, David M., 1950
Fineman, Irving, 1194
Fink, Deborah, 1195
Fink, Gary M., 1196
Fischer, Gloria J., 809
Fischer, Markoosha, 1562
Fischer, Nancy A., 810
Fisher, Dexter, 1197
Fisher, Florrie, 1563
Fisher, Jerilyn B., 1951
Fisher, Minnie, 1564
Fitzgerald, Daniel F., 281
Fitzgerald, Mary P., 1198
Fjellman, Stephen M., 178
Flack, Ambrose, 1952
Fleming, Margaret E., 811
Flynn, Elizabeth Gurley, 1565-1566
Follis, Jane T., 1199
Foner, Nancy, 90
Foner, Philip S., 1200
Fong, Stanley L. M., 1026-1027
Forbes, Kathryn, 1953
Ford, D. M., 1201
Ford, Kathleen, 812-813
Fortune, James, 1202
Fox, Geoffrey, 1028
Frank, Blanche B., 1029
Frank, Dana, 666
Frankau, Pamela, 1567
Freier, Michelle C., 814
Freitag, George, 1954
French, Marilyn, 1955
Fridkis, Ari L., 282
Friedman, Reena S., 283
Frisbie, W. Parker, 284-285
Fritschel, Herman L., 667
Fruchter, Rachel G., 815-816
Frye, Joanne S., 1956
Fuentes, Annette, 489
Fujitomi, Irene, 91
Fuller, Margaret W., 1957
Furio, Colomba M., 490
Gabaccia, Donna R., 179, 286
Gabor, Eva, 1568
Gabor, Jolie, 1569
Gabor, Zsa Zsa, 1570
Gág, Wanda, 1571
Gambino, Richard, 287
Gamble, Lillian M., 1572, 1958
Gamio, Manuel, 1573
Ganguli, B. N., 1203
Gannon, Joseph A., 1204
Ganz, Marie, 1574
Garcia, Céline Frémaux, 1575
Garcia, Mario T., 491, 1205
Garden, Mary, 1576

Garland, Anne W., 1206
Garrison, Dee, 1207
Garrison, Vivian, 180
Gartner, Carol B., 1959
Gaviria, Moises, 817
Gavit, John P., 668
Gebhart, John C., 818-819
Gee, Emma, 92
Gehle, Frederick W., 1208
Gentry, Curt, 492
Gerber, David A., 1209
Geva, Tamara, 1577
Ghahreman, Mahin, 935
Gibbs, Henry, 1210
Gidding, Joshua, 1960
Gil, Carlos, 1211
Gilbert, Anne Hartley, 1578
Gilbert, V.F., 25
Gill, Margaret, 181
Ginger, Ray, 493
Glanz, Rudolf, 93
Glasco, Laurence A., 288
Glass, Beaumont, 1212
Glenn, Evelyn N., 289, 494-497
Glenn, Susan A., 498
Glick, C., 290
Gluck, Gemma La Guardia, 1579
Glueck, Sheldon, 94
Goar, Marjory, 1213
Godoy, Mercedes, 1580
Gold, Michael, 1961
Goldberg, Isaac, 1214
Goldberg, Mark F., 1962
Goldman, Emma, 1581-1583
Goldmark, Josephine, 1584
Goldschieder, Calvin, 820-822
Goldschieder, Frances K., 291
Goldsmith, Margaret, 1215
Goldstein, Ruth T., 1963
Golomb, Deborah G., 669
Gonzalez, Diana H., 823
González, Nancie L., 182-184, 824
Gonzalez, Rosalinda M., 95, 292
Gordon, L. W., 825
Gordon, Linda, 293
Gordon, Monica H., 185
Goritzina, Kyra, 1585
Gornick, Vivian, 1216-1217
Gosselink, Sara E., 1964
Graham, Isabella, 1218, 1586
Graham, Sheilah, 1587-1590
Granowicz, Antoni, 1219, 1965-1966

AUTHORS

Grant, Geraldine, 294
Graves, William W., 1220
Gray, Donna, 936
Gray, Ellen, 295
Green, Archie, 1221
Greenbaum, Lenora, 1222
Greenberg, Blu, 26
Greenberg, Harvey R., 937
Greenburger, Ingrid, 1591
Grey, Donna, 186
Griffen, Clyde, 499
Gringhuis, Richard H., 1967-1968
Grinstein, Alexander, 1030
Griswold del Castillo, Richard, 296
Groneman, Carol, 500-501
Gross, David C., 1223
Grossinger, Tani, 1224
Grubb, Farley, 502
Guest, Avery, 826
Guiney, Louise, 1592
Guinnane, Timothy W., 297
Gull, Caroline, 1593
Gunn, Rex, 1225
Gupta, Omprakash K., 298
Gurak, Douglas T., 96, 299, 827-828
Habe, Hans, 1969-1970
Habers, Christopher G., 938
Haddad, Safia F., 300
Hagopian, Richard, 1971
Haines, Michael, 829
Hall, Elizabeth L., 301
Hamburger, Sonia, 830
Hampsten, Elizabeth, 302
Hancock, Paula, 503
Hanousek, Mary E., 670
Hapgood, Hutchins, 1972
Harbison, Sarah F., 831
Harding, Bertita Leonarz, 1594
Hardy-Fanta, Carol, 939
Hare, Catherine, 1595
Hareven, Tamara, 303-304, 504-506, 832-833
Harper, Jacob C., 1226
Harris, Frank, 1227
Harris, Rachel, 834
Hart, Sara Liebenstein, 1596
Hartman, Harriet, 507
Hartman, May Weisser, 1597
Harzler, Kaye, 305
Hasanovitz, Elizabeth, 1598
Hatfield, Inge, 1599
Haug, Madeleine J., 508
Havighurst, Walter, 1973
Havira, Barbara S., 509
Hawkes, Glenn R., 306

Hayner, Norman S., 307
Healy, Kathleen, 1228
Heer, David, 308
Heifetz, Julie, 1229
Helen Louise, Sister, 1230
Heller, Rita R., 940
Helmbold, Lois R., 309
Henderson, Janet K., 1231
Hendricks, Glenn, 310
Henie, Sonja, 1600
Henney, Nella B., 1232
Henriksen, Louise L., 1233
Henry, Alice, 671-672, 1601
Hepokoski, Carol, 1234
Hernandez, Cibeles, 1031
Hernandez-Peck, Maria C., 835
Herron, Sister Mary E., 673
Herzfeld, Elsa G., 97, 311
Higa, Masanori, 312
Higbee, Blanche, 1602
Hilf, Mary, 1603
Hinding, Andrea, 27
Hines, David, 510
Hirata, Lucy C., 511
Hirayama, Kasumi K., 512-513
Ho, Yuet-fung, 1032
Hobart, Alice T., 1974
Hobbs, Lisa, 1604
Hobson, Barbara M., 514
Hoehling, Mary, 1235
Hoerder, Dirk, 28
Hoffman, Klaus, 515
Hoglund, A. William, 29
Holden, William C., 1236
Holloway, Marcella M., 674
Holt, C. E., 1605
Holte, James C., 30
Hopkins, David D., 836
Horowitz, Ruth, 98
Hotchkiss, Christine Oppeln-Bronikowska, 1606
Houghteling, Leila, 516
Houston, Helen R., 31
Houston, Jean W., 1607-1608
Houstoun, Marion, 187
Hsu, Vivian, 1237
Hua, Chuang, 1609
Hughes, Arthur J., 1238
Hughes, Gwendolyn S., 517
Hughes, Rupert, 1975-1976
Humphrey, Norman D., 313, 518
Humula, Anna J., 1610
Hung, Lucy, 1033
Hunter, Kathleen, 837-838
Hurley, Sister Helen A., 675-676
Hurst, Fannie, 1977

Hvidt, Kristian, 188
Hyman, Colette A., 677
Hyman, Paula, 99, 678
Hynes, Kathleen, 941
Ibrahim, I. B., 839
Ichioka, Yuji, 100-101, 519
Ifkovic, Edward, 1978
Ikeda-Spiegel, Motoko, 1611
Ikels, Charlotte, 314
Ileana, Princess of Rumania, 1612
Infante, Isa M., 679
Inglehart, Babette, 33, 1979
Ireland, Joseph N., 1240
Irwin, Elizabeth A., 520, 942
Isasi-Diaz, Ada, 943
Isely, Elise Dubach, 1613
Ishiguro, Kazuo, 1980
Ishill, Joseph, 1241
Jackson, Pauline, 189
Jacoby, Robin M., 680
Jacques, Karen N., 840
Jaffe, A. J., 841
James, Edward, 34, 1242
Jameson, Elizabeth, 102
Janney, Russell, 1981
Jannopoulo, Helen P., 1614
Jastrow, Marie, 1615-1616
Jean, Sister Patricia, 1243
Jennings, Rosa S., 1244, 1617
Jensen, Joan M., 521, 681
Jeritza, Maria, 1618
Jessey, Cornelia, 1982-1983
Jex, Eliza Goodson, 1619
Joe, Jeanne, 1620
Johnson, Audrey, 522
Johnson, Carmen A., 523, 842
Johnson, Colleen L., 315-317
Johnson, Elizabeth S., 318
Johnson, Nan E., 843
Johnson, Ronald C., 944
Johnston, Malcolm S., 1245
Johnston, Maxene, 945
Jones, Elizabeth O., 1984
Jones, Kay F., 1246
Jones, Mary (Mother), 1621
Jones, Robert C., 319
Jordan, Rosan A., 844
Joseph, Judith L. V., 524
Joyce, Richard E., 525
Juhasz, Suzanne, 1622
Jun, Suk-ho, 946
Jung, B., 190
Jurczak, Chester A., 845
Jurma, Mall, 682
Kahn, Frida, 1623
Kahn, Lisa, 1247
Kaku, Kanae, 846
Kaplan, Louis, 35

Karabatsos, Lewis T., 1248
Karsh, Audrey R., 320
Karvonen, Hilda, 1249
Kataoka, Susan M., 103
Katkov, Norman, 1250
Katz, Naomi, 526
Katzman, David, 527
Kaups, Matti, 191
Kay, Chung Y., 528
Keefe, Susan E., 321
Keith, Henry, 683
Keller, Helen, 1251
Kellor, Frances A., 192, 529
Kelly, Fanny, 1624
Kelly, Gail P., 947-949, 1034
Kelly, Myra, 1985
Kelman, Harold, 1252
Kemble, Fanny, 1625-1630
Kendall, Laurel, 847
Kennedy, J. C., 322
Kennedy, Robert E., 193
Kennedy, Susan E., 36, 104, 530
Kenny, Elizabeth, 1631
Keppel, Ruth, 1253
Kerber, Linda K., 105
Kerst, Catherine H., 37
Kessler-Harris, Alice, 531, 1254
Kessner, Thomas, 532, 1255
Khouzam, Nevine N., 1035
Kibria, Nazli, 1036
Kikumura, Akemi, 323, 1256
Kim, Bok-Lim C., 324-328
Kim, Chong O., 1037
Kim, Elaine H., 533, 1986
Kim, Illsoo, 534
Kim, Kwang Chung, 535
Kim, Sil Dong, 950
Kinel, Lola, 1632
Kingston, Maxine Hong, 1633
Kish, M. Olha, 685
Kitano, Harry H., 329-333
Klaczynska, Barbara M., 536-537
Klausner, Patricia R., 538
Klehr, Harvey, 686
Klein, Gerda W., 1257, 1634
Klein, Herman, 1258
Kleinberg, Susan J., 539-540
Knauff, Ellen Raphael, 1635
Kneeland, George J., 541
Knef, Hildegard, 1636-1637
Kodama-Nishimotot, Michi, 1259
Kohler, Mary H., 687, 1260
Kohut, Rebecca Bettelheim, 687, 1638-1639

AUTHORS

Koren, Else Hysing, 1640
Korfker, Dena, 1990
Koske, Mary, 38
Kossoudji, Sherrie A., 542
Kramer, Sydelle, 1261
Kranau, Edgar J., 1038
Kranitz-Sanders, Lillian, 1262
Kransdorf, Martha, 1263
Krause, Corinne A., 543, 951-952, 1039
Krawczyk, Monica, 1991
Kritz, Mary M., 848
Kryszak, Mary O., 688
Kuchner, Joan R. F., 334
Kumagai, Gloria L., 106-107
Kunnu, Felix B., 953
Kutscher, Carol B., 689
Kuzmack, Linda G., 690
Kuznicki, Sister Ellen M., 954
La Roe, Else Kienle, 1641
Lacovia, R.M., 1992
Lagemann, Ellen, 1264
LaGuerre, Michael S., 108, 194
LaGumina, Salvatore, 1265
Lalli, Michael, 1040
LaLonde, Leona M., 1642
Lam-Phoon, Sally C., 955
Lamarr, Hedy, 1643
Lamphere, Louise, 335, 544-549, 691
Lan, Dean, 550
Landau, Penny M., 1266
Landau, Saul, 1267
Landes, Ruth, 336
Lang, Barbara, 1268
Lang, Lucy Fox Robins, 1644
Langseth-Christensen, Lillian, 1645
Langtry, Lillie, 1646
Laosa, Luis M., 337
Lape, Esther, 956
Larsen, Karen, 1269
Larson, Eric M., 195
Larsson, Gösta, 1993
Lasker, Bruno, 109, 692
Lasser, Carol S., 551-552
Laufer, Pearl D., 1994
Laughlin, Clara E., 553
Lauw, Louisa, 1270
Law, Timothy, 338
Lawrence, Gertrude, 1647
Lawson, Josephine, 1648
Lawson, Ronald, 693
Lawton, Mary, 1649
Le Gallienne, Eva, 1650-1651
Leahy, J. Kenneth, 1271

Lebeson, Anita L., 1272
Lederer, Charlotte, 1995
Lee, Dorothy, 1041
Lee, Sirkka T., 694
Lee, Sung-Ja C., 339
Leeder, Elaine J., 1273
Lehmann, Lilli, 1652
Lehmann, Lotte, 1653-1654
Leiserson, William M., 554
Leitner, Isabella, 1655
Lenihan, Mina Ward, 1656
Lenk, Edward A., 1274
Leon, J. L., 340
Leonard, Karen, 341-342
Leonetti, Donna L., 849-851
Lerner, Elinor, 695-696, 957
Leuchter, Sara, 39
Levenberg, Diane E., 1996
Levin, Alexandra L., 1275-1276
Levin, Marvin, 697
Levin, Meyer, 1997
Levine, Susan, 698
Levinger, Elma E., 1277
Levorsen, Barbara, 555, 1657
Levy, Harriet Lane, 1658
Levy, Julius, 852
Lewandowski, Monica A., 1278
Lewin, Ellen, 343, 853
Lewis, Anna, 1659-1661
Lewis, Janet, 1998
Lewis, Oscar, 1279
Lewisohn, Ludwig, 1999
Li, Lillian, 958
Li, Peter S., 344
Li-Repac, Diana C., 345
Lilienthal, Meta, 1662
Lin, Alice, 1663
Lin, Mao-chu, 1664
Lin, Yu-Taug, 1997
Lindborg, Kristina, 1280
Lindemann, Constance, 854
Lindewall, Arvo, 1281
Lindheim, Irma Levy, 1665
Lindsay, Mela M., 1998
Lindström-Best, Varpu, 959
Ling, Amy, 1282-1283
Linkugel, Wilmer, 1284
Linn, Margaret W., 855-856
Lion, Hortense, 1999
Lipner, Nira H., 960
Lippard, Lucy R., 1285
Lips, Eva, 1666-1667
Litwin-Grinberg, Ruth R., 1286
Liu, William T., 110
Lixl-Purcell, Andreas, 1668
Llanes, José, 1287
Lobodzinska, Barbara, 346

Loeb, Catherine, 40
Logan, Herschel C., 1288
Logan, Lorna, 1289
Logan, Milla Zenovich, 1669-1670
Loggins, Vernon, 1290
Long, Priscilla, 699, 1291
Loo, Chalsa, 700, 961
Loomis, A. W., 111
Lopata, Helen Z., 347-348
Lord, Carmen B., 962
Lorit, Sergio C., 1292
Loucks, Jennie Erickson, 1671
Lowenthal, Marvin, 1293
Lundeberg, Olav T., 2000
Lyman, Stanford M., 349
Lynch, Alice C., 1294
MacLean, Annie M., 112, 556, 1672
Madison, Charles A., 1295
Madrigal, Reyes R., 701
Maeder, Clara Fisher, 1673
Malak, Henry M., 1296
Manansala, Erlinda, 963
Mancuso, Arlene, 557
Mander, Anica Vesel, 1674
Mannin, Ethel, 2001
Manning, Caroline, 558
Manning, Marie, 1675
Maram, Sheldon L., 559
Marcum, John P., 857
Marcus, Jacob R., 113
Marie Therese, Sister, 1297
Maril, Robert L., 858
Marinacci, Barbara, 1298
Markham, Pauline, 1676
Markides, Kyriakos, 350, 964-964
Mars, Amy I., 351
Marsh, Margaret, 1299
Marshall, Catherine A., 1042
Marshall, Harvey H., Jr., 859
Marshall, Mrs. Anne James, 1677
Marshall, Paule, 2002-2003
Martin, Mildred C., 1300
Martindale, Cyril C., 1301
Martinez, Marco A., 352-353
Mason, Karen M., 702
Massey, Douglas S., 196-197
Massiah, Joycelin, 198
Massing, Hede, 1678
Masuoka, Jitsuichi, 354
Mathias, Elizabeth, 1302
Matson, Norman H., 2004
Matsui, Haru, 1679
Matsumoto, Valerie J., 114, 355
Matthews, Ellen, 1043

Mavity, Nancy B., 1303
Maxson, Charles H., 1044
Maynard, Theodore, 1304-1305
Mazow, Julia W., 2005
McAlpine, Dale, 2006
McArdle, Sister Mary A., 1306
McCarthy, T. P., 703
McCormack, Lily Foley, 1680
McCreesh, Carolyn D., 704
McCrosson, Mary, 1307
McCunn, Ruthanne L., 1308-1309
McDannell, Colleen, 966
McDonald, Dorothy R., 1310
McDonald, Julie, 2007
McDonald, Lucile, 1311
McDonald, Sister Grace, 967
McFarland, C. K., 1312
McGoldrick, Monica, 356
McGovern, James R., 1313
McHale, M. Jerome, 705
McInnis, Kathleen M., 560
McIntosh, Karyl, 860
McLoughlin, William G., 1314
McPherson, Aimee Semple, 1681-1684
McSorley, Edward, 2008
Means, Florence, 2009
Medina, Celia, 561
Meier, Matt S., 41
Meir, Golda, 1685
Melloh, Ardith K., 562
Melody, Sister Laura, 357
Meloni, Christine F., 968
Melville, Margarita B., 1045
Mendez, Paz P., 199
Mensch, Jean U., 563
Meredith, William M., 1046-1047
Merriam, Eve, 1315
Meyer, Agnes Ernst, 1686
Meyer, Ruth F., 706
Meyerowitz, Joanne, 200
Meyerowitz, Ruth, 707
Michel, Auguste Marie, 1687
Michel, Sonya, 2010
Michelet, Maren, 1316
Michener, James, 2011
Milinowski, Marta, 1317
Millberg, Karen Schwencke, 1688
Miller, Beth, 2012
Miller, Helen, 2013
Miller, Michael V., 358
Miller, Sally M., 1318-1320
Mindel, Charles H., 359
Miniter, Edith, 2014
Miraflor, Clarita G., 564

Miranda, Manuel R., 969
Mirandé, Alfredo, 115-116, 360
Mitchell, Albert G., 361
Mitchell, Florence S., 117
Mittelbach, Frank G., 362
Miyasaki, Gai, 118
Modell, John, 565
Modjeska, Helen, 1689-1690
Mohr, James C., 861
Moise, Penina, 1691
Molek, Mary, 1321
Momeni, Jamshid A., 42
Monroe, Day, 363
Montenegro, Raquel, 970
Montero, Darrel, 566, 862
Mora, Magdalena, 119, 708
Morante, Elsa, 2015
Morawska, Eva, 120
More, Hermon, 1322
More, Louise B., 364
Morehouse, William M., 709
Morgan, Myfanwy, 365
Mori, Toshio, 2016-2017
Mormino, Gary R. 567-568
Morokvasic, Mirjana, 201
Morris, Edita, 1692
Morrison, Joan, 1323
Mortimer, Delores M., 43, 121
Mueller, Amelia, 1693
Mulder, Arnold, 1694
Murai, Eiko, 1048
Murguia, Edward, 366
Murillo, Nathan, 367
Murphy, Patricia, 1695
Myers, Vincent, 863
Naff, Alixa, 569
Namerow, Pearlina B., 864
Namias, June, 1324
Namioka, Lensey, 2018
Nasaw, David, 570
Nassau, Mabel L., 865
Nathan, Robert, 2019
Negri, Pola, 1696
Neidle, Cecyle, 122
Nelson, David T., 1697
Nelson, Teresa Leopando Lucero, 1698
Nemic, Bozena, 2020
Neu, Irene D., 571
Newby, Elizabeth, 1699
Newlin-Haus, Esther M., 368
Newman, Jacqueline M., 866
Newman, Judith Sternberg, 1700
Nguyen, Thuy T., 572
Nicoll, Bruce H., 1327
Nieh, Hualing,, 2021
Nies, Judith, 1328

Niethammer, Carolyn, 1329
Nin, Anais, 1701-1707
Noisuwan, Samran, 1049
Nolan, Janet A., 202
Nomura, Gail M., 1330
North, Nancy, 1331
Norton, Minervà B., 1332, 1708
Novak, Michael, 710
Novickis, Biruté, 711
Nowicki, Stella, 1709
Nugent, Helen L., 1333-1334
O'Donovan-Rossa, Margaret, 1335
O'Farrell, M. Brigid, 1336
O'Higgins, Patrick, 1337
O'Neal, Mary T., 1710
Oates, Mary J., 971
Odencrantz, Louise, 573
Ogden, Annegret, 574
Oh, Heisik, 369
Oh, Tai K., 203
Ohori, Fumiye, 1711
Okubo, Miné, 1712
Okumara, Taki, 1713
Olsson, Anna, 1714
Ong, Paul M., 575
Ormonda, Czenzi, 2022
Ornitz, Samuel, 2023
Orpen, Mrs., 1715
Orsi, Robert A., 972
Ortiz, Silvia M., 867
Ortiz, Vilma, 576
Orton, Helen, 2024
Osako, Masako M., 868
Osei, Gabriel K., 1050
Oshana, Maryann, 44
Ostenso, Martha, 2025
Otterbein, Keith F., 204
Owen, Harry G., 1338
Owens, Sister M. Lilliana, 1339
Packer, Mrs. Jane Knight, 1716
Padow, Mollie Potter, 1717
Pagano, Jo, 2026
Palacios, Maria, 973
Palisi, Bartolomeo J., 712
Palmer, Phyllis M., 1340
Pang, Henry, 205
Panunzio, Constantine, 370
Papademetriou, Demetrios G., 206
Papanikolas, Helen, 1341
Papashvily, George, 1718
Paradise, Viola, 577
Park, Seong H., 1051
Parker, Cornelia S., 578
Parkman, M. A., 371

Parot, Joseph J., 372
Pascoe, Peggy A., 579
Pasquarelli, John, 2027
Passero, Rosara L., 580
Paul, Almira, 1719
Pauli, Hertha E., 1720
Pavich, Emma G., 869
Pawlowicz, Sala Kaminska, 1721
Payne, Elizabeth, 1342
Peffer, George A., 207
Pehotsky, Bessie, 123
Peiss, Kathy, 1052-1053
Peñalosa, Fernando, 373
Penczer, Lynne O., 581
Penti, Marsha, 1054-1055
Penzik, Irena, 1722
Peragallo, Olga., 1343
Perez, Lisandro, 582
Perkins, Alice J. G., 1344
Perkins, Luch F., 2028
Pernicone, Carol G., 583
Perry, Elisabeth I., 1345
Pesotta, Rose, 1723-1724
Pessar, Patricia R., 374, 584-586
Peterson, Susan C., 713-715, 1056
Petrakis, Harry M., 2029-2032
Petrova, Olga, 1725
Petrovskaya, Kyra, 1726
Petterson, Lucille, 1727
Philipson, Ilene, 1346
Pickford, Mary, 1728
Pickle, Linda S., 124, 716-717
Picon, Molly, 1729
Pido, Antonio J. A., 125
Pienkos, Angela T., 718
Pine, Hester, 2033
Plattner, Elissa M., 719
Pleck, Elizabeth H., 375-377, 587
Plotkin, Sara, 1730
Poirier, Suzanne, 1347
Polasek, Emily M.K., 1731
Pollack, Barbara, 1348
Pollock, Nancy J., 208
Polykoff, Shirley, 1732
Pope-Hennessey, Una, 1349
Porter, Jack N., 1350-1351
Portillo, Cristina, 45
Poston, Dudley L., 588
Pratt, Norma F., 720-721
Preus, Caroline Dorothea Margarethe (Keyser), 1733
Priesand, Sally, 722
Prieto, Yolanda, 589
Prisland, Marie, 1734

Proudian, Armine, 378
Putnam, Frank B., 1352
Puzo, Mario, 2034
Quinn, Jane, 723
Quinn, Susan, 1353
Raaen, Aagot, 1735-1736
Rabine, Leslie W., 2035
Rabinovitz, Lauren H., 1354
Rabinowitz, Benjamin, 724
Rabinowitz, Dorothy, 1355
Racowitza, Elena von Dönniges, 1737
Radzialowski, Thaddeus, 725
Radziwill, Ekaterina Rzewuska, 1738
Rafael, Ruth K., 726
Ragsdale, Crystal S., 126
Ragucci, Antoinette T., 870
Raider, Roberta A., 1356
Ralph, Julian, 2036
Ramos, Luis A., 1357
Ramos, Reyes, 379
Randall, Isabelle, 1739
Randolph, Vance, 2037
Ranney, Susan, 590
Rasmussen, Anne-Marie, 1740
Rasmussen, Janet E., 209, 1358
Ratliff, Bascom W., 380
Reaver, J. Russell, 1359
Reed, Dorothy, 1058
Reed, Ruth, 381
Reichert, Josh, 210
Reichert, William O., 1360
Reid, Ira D., 127
Reifert, Gail, 1361
Reimers, Cordelia W., 591
Reishus, Martha, 727
Reiss, Johanna, 1741
Resnick, Rose, 1742
Rey, Kitty H., 871
Reznick, Allen E., 1362
Reznikoff, Sara, 1743
Rich, B. Ruby, 872
Richards, Marilee, 1744
Richardson, Frank D., 382
Richardson, James B., 1363
Richardson, Mary Walsham Few, 1745
Richmond, Marie L., 383-384
Riddell, Adalijiza S., 728
Rigg, Pat., 974
Rindfuss, R. R., 873
Rios-Bustamente, Antonio J., 592
Rischin, Moses, 2038
Risdon, Randall, 385
Ritter, Darlene M., 1746
Ritter, Ellen, 1364

Robbins, Jane E., 593
Roberts, Carl E., 1365
Roberts, Marjorie, 1058
Robins, Elizabeth, 1747
Robins, Margaret D., 1366
Roboff, Sari, 720
Rodriguez, Richard, 1367
Rodzinski, Halina, 1748
Rogers, Clara K., 1749
Roisdal, Agnes, 1750, 2039
Rolvaag, Ole E., 2040
Romero, Mary, 594
Ronyoung, Kim, 2041
Rooney, Elizabeth, 386
Rosen, Ellen I., 595
Rosen, Ruth, 1751
Rosenberg, Ethel Greenglass, 1752
Rosenberg, Joseph D., 2042
Rosenhouse-Persson, Sandra, 874
Rosenthal, Jean, 1753
Rosenwaike, Ira, 875
Rosicky, Rose, 1368
Rosler, Martha, 1754
Ross, Carl, 730-731
Ross, Dorothy, 1755
Ross, Ishbel, 1369
Rossiliano, Elly L., 2043
Rostenberg, Leona, 1756
Rothbell, Gladys, 387
Rothchild, Sylvia, 1370
Rothluebber, Francis B., 1371
Roucek, Joseph S., 46
Rourke, Constance, 1372
Royce, Sarah, 1757
Ruben, G. Rumbaut, 876
Rubin, Steven, 1758
Rubinstein, Charlotte S., 1373
Rubinstein, Helena, 1759
Rud, Anthony M., 2044
Ruddy, Anna C., 2045
Rudolph, Marguerita, 1760
Ruiz, Vicki L., 596-598
Rushmore, Robert, 1374
Ruskay, Sophie, 1761
Russell, Charles E., 1375
Russell, Matthew, 1376
Ruud, Curtis D., 2046
Ryan, Christine E., 1059
Ryan, Lawrence, 388
Ryan, Mary P., 128, 732
Rybacki, Stella, 1762
Rynearson, Ann M., 129
Saarinen, Aline, 1377
Sabagh, Georges, 877-878
Safa, Helen I., 599
Sahli, Nancy A., 1378

Saiki, Patsy Sumie, 130
Salcido, Ramos M., 1379
Salgado de Snyder, Velia N., 975
Salmon, Lucy M., 600
Salvaneschi, Lenore, 1380
Salvatori, Mariolina, 2047
Salz, Helen A., 1763
Sánchez, Marta E., 1381
Sandberg, Sara, 1764-1765
Sandoz, Mari, 1766-1767
Sanger, Margaret Higgins, 1768-1769
Sargent, Carolyn, 879
Saroff, Sophie, 1770
Saroyan, William, 2048
Sarsfield, Nancy C., 603
Sassen-Koob, Saskia, 211
Savage, Sister Mary Lucia, 733
Scarpaci, Jean V., 131
Scatena, Maria, 976
Scelsa, Joseph V., 977
Schaeffer, Susan F., 2049
Schappes, Morris U., 1382
Scharman, Ralph, 1383
Schatz, Ronald, 734
Schechter, Hope M., 1771
Scheier, Paula, 1384
Schelbert, Leo, 1772
Schenck, Lucy Reissig, 1773
Scheper-Hughes, Nancy, 212-213
Schneider, Aili Gronlund, 1774
Schneider, Dorothee, 602
Schneider, Florence H., 978
Schneiderman, Rose, 1775-1776
Schnepp, Gerald J., 389
Schoen, Carol B., 1385-1386
Schofield, Ann, 1387
Scholten, Pat C., 1388-1389
Schrag, Otto, 2050
Schrode, Georg, 735
Schroeder, Adolf E., 1777
Schroeter, Elizabeth A., 1778
Schulman, Sarah, 736
Schultz, Sandra L., 390
Schwartz, Laura A., 391
Schwarz, Geraldine, 392
Schwieder, Dorothy, 393
Scott, Alma, 1390
Seaver, James E., 1391
Seckar, Alvena V., 1779
Seder, Doris L., 394
Segal, Lore Groszmann, 1780
Segale, Rose M., 1781

Segura, Denise A., 603-604
Seifer, Nancy, 1392
Seivwright, Mary, 214
Seklow, Edna, 1782
Selavan, Ida C., 1393
Selby, Maija L., 880
Seller, Maxine, 132-133, 737, 979-981, 1060, 1394
Seltzer, Mildred, 881
Sermolino, Maria, 1783
Sevier, Christine, 738
Sewell-Coker, Beverly, 1061
Shai, Donna, 882
Shand, Margaret Clark, 1784
Shank, Margarethe E., 2051
Shapiro-Perl, Nina, 739-740
Sharkey, Mary A., 1395
Sharlip, William, 982
Shaw, Anna H., 1785
Sheehan, Susan, 2052
Shepherd, C., 605
Sher, Eva Goldstein, 1786
Shick, Maete Gordon, 1787
Shin, Eui-Hang, 395
Shukert, Elfrieda B., 215
Shulman, Alix K., 1396-1398
Sicherman, Barbara, 1399
Sickels, Eleanor M., 1400
Siddiqui, Musab U., 396
Sidel, Ruth, 1401
Siegal, Aranka, 1788-1789
Siegel, Martha K., 883
Silverman, Ely, 1402
Simkhovitch, Mary K., 134, 1403
Simon, Kate, 1790-1791
Simon, Rita J., 216, 606-609, 1062
Simonian, Leonie B., 1792
Simonielli, Katina, 983
Sinak, Maria, 2053
Sinclair, Upton, 2054
Singer, Joy D., 1404
Siwundhla, Alice (Princess Msumba), 1793-1794
Skardal, Dorothy, 47
Slater, Lisa A., 1795
Slayton, Robert A., 397
Slesinger, Doris P., 884
Sluzki, Carlos E., 984
Smith, Betty, 2055
Smith, Carol J., 610
Smith, Doris, 985
Smith, Gary L., 741
Smith, Jacquelen M., 398
Smith, Judith E., 399-400
Smith, M. Estellie, 217-218
Snow, Carmel White, 1796
Snyder, Robert E., 742

Sochen, June, 743-744
Solberg, S. E., 1405
Soldene, Emily, 1797
Solomon, Barbara M., 745
Solomon, Hannah G., 1798
Solomon, Martha, 1407
Soltow, Martha J., 48
Sone, Monica Itoi, 1799
Song, Cathy, 2056
Soong, Irma Tam, 1800
Soregi, Priscilla Varga, 1801
Sorin, Gerald, 746
Sothern, E. H., 1408
Sourian, Peter, 2057
Spacks, Patricia Meyer, 1802
Spargo, John, 401
Spencer, Ralph W., 1409
Spitzer, Antoinette, 2058
Sponland, Ingeborg, 1803
Stan, Anisoara, 1804
Stanley, Ilse Davidsohn, 1805
Stansell, Christine, 135-136, 611
Staples, Robert, 402
Stauffer, Helen W., 1410-1411
Steel, Edward M., 1412-1413, 1806
Stein, Howard F., 403-404
Stein, Leon, 612
Steinberg, Stephen, 613
Steiner, Dale R., 1414
Steiner, Ruth, 1415
Steinitz, Lucy Y., 1416
Stenhouse, Fanny, 1807
Stern, Elizabeth G., 1808-1810
Stern, Mark J., 885
Stern, Peter, 1417
Stern, Phyllis N., 886
Stjänstedt, Ritta, 747
Stokes, Rose Pastor, 1811-1812
Stoll, Joseph, 1418
Stone, Goldie, 1813
Stone, William L., 1419
Stoner, K. Lynn, 49
Strauss, Anselm L., 405
Strom, Robert, 406
Stromvall, Phyllis, 1420
Strong, Miriam, 748
Stuecher, Dorothea D., 1421
Suckow, Ruth, 2059-2060
Sue, Stanley, 986
Sugimoto, Etsu Inagaki, 1814, 2061-2064
Suhl, Yuri, 1422

Sullivan, Mary L., 1423
Sullivan, Teresa A., 614
Sung, Betty L., 219
Sunoo, Harold Hakwon, 137
Sunoo, Sonia Shin, 138
Surawicz, Frida G., 1424
Suttilagsana, Supattra, 1815
Swenson, Ingrid, 887-888
Swicegood, Gary, 889
Swift, Fletcher H., 1425
Sykes, Hope L., 2065-2066
Symonds, John, 1426
Szapocznik, Jose, 407, 1063
Szymczak, Robert, 749
Tabor, Margaret E., 1427
Tait, Joseph, 1064
Talbot, Jane M., 50
Talbot, Toby, 1428
Tamagawa, Kathleen, 1816
Tamarkin, Stanley R., 1429
Tapping, Minnie Ellingson, 1820
Tarbox, Mary P., 615
Tateishi, John, 1430
Taub, Harold J., 1431
Taves, Ann, 987
Tax, Meredith, 750, 2067
Taylor, Bride N., 1432
Taylor, Elizabeth R., 1818-1819
Taylor, Paul S., 616
Tenison, Eva M., 1433
Tentler, Leslie, 617
Teodor, Luis V., Jr., 139
Terkel, Louis, 1434
Tetrazzini, Luisa, 1820
Tharp, Roland G., 1065
Thoburn, James M., 1435
Thomas, Deborah, 988
Thomas, Dorothy S., 890
Thomas, Evangeline, 51
Thomas, Lately, 1436
Thomas, Trudelle H., 751
Thomas, William J., 1821
Thompson, Ariadne, 1822
Thompson, Goldianne Guyer, 1823
Thomson, Gladys Scott, 1824
Tibbets, Joel W., 1437
Tienda, Marta, 408, 618-619.
Tinker, John N., 409
Toai, Ton That, 989
Tobenkin, Elias, 140, 2068
Toll, William, 410
Tompkins, Leonara Brooke, 1825
Torgoff, Stella de Rosa, 411
Tovar, Ines H., 1438
True, Reiko Homma, 141
True, Ruth S., 1066
Truillo, Roberto G., 52
Tsai, Shih-shan Henry, 142
Tsegga, Asaye, 1067
Tsutakawa, Mayumi, 412
Tucker, Sophie, 1826
Turbin, Carole, 752-755
Turner, Kay F., 990-991
Tyler, Parker, 1439
Tyree, Andrea, 220-221
Uchida, Yoshiko, 1827, 2069-2070
Uhlenberg, Peter, 891
Urdaneta, Maria L., 892
Utley, Freda, 1828-1829
Uyeunten, Sandra, 756
Valanis, Barbara M., 893-894
Van Deusen, John, 413
Van Kleeck, Mary, 620-621, 992
Van Raaphorst, Donna L., 757
Van Tran, Thanh, 993
Vásquez, Richard, 2071
Vazquez, Mario F, 758
Vázsonyi, Andrew, 895
Vega, William A., 994-996, 1068
Velazquez, Loreta J., 1830
Ventura, S. J., 896
Viertel, Salka, 1831
Vogel, Suzanne, 897
von Hassell, Malve, 1440
von Mises, Margit, 1832
von Trapp, Maria A., 1833-1836
Wagenknecht, Edward C., 1441
Wagner, Friedelind, 1837
Wagner, Maria, 1442
Wald, Lillian D., 1838-1839
Walden, Daniel, 2072
Waldinger, Roger, 622-623, 758
Walkowitz, Daniel, 414
Wallach, Erica, 1840
Walsh, Sister Marie, 760
Walska, Ganna, 1841
Walter, I., 1069
Walther, Anna H., 1842
Waltz, Waldo E., 222
Ward, David A., 1443
Ward, Maisie, 1843-1844
Wargelin Brown, K. Marianne, 144, 761, 1444
Waterman, William R., 1445
Waterston, Anna C., 1446
Weatherford, Doris, 145
Webb, Carol P., 762
Webb, Mary G., 1447
Weber, Heidi, 624

298 IMMIGRANT WOMEN IN THE U.S.

Webster, Janice R., 1070
Webster, Margaret, 1845
Weiler, N. Sue, 763
Weinberg, Sydney S., 146, 415, 625, 997
Weiser, Frederick S., 764
Wembridge, Eleanor, 2073
Werstein, Irving, 1448
Wertheimer, Barbara, 626
Westcott, Marcia, 1449
Wexler, Alice, 1450-1451
Wheeler, Thomas C., 1846
Whiffen, Blanche Gaston, 1847
Wiest, Raymond E., 223
Wilber, George L., 627
Wildenhain, Marguerite, 1848
Wilentz, Gay A., 2074
Wiley, Irena, 1849
Willett, Mabel H., 628
Willette, Dorothy D., 2075
William, Ronald L., 898
Williams, Brett., 416
Williams, Gertrude, 1452
Williams, Harvey, 998
Williams, Katherine, 1850
Williams, Phyllis, 417
Williams, Tennessee, 2076
Williams, William C., 2077-2078
Wilson, Carol G., 1453-1454
Wilson, Dorothy C., 1455
Wilson, Philip W., 1456
Wilson, Tracey M., 765
Wing Siu Luk, Judith, 147
Winsey, Valentine Rossilli, 148
Winslow, Catherine Reignolds, 1851-1852
Winston, Clara, 2079
Winter, William, 1457
Winther, Sophus K., 2080-2081
Wise, James W., 1458
Wojciechowska, Maia, 1853
Wold, Clynonia N., 418
Wolfenstein, Martha, 419
Woloch, Nancy, 149
Wong, Anna, 1071
Wong, Bernard, 420
Wong, Diane Yen-Mei, 1854
Wong, Jade Snow, 1855-1856
Wong, Joyce M., 629

Wong, Kay S., 999
Wong, Lorraine, 1857
Wong, Morrison G., 630-631
Wong, Sandra M. J., 421
Woo, Deborah, 632
Woo, Merle, 55
Woods, Robert A., 150
Woodward, Elizabeth A., 1000
Worland, Elizabeth C., 1459
Wormeley, Katharine., 1858
Woroby, Maria, 766
Woytinsky, Emma Shadkhan, 1859
Wyndham, Horace, 1460
Xan, Erna O., 1860, 2082
Yamanaka, Keiko, 633
Yanagida, Evelyn, 1001
Yang, Eun Sik, 151-152
Yanigasako, Sylvia J., 422, 1072
Yans-McLaughlin, Virginia, 423, 634
Yeung, Wai-Tsang, 424
Yeung, Wing Hon, 1073
Yezierska, Anzia, 1861, 2083-2085
Yim, Sun B., 425
Yoshika, Robert B., 153
Young, Ella, 1862
Young-Bruehl, Elisabeth, 1461
Yu, Eui-Young, 426, 767
Yu, Lucy C., 1074
Yung, Judy, 154-155, 224
Yurka, Blanche, 1863
Yzenbaard, John H., 1864
Zaharias, Mildred (Babe) Didrikson, 1865
Zaimi, Nexhmie, 1866
Zakrzewska, Marie E., 1867-1868
Zapata, Vincente S., 1002
Zassenhaus, Hiltgunt, 1869
Zastrow, Erika, 2086
Zavella, Patricia, 635
Zayas, Luis H., 1075
Zeitlin, Rose, 1462
Zelayeta, Elena E., 1870
Zeskind, Philip S., 427
Zinn, Maxine B. 428, 1003

Index of Persons

Adler, Polly, 1463
Ah Toy, 492
Aladjem, Henrietta, 1464
Alessandro, Antonietta Pisanelli, 1394
Allilueva, Svetlana, 1465
Anderson, Hulda, 959
Anderson, Mary, 34, 1166, 1196, 1466
Andres, Chaya R., 1467
Anneke, Mathilde Franziska Giesler, 1421, 1432
Antin, Mary, 1272, 1271, 1468-1470, 1507, 1540, 1758, 1919, 1928, 1950, 1993
Arendt, Hannah, 1156, 1417, 1461
Armaghanian, Arsha L., 1471
Athas, Daphne, 1472
Audobon, Lucy Bakewell, 1173
Barr, Amelia Edith Huddleston, 1474-1475
Barschak, Erna, 1476
Bauer, Mother Benedicta, 1260
Baum, Vicki, 1478
Beaumont, Betty Bentley, 1479
Beh, Siew Hua, 1480
Bellanca, Dorothy Jacobs, 1083-1084, 1196
Belmont, Eleanor Robson, 1481
Bemis, Polly (see Lalu Nathoy)
Bengis, Ingrid, 1482
Bentlage, Mary K., 1484
Berg, Gertrude, 1485
Berg, Rebecca Himber, 1486
Berkowitz, Sarah Bick, 1487
Best, Sophie, 1500
Bethune, Joanna Graham, 1488
Bingle, Alice, 1489-1490
Birkbeck, Elizabeth, 1824
Bisno, Beatrice, 1993
Bjorn, Thyra Ferre, 1491-1492
Blackwell, Elizabeth, 78, 1087, 1140, 1190, 1231, 1245, 1369, 1378, 1427, 1455, 1493
Blavatsky, Helene Petrovna Hahn, 1091, 1107, 1133, 1365, 1426, 1452
Blinde, Patricia Lin, 1497
Blum, Elsa Proehl, 1498
Bonfanti, Maria, 1092
Booth, Evangeline Cory, 1456
Born, Helena, 1299

Boulding, Elise Bior-Hansen, 1499
Bowyer, Edith Nicholl, 1501
Braggiotti, Gloria, 1502
Brand, Sandra, 1503
Briggs, Margaret Yang, 1505
Britten, Emma Hardinge, 1506
Bühler, Charlotte Bertha, 1156
Burke, Billie, 1508
Burland, Rebecca, 1509
Burnett, Frances Eliza Hodgson, 1131, 1510
Burton, Naomi, 1512
Butler, Mother Marie Joseph, 1132, 1271
Cabrini, Mother Frances Xavier, 1102, 1116, 1175, 1292, 1298, 1301, 1305, 1423
Cameron, Donaldina Mackenzie, 579, 1289, 1300, 1454
Carreño, Teresa, 1317
Casal, Lourdes, 1126
Cashman, Nellie, 1144, 1329
Cassiari, Rosa, 1558
Cassini, Marguerite, 1514
Cervantes, Lorna Dee, 1381
Chang, Diana, 1283
Chao, Buwei Yang, 1515
Chennault, Anna, 1517
Chin, Louise, 1518
Chisholm, Shirley, 22, 1123, 1138, 1519-1520
Chou, Cynthia L., 1521
Christian, Barbara T., 1522
Christman, Elisabeth, 1196
Cisneros, Evangelina, 1523
Clarke, Mary Frances, 1151
Cohen, Rose Gallup, 1264, 1525
Cohn, Fannia Mary, 1146, 1196, 1254
Colby, Clara Bewick, 1122
Coleman, Ann Thomas, 1526
Cone, Claribel, 1348
Cone, Etta, 1348
Connelly, Cornelia, 1297
Connolly, Olga Fikotova, 1527
Cope, Mother Marianne, 1274
Cornaby, Hannah Hollingsworth, 1528
Corpi, Lucha, 1381

300   IMMIGRANT WOMEN IN THE U.S.

Crabtree, Lotta, 1097, 1149, 1174, 1372
Cumming, Kate, 1529
Curwell, Laura E., 1530
Cusack, May, 1531
Daché, Lilly, 1532
Dahl, Borghild M., 1533-1534
Dahl, Mary, 1400
D'Aquino, Iva Ikuko Toguri (See Tokyo Rose)
Davies, Mrs. Eliza, 1535
De Hoyos, Angela, 1357
De Hueck, Catherine, 1536-1537
De Wolfe, Elsie, 1538
Del Mar, Marcia, 1539
Demjanovich, Teresa, 1150, 1304
Dennis, Peggy, 1541-1542
Deren, Maya, 1144, 1354
Dessler, Julia Shapiro, 1543
Deutsch, Helene, 1544
Dodd, Bella Visono, 1545
Doering, Bertha-Charlotte, 1546
Dreier, Katherine Sophie, 1377
Dreier, Mary Elisabeth, 1547
Dressler, Marie, 1356, 1548-1549
Drew, Louisa Lane, 1550
Duchesne, Philippine, 647, 1135
Dudzik, Mary Theresa, 1296
Duff, Mary Ann Dyke, 1240, 1266
Dumont, Eleanore, 491
Eastwood, Alice, 1164, 1453
Eaton, Evelyn, 1551-1552
Eaton, Edith, 1282, 1406
Eaton, Winnifred, 1553
Edelman, Fannie, 1554
Edmonds, Jean S., 1555
Edmonds, Sarah Emma Evelyn, 1169, 1235, 1556
Eldridge, Kathleen Tamagawa, 1817-1818
Ellis, Christine, 1557
Endreson, Guri, 1494
Epstein, Helen, 1186
Evosevick, Sarah Vukelich, 1559
Fairfax, Beatrice (See Marie Manning)
Far, Sui Sin (See Edith Eaton)
Fermi, Laura, 1561
Ferraro, Geraldine A., 1238, 1278

Fischer, Markoosha, 1562
Fisher, Florrie, 1563
Fisher, Minnie, 1564
Fiske, Minnie Maddern, 1109
Flynn, Elizabeth Gurley, 1098-1099, 1196, 1389, 1565-1566
Force, Juliana Rieser, 1322
Frankau, Pamela, 1567
Friess, Caroline, 1025
Frohmiller, Ana, 1246
Gabor, Jolie, 1569
Gabor, Eva, 1568
Gabor, Zsa Zsa, 1570
Gág, Wanda Hazel, 1158, 1390, 1571
Gamble, Lillian M, 1572
Ganz, Marie, 1299, 1574
Garcia, Céline Frémaux, 1575
Garden, Mary, 1576
Geva, Tamara, 1577
Gilbert, Anne Jane Hartley, 1578
Gluck, Gemma La Guardia, 1579
Godoy, Mercedes, 1580
Goeppert-Mayer, Maria, 1170
Goldman, Emma, 78, 149, 909, 1120, 1125, 1152, 1177, 1189, 1203, 1215, 1227, 1241, 1347, 1360, 1361, 1396-1398, 1407, 1414, 1441, 1450-1451, 1507, 1581-1583, 1802.
Goldmark, Josephine Clara, 1584
Goritzina, Kyra, 1585
Graham, Isabella Marshall, 1108, 1218, 1586
Graham, Sheilah, 1587-1590
Greenburger, Ingrid, 1591
Grossinger, Jennie, 1224, 1431
Guérin, Mother Theodore, 976
Guiney, Louise Imogen, 1433, 1592
Gull, Caroline, 1593
Hackelmeier, Theresa, 652.
Hannappel, Mary, 1181
Hansteen, Aasta, 1358
Harding, Bertita Leonarz, 1594
Hart, Sara Liebenstein, 1596
Hartman, May Weisser, 1597
Hasanovitz, Elizabeth, 1598
Hatfield, Inge, 1599
Hayden, Mother Mary Bridget, 1198, 1220, 1339
Heck, Barbara Ruckle, 1134

Heckler, Margaret M., 1101
Henie, Sonja, 1600
Henry, Alice, 1196, 1601
Hesse, Eva, 1285
Higbee, Blanche, 1602
Hilf, Mary, 1603
Hillkowitz, Anna, 1076
Hoar, Yvonne, 1248
Hobbs, Lisa, 1604
Holt, C. E., 1605
Holtzman, Fanny. 1104
Honegger-Hanhart, Wilhelmina, 1772
Hopekirk, Helen, 1136
Horney, Karen Danielsen, 1156, 1207, 1252, 1353, 1449
Hotchkiss, Christine Oppeln-Bronikowska, 1606
Housepian, Marjorie, 1088
Houston, Jeanne Wakatsuki, 1607-1608
Hua, Chuang, 1609, 1815
Humula, Anna J., 1610
Ikeda-Spiegel, Motoko, 1611
Ileana, Princess of Romania, 1612
Isely, Elise Dubach, 1613
Jannopoulo, Helen P., 1614
Jastrow, Marie, 1615-1616
Jemison, Mary, 1391
Jennings, Rosa Schreurs, 1617
Jeritza, Maria, 1618
Jessen, Henrietta, 1494
Jex, Eliza Goodson, 1619
Joe, Jeanne, 1620
Jones, Mary (Mother) Harris, 1192, 1196, 1200, 1221, 1291, 1312, 1315, 1328, 1361, 1387-1389, 1400, 1412-1413, 1448, 1621, 1806
Kahn, Frida, 1623
Keene, Laura, 1160
Kelly, Myra, 1950, 1959
Kelly, Fanny Wiggins, 1624
Kemble, Frances Anne (Fanny), 1081, 1114, 1178, 1210, 1250, 1349, 1374, 1625-1630
Kemen, Emilie, 1153
Kennedy, Kate, 1294
Kenny, Elizabeth, 1631
Kinel, Lola, 1632
Kingston, Maxine Hong, 1237, 1473, 1497, 1622, 1633, 1664, 1815, 1986, 2035
Kirby, Charlotte Ives Cobb Godbe, 1100
Klein, Gerda Weissmann, 1634
Knauff, Ellen Raphael, 1635

Knef, Hildegard, 1636-1637
Koenig, Emilie Lohman, 1121, 1504
Kohut, Rebekah Bettelheim, 1084, 1272, 1638-1639
Konikow, Antoinette, 1191, 1319
Koren, Else Hysing, 1640, 1697
Krawcyzk, Monica, 1111, 1891
La Roe, Else Kienle, 1641
LaLonde, Leona M., 1642
Lamarr, Hedy, 1643
Lang, Lucy Fox Robins, 1644
Langseth-Christensen, Lillian, 1645
Langtry, Lillie, 1646
Lappala, Milma, 1234
Larsen, Ingeborg Astrup, 1269
Lawrence, Gertrude, 1647
Lawson, Josephine, 1648
Le Gallienne, Eva, 1650-1651
Lehmann, Lotte, 1212, 1653-1654
Leitner, Isabella, 1655
Lemberg, Rosalia, 1281
Lemlich, Clara (See Clara Lemlich Shavelson)
Lenihan, Mina Ward, 1656
Levorsen, Barbara, 1657
Levy, Harriet Lane, 1658.
Lilienthal, Meta, 1319, 1662
Lin, Alice, 1663
Lindheim, Irma Levy, 1665
Lips, Eva, 1666-1667
Loeb, Sophie Irene, 1400
Logan, Milla Zenovich, 1669-1670
Lohman, Ann Trow, 1079, 1121
Lopez de la Cruz, Jessie, 1137
Loucks, Jennie Erickson, 1671
MacLean, Annie M., 1672
Macy, Anne Sullivan, 1231, 1251
Maeder, Clara Fisher, 1673
Malkiel, Theresa, 909, 1318-1319
Mander, Anica Vesel, 1674
Manning, Marie, 1675
Markham, Pauline, 1676
Marlowe, Julia, 1095, 1375, 1408
Marshall, Mrs. Anne James, 1677
Marshall, Paule, 31, 1894, 1989, 2074

IMMIGRANT WOMEN IN THE U.S.

Marwedel, Emma Jacobina Christiana, 1425
Massing, Hede, 1678
Matsui, Haru, 1679
Mattson, Helmi, 959, 1249
Mayer, Maria Gertrude Goeppert, 1170
McBeth, Susan Low, 1659-1661
McCone, Selma Jokela, 959, 1249
McCormack, Lily Ofley, 1680
McGroarty, Sister Susan (Julia), 1230, 1333
McPherson, Aimee Semple, 1303, 1314, 1436-1437, 1681-1684
Mehegan, Mary Xavier, 1893
Meir, Golda, 1223, 1685, 1802
Mendoza, Lydia, 1211
Meyer, Agnes Elizabeth Ernst, 1686
Michel, Auguste Marie, 1687
Millberg, Karen Schwencke, 1688
Mirikitani, Janice, 1892
Modieska, Helen, 1147-1148, 1219, 1689-1690
Modjeska, Helen (see Modieska, Helen)
Moise, Penina, 1691
Monk, Maria, 1419
Montez, Lola, 1163, 1214, 1279
Morgan, Elizabeth, 1383
Morgan, Agnes Fay, 1364
Morlacchi, Giuseppina, 1092, 1288
Morris, Edita, 1692
Mortimer, Mary, 1332
Morton, Leah (see Elizabeth Stern)
Moskowitz, Belle Lindner Israels, 1345
Mueller, Amelia, 1692
Murphy, Patricia, 1695
Nathoy, Lalu, 1309
Negri, Pola, 1696
Nelson, Teresa Leopando Lucero, 1698
Newby, Elizabeth, 1699
Newman, Judith Sternberg, 1700
Newman, Pauline, 702, 1196
Ney, Elisabet, 1159, 1162, 1202, 1213, 1290, 1373, 1432
Nguyen, Jamie, 1414
Nin, Anais, 1701-1707

Niranen, Margareeta (See Maggie Walz)
Norton, Minerva Brace, 1708
Nowicki, Stella, 1709
Nurmi, Maiju, 1249
O'Neal, Mary T., 1710
O'Reilly, Leonora, 34, 1130
O'Sullivan, Mary Kenney, 657, 1459
Ohori, Fumiye, 1711
Okubo, Miné, 1712
Okumara, Taki, 1713
Oleson, Anna, 1195
Olsen, Tilly, 1893
Olsson, Anna, 1714
Orpen, Mrs., 1715
Ostenso, Martha, 1089, 1128-1129, 1928
Packer, Jane Knight, 1716
Padow, Mollie Potter, 1717
Papashvily, Helen, 1718
Pariseau, Mother Joseph, 1307
Pasanen, Ida, 1444
Patti, Adelina, 1165, 1258, 1270
Paul, Almira, 1719
Pauli, Hertha E., 1720
Pawlowicz, Sala Kaminska, 1721
Penzik, Irena, 1722
Pesotta, Rose, 1254, 1273, 1394, 1723-1724
Petrova, Olga, 1725
Petrovskaya, Kyra, 1726
Petterson, Anna, 1727
Phillipps, Adelaide, 1446
Pickford, Mary, 1728
Picon, Molly, 1729
Plotkin, Sara, 1730
Polasek, Emily M. K., 1731
Polykoff, Shirley, 1732
Portillo, Estela, 1951
Preus, Caroline Dorothea Margarethe (Keyser), 1733
Prisland, Marie, 1734
Raaen, Aagot, 1735-1736
Racowitza, Elena von Dönniges, 1737
Radziwill, Ekaterina Rzewuska, 1738
Ramirez, Sara Estela, 1438
Randall, Isabelle, 1739
Rasmussen, Anne-Marie, 1740
Rautalahti, Thyra, 1444
Rehan, Ada, 1457
Reiss, Johanna, 1741
Resnick, Rose, 1742

Restell, Madame (see Lohmann, Anna Trow)
Reznikoff, Sara, 1743
Richardson, Mary Walsham Few, 1745
Richman, Julia, 909, 1077, 1105-1106, 1263
Ritter, Louise, 1746
Robins, Elizabeth, 1747
Robins, Margaret Dreier, 34, 1196, 1342, 1366
Robinson, Therese, 1421
Rodzinski, Halina, 1748
Rogers, Clara K., 1749
Roisdal, Agnes, 1750
Rose, Ernestine Louise Siismondi Potowski, 1272, 1382
Rosenberg, Ethel Greenglass, 1346, 1752
Rosenthal, Jean, 1753
Ross, Dorothy, 1755
Rostenberg, Leona, 1756
Royce, Sarah Eleanor Bayliss, 1757
Rubinstein, Helena, 1188, 1337, 1759
Rudolph, Marguerita, 1760
Ruskay, Sophie, 1761
Russell, Mother Mary Baptist, 1306, 1376
Rybacki, Stella, 1762
Saehle, Jannicke, 1494
Salz, Helen A., 1763
Sandberg, Sara, 1764-1765
Sandoz, Mari, 62, 1327, 1410-1411, 1766-1767
Sandusky, Hannah, 1393.
Sangalli, Rita, 1092
Sanger, Margaret Higgins, 149, 1169, 1770-1771
Saroff, Sophie, 1772
Schechter, Hope Mendoza, 1771
Schenck, Lucy Reissig, 1773
Schmidt, Minna, 1155
Schneider, Aili Gronlund, 1774
Schneiderman, Rose, 34, 1185, 1196, 1254, 1388, 1775-1776
Schroeter, Elizabeth A., 1778
Schumann-Heink, Ernestine, 1649
Schwimmer, Rosika. 1239
Scripps, Ellen Browning, 1226
Seckar, Alvena V., 1779
Segal, Lore Groszmann, 1780
Segale, Rose M., 1781
Seklow, Edna, 1782

Sembrich, Marcella, 1338
Sermolino, Maria, 1783
Shand, Margaret Clark, 1784
Shavelson, Clara Lemlich, 909, 1382, 1384
Shaw, Pauline Agassiz, 1785
Shaw, Anna Howard Shaw, 1103, 1284, 1291, 1313, 1315, 1409, 1447
Sher, Eva Goldstein, 1786
Shick, Maete Gordon, 1787
Siegal, Aranka, 1788-1789
Simon, Kate, 1790-1791
Simonian, Leonie B., 1792
Siwundhla, Alice (Princess Msumba), 1793-1794
Slater, Lisa A., 1795
Snow, Carmel White, 1796
Soldene, Emily, 1797
Solomon, Hannah Greenebaum, 1272, 1798
Sone, Monica Itoi, 1799
Sonnenschein, Rosa (See Rosa Sonneschein)
Sonneschein, Rosa, 1272, 1350-1351
Soong, Irma Tam, 1800
Soregi, Priscilla Varga, 1801
Stan, Anisoara, 1804
Stanley, Ilse Davidsohn, 1805
Stastny, Olga, 1078
Steiner, Mollie, 1299
Stern, Edith Rosenwald, 1257
Stern, Elizabeth Gertrude, 1315, 1808-1810, 1928
Stettheimer, Florine, 1439
Stokes, Rose Harriet Pastor, 78, 909, 1196, 1388, 1422, 1429, 1811-1812
Stone, Goldie, 1813
Strítecky, Marie, 1743
Sugimoto, Etsu Inagaki, 1814
Sullivan, Anna, 1336
Sutro-Schücking, Kathinka, 1421
Svendsen, Gro, 1414, 1560
Swartz, Maud O'Farrell, 1196
Szold, Henrietta, 689, 697, 909, 1171, 1183, 1194, 1272, 1275-1277, 1293, 1441, 1462
Tamagawa, Kathleen (See Kathleen Tamagawa Eldridge)
Tapping, Minnie Ellingson, 1817
Taylor, Laurette, 1157

Taylor, Elizabeth R., 1818-1819
Tetrazzini, Luisa, 1820
Thoburn, Isabella, 1435
Thompson, Ariadne, 1822
Thompson, Goldianne Guyer, 1823
Tokyo Rose, 1182, 1225, 1443
Tompkins, Leonara Brooke, 1825
Tucker, Sophie, 1823
Uchida, Yoshiko, 1827
Urrea, Teresa, 1236, 1352, 1367
Urso, Camilla, 1093
Utley, Freda, 1828-1829
Van der Schrieck, Louise, 1334
Velazquez, Loreta Janeta, 1830
Viertel, Salka, 1831
Villanueva, Alma, 1381
Vincent, Mary Ann Farlow, 1363
von Mises, Margit, 1832
von Trapp, Maria A., 1833-1836
Waerenskjold, Elise (See Warenskjold)
Wagner, Friedelind, 1837
Wald, Lillian D., 909, 1112, 1152, 1168, 1179, 1204, 1264, 1362, 1441, 1838-1839
Walsh, Mother Mary, 1113
Walska, Ganna, 1841
Walther, Anna H., 1842
Walz, Maggie, 1444
Ward, Maisie, 1843-1844
Warde, Frances, 1228
Warenskjold, Elise, 1119, 1524
Webster, Margaret, 1402, 1845
Wergeland, Agnes Mathilde, 1316
Whiffen, Blanche Gaston, 1847
Wildenhain, Marguerite, 1848
Wiley, Irena, 1849
Williams, Katherine, 1850
Winslow, Catherine Reignolds, 1851-1852
Wise, Louise Waterman, 1458
Wojciechowska, Maia, 1853
Wong, Lorraine, 1857
Wong, Ah So, 1267
Wong, Jade Snow, 1142, 1497, 1507, 1540, 1664, 1815, 1846, 1855-1856, 1986
Wormeley, Katharine Prescott, 1858
Woytinsky, Emma Shadkhan, 1859
Wright, Frances, 78, 149, 1096, 1184, 1199, 1340, 1344, 1445
Xan, Erna Oleson, 1862
Yezierska, Anzia, 878, 1117, 1172, 1233, 1385-1386, 1507, 1540, 1861, 1928, 1950, 1959, 1979, 1991, 1993, 2047
Young, Ella, 1862, 1893
Yurka, Blanche, 1863
Zaharias, Mildred Ella (Babe) Didrikson, 1865
Zaimi, Nexhmie, 1866
Zakrzewska, Marie Elizabeth, 78, 1867-1868
Zassenhaus, Hiltgunt, 1869
Zelayeta, Elena E., 1870
Zemen, Josephine Humjpel, 1394
Zita, Mother Mary, 1405
Zuk, Mary, 735

Group Index

Afghans, 44

Africans, 893, 936, 1209, 1793, 1794. See also Nigerian

Albanians, 1866

Alsatians, 1193, 1250

Antiguans, 1167

Arabs, 300, 359, 568. See also Egyptians, Syrians

Armenians, 378, 1088, 1324, 1471, 1914, 1971, 2048

Asians, 13, 18, 21, 44, 55, 60, 91, 106, 107, 141, 143, 145, 153, 161, 203, 231, 257, 269, 277, 323, 324, 328, 333, 340, 342, 356, 382, 468, 489, 526, 533, 619, 623, 631, 632, 633, 651, 773, 775, 776, 790, 873, 986, 1086, 1124, 1197, 1283, 1443, 1607, 1815, 1854, 1986 (See also Cambodians, Chinese, Hmong, Indians, Japanese, Kampucheans, Khmer, Koreans, Laotians, Sri Lankans, Thai, Vietnamese);

Southeast, 277, 413, 440, 825, 887-888, 900, 955

Australians, 215, 671-672, 1601, 1604, 1631

Austrians, 364, 474, 652, 742, 808, 1206, 1247, 1250, 1618, 1643, 1645, 1833-1836, 2079. See also Jews

Baltic, 682. See also Jews, Lithuanians

Barbadians, 22, 198, 1123, 1138, 1519, 1520, 2003

Belgians, 646, 1334, 1642

Blacks (foreign-born), 11, 170, 184, 462, 522, 1522, 2002

Bohemians, 439, 480, 592, 763, 1368, 1415, 1731, 1863, 1909-1911. See also Czechs

Bolivians, 1038

British, 97, 236, 304, 356, 414, 499, 514, 723, 1161. See also English, Irish, Scots, Welsh

Bulgarians, 1464

Cambodians, 117, 251, 413

Canadians, 200, 240, 514, 723, 832, 1145, 1164, 1169, 1235, 1303, 1314, 1356, 1391, 1419, 1436-1437, 1453, 1488, 1538, 1548, 1549, 1551-1552, 1555-1556, 1605, 1624, 1672, 1681-1684, 1695, 1716, 1719, 1728, 1774;

English Canadians, 247;

French Canadians, 94, 237, 304, 356, 365, 414, 446, 480, 485, 506, 549, 648, 656, 658, 665, 971, 1248, 1311

Caribbean, 3, 14, 172, 176, 181, 185, 186, 204, 489, 522, 619, 623, 683, 796, 813, 815, 816, 863, 893, 894, 1050, 1167. See also Antiguans, Barbadians, Cubans, Dominicans, Haitians, Jamaicans, Tobagoans, Trinidadians

Carpatho-Ruthenians, 1150

Central Americans, 19, 172, 343, 408, 489, 591, 618, 623, 813, 841, 853. See also Chicanas, El Salvadorans, Garifunas, Guatemalans, Hondurans, Mexicans, Nicaraguans

306 IMMIGRANT WOMEN IN THE U.S.

Chicana, 5, 7, 19, 40-41, 45, 50, 52, 66, 83, 95, 98, 115-116, 272, 275, 292, 296, 337, 360, 428, 444, 459, 482, 491, 561, 594, 603-604, 635, 653, 701, 728, 837, 838, 856, 869, 877, 892, 924-925, 1080, 1086, 1205, 1381, 1951, 2012, 2071. See also Mexican

Chinese, 60, 76-77, 86, 91, 102, 111, 142, 154-155, 174, 190, 207, 219, 224, 234, 252-253, 277, 289-290, 307, 314, 332-334, 338, 344-345, 349, 356, 359, 370, 385, 398, 420-421, 424, 431, 438, 459, 467, 481, 484, 492, 510, 511, 528, 550, 575, 579, 605, 623, 629-631, 633, 650, 700, 836, 843, 848, 859, 866, 876, 910, 920, 944, 958, 961, 986, 999, 1012-1013, 1018, 1026, 1027, 1032-1033, 1046, 1059, 1067, 1071, 1073-1074, 1086, 1124, 1142, 1237, 1255, 1259, 1282, 1283, 1289, 1300, 1308-1309, 1406, 1454, 1480, 1497, 1505, 1515, 1517-1518, 1521, 1553, 1609, 1620, 1622, 1633, 1663-1664, 1800, 1846, 1855-1857, 1917, 1943, 1986, 1997, 2018, 2021

Color, people of, 12, 44

Colombians, 19, 74, 96, 299, 464, 548-549

Croatians, 244, 1187

Cubans, 10, 19, 60, 87, 197, 225, 228-229, 232, 250, 274, 279, 285, 356, 359, 383-384, 407, 427, 459, 462, 487-488, 508, 582, 589, 591, 599, 615, 619, 627, 748, 779, 781, 799, 813, 823, 828, 834-835, 837, 841, 848, 855-856, 864, 872, 882, 896, 943, 962, 1009, 1021, 1028, 1031, 1038, 1126, 1287, 1523, 1539, 1580, 1830

Czechs, 388, 1078, 1158, 1368, 1390, 1394, 1527, 1571, 1635, 1744, 1944, 1952, 1984, 1990, 2022. See also Bohemian

Danes, 188, 1688, 1842, 1957, 2007, 2080-2081

Dominicans, 19, 96, 180, 183, 195, 299, 310, 374, 584-586, 610, 679, 824

Dutch, 686, 1181, 1244, 1253, 1260, 1617, 1694, 1864, 1931, 1947, 1964, 1967-1968, 1987, 2028. See also Jews

Eastern Europeans, 70, 120, 240, 452, 558, 658, 710, 802, 940, 1725, 1762, 2053. See also Baltic, Bohemians, Bulgarians, Carpatho-Ruthenians, Croatians, Czechs, Hungarians, Jews, Lithuanians, Poles, Rumanians, Russians, Slovaks, Slovenians, Ukrainians

Egyptians, 772

El Salvadorans, 926, 941, 984

English, 88, 160, 215, 364, 437, 480, 549, 762, 1079, 1081, 1087, 1095, 1097, 1100, 1103, 1109, 1114, 1121-1122, 1131, 1140, 1149, 1160, 1161, 1173-1174, 1178, 1190, 1201, 1208, 1210, 1226, 1231, 1240, 1245, 1266, 1282, 1284, 1297, 1299, 1313, 1315, 1325, 1332, 1349, 1363, 1364, 1369, 1372, 1374-1375, 1378, 1383, 1402, 1406, 1408-1409, 1427, 1446-1447, 1455-1456, 1474-1475, 1479, 1481, 1489-1490, 1493, 1501, 1506, 1508-1509, 1510, 1512, 1526, 1528, 1530, 1550, 1553, 1567,

GROUPS 307

1576, 1578, 1587-1588, 1589-1590, 1595, 1619, 1627-1630, 1635, 1639, 1646-1647, 1673, 1675-1677, 1708, 1715, 1719, 1739, 1745, 1747, 1749, 1755, 1757, 1780, 1785, 1797, 1807, 1818-1819, 1824, 1828-1829, 1837, 1843, 1844-1845, 1847, 1851, 1852, 1858, 1877, 1885, 1930, 1933, 1974

Eurasians, 1283

European-Americans, 18, 102, 263

Filipinas, 44, 60-61, 75, 109, 125, 139, 157, 175, 199, 259, 295, 370, 385, 443, 459, 525, 564, 601, 619, 631-633, 790, 791, 839, 859, 886, 986, 1124, 1154, 1259, 1698

Finns, 38, 144, 191, 694, 730-731, 747, 761, 959, 1054-1055, 1234, 1249, 1281, 1444, 1135, 1145, 1153, 1671, 1774, 1877, 2000, 2013

French, 364, 544, 647, 658, 659, 664-665, 674-676, 719, 723, 733, 751, 848, 930, 976, 1307, 1324, 1392, 1532, 1575, 1602, 1650-1651, 1687, 1701-1707, 1793, 1949, 1972, 1974, 2024, 2050

Garifunas, 182, 824

Germans, 97, 124, 126, 135-136, 215, 240, 288, 302, 311, 356, 364, 377, 381, 437, 439, 461, 480, 484, 499, 502, 515, 583, 600, 602, 611, 621, 642, 664-665, 667, 682, 698, 706, 716, 732, 738, 764, 804, 861, 930, 942, 967, 992, 1010, 1025, 1066, 1085, 1134, 1145, 1155-1156, 1159, 1162, 1170, 1202, 1207, 1212-1213, 1247, 1252, 1268, 1274, 1290, 1322, 1327, 1342, 1353, 1366, 1371, 1373, 1377, 1410-1411, 1417-1418, 1421, 1425, 1432, 1434, 1442, 1461, 1484, 1498, 1504, 1514, 1516, 1547-1549, 1591, 1599, 1635-1637, 1641, 1649, 1654-1653, 1654, 1662, 1666-1667, 1686, 1693, 1696, 1737, 1746, 1766, 1767, 1772-1773, 1777, 1796, 1824, 1832, 1837, 1840, 1848, 1867-1869, 1921, 1936, 1948, 1954, 1969-1970, 1972, 2033, 2036, 2051, 2058-2060, 2068, 2077, 2086 (See also Jews);

  Bavarians, 670, 1025, 1999;

  Saxons, 717;

  German-Russians, 302, 515, 1778, 1948, 1998, 2037, 2065-2066

Greeks, 56, 277, 304, 356, 390, 394, 848, 929, 1041, 1324, 1341, 1472, 1614, 1822, 2029-2032, 2057

Guatemalans, 926, 1324

Guyanians, 22, 1138, 1519-1520

Haitians, 71, 108, 178, 194, 277, 816, 871, 1127

Hispanics, 17, 19, 196, 197, 232, 279, 285, 408, 476, 487, 559, 576, 591, 599, 610, 618, 781, 796, 799, 805, 809, 828, 884, 896, 918, 939, 943, 1035, 1038, 1075, 2012. See also Bolivians, Chicanas, Colombians, Cubans, Dominicans, El Salvadorans, Guatemalans, Hondurans Mexicans, Nicaraguans, Peruvians, Venezuelans

Hmong, 368, 413, 510, 876, 888, 1018, 1047

308   IMMIGRANT WOMEN IN THE U.S.

Hondurans, 1255

Hungarians, 391, 480, 496, 568-570, 1594, 1801, 2073. See also Jews

Indians, Asian, 257, 298, 342, 396, 633, 900, 988, 1825

Indochinese, 836, 876, 1018, 1059, 1069. See also Cambodians, Hmong, Kampuchean, Khmer, Laotians, Thai, Vietnamese

Iranians, 356, 433, 935

Irish, 85, 94, 97, 135-136, 150, 162, 189, 193, 200, 202, 212-213, 230, 236, 240, 247, 276, 288, 293, 297, 301, 308, 311, 314, 356, 359, 361, 364, 365, 377, 381, 414, 429, 437, 446, 449, 456-457, 461, 480, 484, 499-502, 513, 516, 520, 526, 535-536, 540, 550-552, 582, 599, 611, 613, 615, 621, 642, 644, 655, 657-658, 663, 664-665, 673, 676, 698, 704-705, 713, 715, 729, 752, 753-755, 760, 762, 802, 804, 808, 832-833, 865, 914, 922, 942, 957, 966, 985, 987, 1010, 1056, 1068, 1085, 1090, 1098-1099, 1101, 1113, 1130, 1132, 1134, 1144-1145, 1151, 1157, 1163, 1170, 1176, 1192, 1198, 1214, 1220-1221, 1228, 1230, 1232, 1243, 1246, 1251, 1255, 1271, 1279, 1291, 1294, 1306, 1312, 1315, 1324, 1328-1329, 1333, 1335-1336, 1339, 1361, 1376, 1387, 1389, 1395, 1401, 1405, 1412-1413, 1433, 1448, 1457-1460, 1511, 1531, 1565-1566, 1592, 1621, 1680, 1768-1769, 1798, 1816, 1862, 1872, 1886, 1895, 1907, 1920, 1922-1925, 1929, 1934-1936, 1938, 1941, 1954, 1959, 1985, 2008, 2036, 2052, 2054-2055

Israelis, 960

Italians, 9, 73, 89, 131, 148, 150, 179, 215, 230, 235-236, 244, 255, 266, 267-268, 273, 277, 286-287, 293, 301, 317-318, 356, 359, 364, 391, 393, 399-400, 417, 423, 437, 439, 448, 456, 472, 480, 490, 520, 532, 537, 543, 549, 557, 567-568, 573, 580, 587, 612-613, 620, 628, 634, 636, 640, 648, 677, 681, 685, 712, 741-742, 759, 763, 784, 786, 802, 804, 818, 819, 852, 860, 870, 875, 905-906, 921-922, 942, 952, 957, 972, 977, 1020, 1039-1040, 1057-1058, 1064, 1090, 1092-1094, 1102, 1110, 1116, 1165, 1175, 1238, 1258, 1265, 1270, 1278, 1288, 1292, 1298, 1301-1302, 1305, 1324, 1343, 1392, 1394, 1401, 1403, 1420, 1423, 1502, 1545, 1561, 1579, 1674, 1782, 1783, 1820, 1820, 1885, 1902, 1913, 1916, 1927, 1945, 2026-2027, 2034, 2045, 2076

Jamaicans, 90, 164, 165, 167, 208, 214, 1005, 1167

Japanese, 44, 60, 91-92, 100-103, 114, 130, 174, 205, 215, 252-253, 262, 269, 270, 278, 281, 290, 295, 312, 315-316, 323-325, 329-330, 333, 351, 354-355, 359, 370, 385, 389, 405, 409, 412, 422, 459, 494-497, 519, 631, 633, 756, 769, 773, 803, 827-828, 839, 843, 846, 848-851, 859, 862, 868, 878, 890, 897, 903-904, 944, 968, 986, 1001, 1014-1015, 1023, 1042, 1048, 1072, 1086, 1124, 1182, 1225, 1256, 1259, 1282, 1310, 1324, 1330, 1430, 1434, 1553, 1607, 1608, 1611, 1679, 1711-1713, 1799, 1814, 1816, 1827, 1892, 1980, 2009, 2011,

GROUPS 309

2016-2017, 2051, 2061, 2062-2064, 2069-2070

Jews, 8, 23, 26, 39, 54, 65, 89, 113, 133, 239, 241, 242, 266, 320, 348, 359, 387, 391, 399, 400, 415, 419, 498, 524, 536, 537, 543, 577, 609, 613, 620, 637, 641, 685, 687, 689, 692-693, 695-696, 722, 741, 743-744, 745, 763, 820, 822, 883, 952, 957, 979, 992, 997, 1039, 1083-1084, 1104, 1110, 1223-1224, 1262, 1272, 1324, 1326, 1394, 1401, 1415, 1431, 1441, 1485, 1503, 1507, 1544, 1564, 1615, 1623, 1634, 1638-1639, 1655, 1691, 1717, 1720-1722, 1730, 1751, 1753, 1786-1788, 1808, 1813, 1831, 1893, 1901, 1946, 1959, 1983, 1993, 1996, 2001, 2005, 2010, 2023, 2084;

Austrian, 1104, 1224, 1431, 1478, 1574, 1584, 1678, 1764-1765, 1780;

Dutch, 1741;

Eastern European, 89, 93, 146, 238, 248, 282-283, 336, 442, 456, 532, 541, 553, 563, 571, 612, 620, 625, 628, 639, 660, 666, 677-678, 681, 704, 720, 736-737, 745, 746, 759, 804, 881, 909, 921, 937, 942, 1008, 1019, 1030, 1060, 1076, 1191, 1217, 1254, 1286, 1318, 1345, 1346, 1384, 1429, 1467, 1541, 1542, 1563, 1564, 1732, 1752, 1782, 1790-1791, 1812, 1878, 1888, 1903, 1960, 1961, 1962, 1985, 1994, 2042, 2067, 2083;

German, 93, 410, 571, 662, 669, 690, 724, 726, 745, 1007, 1076, 1077, 1105, 1106, 1112, 1152, 1156, 1168, 1179, 1204, 1257, 1263, 1264, 1285, 1315, 1348, 1350, 1351, 1362, 1439, 1458, 1476, 1596, 1658, 1665, 1668, 1674, 1700, 1756, 1763, 1798, 1805, 1808-1810, 1838-1839;

Hungarian, 697, 1034, 1171, 1183, 1194, 1239, 1275-1277, 1293, 1462, 1639, 1655, 1788;

Latvian, 1082-1083;

Lithuanian, 244, 1393, 1543, 1717, 1787, 1813;

Orthodox, 721, 821, 1029;

Polish, 1172, 1185, 1233, 1382, 1386, 1422, 1428, 1487, 1503, 1544, 1634, 1721-1722, 1831, 1861, 1874, 1979, 2049, 2084;

Rumanian, 1753;

Russian, 97, 267, 439, 480, 702, 1146, 1152, 1177, 1189, 1203, 1215, 1216, 1223, 1241, 1261, 1264, 1273, 1295, 1299, 1347, 1360, 1312, 1382, 1396, 1397, 1398, 1400, 1407, 1414, 1450, 1451, 1463, 1468-70, 1482, 1483, 1485, 1525, 1581-1583, 1597-1598, 1603, 1644, 1685, 1723-1724, 1729, 1742, 1743, 1761, 1770, 1775-1776, 1809, 1811, 1826, 18659 2001;

Sephardic, 721, 1118;

Serbian, 1615-1616;

Soviet, 606, 609, 1062, 1222, 1370;

Turkish, 1118;

Ukrainian, 1623, 1724;

West Indian, 1691

Kampucheans, 825

Khmer, 510, 876, 879

Koreans, 63, 137, 138, 151-152, 261, 264, 324-327, 331, 333, 339, 359, 369, 371, 380, 395, 406, 425-426, 450, 465, 469, 534-535, 538, 633, 767, 803, 847-848, 919, 946, 950, 968, 1037, 1051, 1139

Laotians, 129, 251, 413, 510, 825, 876, 1047

Latin-Americans, 44, 173, 231, 343, 538, 619, 797, 853, 902, 918, 1035, 1401; Latinas, 17, 49, 79, 463, 798, 805. See also Bolivians, Chicanas, Cubans, Dominicans, El Salvadorans, Haitians, Hondurans, Mexicans, Nicaraguans, Peruvians, Venezuelans

Lebanese, 62

Lithuanians, 322, 480, 685, 711, 1011, 1359. See also Jews

Malaysians, 1480

Mexicans, 6-7, 17, 19, 41, 44, 60, 66, 82, 95, 102, 115, 119, 156, 159, 163, 168, 196-197, 210, 221, 223, 226, 232-233, 245, 256, 258-259, 263, 271-272, 280, 284-285, 292, 295, 305-306, 308, 313, 319, 321, 341, 343, 350, 352-353, 356-359, 362, 366-367, 370, 373, 379, 397, 402, 408, 416, 445, 454, 458-459, 463, 466, 475, 478, 482, 487, 491, 503, 518, 523, 542, 588-590, 591-592, 594, 596-598, 603, 607-608, 614, 616, 618, 627, 649, 653-654, 685, 708, 728, 758, 770-771, 774-783, 785, 787-788, 792-795, 799, 806-807, 809-810, 812, 814, 817, 827-828, 830, 838, 840-842, 844, 853-854, 857-858, 867, 869, 874, 877, 880, 882, 884, 889, 891-892, 896, 898, 907-908, 915, 917, 923-924, 928, 941, 943, 945, 964-965, 969-970, 973-975, 983-984, 990-991, 994-996, 1002-1003, 1022, 1038, 1045, 1065, 1068, 1080, 1197, 1205, 1211, 1236, 1280, 1324, 1357, 1367, 1379, 1381, 1438, 1573, 1580, 1699, 1754, 1771, 1870, 1982, 2071. See also Chicano

Negroes, 127

New Zealand, 1289, 1300, 1454, 1655

Nicaraguans, 926, 941

Nigerians, 249, 953

Norwegians, 209, 240, 392, 555, 727, 1089, 1119, 1128, 1129, 1195, 1269, 1316, 1331, 1358, 1361, 1400, 1414, 1494-1495, 1524, 1533-1534, 1560, 1572, 1600, 1640, 1657, 1697, 1733, 1735-1736, 1740, 1750, 1803, 1817, 1860, 1865, 1890, 1897, 1906, 1915, 1926, 1953, 1958, 1974, 1990, 2004, 2025, 2040-2041, 2046, 2051, 2077-2078, 2082

Pacific, 21. See also Filipinas, Malaysians, Samoans

Persians, 44

Peruvians, 1038, 1255

Poles, 72, 200, 235-236, 243-244, 246, 301, 304, 322, 346-348, 356, 359, 372, 377, 381, 386, 391, 397, 439, 448, 456, 479-480, 516-517, 536-537, 544, 549, 645, 681, 685, 688, 707, 718, 725, 735, 742, 749, 763, 845, 860, 899, 922, 954, 1010, 1111, 1115, 1147, 1148, 1188, 1206, 1219, 1296, 1337, 1338, 1420, 1557, 1606, 1689-1690, 1696, 1709, 1759, 1821, 1841, 1849,

GROUPS 311

1853, 1867-1868, 1871, 1873, 1881-1882, 1891, 1896, 1904, 1908, 1918, 1937, 1955, 1965-1966, 1975, 1981, 1989, 2006, 2014, 2019, 2043. See also Jews

Portuguese, 94, 217-218, 234, 335, 356, 483, 544-546, 548-549, 581, 595, 691, 739-740, 915-916

Rumanians, 1612, 1804. See also Jews

Russians, 236, 301, 381, 480, 808, 1091, 1107, 1133, 1143, 1354, 1365, 1404, 1426, 1452, 1465, 1514, 1516, 1536-1537, 1562, 1577, 1585, 1632, 1718, 1726, 1738, 1828-1829. See also Jews

Samoans, 227, 295, 432, 831

Scandinavians, 47, 67, 200, 364, 480, 484, 685, 706, 1070, 1499, 1910, 2044. See also Danes, Finns, Norwegians, Swedes

Scots, 364, 493, 1096, 1108, 1136, 1184, 1199, 1218, 1289, 1300, 1340, 1344, 1435, 1445, 1454, 1529, 1535, 1586, 1659-1661, 1784, 1872, 1995

Serbians, 1559, 1669, 1670. See also Jews

Slavs, 64, 123, 254, 267, 429, 456, 543, 742, 950-952, 1039. See also Albanians, Bulgarians, Carpatho-Ruthenians, Croatians, Poles, Rumanians, Russians, Serbians, Slovaks, Slovenians, Ukrainians

Slovaks, 322, 391, 403-404, 1779, 1887, 1992

Slovenians, 244, 1110, 1321, 1734

South Americans, 19, 172, 408, 591, 618, 623, 813, 841, 893. See also Bolivians, Colombians, Guyanians, Peruvians, Venezuelans

Southern Europeans, 452, 558, 940. See also Albanians, Greeks, Croatians, Italians, Portuguese, Serbians, Spanish

Spanish, 18, 245, 277, 341, 352, 561, 627, 841, 898, 918, 923, 928, 941, 945, 1065, 1165, 1258, 1270, 1434, 1539, 1555, 1699, 1870

Sri Lankans, 900

Swedes, 439, 562, 1006, 1166, 1327, 1410-1411, 1466, 1477, 1491-1492, 1546, 1648, 1692, 1714, 1880, 1889, 1898, 1899-1900, 1905, 1911-1912, 1977

Swiss, 364, 716, 1500, 1593, 1613, 1746, 1766-1767

Syrians, 150, 648

Thai, 1049

Tobagoans, 176

Trinidadians, 170, 176, 1324

Turks, 44. See also Jews

Ukrainians, 643, 684-685, 766, 1760. See also Jews

Venezuelans, 1317

Vietnamese, 110, 295, 324, 356, 359, 413, 418, 436, 510, 512-513, 654, 771, 825, 939-949, 989, 993, 1018, 1034, 1936, 1043, 1046, 1062, 1071, 1324, 1414

Welsh, 160, 449, 1710, 2075

West Indians, 44, 356, 381, 473, 936, 1061, 1255, 1850. See also Antiguans, Barbadians, Trinidadians

Subject Index

abortion, 774, 861, 874, 892, 1079, 1121

adventuress, 1144, 1163, 1214, 1279, 1329, 1460, 1511, 1784

aging and old age, 314, 316, 318, 339, 835, 837, 855, 862, 865, 868, 881, 883, 922, 965, 998, 1286

Alaska, 1329, 1747, 1784

anti-communism, 1514, 1678, 1722, 1795, 1828-1829

archives, 2, 15, 27, 32, 34, 38, 39, 51, 54

Arizona, 296, 1329

Arkansas, 1677, 2037

athletes, 1527, 1600, 1865

autobiography, 1, 16, 30, 35, 1237, 1250, 1463-1870, 1883

Baltic Women's Council, 682, 711

bibliography, 1-55, 527, 1407, 1950

biography, 16, 689, 702, 709, 722, 751, 909, 930, 976, 1025, 1076-1462, 1560, 1640, 1735, 1757, 1806, 1810

birth and pregnancy, 123, 248, 249, 483, 784, 804, 814, 817, 819, 824, 834, 860, 879, 880, 886, 888, 893-894, 896, 898, 1023, 1073

birth control, 709, 723, 790-791, 838, 856, 864, 867, 887, 1170, 1768-1769

boarders and boarding, 123, 265, 361, 452, 457, 479, 516, 565, 624, 895, 1329

body image, 773

business and businesswomen, 528, 571, 1144, 1155, 1188, 1224, 1329, 1337, 1420, 1479, 1538, 1559, 1603, 1695, 1732, 1756, 1759, 1761, 1787, 1804, 1870;

   family businesses, 289, 433, 496

California, 111, 233, 245, 321, 341, 503, 575, 596, 598, 700, 767, 843, 859, 898, 1147, 1279, 1425, 1546, 1605, 1737, 1757, 1784, 1792, 1848, 1965, 1974, 2017, 2026, 2069, 2071;

   Encina, 1995;

   Hollywood, 1104, 1587-1590, 1632, 1831, 1981;

   Los Angeles, 252, 259, 296, 337, 370, 385, 436, 478, 487, 559, 607, 616, 1982;

   Sacramento, 269;

   San Diego, 794;

   San Francisco, 343, 294, 492, 629-630, 726, 1187, 1294, 1454, 1658, 1669, 1953;

   Silicon Valley, 489, 526;

   Stockton, 1320

charity and welfare, 301, 379, 503, 560, 610, 876, 1108, 1218, 1488, 1586. See also social work

Chicanismo, Movimiento, 701, 728

childhood, 16, 401, 570, 871, 1642, 1714, 1715, 1724, 1735, 1750, 1761, 1764-1765, 1773, 1782-1783, 1786, 1789, 1791, 1823, 1855, 1890;

   girlhood, 57, 150, 581, 992, 1061, 1065, 1312, 1484, 1486, 1520, 1580, 1615, 1629, 1856, 1871, 1873, 1877-1878, 1880, 1886, 1890, 1897-1898, 1906, 1909-1911, 1916, 1918, 1920, 1922, 1925-1927, 1931, 1934, 1936, 1937, 1940, 1954, 1963, 1966, 1967-1968, 1973, 1977, 1981, 1985, 1987, 1994, 1998, 2000, 2003, 2013, 2024-2025, 2037, 2053, 2057, 2070, 2073, 2082-2083, 2085-2086;

   adolescence, 258, 262, 274, 782-783, 854, 864, 888, 939, 1002, 1062, 1790

childrearing, 70, 234, 242, 249, 263, 266, 274, 279, 295, 298, 312, 329-330, 334, 337-338, 343, 345, 351, 352-353, 357, 363, 368, 404, 406, 419, 427, 610, 791, 941, 1051;

   feeding of children, 249-250, 264, 801, 842, 945

citizenship and naturalization, 127, 161, 1044;

   Cable Act, 166, 222, 1044. See also immigration law

clerical work, 170, 470, 1632

colleges, 902, 936, 1132, 1271, 1209, 1468, 1708, 1714, 1736, 1793

Colorado, 699, 1983, 2025, 2066;

   Denver, 1076, 1685;

   Ludlow, 1387, 1710

community activists, 721, 743-744, 761, 1084, 1105, 1118, 1137, 1176, 1206, 1257, 1275-1277, 1293, 1351, 1368, 1392, 1401, 1444, 1638-1639, 1661, 1730, 1734, 1797, 1808, 1810, 1813

Connecticut, 235, 1944;

   Hartford, 765, 1005

consumer behavior, 70, 300, 322, 364, 516, 585, 602, 666, 678

courtship, 402, 910, 1009, 1019, 1033, 1040, 1058

criminal behavior and delinquency, 94, 127, 258, 360, 808, 917, 1010, 1566, 1840

culture change and acculturation, 271, 305, 313, 345, 383, 601, 792, 854, 869, 923, 953, 968, 973, 975, 1004-1075, 1672;

   Americanization, 89, 146, 267, 847, 956, 1017, 1022, 1024, 1029, 1052, 1070, 1105, 1879, 1948;

   cultural conflict, 354, 1043, 2044

Dakota, 715, 1734, 1926

diaries, 1285, 1471, 1489, 1571, 1640, 1659, 1661, 1697, 1702-1707, 1733

divorce, 227, 285, 386, 964, 996

drugs and alcohol, 293, 823, 858, 863, 924, 1563

education, 16, 115, 134, 146, 472, 564, 572, 662, 674, 906, 911-912, 916, 921, 925, 928, 931, 947-948, 949, 955, 970, 974, 976-978, 980-982, 985, 988, 992-993, 997, 1000, 1003, 1018, 1038, 1115,

1146, 1176, 1204, 1245, 1264, 1275, 1425, 1468; (See also colleges, schools);

influence on fertility, 523, 777-778, 884;

influence on work, 475, 576, 589, 632

espionage, 1182, 1235, 1346, 1443, 1556, 1652, 1678, 1830, 1840

familism, 255, 1065

family, 16, 50, 79, 85, 115, 116, 134, 225-428, 447-449, 554, 569, 584, 617, 634, 694, 754, 797, 1036, 1043, 1071, 1939; (See also business, childrearing, familism, family roles, family sagas, household, immigration law, intermarriage, kinship, machismo, marriage, patriarchy, sex roles, violence);

decision-making, 272, 306, 378, 383, 421, 557, 585-586;

desertion, 247, 268, 282-283, 563, 1710, 2076;

division of labor, 261, 305, 319, 488, 512-513, 515, 535;

economy, 309, 477, 485;

size, 280, 1002;

strategies, 548

family roles, 10, 156, 238, 356, 360-361, 367, 1280, 1827;

daughters, 498, 532, 625, 1879, 1887, 1889, 1905, 1983, 1997, 2010, 2922, 2028, 2055, 2061-2063, 2065, 2064, 2067, 2073;

grandmothers, 543, 881, 952, 1261, 1962, 2020, 2064;

mothers, 136, 225-226, 241-242, 273, 311, 373, 437, 452, 475, 478, 483, 498, 517, 548, 587, 1031, 1037, 1049, 1403, 1883, 1916, 1924-1925, 1942, 1948, 1952-1953, 1961, 1971, 1984, 1997, 2026, 2034, 2040, 2041, 2081;

mothers/daughters, 246, 251, 318, 320, 341, 415, 547, 549, 845, 868, 962, 1062, 1874, 1955, 2010, 2042, 2048;

widows, 277, 347, 1921, 1938, 1944, 1947, 1996, 2029-2031;

wives, 294, 300, 350, 394, 420, 699

family sagas (fictional), 1889, 1895, 1899, 1925, 1929, 1945, 1952, 1953, 1955, 1958, 1983, 1997, 2004, 2006, 2009, 2014, 2022, 2025, 2026, 2033, 2040, 2044, 2051, 2059-2060, 2065, 2068, 2070-2071, 2080-2082

farming, 306, 355, 496, 521, 555, 562, 619, 1195, 1331, 1501, 1560, 1602, 1613, 1640, 1642, 1693, 1715, 1735, 1750, 1786, 1824, 1860, 1905, 1908, 2064. See also frontier

feminism, 13, 637, 651, 653, 660, 679, 683, 731, 750, 936, 970, 1006, 1060, 1622;

316   IMMIGRANT WOMEN IN THE U.S.

feminists, 1082, 1096, 1103, 1122, 1130, 1138, 1155, 1191, 1201, 1239, 1249, 1282, 1284, 1313, 1315, 1351, 1358, 1366, 1382, 1397, 1409, 1422, 1438, 1447, 1520, 1547;

women's rights and suffrage, 209, 695-696, 755, 957, 1122, 1325, 1868

fertility, 19, 127, 284, 288, 291, 365, 523, 771, 775, 776, 777-781, 785-786, 790-791, 799, 806-807, 810-812, 820-822, 825-829, 831-833, 836, 841, 843, 846, 848-851, 854, 856-857, 859, 873, 875-878, 884-885, 887, 889-890. See also childbirth and pregnancy, education, family size

fiction, 33, 46-47, 52, 55, 115, 1086, 1283, 1871-2086

fine arts, 471, 1158, 1159-1160, 1162, 1202, 1213, 1285, 1322, 1348, 1358, 1373, 1377, 1390, 1439, 1571, 1849, 1912

Florida, 178, 1035;

Miami, 384, 462, 487, 508;

Tampa, 567-568, 723

folklore, 20, 37, 388, 417, 844, 846, 860, 895, 945, 958, 990-991, 1041, 1054-1055, 1302, 1359. See also handicrafts, healers

food processing, 429, 456, 463, 596, 598, 635, 649, 654

food and food preparation, 254, 416, 479, 486, 555, 572, 602, 666, 678, 693, 735, 866, 1049. See also childrearing

friendship, 266, 321, 900

frontier, 24, 67, 126, 1056, 1201, 1253, 1135, 1309, 1330, 1400, 1411, 1494-1495, 1500, 1513, 1526, 1560, 1602, 1613, 1693, 1757, 1767, 1785, 1801, 1817, 1823-1824, 1858, 1860, 1872, 1875, 1910, 1911, 1939, 1940-1941, 1973, 2040, 2046. See also farming

garment industry, 183, 431, 456, 470, 489, 490, 498, 508, 546, 559, 577, 580, 585, 616, 622-623, 637, 661, 681, 700, 702, 704, 736-737, 763, 765, 1532, 1598, 1743, 1745, 1771, 1842, 1901; (See also labor, Women's Trade Union League);

homework, 451, 628;

sweatshops, 372, 439, 455, 550, 611, 630, 1318, 1886.

Georgia, 1628

Hadassah, 689, 697, 1171, 1194, 1276, 1277, 1293, 1462

handicrafts, 59, 486, 931, 990-991, 1804, 1848

Hawaii, 60, 118, 130, 139, 152, 157, 234, 261, 262, 290, 312, 340, 354, 371, 465, 839, 843, 859, 944, 1023;

Honolulu, 315-316, 847, 919, 1001, 1140, 1259, 1274, 1713

healers, 770, 830, 1236, 1352, 1367, 2045

health and illness, 79, 97, 134, 784, 787-788, 792, 794-798, 800, 815-819, 845, 847, 853, 870, 893, 897, 941, 945, 1012, 1039, 1464, 1534. See also healers, mental health

Holocaust, 39, 54, 1186, 1229, 1355, 1416, 1262, 1487, 1503, 1634, 1700, 1721, 1788-1789, 1888, 2049

household, 310, 397;

  female-headed, 110, 275-276, 296, 365, 379, 408, 444, 560;

  structure, 96, 184, 194, 284, 288, 440, 466

housework and housewives, 71, 97, 289, 339, 348, 497, 518, 532, 539-540, 574, 602, 666, 1022, 1029. See also boarders and boarding

Idaho, 2013

identity and personality, 231, 246, 251, 273, 701, 905, 915, 920, 922, 925, 932, 944, 950, 953, 960, 961, 975, 989, 993, 999, 1001, 1015, 1027, 1030, 1064, 1237

ideology about women, 287, 910, 933, 979, 1028, 1036, 1053, 1477

illegitimacy, 245, 381, 1809, 1916

Illinois, 716, 914, 1509, 1602, 1824;

  Chicago, 56, 140, 200, 251, 260, 300, 322, 348, 363, 372, 429, 439, 516, 577, 641, 677, 688, 763, 768, 1028, 1154, 1296, 1364, 1400, 1415, 1558, 1596, 1620, 1709, 1873, 1898-1900, 1994, 2006, 2032

immigration law,

  Chinese Exclusion Act, 207, 344;

  family re-unification, 175, 177, 221. See also citizenship and naturalization

income, 435, 468, 588, 591, 627, 631, **841**

Indians (Native Americans), 1198, 1220, 1391, 1494, 1624, 1659-1661

Indiana, 652

industrial work, 462, 529, 548-549, 573, 617, 620-621, 698, 1312, 2073;

  cigar workers, 567-568, 593;

  electronics plants, 489, 526;

  factories, 487, 509, 536, 544, 608, 2059; textiles, 493, 520, 762, 1110. See also garment industry

intermarriage, 109, 127, 230-231, 236, 240, 252, 259, 278, 290, 323, 325, 327-328, 331-333, 340, 341, 358, 361-362, 366, 370, 385, 390, 395, 409, 424, 950, 1920, 1937, 1954, 2077-2078, 2085. See also marriage.

internment (of Japanese during World War II), 1310, 1430, 1607-1608, 1712, 1799, 1827, 1892, 2009, 2069

Iowa, 562, 1244, 1331, 1484, 1640, 1697, 1964, 2007, 2059-2060

Kansas, 272, 1613, 1693, 1948, 2037

Kentucky, 719, 1535

kinship, 178-180, 244, 315-316, 321, 335, 404, 422, 557, 1009, 1020, 1072. See also family labor, 48, 446, 545, 546, 635, 678, 681, 691, 729, 739-740, 747, 753-754, 756, 940, 978;

   activists, 672, 761, 1082-1083, 1098-1099, 1130, 1166, 1185, 1192, 1196, 1200, 1221, 1248-1249, 1254, 1273, 1281, 1312, 1318, 1328, 1336, 1342, 1361, 1364, 1366, 1382-1384, 1388, 1389, 1394, 1412-1413, 1438, 1459, 1466, 1547, 1557, 1565, 1566, 1598, 1601, 1621, 1717, 1723-1726, 1771, 1775, 1776;

   Amalgamated Clothing Workers, 1083;

   Industrial Workers of the World, 694, 742, 1110;

   International Ladies Garment Workers Union, 741, 758, 759, 1146, 1254, 1273;

   strikes, 265, 470, 491, 6398 641, 648, 649, 698, 699, 704, 708, 710, 735, 737, 742, 762-763, 765, 1384, 1710, 1901, 2054;

   unions, 598, 637, 671, 734, 736, 752, 755, 757; (See also Women's Trade Union League);

   United Automobile Workers, 707

language learning and use of English, 436, 523, 608, 677, 783, 884, 889, 923, 927, 947-949, 968, 993, 1034, 1071, 1358, 1443

leisure, 134, 150, 570, 1004, 1024, 1051-1052, 1057

letters, 1465, 1477, 1494-1495, 1500, 1504, 1524, 1560, 1581, 1586, 1592, 1595, 1660, 1689, 1727, 1744, 1746, 1752, 1772, 1777, 1806, 1821, 1824,

Louisiana, 1575

machismo, 50, 116, 358, 428, 924. See also family, patriarchy

male impersonator, 1169, 1256, 1719. See also soldier

marriage, 21, 50, 146, 193, 228-229, 248, 256, 291, 297, 299, 308, 310, 314, 342, 346, 479, 396, 413, 961, 1023, 1047, 1065, 1068, 1619, 1807, 1882; (See also divorce, intermarriage);

   common law marriage, 245;

   military and war brides, 21, 174, 205, 215, 270, 281, 324, 326, 380, 382, 389, 405, 497, 1434, 1634-1635, 1825, 1885, 1902, 1917, 1930, 1933, 1969-1970, 1980, 2011, 2015, 2050;

   picture brides, 106, 152, 919, 1139, 2056;

   wedding ceremony, 271, 1779

Maryland, 1276, 1923

Massachusetts, 483, 832, 897, 1785, 2019;

   Boston, 514, 729, 745, 833, 1934;

   Holyoke, 365, 493, 1925;

   Lawrence, 648, 802;

   Lowell, 762, 1248, 1420, 1871

mental health, 110, 929, 951, 968, 984, 986, 1012, 1039;

   counseling and therapy, 227, 356, 369, 418, 907-908, 923, 938, 969, 973, 1042, 1047;

depression, 939, 964-965, 975, 994-996, 1001, 1068;

   stress, 79, 463, 512-513, 797, 823, 886, 926, 941, 963, 1045, 1073-1074;

   suicide, 1039, 1075

Michigan, 702, 1253, 1602, 1785, 1880, 1890;

   Detroit, 313, 518, 735

middle class, 316, 334, 585, 589, 616, 1007, 1575, 1765

midwestern U.S., 67, 795, 1280, 1393, 1921, 1939

midwives, 57, 123, 768, 802, 804, 852. See also birth and pregnancy, healers

migration, 3, 11, 14, 43, 79, 85, 103, 123, 434, 497, 795, 798, 973, 1280, 1509, 1584, 1614, 1697, 1699, 1733, 1772, 1866, 1998;

   brain drain, 173, 186, 203, 936;

   return migration, 1054-1055, 1209, 1378, 1472, 1502, 1562, 1606, 1670, 1679, 1840, 1874, 1998, 1922, 1966;

   sex ratios, 69, 71, 109, 158, 160-161, 163, 169, 174, 176, 187, 189-91, 197, 205, 210, 219, 221, 307, 344, 349, 370, 730;

   undocumented, 159, 163, 168, 196, 206, 441, 458, 503, 542, 559, 594, 607-608, 758, 794, 806-807, 1045, 1379;

   women left behind, 156, 198, 204, 208, 212-213, 223

mining, 112, 393, 829, 1110, 1329, 1710, 1762

Minnesota, 237, 675-676, 967, 1500, 1817, 1897, 1905, 2000

Mississippi, 1479

Missouri, 124, 1339, 1380, 1823;

   St. Louis, 129, 647, 674, 733, 1229

mobility, 146, 172, 454, 509, 603, 614, 842, 857

Montana, 1739

mortality and death, 97, 787, 852, 882

National Council of Jewish Women, 662, 1350-1351, 1798

Nebraska, 1078, 1327, 1368, 1746, 1872, 1910, 2080-2081

New Jersey, 243, 589, 601, 1395, 1786, 2077;

   Newark, 852;

   Paterson, 1110, 1881-1882

New England, 217, 304, 447, 545, 548-549, 551-552, 581, 656, 1716, 1877, 1914, 1945, 2014, 2050

New Mexico, 296, 1501, 1781

New Hampshire, 505, 1745, 1904

320   IMMIGRANT WOMEN IN THE U.S.

New York (City), 69, 71, 74, 96, 135-136, 170, 182, 268, 283, 299, 420, 441, 461, 464, 470, 472, 500-502, 514, 520, 534, 538, 573, 583, 585, 593, 610-611, 637-638, 640, 660-661, 665, 683, 692-693, 695-696, 736, 760, 804, 818-819, 865, 921, 957, 972, 1085, 1106, 1113, 1123, 1263, 1531, 1585, 1615, 1618, 1655, 1695, 1750, 1764-1765, 1782-1783, 1879, 1895, 1906, 1922, 1938, 1949, 1955, 1963, 1975-1977, 1985, 1990, 1999, 2003, 2023, 2036, 2039, 2043, 2055, 2067

New York (State), 255, 414, 479, 499, 698, 742, 860, 954, 1153, 1884;

Buffalo, 288, 1935;

Rochester, 681, 786;

Troy, 752-755

North Dakota, 302, 1056, 1657

northwestern U.S., 138

nuns, 664-665, 716, 723, 912, 1025, 1102, 1116, 1132, 1135, 1150-1151, 1153, 1175, 1228, 1230, 1243, 1271, 1292, 1297, 1301, 1305-1306, 1333-1334, 1339, 1376, 1405, 1423, 1531, 1781, 1833-1836, 1871. See also sisterhoods

Ohio, 663, 1193, 2075

Oklahoma, 1671, 1801, 2037

oral histories, 15, 54, 146, 244, 336, 391-392, 415, 479, 506, 567-568, 625, 952, 997, 1090, 1110, 1118, 1139, 1205, 1229, 1248, 1255, 1259, 1261-1262, 1265, 1280, 1320, 1323-1324, 1326, 1331, 1370, 1392, 1420, 1430, 1434, 1564, 1709, 1730, 1763, 1770-1771

Oregon, 410, 836

organizations, community, 693;

women's ethnic 70, 112, 524, 643, 656, 669, 687, 690, 711-712, 718, 723, 745, 749, 766, 911, 1115, 1368, 1827;

women's religious, 641, 667, 706, 722, 764, 919, 987, 1368, 1456. See also Baltic Women's Council, Hadassah, National Council of Jewish Women, Polish Women's Alliance, Young Women's Hebrew Association, Zionism

patriarchy, 292-293, 306-307, 313, 346, 375, 433, 447, 867, 970, 1540. See also machismo

Pennsylvania, 112, 120, 254, 449, 477, 748, 829, 1025, 1297, 1593, 1762, 2024;

Philadelphia, 502, 514, 517, 580, 1312;

Pittsburgh, 456, 539-540, 615, 705, 1326, 1887

performing arts, actresses, 1081, 1095, 1097, 1109, 1114, 1147-1149, 1157, 1160, 1174, 1178, 1210, 1214, 1219, 1240, 1250, 1266, 1340, 1363, 1372, 1374-1375, 1408, 1446, 1457, 1460, 1481, 1485, 1508, 1511, 1548-1550, 1568-1569, 1578, 1625-1630, 1636-1637, 1643, 1646-1647, 1650-1651, 1673, 1676, 1689-1690, 1696, 1725, 1728-1729, 1737, 1747, 1797, 1818-1819, 1831-1832, 1845, 1847, 1851-1852, 1863, 1965, 1981;

dancers, 1092, 1288, 1577-1578;

SUBJECTS

musicians, 1092, 1136, 1317, 1498, 1742;

singers, 1165, 1211-1212, 1258, 1270, 1338, 1446, 1576, 1618, 1636-1637, 1649, 1652-1653, 1654, 1673, 1680, 1749, 1792, 1797, 1820, 1826, 1833-1836, 1841;

theater and film, 1143, 1354, 1394, 1402, 1478, 1753, 1845

Polish Women's Alliance, 688, 725

politics, 134, 636, 650, 668, 679, 683, 701, 957;

political activists, 22, 655, 1101, 1138, 1152, 1345, 1223, 1238-1239, 1246, 1278, 1517, 1519-1520, 1679, 1685, 1763. See also radicals, reformers

press, 28, 47, 901, 937, 946, 959, 979, 1007-1008, 1060, 1226, 1350, 1442, 2038. See also journalists

professionals, 21, 170, 462, 522, 561, 609, 983, 1076, 1476, 1529;

doctors, 1078, 1087, 1140, 1190, 1201, 1231, 1245, 1369, 1378, 1404, 1427, 1455, 1493, 1640, 1687, 1867-1869;

educators, 1077, 1105-1106, 1230, 1263;

lawyers, 1104, 1545;

nurses, 177, 214, 432, 443, 469, 525, 564, 601, 615, 1112, 1168, 1179, 1204, 1235, 1362, 1415, 1489-1490, 1555-1556, 1593, 1631, 1687, 1698, 1803, 1838, 1858;

psychologists, 1207, 1252, 1353, 1424, 1449, 1476, 1544;

scholars, 1126, 1156, 1160, 1164, 1170, 1417, 1433, 1417, 1453, 1461, 1499, 1666, 1778;

teachers, 1232, 1251, 1263, 1265, 1294, 1332, 1434, 1677, 1708, 1814, 1904, 1959, 1985;

welfare workers, 1265, 1596, 1639. See also social work

prostitution, 21, 101, 183, 434, 438, 467, 481, 492, 511, 519, 524, 538, 541, 563, 579, 605, 629, 639, 1267, 1289, 1300, 1309, 1454, 1463, 1563, 1751, 1873, 1878. See also sexuality, social work

radicals, 4, 694, 720-721, 736, 744, 746, 761, 766, 1096, 1098-1099, 1152, 1177, 1184, 1191-1192, 1199, 1203, 1217, 1221, 1241, 1291, 1295, 1328, 1344, 1396-1398, 1429, 1438, 1445, 1450-1451, 1523, 1542, 1557, 1565-1565, 1574, 1581-1583, 1621, 1709, 1811-1812;

anarchists, 1152, 1177, 1189, 1203, 1215, 1241, 1273, 1291, 1299, 1347, 1360-1361, 1396-1398, 1407, 1450, 1541, 1574, 1581-1583, 1972;

Communists, 685, 1217, 1541-1542, 1545, 1722, 1840;

Socialists, 641-642, 666, 979, 1060, 1319, 1685

reformers, 1106, 1152, 1168, 1264, 1294, 1340, 1366, 1596, 1768. See also temperance

322 IMMIGRANT WOMEN IN THE U.S.

refugees, 53, 117, 129, 368, 460, 471, 510, 512-513, 566, 606, 609, 748, 876, 879, 913, 947-949, 1016, 1018, 1034, 1043, 1046, 1059, 1062, 1069, 1156, 1222, 1370, 1476, 1514, 1516, 1539, 1562, 1609, 1726, 1738, 1800, 1828-1829, 1853

religions, 369, 341, 1234, 1531, 1595, 1866;

   Adventist, 955, 1648;

   Catholic, 51, 230, 348, 640, 658, 664, 685, 703, 714, 771, 874, 877, 912, 918, 954, 966-967, 971, 987, 1056, 1145, 1419, 1459, 1512, 1536-1537, 1545, 1843-1844;

   Jewish,

      autobiographies, 1463, 1467-1470, 1476, 1478, 1482-1483, 1485, 1487, 1503, 1507, 1525, 1541-1544, 1563-1564, 1574, 1581-1584, 1596-1598, 1603, 1615-1616, 1623, 1634, 1638-1639, 1644, 1655, 1658, 1665, 1668, 1674, 1678, 1685, 1691, 1700, 1717, 1720-1724, 1729-1730, 1732, 1741-1743, 1751-1753, 1756, 1761, 1763-1765, 1770, 1775-1776, 1780-1782, 1786-1788, 1790-1791, 1798, 1805, 1808-1810, 1811-1813, 1826, 1831, 1838-1839, 1859, 1861;

      bibliographies, 8, 23, 26, 39, 54;

      biographies, 1076-1077, 1082-1084, 1104-1106, 1110, 1112, 1118, 1146, 1152, 1156, 1168, 1171-1172, 1176, 1179, 1183, 1185, 1189, 1191, 1194, 1203-1204, 1215-1217, 1222-1224, 1233, 1239, 1241, 1254, 1257, 1261-1264, 1272-1273, 1275-1277, 1285-1286, 1293, 1295, 1299, 1315, 1318, 1324, 1326, 1345-1348, 1350-1351, 1360-1362, 1370, 1382, 1384, 1386, 1393-1394, 1396-1398, 1400-1401, 1407, 1414-1415, 1422, 1428-1429, 1431, 1439, 1441, 1450-1451, 1458, 1462;

      collective action, 637, 639, 641, 660, 662, 666, 669, 677-678, 681, 685, 687, 689-690, 692-693, 695-697, 702, 704, 720-722, 724, 726, 736-737, 741, 743-746, 759, 763;

      cultural change, 1007-1008, 1019, 1029-1030, 1034, 1039, 1060, 1062;

      family, 238, 239, 241-242, 244, 248, 266-267, 282-283, 320, 336, 348, 359, 387, 391, 399, 400, 410, 415, 419;

      fertility and health, 804, 820-822, 881, 883;

      fiction, 1874, 1878, 1893, 1901, 1903, 1946, 1959-1962, 1979, 1983, 1985, 1993-1994, 1996, 2001, 2005, 2010, 2023, 2042, 2049, 2067, 2083-2084;

      general works, 65, 89, 93, 97, 113, 133, 146;

      mind, 909, 921, 937, 942, 952, 957, 979, 992, 997;

      work, 439, 442, 456, 480, 498, 524, 532, 536-537, 541, 543, 553, 563, 571, 577, 606, 609, 612-613, 620, 625, 628;

   Lutheran, 667, 706, 727, 764, 1380, 1504, 1803;

   Mennonite, 1693, 1778, 1948;

SUBJECTS   323

Methodism, 919, 1134, 1713;

Mormon, 1528, 1619, 1807

religious beliefs, 134, 237, 771, 837, 874, 877, 909, 943, 951, 966, 972, 990-991, 1480, 1512

religious work and workers, 928, 1418, 1456, 1536-1537, 1545, 1803, 1843-1844;

    evangelists, 1303, 1314, 1436-1437, 1682-1684, 1691;

    ministers, 1103, 1201, 1234, 1284, 1325, 1409, 1447, 1595;

    missionaries, 1102, 1134-1135, 1175, 1198 1220, 1292, 1298, 1300-1301, 1305, 1339, 1423, 1435, 1454, 1535, 1546, 1555, 1659-1661, 1713, 1793. See also nuns, organizations, sisterhoods

schools, 715, 723, 899, 914, 940, 942, 954, 967, 971, 1056, 1106, 1132, 1263, 1271, 1275, 1311, 1332

second generation,

    autobiographies, 1466, 1472, 1482-1485, 1498-1499, 1502, 1519-1520, 1533-1534, 1538, 1541-1542, 1547, 1557, 1563, 1565-1566, 1571-1572, 1575, 1579, 1592, 1596-1597, 1617, 1622, 1633, 1645, 1657-1658, 1662, 1665, 1669, 1670-1671, 1675, 1686, 1691, 1693, 1709, 1712, 1717, 1729, 1732, 1742, 1750-1753, 1756, 1763-1769, 1771, 1773-1774, 1782-1783, 1786, 1798-1799, 1808-1810, 1817, 1822-1823, 1838-1839, 1846, 1855, 1860, 1863, 1865;

bibliographies, 19, 22, 34, 54;

biographies, 1076-1077, 1085, 1090, 1094, 1097-1099, 1101, 1104-1106, 1110, 1112, 1115, 1123-1124, 1128, 1130, 1138, 1142, 1149-1150, 1152, 1157-1158, 1168, 1170-1171, 1174, 1179-1180, 1182, 1186, 1194, 1196-1197, 1204-1206, 1216-1217, 1232, 1237, 1242, 1246, 1248, 1250-1251, 1257, 1259, 1263-1265, 1276, 1278, 1293, 1304, 1310, 1315, 1322, 1327, 1331, 1342-1343, 1345-1346, 1348, 1350-1351, 1362, 1366, 1372, 1377, 1381, 1390, 1392, 1399, 1401, 1410-1411, 1420, 1434-1435, 1439, 1459, 1462;

collective action, 640, 642, 655-656, 662, 667, 673, 676, 697-698, 704, 706-707, 721, 724, 726, 734-735, 741, 743-745, 749, 763-764;

cultural change, 1004, 1007, 1009, 1019-1020, 1024, 1026, 1029-1030, 1040, 1052-1053, 1057, 1064, 1066, 1072, 1075;

family, 234, 235, 240, 258, 263, 266, 272, 308, 309, 315, 317, 318, 320, 329, 336, 341, 348, 358, 359, 360, 363, 378, 390, 392, 400, 410, 419, 428;

fertility and health, 818, 821, 832-833, 845, 849-851, 854, 860, 868, 875, 890;

324   IMMIGRANT WOMEN IN THE U.S.

   fiction, 1871-1872, 1874, 1877, 1879, 1880, 1886, 1890, 1893, 1898, 1910, 1912, 1916, 1918, 1921, 1925, 1927, 1929, 1936-1937, 1954, 1959, 1963, 1966, 1968, 1972, 1975-1977, 1981, 1985, 2003, 2005, 2028, 2036, 2044, 2052, 2055, 2070, 2082;

   general works, 58, 59, 93, 94, 98, 102, 113, 135, 136, 149;

   mind, 912, 917, 921, 939-940, 954, 978, 982-983, 985, 992, 1002;

   work, 437, 449, 451, 457, 461, 517, 532, 540, 557, 570, 621, 631, 635

servants and domestic service, 183, 434, 470, 473, 474, 484, 491, 494-496, 502, 527, 529, 551-552, 594, 597, 600, 613, 730, 755, 757, 980, 1006, 1054-1055, 1069, 1155, 1585, 1740, 1754, 1763, 1926, 1977, 2041

sex roles, 21, 90, 234, 239, 257, 355, 407, 611, 949, 962, 965, 986, 1014, 1026-1027, 1034, 1038. See also family

sexuality, 98, 109, 149, 239, 265, 269, 287, 310, 553, 769, 783, 793, 805, 808, 867, 869, 871-872, 895, 1922, 1931, 2012. See also prostitution

sisterhoods, 51, 644-645, 647, 652, 658, 670, 684, 703, 714, 732, 751, 914, 930, 967, 971, 976, 1056, 1113, 1145, 1151, 1153, 1181, 1297, 1301, 1371;

   Dominican Sisters, 686, 738, 748, 1260;

   Felician sisters, 899, 954, 1115;

   Franciscan Sisters, 1274, 1296;

   Presentation Sisters, 713, 715;

   Sisters of Charity, 760, 1304, 1395;

   Sisters of the Divine Providence, 719, 1307;

   Sisters of Mercy, 663, 673, 705, 1228, 1306, 1376;

   Sisters of Notre Dame de Namur, 646, 1230, 1334;

   Sisters of Saint Joseph of Carondelet, 659, 674-676, 723, 733

social work: 690, 904, 1061, 1415, 1597, 1809;

   "rescue" work, 579, 1289;

   settlement houses, 1017, 1112, 1168, 1179, 1204, 1362, 1558, 1838-1839. See also charity and welfare, professionals

soldiers, 1169, 1235, 1830

South Dakota, 713

southwestern U.S., 1236, 1352

spiritualists, 1091, 1107, 1133, 1365, 1426, 1452, 1506, 1716

stereotypes, 44, 124, 132, 141, 153, 387, 1664, 1893

temperance, 1745, 1827

Tennessee, 1529

Texas, 126, 454, 844, 1119, 1432, 1474, 1513, 1524, 1526, 1693, 1699, 1755, 1823, 1865;

El Paso, 491, 597;

Houston, 458, 1045, 1159, 1162;

San Antonio, 296, 654

Utah, 1528, 1619, 1807, 2026

Vermont, 1825, 1908

violence, 265, 293, 360, 375-377, 818, 907, 1018;

battered wives, 425, 840

Virginia, 1535

Washington, 1311, 1330, 1602;

Seattle, 1070, 1118, 1799

Washington, D.C., 249

western U.S., 62, 95, 102, 579, 1161, 1307, 1311, 1329, 2065

West Virginia, 1389, 1779

Wisconsin, 1025, 1860, 1973;

Milwaukee, 670, 718, 1223, 1371, 1603, 1685;

Racine, 686, 1260

Women's Bureau, 1166, 1466

women's culture, 648

Women's Trade Union League, 34, 638, 657, 660-661, 680, 704, 750, 1130, 1185, 1342

work and wage-earning, 10, 97, 103, 106, 115, 146, 232, 243, 261, 286, 289, 301, 303, 304, 311, 322, 363, 372, 429-635, 823, 992, 997, 1003, 1564;

labor force participation, 440, 459, 475-476, 503, 510, 566, 575-576, 589, 599, 631-633, 851;

labor market segmentation, 494, 507, 604, 631;

unemployment, 784. See also particular industries and types of work

working class, 36, 104, 135, 280, 309, 414, 500, 531, 616, 626, 750, 932, 957, 1392, 1401

writers, 47, 720, 1086, 1088, 1094, 1096, 1111, 1119, 1128-1129, 1131, 1142, 1167, 1172, 1184, 1186, 1197, 1199, 1226, 1233, 1268, 1282-1283, 1327, 1340, 1343-1344, 1358, 1385, 1386, 1390, 1406, 1410-1411, 1419, 1421, 1442, 1445, 1468-1470, 1497, 1507, 1510, 1515, 1552-1553, 1571, 1592, 1594, 1604, 1606, 1622, 1633, 1691, 1701-1707, 1725, 1845, 1861-1862, 1870;

journalists, 1394, 1587-1590, 1686, 1783, 1796;

novelists, 1089, 1129, 1474-1475, 1491-1492, 1533-1534, 1567, 1692, 1766-1767;

poets, 7, 1124, 1154, 1357, 1381, 1416, 1433, 1438, 1592, 1763, 1862

Young Women's Hebrew Association, 724, 726

Zionism, 1171, 1183, 1275, 1277, 1351, 1665

About the Compiler

DONNA GABACCIA is Associate Professor of History at Mercy College. She is the author of two books, *Militants and Migrants,* and *From Sicily to Elizabeth Street,* and numerous articles.

LIBRARY USE ONLY
DOES NOT CIRCULATE